CONTROLLING

Herausgegeben von Prof. Dr. Volker Lingnau, Kaiserslautern, Prof. Dr. Albrecht Becker, Innsbruck, Prof. Dr. Rolf Brühl, Berlin, und Prof. Dr. Bernhard Hirsch, München

Band 18
Jörn Sebastian Basel
Heuristic Reasoning in Management Accounting – A Mixed Methods Analysis
Lohmar – Köln 2012 • 268 S. • € 57,- (D) • ISBN 978-3-8441-0160-7

Band 19
Sabrina Buch
Shared Knowledge – The Comparability of Idiosyncratic Mental Models
Lohmar – Köln 2012 • 320 S. • € 62,- (D) • ISBN 978-3-8441-0186-7

Band 20
Michael Hoogen
Organisations- und wissenschaftstheoretische Implikationen für die Controllingforschung
Lohmar – Köln 2013 • 288 S. • € 58,- (D) • ISBN 978-3-8441-0235-2

Band 21
Max Kury
Abgabe von Rechenschaft zum Wiederaufbau von Vertrauen – Eine empirische Untersuchung der Berichterstattung von Banken
Lohmar – Köln 2014 • 308 S. • € 59,- (D) • ISBN 978-3-8441-0306-9

Band 22
Robert Huber
Nachhaltigkeitsorientierte Anreizsysteme – Eine empirische Analyse zu Gestaltung und Verhaltenswirkungen
Lohmar – Köln 2014 • 232 S. • € 56,- (D) • ISBN 978-3-8441-0339-7

Band 23
Michael Hanzlick
Management Control Systems and Cross-Cultural Research – Empirical Evidence on Performance Measurement, Performance Evaluation and Rewards in a Cross-Cultural Comparison
Lohmar – Köln 2015 • 304 S. • € 59,- (D) • ISBN 978-3-8441-0380-9

JOSEF EUL VERLAG

Reihe: Controlling · Band 23

Herausgegeben von Prof. Dr. Volker Lingnau, Kaiserslautern,
Prof. Dr. Albrecht Becker, Innsbruck, Prof. Dr. Rolf Brühl, Berlin,
und Prof. Dr. Bernhard Hirsch, München

Dr. Michael Hanzlick

Management Control Systems and Cross-Cultural Research

Empirical Evidence on Performance Measurement, Performance Evaluation and Rewards in a Cross-Cultural Comparison

With a Foreword by Prof. Dr. Rolf Brühl,
ESCP Europe Business School Berlin

Bibliografische Information der Deutschen Nationalbibliothek

Die Deutsche Nationalbibliothek verzeichnet diese Publikation in der Deutschen Nationalbibliografie; detaillierte bibliografische Daten sind im Internet über <http://dnb.d-nb.de> abrufbar.

Dissertation, ESCP Europe Business School Berlin, 2014

ISBN 978-3-8441-0380-9
1. Auflage Januar 2015

© JOSEF EUL VERLAG GmbH, Lohmar – Köln, 2015
Alle Rechte vorbehalten

JOSEF EUL VERLAG GmbH
Brandsberg 6
53797 Lohmar
Tel.: 0 22 05 / 90 10 6-6
Fax: 0 22 05 / 90 10 6-88
E-Mail: info@eul-verlag.de
http://www.eul-verlag.de

Bei der Herstellung unserer Bücher möchten wir die Umwelt schonen. Dieses Buch ist daher auf säurefreiem, 100% chlorfrei gebleichtem, alterungsbeständigem Papier nach DIN 6738 gedruckt.

Foreword

Although companies face major challenges of internationalization and globalization, research in management control has not significantly investigated these phenomena. This is surprising because companies that organize their activities worldwide usually share common problems in management control. On the agenda of international management control departments is the question whether they should try to implement a system of management control, which is standardized – and usually that system is originally from the home base of these companies. Or should these companies adapt their management controls to the local specificities? As management control is seen as a decisive tool of managers to keep their companies on track, it seems to be a worthwhile endeavour to have a closer look on management control systems in different countries.

This is where Michael Hanzlick positions his dissertation and consequently he states his general research objective: "whether there are cultural differences among organizations in their respective control practices, in particular in performance measurement, performance evaluation and reward schemes" (p. 11). As these subsystems are core systems of any management control systems, he aims at a highly relevant research endeavour, which is not only of interest to researchers but also to practitioners in the field.

Two aspects in respect to culture are important to note: First, Michael Hanzlick (together with other team members) collects original data for the cultural values, and gives good reasons to do this. Second, he chooses to do the survey in four countries (Belgium, Canada, Germany and Poland) which should reveal enough variation on cultural values because they represent different cultural areas. Additionally Poland, representing one of the East European emerging market countries has not been in previous studies on management control systems.

Overall, Michael Hanzlick could show that culture matters in many instances. However, no simple picture showed up. This should not be astonishing because it corroborates the findings of previous research. In published articles of cross-cultural research in management control, usually a bit less than 50% of the hypotheses could be supported. Therefore, this research stream is far from being in a state of consolidation. Looking at the results of this thesis, one could give researchers the clear advice to closely examine each design variable separately.

Broad based assumptions about the link between cultural values and management control are doomed to fail.

Only one group of results should be highlighted here. Michael Hanzlick indicates that a variety of cultural values have an influence on the design of performance management and rewards. Because of his fine-grained analysis, he is able to show that especially the mix of financial and non-financial measures is likely to be influenced by cultural values. This is an intriguing finding because discussions of this mix are focused on the appropriate performance model, which fits to the strategy of organisations. There is less discussion about taken-for-granted influences like culture. This is important because it indicates that organizations tend to use a mix of measures depending on the cultural values (uncertainty avoidance, future orientation). The influence holds under various conditions. Although traditionally, in the (economic) literature one can find a bias towards financials, in recent contributions non-financials are emphasized: In settings with information asymmetry and uncertainty, they capture the noise. As this dissertation shows additionally, cultural values have to be looked at and that they may accompany the effects of economic uncertainty. This is also corroborated by the (positive) influence of future orientation on the mix towards non-financials; in this case, economic uncertainty has a major impact as well.

To sum up, Michael Hanzlick's thorough and innovative dissertation picks up an up-to-date topic in management control research which not only is of relevance for researchers but as well for practitioners. I am convinced that both researchers and practitioners will benefit from reading this fine piece of research and I wish this book all the success it deserves.

Berlin, December 2014   Prof. Dr. Rolf Brühl

Preface

The topic of my thesis was mainly motivated by a keen interest in management controls and cultural phenomena which I came across in my first years in business as well as during my previous studies in an international context.

Management controls are a crucial tool for steering organizations and regulating the behaviour of the subordinates of top management. As a natural consequence to increased globalization, companies are exposed to increasingly multicultural surroundings. In going abroad these firms face the question of whether to use the standardized form of control similar to that used in their home setting, or whether to adapt their control elements to the local specificities. In a nutshell, the thesis deals with the impact of cultural phenomena on management controls. Strikingly, empirical research that helps to understand how companies organize their control activities with regard to cultures other than their own is rather thin.

This thesis extends previous studies on management controls and culture in several ways by. I widened the focus on control elements and incorporated performance evaluation and rewards in close collaboration with performance measures. In the present study, I extended the current state of cultural investigation in the domain of performance measurement, evaluation and rewards. This thesis looks into the control elements of four different countries, among them Poland, which until now has not been studied with regard to management control elements. Furthermore, I addressed the GLOBE framework instead of the older Hofstede paradigm. From a managerial perspective, my research aims to offer practical advice to executives on how to design management controls across different cultures.

I would like to invite the reader to immerse him/herself in further reading. The thesis has a classic structure: the introduction is followed by a theory section, followed in turn by the development of hypotheses, methodologies, results and discussion. By reading the book the reader may learn that the broad claim "culture matters" needs to be resolved. My advice is to examine the influence of culture on the different control variables in very fine-grained steps.

Berlin, January 2015   Michael Hanzlick

Acknowledgments

Like many other research quests, my thesis presents the culmination of findings generated over a four-year time span as a researcher at ESCP Europe Business School Berlin. During this time I was involved with many persons who were instrumental in the writing of my thesis. I owe these immeasurable thanks and deep gratitude.

First and foremost, I am extremely grateful that Prof. Dr. Rolf Brühl supervised my thesis and acted as a stimulating mentor and true "Doktorvater" during the four years at his Chair of Management Control. His enthusiasm for research was very contagious and motivational for me. He has always been more than willing to function as a necessary sparring partner, and encouraged me to address the research topic of management control from a cultural angle. I greatly benefited from his expertise, inspiring guidance and insightful comments during the whole process of the writing of the dissertation, paired with providing me with the essential leeway needed to cope with the project requirements. He challenged me to reflect critically on each main step of the project. Next, I was very glad that Prof. Carsten Rohde from the Department of Accounting and Auditing of the Copenhagen Business School accepted the role of second supervisor. He has been involved in the overall international research project and has been well aware of the challenges we faced during those years. I also want to thank Prof. Dr. Sylvie Geisendorf for acting as the Chair of the Evaluation Committee.

Writing about this topic would not have been possible without Prof. Teemu Malmi and Mikko Sandelin from Aalto University. I am indebted for their passion with regard to shedding light on the coupling and configurations of management control systems, and their initiation of the overall research project on management controls. Furthermore, I am sincerely grateful to three research partners, Dr. Piotr Bednarek from Wrocław University of Economics, Prof. Maurice Gosselin from Université Laval in Québec and Prof. Sophie Hoozée from the Erasmus School of Economics in Rotterdam for joining me in the cross-cultural effort, for sharing their data and for sharing their truthful and illuminating views on a number of issues related to the cross-cultural project. I especially enjoyed the close research collaboration with Sophie. She raised many precious points in our lively discussions. Appreciation goes to Prof. Dr. Otto Janschek from Vienna University of Economics and Business who was a valuable research partner in the early stages of the research project. I also want to express my warm thanks to

Prof. Dr. Robert Wilken from ESCP Europe in Berlin who kindly assisted with some statistical questions.

I gratefully acknowledge the financial contribution of ESCP Europe and CIMA. Without their funding the whole project would have been a costly endeavour for me. I am grateful that they granted me the necessary academic trust and covered the research expenses. I have collaborated with many practitioners, i.e. managers, who were willing to participate in my research project. Without their interest in the subject and the precious time they devoted to the interviews, this thesis would have never been accomplished.

I profited from several research colloquia and conferences. I had stimulating discussions and intensive talks with the participants of the Berlin doctoral program of ESCP Europe, within the yearly research talks in collaboration with the Chair of Management Control at the University of the German Armed Forces in Munich, and within the ACMAR Doctoral Colloquium in Vallendar. These platforms forced me to sharpen the research focus and the theoretical foundation of my thesis. I thank participants of the Conference on New Directions in Management Accounting in Brussels for valuable comments on cross-cultural management control research.

During the time at our Chair I had the pleasure to get to know Dr. Max Kury who not only spent many lunch sessions at our beloved "Cordoba", but was also an enthusiastic researcher to whom I could address concerns and ask about obstacles I faced during this time. Additionally, Dr. Jörn Basel, who shared my passion for running long distances, was a colleague I really appreciated. A warm "thank you" goes to the zealous and conscientious research assistants associated with my dissertation project, namely to Stefanie Friedemann, Robin Hahn, Anne Kollien, Georg Schmidtgen and Nils Plambeck. Besides their responsibility for numerous administrative tasks, they assisted in the preparation of data collection, data transfer, and initial statistical set-ups, as well as for drafting research reports.

I am especially grateful to those persons who enriched my time at ESCP Europe and created many memorable moments. In particular, I would like to mention Tayfun Aykac, Philipp Bartholomä, Aaron W. Bauer, Katherina Bruns, Kyung-Hun Ha, Christian Klippert, Dr. Angela Kornau, Eva Kreibohm, Dr. Erik Maier, Florian Reichle and Dr. Lynn Schäfer.

Acknowledgments

Finally, I would like to acknowledge friends and family who supported me during this time. I would like to express my deep gratitude to my parents, Angelika Hanzlick and Dr. Joachim Hanzlick, to my sister, Susanne Hanzlick, and to my parents-in-law, Christa Buchholz and Dr. Manfred Buchholz, for their unfailing encouragement, and my sincere thanks to Christa for her diligent lectorate. Most importantly, I would like to devote cordial gratitude to my wife, Dr. Friederike Hanzlick, who strongly encouraged me in my academic quest and always provided unstinting support.

Berlin, January 2015   Michael Hanzlick

Contents

Contents XIII

List of Figures XVII

List of Tables XIX

List of Abbreviations XXIII

1	**Introduction** 1	
1.1	**Motivation** 1	
1.2	**Research background and guiding research question** 6	
1.3	**Outline of the thesis** 13	
2	**Fundamental terms and theoretical framework** 21	
2.1	**Culture** 21	
2.1.1	Complexity of the cultural phenomenon 21	
2.1.2	Major cultural frameworks 22	
2.1.3	Hofstede framework 24	
2.1.4	GLOBE framework 25	
2.1.4.1	Overview of the GLOBE study 25	
2.1.4.2	GLOBE dimensions 26	
2.1.4.3	Critical appraisal of the GLOBE study 28	
2.2	**Management control systems' framework** 32	
2.3	**Performance measurement, performance evaluation and rewards** 34	
2.3.1	Performance measurement 34	
2.3.1.1	Nature and purpose of performance measures 34	
2.3.1.2	Categories of performance measures 36	
2.3.1.3	Performance measurement as an entity: The Balanced Scorecard 39	
2.3.1.4	Benefits of a holistic use of performance measures 41

2.3.2	Performance evaluation	43
2.3.2.1	Nature and purpose of performance evaluation	43
2.3.2.2	Features and process of performance evaluation	45
2.3.3	Rewards	49
2.3.3.1	Nature and purpose of rewards	49
2.3.3.2	Categories of rewards	51
2.4	**Theories**	**53**
2.4.1	Contingency-based approach	53
2.4.2	New institutionalism	55
2.4.3	Stakeholder theory	60
2.4.4	Agency theory	62
2.4.5	Synthesis of theoretical approaches	63
3	**Research overview and hypotheses**	**67**
3.1	**Methodology of literature review**	**67**
3.2	**Research overview**	**69**
3.3	**Research hypotheses**	**72**
3.3.1	Hypotheses development	72
3.3.2	Hypotheses related to power distance	74
3.3.3	Hypotheses related to future orientation	75
3.3.4	Hypotheses related to assertiveness	77
3.3.5	Hypotheses related to individualism/collectivism	78
3.3.6	Hypotheses related to uncertainty avoidance	82
4	**Research methodology**	**87**
4.1	**Sample**	**87**
4.2	**Questionnaire design**	**90**
4.2.1	Management control systems' questionnaire	90
4.2.2	GLOBE questionnaire	92

4.3	**Data collection**	94
4.3.1	Methods of data collection	94
4.3.2	Acquisition process	95
4.3.3	Interview process	96
4.4	**Variables and measures**	**101**
4.4.1	Management control variables	101
4.4.2	Cultural dimensions	103
4.4.3	Control variables	104
4.5	**Tests of and remedies for measurement error**	**107**
4.5.1	Missing data	107
4.5.2	Outlier analysis	109
4.5.3	Test of normality, homogeneity, skew and kurtosis	110
4.5.4	Common-method bias	110
4.5.5	Construct analysis	111
4.5.5.1	General remarks on construct validity	111
4.5.5.2	Performance evaluation and reward constructs	112
4.5.5.3	GLOBE constructs	115
5	**Results**	**121**
5.1	**Descriptive statistics**	**121**
5.1.1	Report on interviews	121
5.1.2	Respondent demographics	122
5.1.3	Industry composition	124
5.1.4	Firms' characteristics	126
5.1.5	GLOBE scores	128
5.2	**Multivariate analysis**	**134**
5.3	**Robustness tests**	**139**
5.4	**Summary of hypotheses**	**147**

6	Discussion and conclusion	151
6.1	Discussion of results	151
6.2	Contributions to theory and former research	160
6.3	Managerial and practical implications	164
6.4	Limitations	166
6.5	Avenues for future research	170
6.6	Conclusion	173
Appendix		175
References		235

List of Figures

Figure 1: Building blocks of cross-cultural research and MCS 13
Figure 2: Performance measurement, evaluation and reward process 15
Figure 3: Overview of cultural frameworks 23
Figure 4: MCS package framework of Malmi and Brown (2008) 33
Figure 5: Organizational survival 56
Figure 6: Pillars of institutions 57
Figure 7: Modes of survey administration 94

List of Tables

Table 1: Definition of GLOBE dimensions 27
Table 2: Origins of the nine GLOBE dimensions 28
Table 3: Total rewards... 51
Table 4: Sections of the MCS questionnaire 91
Table 5: Questionnaire constructs on performance evaluation 102
Table 6: Questionnaire constructs on rewards 102
Table 7: Questionnaire constructs on performance areas... 103
Table 8: Little MCAR-Test for GLOBE data 108
Table 9: Performance evaluation and reward scale items 114
Table 10: Cut-off criteria for fit indices 116
Table 11: CFA reports on GLOBE dimensions 117
Table 12: Steps to assess measurement invariance 118
Table 13: Period of interviews 121
Table 14: Form of interview and interviewers 122
Table 15: Demographic data (part 1) 123
Table 16: Demographic data (part 2) 124
Table 17: Industry composition.. 125
Table 18: Firms' headquarters.. 127
Table 19: Employees and financial indicators of sample firms 128
Table 20: GLOBE scores for the dimensions of national culture 129
Table 21: Deviations of GLOBE scores to the original study.................................... 130
Table 22: Bandwidth and group distance of GLOBE scores 132
Table 23: GLOBE scores for low and high level 133
Table 24: Means, SD, ANOVA, and effect size for high and low cultural levels (1)............ 135
Table 25: Means, SD, ANOVA, and effect size for high and low cultural levels (2)............ 136
Table 26: Variable definitions and descriptive statistics.. 140
Table 27: F-values of control variables for low and high level cultural dimensions'............ 141

Table 28: Correlations of covariates, performance evaluation and reward variables (1) 143
Table 29: Correlations of covariates, performance evaluation and reward variables (2) 144
Table 30: Summary of hypotheses' testing on performance evaluation 148
Table 31: Summary of hypotheses' testing on rewards (1) 149
Table 32: Summary of hypotheses' testing on rewards (2) 150
Table 33: Definition of management control systems 177
Table 34: Six steps of literature review 187
Table 35: Search operationalization 189
Table 36: Classification scheme 190
Table 37: Coding categories literature review 190
Table 38: Journals included in the literature review 191
Table 39: Publications of literature review by journal source and year 193
Table 40: Summary of articles from literature review (1) 195
Table 41: Summary of articles from literature review (2) 196
Table 42: Summary of articles from literature review (3) 197
Table 43: Summary of articles from literature review (4) 198
Table 44: Summary of articles from literature review (5) 199
Table 45: Summary of articles from literature review (6) 200
Table 46: GLOBE cultural clusters on societal practices scores 201
Table 47: Means, SD, ANOVA, and effect size by country – performance evaluation 220
Table 48: Means, SD, ANOVA, and effect size by country – rewards 221
Table 49: ANCOVA tests (1) 222
Table 50: ANCOVA tests (2) 223
Table 51: ANCOVA tests (3) 224
Table 52: ANCOVA tests (4) 225
Table 53: ANCOVA tests (5) 226
Table 54: ANCOVA tests (6) 227
Table 55: ANCOVA tests (7) 228
Table 56: ANCOVA tests (8) 229

List of Tables

Table 57: ANCOVA tests (9) 230
Table 58: ANCOVA tests (10) 231
Table 59: ANCOVA tests – only heterogeneous regression slopes (1) 232
Table 60: ANCOVA tests – only heterogeneous regression slopes (2) 233
Table 61: ANCOVA tests – only heterogeneous regression slopes (3) 234

List of Abbreviations

Abbreviation	Meaning
AGFI	Adjusted Goodness-of-Fit Index
ANCOVA	Analysis of covariance
ANOVA	Analysis of variance
AOS	Accounting, Organizations and Society (Journal)
BSC	Balanced Scorecard
BRIC	Brazil, Russia, India, China
CAR	Contemporary Accounting Research (Journal)
CEO	Chief Executive Officer
CFA	Confirmatory Factor Analysis
CFI	Comparative Fit Index
CFO	Chief Financial Officer
COO	Chief Operating Officer
CRANET	The Cranfield Network on International Human Resource Management
CMV	Common method variance
df	Degrees of freedom
EAR	European Accounting Review (Journal)
EBIT	Earnings Before Interest and Taxes
EFA	Exploratory Factor Analysis
EVA	Economic Value Added
GFI	Goodness-of-Fit Index
GLOBE	Global Leadership and Organizational Behavior Effectiveness
HLM	Hierarchical Linear Modelling
HRM	Human Resource Management
IT	Information Technology
JAR	Journal of Accounting Research (Journal)
JMAR	Journal of Management Accounting Research (Journal)
KMO	Kaiser–Meyer–Olkin (statistical measure)
M	Mean
MAD	Median Absolute Deviation

Abbreviation	Meaning
MAR	Management Accounting Research (Journal)
MAS	Management Accounting Systems
MCAR	Missing Completely At Random
MIT	Massachusetts Institute of Technology
MCS	Management Control Systems
MNC	Multi-National Corporations
N	Size/Number of group
NACE	Nomenclature générale des Activités économiques dans les Communautés Européennes (General Industrial Classification of Economic Activities
ORBIS	Database from the Bureau van Dijk that contains financial information
p	Significance level
PA	Percent Agreement
PMS	Performance Management Systems
RMSEA	Root Mean Square Error of Approximation
ROA	Return on Assets
ROE	Return on Equity
ROS	Return on Sales
SBU	Strategic Business Unit
SD	Standard deviation
SEM	Structural Equation Modelling
SIC	Standard Industrial Classification
SPSS	Statistical Package for the Social Science
SRMR	Standardized Root Mean Square Residual
TAR	The Accounting Review (Journal)
TLI	Tucker-Lewis Index
TMT	Top Management Team
UK	United Kingdom
US	United States

1 Introduction

1.1 Motivation

Globalization has a growing and on-going impact on the nature and operation of companies (Simon, 2012). It intensifies relationships between social actors across the world in the way local events are even affected by actions far away. In the same vein, globalization increases the inter-linkages of countries and companies. Whatever happens locally has implications for far-off destinations and vice versa (Giddens, 1990). On-going globalization is driven through increasing numbers of countries participating in the 'market' mentality. These include former developing countries (e.g. the BRIC states Brazil, Russia, India, China), which are predicted to gain in importance (Nudurupati et al., 2011; Wilson & Purushothaman, 2007; Wilson et al., 2011). Businesses have witnessed huge shifts and advancements in technological developments, together with a surging market liberalisation that has worked as a clear catalyst for globalization (Govindarajan & Gupta, 2000). Large corporations have been actively involved in international operations for quite some time, but medium-sized corporations are increasingly internationalizing and expanding their businesses abroad too.[1] In doing so, these companies face different markets and also different cultures. For those multinational organizations, the necessity to implement and sustain effective control mechanisms has grown.

A fundamental challenge that management faces in the twenty-first century is how to exercise adequate control in the organization and its respective strategic business units (SBUs). This holds true not only for companies experiencing massive transformative processes (Ghoshal & Bartlett, 1996), but for all companies that are striving for success. Thus, the overall success of a company is orchestrated by efficient and effective management control systems (MCS). They are an overarching concept and comprise a variety of organizational practices and instruments that executives pursue "for the ultimate purpose of implementing the organiza-

---

[1] Simon (1996; 2009) identified a multitude of "hidden champions" and unveiled the success stories of these midsize niche players. The majority of these firms operate in German speaking and Scandinavian countries. These hidden champions have huge global market shares and are intensively active abroad.

tion's strategy" (Adler, 2011, p. 251).[2] The common feature in the meaning and understanding of MCS is the dealing with control. Various definitions of MCS (see Appendix 1, p. 176ff.) acknowledge that managers employ and enforce measures, the so-called controls, to keep their organization running and to enable subordinates to contribute to the success of the company. Various definitions state that powerful organizational actors (management, dominant coalition) strive to guide and direct the behaviour of their subordinates (middle managers, employees) in orchestrating and exercising authority over them (Kärreman & Alvesson, 2004). The desired intention is facilitated by directing subordinates' attention to relevant subjects, and motivating employees towards congruence of personal behaviour and organizational strategies. MCS should convey both financial and non-financial information to management for decision making and control. These systems should be particularly tailored for the use and benefit of management.

Consequently, MCS are the major vehicle for organizational actions to reach the given objectives of the firm. It is quite obvious that managers who are in charge of the organizations cannot do everything on their own and, therefore, rely on their subordinates to execute their intentions. Managers who head organizations have to build a solid architecture for the implementation of the firm's strategy. In doing this they will allocate resources and take decisions on how their subordinates should best spend their time to work on those decisions (Simons, Dávila & Kaplan, 2000). In order to reach the overall objectives of the firm, managers and organizations employ a variety of MCS (Malmi & Brown, 2008). These deliberations stress the highly practical relevance of the MCS subject.

Management decisions are subject to various influencing factors, such as availability of resources, demographics, internal processes, capabilities, technology, ecological concerns, health and safety regulations or capital availability. However, companies are affected by their national cultural surroundings too (Bearden, Money & Nevins, 2006; Nørreklit & Schoenfeld, 2000). The message of studies and literature reviews (Harrison & McKinnon, 1999; Kirkman, Lowe & Gibson, 2006) is "that culture matters" (Caprar & Neville, 2012, p. 236).

---

[2] Anthony (1965) laid the intellectual basis for the design and use of MCS. Appendix 1 (p. 173ff.) exemplifies a broad list of MCS definitions. Appendix 2 (p. 176ff.) presents a main selection of MCS frameworks.

Culture surrounds firms and clearly impacts everyday life in business organizations and societies (Steel & Taras, 2010). Though the performance of companies is dependent on various factors such as strategy, organizational structure and systems, as well as the management's leadership skills, national culture is a crucial variable for managing people (Gerhart, 2008).

Humans have always expressed a strong interest in the cultural settings of other humans. "Researchers have long sought to understand the nature of culture and its potential influence on human activity" (Earley, 2006, p. 922). A fundamental question is how culture generates an influence on MCS. In a nutshell, the behaviour and actions of managers, and other stakeholders, are ingrained in their cultural context. Humans learn and derive cultural norms consciously and unconsciuosly. Managers, and thus organizations, rely on those cultural norms, standards and mechanisms of their respective organizational surroundings. Business and business research, and thus management scholars, are intriguingly investigating "cultural similarities and differences" and their consequences of "how to transfer management practises" across societies (Kara & Peterson, 2012, p. 342). It can be argued that people from different countries perceive management activities and control systems in diverse ways (Chow et al., 1997; Harrison, 1992) since they are confronted with different cultural norms, standards and mechanisms. This implies that management practices that are effective in one surrounding may be ineffective in another (Chow, Kato & Merchant, 1996), thus "managers are increasingly interested in knowing whether the control practices which are effective in one country can be used effectively in another" (Merchant, Chow & Wu, 1995, p. 619). The underlying logic that individuals (and thus organizations) are affected by culture in implementing control elements in the same fashion within one culture is traced back to "internalised core cultural values which are shared extensively enough by virtue of their membership in a wider national society" (Bhimani, 1999, p. 417). Almost two decades ago Chow, Kato and Merchant (1996, p. 189) nicely summarized that "each individual simultaneously embodies all the dimensions of national culture. Furthermore, just as controls have the potential to complement or substitute for one another, multiple cultural dimensions may affect individuals' preferences for, and/or reactions to a given control".

However, the cultural effect is not solely directed to different cultural preferences, but also to organizational practices. Hope and Fraser (2003) see huge differences in incentive systems across countries. Bhimani (1999, p. 417) states that "there is much systematic evidence suggesting that the pursuit of formally identical tasks or goals takes place in dissimilar ways from one national society to another"; therefore, he assumes "nationally specific solutions to problems of management control design". "That is, something that 'works' in one country will not necessarily work in another" (Murray, Jain & Adams, 1976, p. 50). This ultimately leads to the question of whether firms should adopt their MCS to local needs or whether they can apply a more generalized MCS within the firm's borders across cross-cultural frontiers. The question of whether and how becomes salient. Advice ranges from universal best practices to very fine-grained local adaptation. There is much learning potential for either "local best fits" or "universal best practises" (Jansen, Merchant & van der Stede, 2009; Long & Shields, 2005; Merchant et al., 2011). The research topic is of great importance as firms are increasingly globalizing and thus face cultural-based challenges. It will be interesting to investigate the extent to which there are national differences in the design and use of MCS.

Globalization has certainly paved the prominence of national culture studies over recent decades (Leung et al., 2005). Cultural effects on the design and effectiveness on MCS have been highlighted in a number of studies (see Harrison and McKinnon (1999) for a literature review from 1980 – 1996). In particular, Otley (1999) stresses the importance of studying the cultural aspects of MCS. He emphasizes that management controls, and other performance measurement practices, should be judged not just from an economic perspective but also from a social, behavioural and managerial position, within an overall organizational context. Social, cross-national and cultural aspects make the study of control systems more fascinating.

An examination of various MCS elements will certainly help to answer Harrison's (1992) long-standing research question that

> it is unlikely that all MAS and control systems characteristics are generalizable and transferable across nations, but equally unlikely that none is. In addition, it is likely that some characteristics are generalizable to some groups of nations but not to others. It is therefore also important to know what commonalities certain groups of nations possess that permit or preclude such generalizability. (p. 1)

The scientific calls for the relevance of the cultural subject, and the proven influence of national culture, should consequently complement the models of MCS design (Harrison & McKinnon, 1999).

The widespread practical use of the different elements of management control, which companies actively adapt, and sometimes experiment with to further develop the specific needs of their surroundings, has stimulated many researchers of psychology, human resources, organization, international management, as well as management control, to gain insight into the fundamentals of these control practices (a list of papers is presented in Appendix 5 (p. 192ff.)). Given the vast research area of the MCS domain, a concentration of the research focus is certainly reasonable. This thesis focuses on three main elements of the overall MCS, namely, performance measurement, performance evaluation and rewards. Since these controls are deeply embedded in the overall MCS context, and placed at the core of many frameworks and of business reality, they are worth examining.

A reason to narrow down the topic to certain elements of MCS follows the idea to concentrate on the major and most conventional components of the overall MCS. First, performance measurement is at the very heart of an organization and delivers a set of financial and non-financial indicators to enable the quantification of results. Management relies on thorough and topical information to steer the business. Hence, the quality and composition of performance measures are vital for organizations (Evans, 2004; Grafton, Lillis & Widener, 2010; Haas & Kleingeld, 1999; Kaplan & Norton, 1992; Petersen, 2007). According to Malina and Selto (2004, p. 442) "performance measurement allows a firm to effectively describe and implement strategy, guide employee behavior, assess managerial effectiveness, and provide the basis for rewards". Thus, they are vital "in translating an orgnization's strategy into desired behaviors and results" (van der Stede, Chow & Lin, 2006, p. 185). Second, performance evaluation, both objectively and subjectively, is a vital control function within organizations and is nearly a universal feature (Wong-On-Wing et al., 2007). It serves multiple purposes, including provision of feedback, salary and bonus administration, promotion, training and development (Murphy & Cleveland, 1995). Third, Liu and Leitch (2013), as well as Indjejikian and Nanda (2002), highlight that incentive systems and bonuses are a fundamental component of the overall MCS. Also, Murphy (2001, p. 246) indicates that "annual bonuses are a ubiquitous component of managerial compensation". Gibbs et al. (2004) found that rewards can constitute a substantial portion of the total compensation. The authors found almost equal base salary and rewards for department managers in car dealerships. Although this finding cannot be generalized – car dealerships are an industry with quite high incentives – it stresses the importance of this control system. Jansen, Merchant and van der Stede (2009, p. 59) point out that incentive compensation systems are a very important element for organizations, "because they presumably provide the primary means by which organizations elicit and reinforce desired behaviors".

Otley and Fakiolas (2000, p. 509) emphasize the fundamentality of "performance measurement and the use of performance measures in performance evaluation … as key management issues". Performance measures determined for the evaluation of employees have to be carefully selected, as motivation, job satisfaction, organizational commitment and job performance is affected (Lau & Moser, 2008; Tan & Lau, 2012). Dossi, Patelli and Zoni's (2010, p. 532) remark of an "explosion of academic research regarding performance measurement and compensation", although mainly researched for a narrow set of companies (large, public traded firms within highly established financial markets), stresses the academic relevance. Van Veen-Dirks (2010) states that performance evaluation and rewards are normally seen as one side of the coin in the accounting world. In this vein Ding and Beaulieu (2011) provide evidence for the role of financial incentives in performance evaluations. Cardinaels and van Veen-Dirks (2010) concluded that organizations should be careful in the way they compile and present performance measures for evaluation purposes. Grafton, Lillis and Widener (2010) recently studied the role of performance measurement and evaluation, and provide evidence that measures should be reflected in the evaluation scheme.

The topic of performance measurement, performance evaluation and rewards is tinged with cultural questions for many organizations. As a consequence, the interplay between these strands – influence of cultural aspects on performance measurement, performance evaluation and rewards – is of great relevance for both researchers and practitioners.

1.2 Research background and guiding research question

The scientific world greatly acknowledges research in the field of MCS. The special issue of the Journal of Management Control recently targeted MCS as "one of the core topics of academic accounting research for decades" (Malmi, 2013, p. 229) that deserves intense research attention. There have been a vast number of studies on the topic of MCS in recent decades, and scholars regularly study this phenomenon (Chenhall, 2003, 2007). Additionally, further research, which increases the academic footprint to understand even more fine-grained practical challenges and questions, is often mentioned. There are voices that underline the need for more conceptual work (e.g. Malmi, 2013). Instead of efforts to always fabricate new frameworks, Hanzlick and Brühl (2013) advocate facilitating empirical research. As conceptualizations in MCS have attained a certain level of maturity, the time is ripe for more quantitative and qualitative research (Langfield-Smith, 2007; Malmi & Brown, 2008). Ferreira and Otley (2009) acknowledge that more research and empirical evidence is needed to test the MCS concept. In particular, they advocate more case studies. It is clear that more quantitative research on MCS will also strongly benefit the development of this research field. In terms of research execution, Berry et al. (2009, p. 2) state that "it seems essential to place more emphasis on research which attends more specifically to the relationship of control practice and theory which will require more embedded and collaborative research processes".[3]

Sunder (2002) expresses the sporadic nature of research into culture, within the context of management control. Gerhart and Fang (2005, p. 982) outline that "it is important to identify these *[cultural differences – note of the author]* in academic work and to make managers aware of them". There have been many calls to study culture and control, but up to now only a few studies have researched the relationship between culture and MCS (Berry et al., 2009). Scott (2009) stresses the sparse number of studies into cultural forces. "Research progress in this area has been slow in large part because of the inherent difficulty in conducting cross-national studies" (Jansen, Merchant & van der Stede, 2009, p. 59). Lowe et al. (2002) list some general reasons for scarce cross-cultural comparisons: (1) huge technical and methodological prerequisites to ensure equivalent survey questions across countries, (2) necessity to gain access to survey respondents in several countries at the same time, and (3) challenge to maintain sample comparability across countries. The lack of sufficient scientific rigour in terms of methodological equivalence, and the high complexity to install and pursue a cross-cultural project would prohibit the publication aims of the researchers, and thus limit large-scale cross-cultural studies.

The literature review of Harrison and McKinnon (1999), which targeted cultural influences on MCS, came up with only a tiny collection of articles. Even a deeper look at more recent

---

[3] In order to expand the understanding on the configuration of MCS, Teemu Malmi and Mikko Sandelin have initiated a large international research project. Fifteen research teams in eleven countries from universities across Scandinavia, parts of Western, Eastern and Southern Europe, Australia and Canada joined their research efforts in December 2010 on the topic "Management Control Systems as a package". The project aims to explore the nature and the interrelationships and designs of MCS packages. The enquiry for possible configurations of MCS is at the core of the research.

publications, which will be presented in Chapter 3.2 (p. 69f.), leaves much room for unchartered research territory. Thus, the research gaps are manifold. Generally, they can be attributed to elements of management control and culture, in particular, cultural aspects of control elements. To complement gaps in the thematic research, I also present the main gaps related to research methodology.

First, and to the best of my knowledge, I found no studies that target cultural influences on the amount of performance measures in reward contracts and schemes of performance evaluation. No previous cultural research has dealt with the hierarchical organizational level to which performance measures are tied. Furthermore, I could not identify any cultural study that concentrated on rewarding purpose or importance. Additionally, I found no cultural study related to the level of objectivity or subjectivity in performance evaluation.

Second, a main area of investigation in this thesis deals with the components of performance measures in rewarding schemes. Even in non-cultural studies, relatively few studies have directly examined the relative weights placed on financial and non-financial measures for compensation purposes (Ittner, Larcker & Meyer, 2003). Abdel-Maksoud, Dugdale and Luther (2005) reported on the application and degree of importance of non-financial performance measures within British manufacturing companies. Gosselin (2005) analysed the extent to which firms use financial and non-financial performance measures among 101 Canadian organizations. He showed that financial measures were more often used than non-financial measures. This study mentioned no reference to the use of performance measures within reward settings. The study by Ittner, Larcker and Rajan (1997), which is limited to US firms, investigated factors that determine the relative weighting of financial and non-financial measures of CEO bonuses. Thirty-six percent of the firms incorporated non-financial measures in the CEO bonus scheme, whereas the remaining 64% employed only financial indicators. The cultural study of Schuler and Rogovsky (1998) targeted financial rewards only. Van der Stede (2003) looked at the influence of national culture on the design of management control and reward systems. He was interested in the extent of intracorporate isomorphism within 37 diversified firms and their business units headquartered in Belgium. Indjejikian and Nanda (2002, p. 795) exemplify that, "unfortunately, researchers rarely have access to performance measure and performance standard data on a large scale, because firms almost never disclose such proprietary details". Ittner, Larcker and Meyer (2003, p. 731) state that "relatively few psychology-based performance evaluation studies directly examine the relative weights placed on financial and non-financial measures for compensation purposes". I gained access to large-scale performance data and to the relative weights placed on performance measures. Earlier research showed the relevance of cultural differences to aspects of performance evaluation and rewards, but did "not consider the broader spectrum of rewards being used in today's organizations (e.g. both financial and non-financial rewards)" (Chiang & Birtch, 2007, p. 1295).

Third, previous MCS research targeted single themes or control elements, i.e., examined MCS in isolation (Chenhall, 2003, 2007). However, in business reality it is clear that organizations rely on different combinations of control mechanisms. Most of the previous research only addressed single MCS characteristics one at a time. Rare exceptions are the studies by Widener (2007) or Sandelin (2008). Consequently, only a few studies have so far examined both performance measurement and performance evaluation (e.g. Cardinaels & van Veen-Dirks, 2010; Grafton, Lillis & Widener, 2010), or performance evaluation and rewards (e.g. Bushman, Indjejikian & Smith, 1996), often in form of compensation according to peer performance (e.g. Aggarwal & Samwick, 1999; Albuquerque, 2009; Antle & Smith, 1986; Gibbons & Murphy, 1990; Gong, Li & Shin, 2011; Matsumura & Shin, 2006). Although I will not study the subject of control configurations, I will focus on several topic areas, i.e. performance measurement, performance evaluation and rewards.

I complete a fourth research gap by concentrating on management controls practices from a cultural angle, as a vast amount of previous studies targeted control preferences. One of the representatives with many contributions, Chiang and Birtch (2005; 2006; 2007; 2012) asked for reward type preferences, but did not ask for the actual practices. None of the four studies, focusing on certain control preferences, provide a picture of how things actually happen. The 'should be' condition provides hints for the actual state, but only inconclusively. The articles of Bonache et al. (2012), Chiang and Birtch (2010), Jansen et al. (2009), Lowe et al. (2002), Merchant et al. (2011), Peng and Petersen (2008) and Van der Stede (2003) investigated practices of performance evaluations and rewards across cultures.

Fifth, scrutinizing the topic of rewards, the focus of the literature in non-cultural studies lies mostly on the CEO and on top management (e.g. Brick, Palmon & Wald, 2006; Conyon & Schwalbach, 2000; Cronqvist & Fahlenbrach, 2013; Höppe & Moers, 2011; Jensen & Murphy, 1990a, 1990b, Mehran, 1995; Murphy, 1999). Only a limited number of studies look at the direct subordinate layer, namely middle managers, often because there is publicly available data, particularly for the top management. Seldom can researchers gain access to sensitive information on rewards (Merchant & Otley, 2007; Prendergast, 1999). Indjejikian and Nanda (2002) illustrate rare knowledge of the ingredients of a bonus plan, and the corresponding performance measures especially for middle managers. A rare exception for the subordinate layer is Gibbs (1995). The majority of employees who receive a financial reward belong to the hierarchical level below top management. Thus, it is interesting to understand how rewards are translated into the contracts of subordinates of top management. To answer these questions, scholars infrequently opt for high level (i.e. top management) respondents in their studies.

A sixth research gap targets the cultural samples investigated in this thesis. Previous literature has only incorporated a handful of countries in their investigations. Studies mainly focused on two country comparisons with strong focus on the US and Asia (see Chapter 3.2 (p. 69f.)), mainly for two reasons. Cross border research projects are difficult to start and a challenge to execute in terms of project management, sampling opportunities, timing, complexity and cost. Therefore, research is mainly limited to two country comparisons. Several reasons made these comparisons of interest: the supposed high cultural contradictions of the USA and Asian countries, and the rising importance of Asian economies. Former Asian roots among some US-based researchers certainly facilitated this research agenda. Studies rarely focused on a larger cultural set with more discernible cultural differences. Real opportunities are offered for the transition economies in Eastern Europe.

A seventh research gap area involves the limited scope of the existing cultural framework. Many cross-cultural studies have followed the Hofstede model, though other cultural frameworks (e.g. Schwartz, Trompenaars, GLOBE[4]) exhibit different contents, specific particularities, richer and more far-reaching approaches, or simply newer models to understand cross-cultural similarities and differences.

There is still much to learn about the intermingling of MCS and culture. From the research point of view, I have highlighted several arguments concerning the worth of MCS.

---

[4] GLOBE is an acronym for Global Leadership and Organizational Behavior Effectiveness.

Recognizing the relevance of the interweaving of MCS and culture, there are vast research options. Though stimulating ideas have been provided and many ideas and findings generated, there is still much uncharted research. Hence, the research gaps indicate potential research areas that are of interest for cross-cultural research. The various research gaps that I have identified further highlight the importance of integrating cross-cultural analysis in research to analyze differences between MCS across various cultures. This in turn will fuel research on the impact of culture on management styles and MCS. As a consequence, and to fill this research gap, this work contrasts MCS and three major elements – performance measurement, performance evaluation and rewards – through a cultural lens. This work will shed light on the functioning of these different control devices by means of cultural comparisons. However, to outline the demarcation, this work will not address control packages (Malmi & Brown, 2008) in their entirety in terms of different functionality (Speklé, 2001).[5]

The two strands of literature, MCS and culture, when considered simultaneously, raise the following research objective:

> The general research objective of this thesis is whether there are cultural differences among organizations in their respective control practices, in particular in performance measurement, performance evaluation and reward schemes.

The objectives of the study concern the contingent nature and the design of management control elements across different cultures. The thesis concentrates on cultural differences along a continuum of cultural dimensions for performance evaluation and rewards schemes that are tightly coupled with performance measures. Performance measures are vital ingredients in both performance evaluation and reward schemes. The object of investigation is the subordinate layer to the top management of a stand-alone company or SBU. The research objective is embedded in the question: how top management guides and directs subordinate behaviour. This question in turn is looked at from a comparative cultural stand-

---

[5] Within organizations the various MCS elements form a package of different systems. However, the idea of the package is in its infancy. There have been few published theoretical contributions (Grabner & Moers, 2013; Malmi & Brown, 2008).

point. I will not address the aspect of control effectiveness as the research objective targets cultural differences for various control elements and, therefore, assumes a similar degree of effectiveness across cultures. From the perspective of contingency theory, with the practices of management control as the dependent variables and culture as the independent variable, this study is a 'level 1' study (Fisher, 1995; van der Stede, 2003).

In a nutshell, the thesis deals with the impact of cultural phenomena on control systems. Companies are embedded in relationships with different stakeholders. Managers who lead these companies strive to create value for stakeholders, which can be financial, though not necessarily. In order to monitor the value created by managers, performance is measured and evaluated. Corresponding monetary and non-monetary incentives are set by means of reward systems. These systems, performance measurement, performance evaluation and reward systems are part of a larger MCS. Specific variables, which are considered critical from the perspective of theory and practice, span these three core parts of the MCS. Some of these variables change when companies operate in a different culture. I will demonstrate which variables are affected by culture and how their influence manifests, i.e. address the direction of cultural differences. The meaningless claim "culture matters" is resolved. I aim to provide more specific information about which individual subsystem variables are influenced by culture, or more precisely by a specific cultural dimension. Acknowledging the integrative efforts that should be undertaken to advance and complement institutional theory (Tihanyi, Devinney & Pedersen, 2012), stakeholder theory (Freeman, Harrison & Wicks, 2007; Freeman et al., 2010), contingency theory (Chenhall, 2003, 2007) and cultural deliberations, this thesis aims to use these theories to understand how practices of management control are composed and how they appear in different environments and cultures.

I found that performance standard's objectivity, purpose and frequency show cultural differences in the area of performance evaluation. I found differences in the balance of performance areas. I further found many cultural differences for reward systems. In particular, reward systems differ in the amount of measures, component and level structure, objectivity, equality, nature and importance of rewards. I found a certain degree of similarity in the extent of subjective evaluation and rewarding purpose. Additionally, I found an effect of a variety of contextual factors on the design and use of performance evaluation and reward systems. This thesis extends the extant literature on MCS and culture in several ways. First, prior studies concentrated on a narrow view of MCS. This study incorporates performance evaluation and rewards in close collaboration with performance measures. In contrast to many studies, this thesis looks into the control elements of four different countries, among them Poland, which until now has not been studied for management control elements. Furthermore, the thesis turns to the much newer GLOBE framework and thus abandons the Hofstede paradigm. From a managerial perspective, my research also aims at giving practical advice to executives in how to design MCS across different cultures to improve organizational effectiveness. I aim to provide findings that assist managers to achieve their goals and hence those of their organization to a greater degree. Due to globalization, and increasing multi-national operations, the cross-cultural data could enable managers to analyze how national culture affects MCS.

1.3   Outline of the thesis

Figure 1 illustrates the building blocks of the thesis: (1) Cultural dimensions, (2) MCS and their subsystems, and (3) the institutional, organizational and individual context.

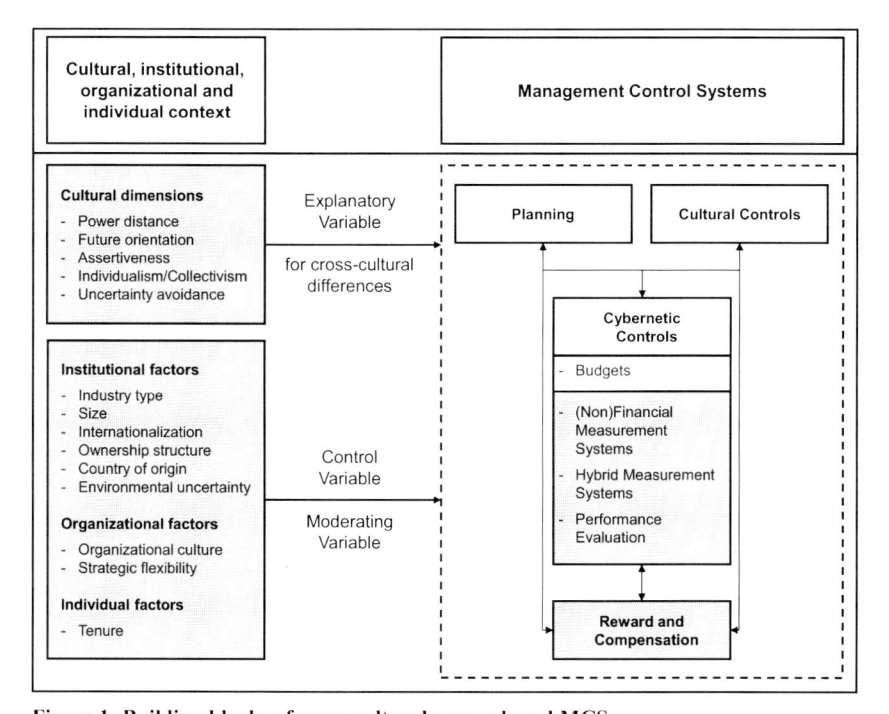

Figure 1: Building blocks of cross-cultural research and MCS

The upper part of the left hand side in Figure 1 portrays cultural dimensions as differentiating variables. The lower part pictures institutional context factors, organizational variables and demographic factors, which serve as control variables. It is crucial to control for alternative explanations in cross-cultural research because national differences may be contingent on other societal or economic factors (Aycan, 2000). Without taking these context factors into consideration, cross-cultural studies on MCS or related parts would, consequently, reduce their explanatory power because they omit important variables. It has been shown that contingency factors (Chenhall, 2003, 2007) as well as demographic variables (Burkert & Lueg, 2013) have an impact on MCS. The different kinds of ownership structure over different countries and the way how control is exercised may affect the steering of companies (Whitley, 1999). Webster and White (2010) found that national culture exerts organizational culture. As there is evidence for a relationship between national culture and organizational culture, and "94 percent of the variance in organizational culture is not explained by national culture in the GLOBE research" (Gerhart, 2009b, p. 254), the real magnitude of this relationship remains unclear. I could imagine that the organizational level of culture influences MCS design; as a consequence, the interplay has to be controlled. These deliberations urged me to include institutional factors, organizational variables and demographic factors as part of the non-cultural context in Figure 1.

While there is a conceptual difference between nation and culture, respectively international and intercultural, or even cross-cultural (Hantrais & Mangen, 1996), there is a common overlap of the "shared aspect of human action and institution" (Earley & Singh, 1995, p. 330). Nations determine cultural groups. Therefore, culture is often equated with the nation-state (Boyacigiller et al., 2004; Kennedy, Fu & Yukl, 2003). I follow this classification. According to Schaffer and Riordan (2003), 79% of cross-cultural research studies used nationality or country of residence as a proxy for national culture. Steel and Taras (2010) acknowledged that geographic boundaries or nationality are appropriate in determining national cultures, if national culture and not the individual is the predictor of the examined differences.

On the right hand side, an overall MCS framework depicts the core ideas and the synthesis of existing frameworks. Part of the cybernetic control system (performance measurement and performance evaluation), as well as the rewards system, will be addressed in the thesis. I see MCS in a broader perspective and refer to Malmi and Brown (2008) as they understand management control as all those practices, procedures and rules to direct and influence employee behaviour. The broad view is substantiated by the variety of control elements with which managers try to achieve management control objectives. This theoretical framework may be applied to advance our knowledge of the interrelation of MCS and cultural phenomena to the benefit of scholars, managers and organizations.

Figure 2 (slightly adapted from Bourguignon and Chiapello (2005, p. 687) and placed in a wider context) concentrates on the core areas of management controls that are targeted in this thesis. The figure summarizes the three-step approach where performance measurement, evaluation and rewards are placed in a logical chain.

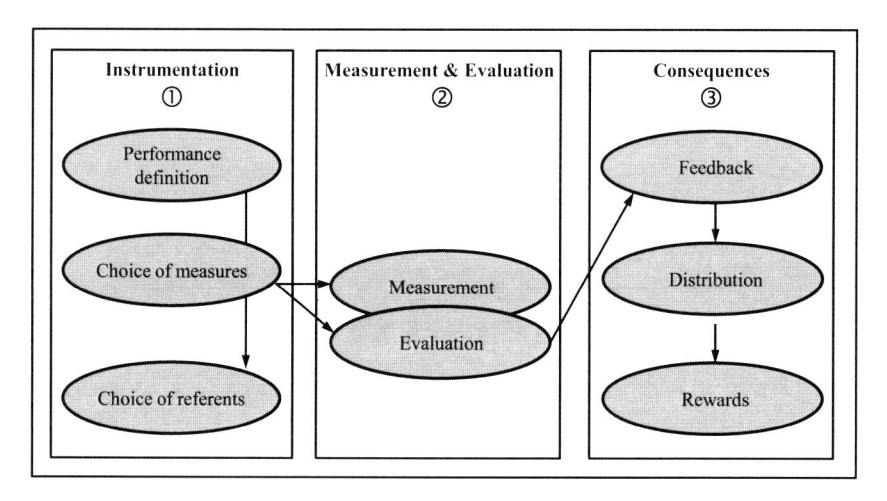

Figure 2: Performance measurement, evaluation and reward process

Performance measures are derived from the instrumentation phase and form the base for performance measurement. Evaluation takes place based on instruments (definition of performance, categorization and selection of measures, references for the measures) and the result of the measurement process. Hence, the first process step serves as the basis for measurement and judgment, which for their part depend on the created information output, the references and judge. In contrast to the original figure, I placed feedback to the last column of the figure since this vehicle serves as the means of transportation of the evaluation to the one being assessed (Bonner et al., 2000). Feedback in form of an appraisal interview communicates the decisions of the supervisors and the consequences for the subordinates in terms of income, social standing and future resource allocations; hence, to the best of my understanding, this should be part of the post evaluation phase. Lawler III (2003) argued that the results of performance evaluations should be strongly tied to the reward system, because first and foremost evaluations are taken seriously and the motivation of those being compensated is potentially rising.

The purpose of my research in terms of progressing scientific knowledge is insulated on explaining unknown phenomena and least studied facts. I am thereby addressing "why" and "how" questions. The major research purpose, the explanatory element, is covered by testing a variety of hypotheses that are derived by theory. The emphasis lies in the context of justification (Reichenbach, 1938). Beside this major research purpose, I also touch on descriptive and exploratory elements. In a descriptive manner I will portray and document business practices in different cultural surroundings. In exploratory fashion I want to show the impact of cultural elements on organizational practices not previously studied.

A major aim of my cross-cultural comparison of the various management control elements is to achieve generalizability of findings. That is why I do not follow the qualitative paradigm in the form of a case-based research, but rather position the study with a quantitative research strategy. Within the quantitative research paradigm, I follow a cross-sectional design in a comparative fashion. Such a design exhibits the collection of more than one case, indeed of many cases, and the reception of quantifiable data of one respondent in one step and an ambiguous pattern of the association between the observed variables in the form of causal inferences (Bryman, 2008). The comparative character of the thesis is exemplified by the cross-cultural setting. Hantrais and Mangen (1996, p. 1) specify the understanding of cross-cultural research by stating that "individuals or teams should set out to study particular issues or phenomena in two or more countries with the express intention of comparing their manifestations in different socio-cultural settings, using the same research instruments".

A theoretical foundation is crucial in research. Luft and Shields (2003; 2007) highlight that a study must align the 'level of theory', 'the level of variable measurement' and 'the level of data analysis'. My level of analysis is the organization for management control elements and the society for the cultural elements. Although culture is a cross-level phenomenon and could be analyzed accordingly, this study focuses on the comparison of management control practices at the singular level of the organization, while the explanatory power to derive the suspected degree of the practices derives from national cultural scores.

As the study is situated at a higher than individual level, I have to apply different steps for measurement and analysis to ensure appropriate alignment. The survey questions for the management control practices target organizational attributes, whereas the cultural questions that are aggregated from the individual level incorporate a societal focus in their questioning. There are a multitude of theoretical approaches, from cognitive theories over organizational thoughts to economic theories, which are generally taken to predict or explain performance evaluation and reward practices (Bonner & Sprinkle, 2002). The focus in my work cannot be an individual theory, e.g. an individual preference or practice applied to certain performance measures in reward contracts, or to follow a distinct pattern of performance evaluation. Rather I am positioned at the organizational level, with a beyond-organizational element related to cross-cultural facts. Many theories from the organizational level tend to state similarities across cultures. Inherently, these theories inhibit a generalizing viewpoint and thus do not provide explanations for cultural differences. Theories that more explicitly incorporate a notion or explanation of cultural differences (e.g. new-institutionalism) have rarely been applied to the research context of cross-cultural studies. Often, the authors of cross-cultural studies merely argue with a "cultural" theory, which they relate to one of its main representatives (e.g. the Hofstede paradigm). As an overall comprising cultural theory does not exist, such an approach is often regarded as the only possible way. To better understand the cultural effects, this thesis integrates both the cultural paradigm and organizational theories to deepen the argumentation and bring in more valid deliberations for cross-cultural differences. There remains the question of how organizations choose and use particular control elements. Organizational theories help to deal with questions of how and why organizations act as they do.

This thesis studies how culture affects MCS, in particular, performance evaluation and reward schemes with close association of performance measures. In attempting to answer this question, Chapter 2 (p. 21ff.) presents the fundamental terms and the theoretical framework. In Chapter 2.1, I show the complexity of the national cultural acumen, present the two major frameworks of potential interest, and unbundle the cultural concept into sub-dimensions. Next, I shed light on the relevant MCS framework, before outlining the single concepts that build the research subject of my thesis. Chapter 2.2 highlights the concept of MCS and the framework in use. Chapter 2.3 focuses on those subsystems – performance measurement, performance evaluation and reward schemes – that are particularly examined in the analysis. Chapter 2.4 provides insights into the theoretical justification of the thesis. Chenhall (2003; 2007) points out the necessity of applying a culture-specific framework to the testing and assessment of cultural values. I complement the theoretical study of culture with contingency thoughts (Chapter 2.4.1), the new institutionalism (Chapter 2.4.2), stakeholder theory (Chapter 2.4.3) and agency theory (Chapter 2.4.4). Chapter 2.4.5 brings a synthesis of the theoretical approaches. This chapter also explains how culture manifests into organizational and managerial actions.

Chapter 3 (p. 67ff.) captures previous cross-cultural MCS research and details those studies by means of a literature review on national culture and performance evaluation and reward schemes. As I will demonstrate in the literature review on cultural studies, there are multiple starting points for analysis to extend the existing literature. Chapter 3.1 provides the methodology of the literature review, while Chapter 3.2 presents the main research papers. Based on theory, previous research and gaps in the literature, Chapter 3.3 develops hypotheses on the basis of five cultural dimensions of the cultural framework. In this, the hypotheses combine the link between the management control practices and the cultural context.

Chapter 4 (p. 87ff.) details the research methodology of the cross-cultural research. I executed my approach as follows. After recruiting three other group members, I coordinated the four teams of researchers. All scholars collected data independently in their own country and followed an identical methodological approach. I present information on the sample characteristics (Chapter 4.1), the questionnaire design (Chapter 4.2), the data collection (Chapter 4.3), as well as the measures (Chapter 4.4). I also provide a specific notion (Chapter 4.5) on assessing the quality of the measurement.

Chapter 5 (p. 121ff.) concentrates on the research question by means of an empirical study. Data were investigated using SPSS version 21.0 (IBM Corp., Armonk, NY, USA) and the R package lavaan[6] (Rosseel, 2012). The chapter presents the descriptive results (Chapter 5.1), examines the univariate analyses of the key differences between the performance evaluation practices and reward schemes in four countries (Chapter 5.2) and applies further tests of robustness (Chapter 5.3). The empirical chapter aims at deriving differences among organizations across different cultures in their respective performance evaluation and reward schemes.

Chapter 6 (p. 151ff.) offers explanations of the findings, highlights the contributions towards theory, former research and practice, discusses limitations and offers prospects for future research.

---

[6] Further information can be found here: http://cran.r-project.org/web/packages/lavaan/index.html. Retrieved June 21, 2014.

2 Fundamental terms and theoretical framework

2.1 Culture

2.1.1 Complexity of the cultural phenomenon

"Culture is a fuzzy construct. If we are to understand the way culture relates to social psychological phenomena, we must analyze it by determining dimensions of cultural variation" (Triandis et al., 1988, p. 323). This quotation underlines that culture is a concept, which is difficult to grasp. Culture is a complex social concept and from the nature of the matter there exist no common definitions (Taras, Rowney & Steel, 2009). A variety of 164 definitions [7] compiled by Kroeber and Kluckhohn (1952) reveals a great complexity. Traditional starting points are found in anthropology and archaeology. Later, an increasing cultural mixture in daily living and rising globalization shifted the focus to management, psychology, and education, too (Taras, Rowney & Steel, 2009).

Looking at the starting points from the anthropological point of view, Kluckhohn (1951, p. 86) defined culture as "patterned ways of thinking, feeling and reacting, acquired and transmitted mainly by symbols, constituting the distinctive achievements of human groups, including their embodiments and artifacts". A similar definition delivered by Geertz (1973, p. 89) saw culture as "an historically transmitted pattern of meanings embodied in symbols, a system of inherited conceptions expressed in symbolic forms by means of which men communicate, perpetuate, and develop their knowledge about and attitudes toward life". Also Kaplan (1965, p. 960) states that "cultures are build up out of patterned and interrelated traditions". Put even shorter, Kuper's (2000, p. 227) view of culture is "a matter of ideas and values, a collective cast of mind". Kluckhohn (1951) and Kaplan (1965) stress the time-related aspect since culture is transferred over time.

Culture is also a multi-level phenomenon. The different levels of culture comprise the individual, organizational and national level. Hofstede (1990) introduced a graphical representation of the different manifestations of culture (unconscious values and conscious

---

[7] The 164 definitions are catalogued among the different groups: descriptive (21), historical (22), normative (27), psychological (38), structural (9), genetic (40) and incomplete (7).

practices) in form of his onion diagram. Apart from the fact that culture is mostly researched at the national level (Caprar & Neville, 2012), I will be dealing with the concept of national culture following the logic of the overarching research question.

From the management field, Hofstede defines national culture as "the collective programming of the mind that distinguishes the members of one group or category of people from others" (Hofstede, Hofstede & Minkov, 2010, p. 6). The GLOBE[8] project declares culture as "shared motives, values, beliefs, identities, and interpretations or meanings of significant events that result from common experiences of members of collectives that are transmitted across generations" (House & Javidan, 2004, p. 15). While beliefs, which reflect actual practices, express people's perceptions of how things are ideally done, values, which reflect desired practices, measure people's aspirations about the way things should be done (Chui & Kwok, 2009). The common denominator of these definitions is that culture is a collective pattern of beliefs and values that is learned and transferred within a community. Culture is deeply embedded in members of a community. Norms, values and standards that are inherent in the respective culture shape the behaviour of social actors.

2.1.2 Major cultural frameworks

Although a vast amount of alternative models to measure culture received recognition and increased popularity (Taras, Rowney & Steel, 2009) I have to choose an instrument for the analysis. Given the great heterogeneity of cultural frameworks which come along with different research instruments, the rationale for my decision is as follows. The research question on MCS design across cultures is targeted with a large-scale quantitative study leaving aside qualitative and descriptive cultural frameworks, ethnography and anthropological oriented frameworks and frameworks, which lack a clear possibility to distinguish cultural dimensions.

---

[8] Information including some GLOBE publications is collected at the official GLOBE website: http://business.nmsu.edu/programs-centers/globe. Retrieved June 21, 2014.

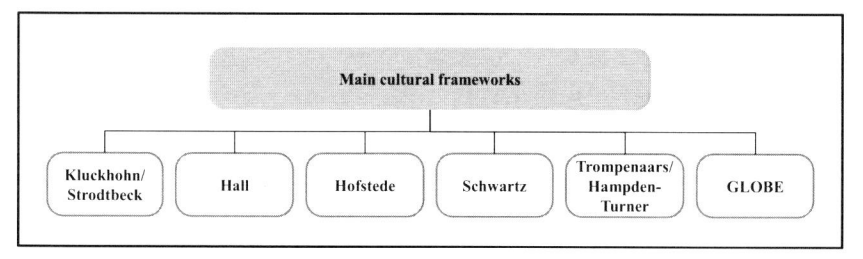

Figure 3: Overview of cultural frameworks

Figure 3 lists the most important cultural frameworks: Kluckhohn and Strodtbeck, Hall, Hofstede, Schwartz, Trompenaars and Hampden-Turner as well as the GLOBE project (Crossland & Hambrick, 2007, p. 771-772; Kutschker & Schmid, 2011, p. 702f.).

Kluckhohn and Strodtbeck were situated in ethnography and empirically studied their value orientation framework with Native American tribes. My methodology does not apply to this approach. For Hall, communication plays a crucial role which is explicitly stated by the words "culture is communication and communication is culture" (Hall, 1990, p. 186). Hall separates cultures along their way they communicate. This makes Hall's four cultural dimensions more applicable in communication studies (Kutschker & Schmid, 2011).

Schwartz' value orientation study[9] (Schwartz, 1994, 1999, 2006) could be a first starting point since his framework is increasingly acknowledged in management literature (Drogendijk & Slangen, 2006). However it has a low appearance in management control and is rather marketing (e.g. Funk et al., 2009; Rubera, Ordanini & Griffith, 2011; Sousa, Ruzo & Losada, 2010) or finance related (e.g. Li et al., 2011; Shao, Kwok & Guedhami, 2009). Schwartz derived his seven value dimensions by surveying teachers and students; later on Schwartz validated his scales with a large-scale and broad sample. What inhibits me most to consider his approach is his limited focus on managerial implications and the appropriateness for individual-level analysis (Funk et al., 2009). However, our research focuses on the organizational and national level.

---

[9] The early studies with teachers and students can be found in Schwartz and Bilsky (1987; 1990).

Trompenaars (1993), later together with Hampden-Turner (1998; 2012), has conducted a cultural study which was published in the book 'Riding the Waves of Culture'. However, they are criticized as being merely anecdotal. The authors develop seven dimensions which are distinct from the Hofstede/GLOBE-tradition but their methodology in generating and operationalizing the cultural dimensions remains unclear. They follow rather an eclectical approach. Moreover, a lack of reliability of their measures led to inconclusive results regarding the cultural dimensions (Kutschker & Schmid, 2011).

In order to increase explanatory power of the cultural influence on MCS it is necessary to unbundle culture into interpretable dimensions and subcomponents (Harrison, 1992; Leung, 2008; Schwartz, 1994), "if culture is seen as a complex, multidimensional structure rather than as a simple categorical variable" (Clark, 1987, p. 461). The unpackaged culture in form of these dimensions can then facilitate to interpret the value and practice patterns. Among the cultural frameworks addressing culture from a quantitative point of view, in form of cultural dimensions, are the Hofstede and the GLOBE framework which are both cross-cultural studies of high prestige (Venaik & Brewer, 2010). In his editorial, Leung (2006, p. 881) speaks of both as titans who introduced "one of the most influential frameworks" (i.e. Hofstede) or undertook "the most sophisticated project" (i.e. GLOBE) in international business. Undoubtedly, the GLOBE study is the most recent and comprehensive examination of culture and leadership systematically approaching cross-cultural research (Steel & Taras, 2010; Tsui, Nifadkar & Ou, 2007).

2.1.3 Hofstede framework

The impact of Hofstede with his path breaking seminal work "Culture's Consequences" is unquestionable (Tung & Verbeke, 2010). Hofstede has been frequently used to measure the influence of national culture on MCS (Williams & van Triest, 2009). This highly respective oeuvre has been the first cultural study which conducted cultural comparisons in a large international extent (Festing et al., 2011). The 'Web of Science' lists Hofstede with a remarkable citation frequency of more than 5.000 (Steel & Taras, 2010, p. 212) which categorizes him as a super classic (Baskerville, 2003). Hofstede investigated the work-attitudes of 116,000 IBM employees comprising both sales and services personnel. He came up with country rankings of 40, later 53 countries, based on average figures for cultural dimensions (Hofstede, 2001, 2006; Hofstede, Hofstede & Minkov, 2010). He was the first to introduce cultural dimensions in which nations meaningfully differ (Hofstede, 2006).

Hofstede related culture in a four-dimensional way (power distance, individualism-collectivism, masculinity-femininity, uncertainty avoidance) which he later complemented by a fifth dimension (long-term versus short-term orientation) (Hofstede, 1980, 1983, 1984; Hofstede & Bond, 1984; Hofstede & Hofstede, 2005; Minkov & Hofstede, 2011). The enormous interdisciplinary use of Hofstede's dimensions reaches from management, accounting, strategy, marketing, organization, human resources, business ethics to psychology (Sivakumar & Nakata, 2001; Søndergaard, 1994). Some researchers see his study not primarily oriented towards scientific community (Kieser, 1994), others grant him "meticulous scholarship" (Smith, 2002, p. 119). Hofstede (1998) proclaimed his cultural dimensions as normal science in a Kuhnian sense. The popularity of the Hofstede study can be ascribed to both rigour and relevance, i.e. scientific quality, adaptability and applicability (Søndergaard, 1994). However the Hofstede framework has been hardly criticized (Baskerville, 2003; Harrison & McKinnon, 2007, McSweeney, 2002a, 2002b, Myers & Tan, 2002; Smith, 2002). Most critique targeted the missing representativeness (exclusive data from a single company, narrow respondents), the out-datedness of the study, the equation of nation with culture, the failed replicability of findings, the non-existent differentiating of national and organizational culture, and the non-exhaustiveness and simplistic nature of cultural dimensions. Hofstede (1998; 2001; 2002; 2003) tried to invalidate the main five criticisms, however large concern remained (Baskerville-Morley, 2005).

2.1.4 GLOBE framework

2.1.4.1 *Overview of the GLOBE study*

The GLOBE study (House et al., 2004) which is favoured and employed in this research context is a multi-phase, multi-method project exploring the interrelationships between organizational culture, national culture and leadership (Dorfman et al., 2012; Javidan & Dastmalchian, 2009). The GLOBE study, which was initiated in the early 1990s, comprised more than 170 social scientists and management scholars in 62 countries or regions. More than 17,000 middle managers in 951 organizations across three industries (financial services, food services and telecommunications) were surveyed. The GLOBE study identified nine cultural dimensions encompassing both organizational and society practices ('As Is') and values ('Should Be')[10]. These dimensions are power distance, uncertainty avoidance, institutional collectivism, in-group collectivism, gender egalitarianism, assertiveness, performance orientation, future orientation and human orientation (House et al., 2004).

2.1.4.2 GLOBE dimensions

The GLOBE study lists nine cultural dimensions. Subsequently, I follow the order of House et al. (2004). In Table 1 I provide mainly literal quotes and rely on the definitions of House et al. (2004, Chapter 12 - 19; 2002, p. 5-7), Javidan and Dastmalchian (2009, p. 45-48), Javidan and Dorfman (2001, p. 495-498), and Javidan and House (2001, p. 293-301).

Uncertainty Avoidance	Uncertainty Avoidance is defined as the extent to which members of an organization or society strive to avoid uncertainty by reliance on social norms, rituals, and bureaucratic practices to alleviate the unpredictability of future events. It refers to the extent to which its members seek orderliness, consistency, structure, formalized procedures and laws to cover situations in their daily lives. Societies with high scores on Uncertainty Avoidance value orderliness and consistency, structured lifestyles and rules and laws to govern situations. Societies scoring low on this dimension have a strong tolerance for ambiguity and uncertainty, live less structured lives and are less concerned about following rules.
Power Distance	Power Distance is defined as the degree to which members of an organization or society expect and agree that power should be unequally shared. It represents the extent to which a community maintains inequality among its members by stratification of individuals and groups with respect to power, authority, prestige, status, wealth, and material possessions. It also reflects the establishment and maintenance of dominance and control of the less by the more powerful. Societies that are high on Power Distance distinguish between those with power and status and those without, and expect obedience towards superiors. Societies scoring low on Power Distance expect less differentiation between those in power and those without.
Collectivism I: Institutional or Societal Collectivism	Collectivism I: Institutional or Societal Collectivism reflects the degree to which organizational and societal institutional practices encourage and reward collective distribution of resources and collective action. This dimension reflects the degree to which individuals are encouraged by societal institutions to be integrated into groups within organizations and society. Organizations in collective countries emphasize group harmony, cohesion and co-operation and reward the group and not the individual. In societies that are more individualistic autonomy, self-interest and individual freedom are valued and organizations tend to reward individual performance.

---

[10] Hofstede distinguished between values (national cultures) and practices (organizational cultures) (Hofstede, 2006). Values are invisible; practices are visible form of appearance for symbols, heroes and rituals (Hofstede, 2001).

Collectivism II: In-Group Collectivism	Collectivism II: In-Group Collectivism reflects the degree to which individuals express pride, loyalty and cohesiveness in their organizations or families. This dimension is different from the above dimension entitled Collectivism I: Institutional or Societal Collectivism. While the former reflects the extent to which institutions of a society favor autonomy versus collectivism, this dimension refers to the extent to which members of a society take pride in membership in small groups such as their families and circles of close friends, and the organizations in which they are employed. Countries scoring high on this cultural practice are societies where being a member of a family and a close group of friends (an in-group) is very important to people. Satisfying the expectations of the 'in-group' is important to people. In contrast, in societies where cultural practice of in-group collectivism is low family members and friends do not expect any type of special treatment and people do not feel obliged to ignore rules to take care of their close friends and family members.
Gender Egalitarianism	Gender Egalitarianism is the extent to which an organization or a society minimizes gender role differences and gender discrimination. Countries high on this dimension view women's status as being higher and their involvement in decision-making stronger compared to more male-dominated societies. The latter group has a higher status for men and has relatively few women in positions of authority.
Assertiveness	Assertiveness is the degree to which individuals in organizations or societies are assertive, confrontational, and aggressive in social relationships. In countries scoring high on this cultural practice people have more of a 'can-do' attitude and tend to be more competitive in business. In countries where this cultural practice is low there is likely to be more sympathy for the weak, more emphasis on harmony and loyalty.
Future Orientation	Future Orientation is the degree to which individuals in organizations or societies engage in future-oriented behaviours such as planning, investing in the future, and delaying gratification. In high future-oriented cultures there is a tendency to have a longer time horizon for decision-making and more systematic planning processes. In less future-oriented cultures there tends to be less systematic planning and more preference for opportunistic behaviours and actions.
Performance Orientation	Performance Orientation refers to the extent to which an organization or society encourages and rewards group members for performance improvement and excellence. In countries which score high on this cultural practice, organizations are likely to emphasize training and development. In countries where the score on this dimension is low, family connections and background are more emphasized.
Human Orientation	Human Orientation is the degree to which individuals in organizations or societies encourage and reward individuals for being fair, altruistic, friendly, generous, caring, and kind to others. In countries high on this cultural practice, human relations, support for others and sympathy for others (especially the vulnerable) are highly valued. People value belongingness and caring for the well-being of others. Paternalistic and patronage associations and relationships are common and children are expected to be obedient. In cultures scoring low on Human Orientation, more emphasis is placed on power, material possessions, self-enhancement and independence. People prefer to solve their own problems and children are more likely to be independent.

Table 1: Definition of GLOBE dimensions

The GLOBE framework is mainly rooted in the previous work of Hofstede complemented by ideas and instruments from Kluckhohn and Strodtbeck, McClelland and Putnam (House & Javidan, 2004; Koopman et al., 1999). Table 2 highlights the cultural sources of GLOBE.

GLOBE dimension	Source
Uncertainty Avoidance	Hofstede (Uncertainty Avoidance)
Power Distance	Hofstede (Power Distance)
Collectivism I: Institutional or Societal Collectivism	Hofstede (Individualism/Collectivism)
Collectivism II: In-Group Collectivism	Hofstede (Individualism/Collectivism)
Gender Egalitarianism	Hofstede (Masculinity)
Assertiveness	Hofstede (Masculinity)
Future Orientation	Kluckhohn and Strodtbeck (Time: Past, Present, Future) Hofstede (Long-Term Orientation)
Performance Orientation	McClelland (Need for Achievement)
Human Orientation	Kluckhohn & Strodtbeck (Human Nature) Putnam's (civic society) McClelland (Need for Affiliation)

Table 2: Origins of the nine GLOBE dimensions

2.1.4.3 Critical appraisal of the GLOBE study

The GLOBE project has been exposed to several criticisms as well (Brewer & Venaik, 2010, 2011; Earley, 2006; Graen, 2006; Hofstede, 2006, 2010; Peterson, 2004; Smith, 2006; Venaik & Brewer, 2010). Some authors provided helpful comments (Maseland & van Hoorn, 2008, 2010; Taras, Steel & Kirkman, 2010). The GLOBE scholars wrote some clarifications on their own (Hanges & Dickson, 2006; Javidan et al., 2006). There is a lively debate on anomalies and contradictions of the GLOBE model around the following themes.

Graen (2006) sharply criticized the representativeness of the sample. He indicates that a target group of 300 managers in one nation cannot show the heterogeneity of culture. The generalizability of the results to the whole population is doubted. The mere aggregation of a small and homogenous part of a society falls short of the mark. However, GLOBE reports that "the dimensions are strongly and significantly correlated with unobtrusive measures that reflect the broader society" (House & Javidan, 2004, p. 20) and thus "the constructs measured by the GLOBE scales generalize beyond the sample from which the data were obtained (middle managers from one of three industries)" (House & Hanges, 2004, p. 101), which in my understanding suspends this suspicion.

A second critique is illustrated by the fact that the questionnaire was developed from an Anglo-American perspective and questions were written in English. Western thinking dominated which clearly is not beneficial in an intercultural topic. Although the GLOBE network was truly international, the US hegemony is present in project structure and data analysis (Hofstede, 2006). An additional critique targets the cultural clusters. The commonalities of many countries in each category are counterintuitive. This can be exemplified by the diverse US business that has not much in common with the British heritage (Graen, 2006).

Further, Hofstede (2006) questioned the operationalization of values and practices. He remarked the high abstraction of the wording and assumes a difficult interpretation of the respondents. Smith (2006, p. 916) doubted the appropriateness of using "the respondents' perceptions of their organizational and national contexts" instead of merely aggregating "individuals' self-reported values". He raised the concern that an objective individual view is not possible and the answer will always be guided by previous experience.

Another critique relates to the amount of dimensions. Although Smith (2006) noticed that the genesis in deriving the nine cultural dimensions was theory-driven (Hanges & Dickson, 2006; House & Javidan, 2004), he stated that the GLOBE dimensions should be consolidated to a larger extent, mainly to address the multicollinearity of future orientation, uncertainty avoidance, performance orientation and power distance practice scores. After examining the content validity of the questionnaire wording, Brewer and Venaik (2011) also proposed to re-label the In-Group Collectivism dimension as Family Collectivism.

The operationalization debate has started with a major exclamation concerning the negative correlation between practices and values for seven dimensions[11] (Hanges, 2004), which

---

[11] The dimensions which showed a negative correlation are: uncertainty avoidance ($r=-0.62$), institutional collectivism ($r=-0.61$), power distance ($r=-0.43$), future orientation ($r=-0.41$), human orientation ($r=-0.32$), performance orientation ($r=-0.28$) and assertiveness ($r=-0.26$). All these correlations were significant at the 5% level. Only gender egalitarianism ($r=0.32$) showed a significantly positive correlation. In-group collectivism showed a positive but insignificant correlation (Hanges, 2004, p. 736).

surprised the GLOBE researchers (Javidan et al., 2006). Maseland and van Horn (2008) explained the counterintuitive negative correlation with the insight of diminishing marginal utility (i.e. societies with lower levels in practices have a marginal preference for a higher level in values than societies with a higher amount of the same dimension). Brewer and Venaik (2010) examined the verbal statements of all GLOBE questions related to values. They found low evidence in GLOBE's framing of the questions and thus ruled out the explanation of Maseland and van Horn (2010). In their commentary, they argued that the formulation of the questions was not important. This hot debate went on and was content wise complemented by alternative approaches and interpretations of Taras, Steel and Kirkman (2010).

It is my understanding that the critique points are very similar to the ones directed at Hofstede one to two decades ago. Acknowledging the controversial debate of the GLOBE model which also shows the influential position of the project (Peterson, 2004), I point out arguments of the main advantages in using the GLOBE taxonomy rather than Hofstede's. Although cultural manifestations change slowly over time (Triandis et al., 1988), Hofstede might be out-dated, since he did his research in the early 1980s, which is almost 30 years ago while GLOBE scores were collected in the (late) 1990s. Life and world has changed a lot since that time. Thus it is questionable whether the Hofstede concept is still viable today (Scandura & Dorfman, 2004). Olivas-Luján, Harzing and McCoy (2004) showed that a major event as the 9/11 attack had an impact on cultural values, specifically to power distance. This suspends the cultural stability assumption (Shenkar, 2001). Besides, research has documented changes in culture (Taras, Kirkman & Steel, 2010).

Second, GLOBE contains additional cultural dimensions which were not part in Hofstede's analysis (Chui & Kwok, 2009; Hofstede, 2006). GLOBE substituted gender egalitarianism and assertiveness for Hofstede's masculinity-femininity dimension and included performance orientation and human orientation. Additionally, future orientation does not bear the connotation of the Confucian Work Dynamism. The dimension individualism/collectivism in the GLOBE concept incorporates the new concept of institutional collectivism (House & Javidan, 2004). Third, GLOBE distinguishes between values and practices and considers multi-level cultural data. Whereas Hofstede only aimed at values derived from attitudes, GLOBE considers both questions in the As Is and Should Be format. GLOBE bases culture on a broader foundation and collects both national and organizational culture to control for relationships.

Fourth, GLOBE addressed almost 1,000 companies from three different sectors while Hofstede only focused on one company. This has the advantage of addressing the interplay between organizational and societal culture: This refers to the question whether one measures the societal culture when questioning the employees or whether the organizational culture is dominating and impeding the answers. There are contrary views on whether societal culture constrains people's behaviour or not (Naor, Linderman & Schroeder, 2010). Webster and White (2010) notice an interaction effect of both culture levels and an impact of national culture on organizational culture. Gerhart (2009b) finds only a small effect for the influence of national culture on organizational culture. His re-analysis of the GLOBE data shows only a minor effect of national culture on organizational culture. He concludes that national culture is "no major constraint on organizational culture" as many scholars have often thought (Gerhart, 2009b, p. 252).

Fifth, GLOBE relied on a better way to measure culture. They included former work and new ideas which they extensively validated with statistical measures (Gupta, Luque & House, 2004; Hanges & Dickson, 2004; House & Javidan, 2004). Hofstede (1980) summarized national cultures only by average scores and did not integrate other statistical measures, such as standard deviations, ranges (Taras, Rowney & Steel, 2009) or validity checks (Smith, 2002). The GLOBE questionnaire has been developed by a larger team and uses many best practice approaches for questionnaire design (Harkness, van de Vijver & Johnson, 2002), questionnaire translation (Harkness, 2002; Harkness & Schoua-Glusberg, 1998) and validation of the research instruments (Schaffer & Riordan, 2003).

Practically, the GLOBE questionnaire is already available in different languages (among German, English, French, Dutch and Polish). Summing up, "it does provide us with the most recent set of cross-cultural data" (Drogendijk & Holm, 2012, p. 390). Furthermore, "the GLOBE study provides cultural scholars with an important set of measures, which should support a wealth of future culture research" (Brewer & Venaik, 2010, p. 1319). Balancing the arguments in favour and against Hofstede and GLOBE, I favour the use of the conceptual and methodological sound GLOBE framework (Chiang & Birtch, 2010), which is the most recent and comprehensive examination of culture and leadership (Alas, Kraus & Niglas, 2009; Sarala & Vaara, 2010).

2.2 Management control systems' framework

Malmi and Brown's (2008) framework summarizes past research and integrates former MCS frameworks. Their concept of MCS operating as a package is not a new phenomenon since Otley (1980) and Flamholtz (1983) have introduced this terminology. The existing frameworks provide insights into what constitutes an MCS package, but they do not address why particular management control elements should be expected to occur together and how they are or should be linked to each other (Malmi & Brown, 2008). Research has targeted explicit theories or large empirical studies on this topic very scarcely (e.g. Abernethy & Brownell, 1997; Alvesson & Kärreman, 2004; Chenhall, 2003, 2007; Dávila, 2005). Previous MCS research studied single themes or control elements and thus examined MCS in isolation (Chenhall, 2003, 2007). But in business reality "it is clear that organizations rely on different combinations of control mechanisms in any given setting, yet virtually nothing is known about how the effects of any one control are governed by the level of simultaneous reliance on other forms" (Abernethy & Brownell, 1997, p. 246). As a consequence theory on management control should shed light on the functioning of these configurations of control devices, and theory should be able to address these control packages in their entirety in terms of differential functionality (Spekle, 2001). I do not address control packages (Malmi & Brown, 2008) in this thesis.

In their own words, Malmi's and Brown's framework

> broadly maps the tools, systems and practices managers have available to formally and informally direct employee behaviour. In establishing the tools and systems managers have available to direct behaviour, our typology contains more recent developments in MCS design (such as hybrids like the BSC), and includes forms of control that have received less attention in empirical research, such as cultural control. (p. 295)

The main constituents of the Malmi and Brown (2008) framework comprise planning, cybernetic controls, reward and compensation, administrative and cultural controls. Planning takes the form of long-term strategic planning where objectives and the strategic direction of the firm are clarified as well as short-term oriented action planning where objectives and action plans for the nearer future, mainly the next year, are set. Malmi and Brown (2008) plead for a more differentiated view and treat both strategic and operational planning as a separate system in their framework. They argue that planning can occur with almost no reference to financials and that is why it should be separated. Organizations use some form of strategic and operational planning which is then monitored by key performance indicators.

Cultural Controls						
Clans			Values			Symbols
Planning			Cybernetic Control			
Long range planning	Action planning	Budgets	Financial Measurem. Systems	Non-Financial Measurem. Systems	Hybrid Measurem. Systems	**Reward and compensation**
Administrative Controls						
Governance Structure			Organization Structure			Policies and Procedures

Figure 4: MCS package framework of Malmi and Brown (2008)

Cybernetic controls[12] comprise budgets, financial and non-financial measures as well as hybrid performance measurement systems (e.g. the BSC). This element covers measures to compare the current financial and non-financial achievement with the planned goals and to take, if necessary, corrective actions. Next to performance measurement, ex-post performance evaluation forms part of the cybernetic element. This closes the feedback circle since budgets often integrate evaluation criteria (Malmi & Brown, 2008). Variance analysis is a tool which is often deployed to outline the differences between actual and planned performance and to evaluate the course of action. Budgets act as tools that "weave together all the disparate threads of an organization into a comprehensive plan that serves many different purposes, particularly performance planning and ex post evaluation of actual performance vis-a`-vis the plan" (Hansen, Otley & van der Stede, 2003, p. 96). Performance evaluation with a corresponding reward system further provides feedback, incentivises behaviour and aligns the interests of shareholders, managers and employees. Although reward and compensation are strongly linked to performance measurement and evaluation, they are treated as an individual MCS element since organizations distribute them for various

---

[12] Going back to the work of Wiener (1948/1994), the cybernetic concept (the Greek "κυβερνήτης" is translated to the steersman of a ship) is understood as "a process in which a feedback loop is represented by using standards of performance, measuring system performance, comparing that performance to standards, feeding back information about unwanted variances in the system, and modifying the system's comportment" (Green & Welsh, 1988, p. 289) and therefore forms a basic element of control.

reasons. Administrative controls comprise those systems that guide employees by organizational design and structure, governance structures as well as policies and procedures. They give guidance on the organizational set-up, management processes, information flows, the extent of authority and specific rules. Cultural controls include the collection of norms, values and beliefs (Flamholtz, 1983). "The term 'social control' refers to any kind of disapproval reaction that a person might express toward someone who transgresses a social norm" (Brauer & Chaurand, 2009, p. 490). In other terms one could speak of social controls in the sense of a regulating mechanism to achieve common principles and values towards morally acknowledged and conformal behaviour amongst organizational members (Cusson, 2001; Janowitz, 1975).

2.3 Performance measurement, performance evaluation and rewards

2.3.1 Performance measurement

2.3.1.1 *Nature and purpose of performance measures*

Performance measurement is a vital source for the management of a company (Melnyk et al., 2014). Performance from an organizational point of view[13] is the result from the managerial actions and the subordinates' execution of the managers' directives (Carton & Hofer, 2006). Measurement is the assignment of numbers to phenomena (Micheli & Mari, 2014). Hence, performance measurement aims at examining and analyzing the achievement of the firm's objectives, more specifically "to determine the effectiveness of the managerial decisions" (Carton & Hofer, 2006, p. 39). Neely, Gregory and Platts (1995, p. 80) define performance measurement "as the process of quantifying the efficiency and effectiveness of action". Hence performance measurement identifies areas for organizational improvement and gives guidance for managerial interventions. Hence performance measures should be treated as "just indicators of performance and not real performance" (Bourne et al., 2014, p. 118). Performance measures are based on "a formula or rule that enables quantification of performance" (Haas & Kleingeld, 1999, p. 234).

---

[13] The level of analysis is the organization or the business unit. Assessing team and individual performance is not addressed here. The assessment of the individual performance by means of performance measures is rather part of Chapter 2.3.2 (p. 42ff.).

The purpose of performance measurement is grounded in the determination of the amount of value creation. Multiple stakeholders have an interest in receiving information about the well-being of a company. Two important parties that provide and invest funds in a company are debt- and equity-holders, i.e. owners and financiers (banks, bondholders, etc.). These interest groups are normally[14] only willing to provide monetary funds to the firm if they expect to receive a satisfactory amount of return to compensate for their risk. Organizations have to deliver a real contribution in return for the provision of funds. Performance measures can show (mostly ex-post) whether the needs of both debt and equity lenders are satisfied. Funds will be only left in those companies in which the realized value creation by the firm exceeds the initial value contribution from the stakeholders. The funds, which are by means of investments converted to assets or used for payments to suppliers and employees, are logically necessary for the firm to produce or deliver goods or services. As a consequence, money remains in those organizations, which create a positive value. They in turn have then the necessary funds to further run their operations. If the money was withdrawn the firm would run into financial distress and bankruptcy (Alchian & Demsetz, 1972; Holmstrom & Tirole, 1989; Jensen & Meckling, 1976; Otley, 2007). Coming back to the purpose of performance measurement, one can state that performance measurement is essential in order to determine the extent of the exact value creation and to communicate this to the key stakeholders (Micheli & Mari, 2014).

Henry (2006b) distinguished four purposes for performance measurement: monitoring, attention focusing, strategic decision-making and legitimization. Encapsulating his thoughts, monitoring circles around the provision of feedback about the well-being of the companies' performance. Managers send signals as a mean to focus the attention of their subordinates towards the organizational objectives. Additionally, performance measures should facilitate the strategic course of action stressing a learning perspective and a problem-solving perspective. In collecting information about performance, managers want to provide reasons for their past, current and future action steps in order to legitimize their decisions. Performance measures help to evaluate how well organizations work and whether they deliver value for their stakeholders. Melnyk, Stewart and Swink (2004) state three purposes

---

[14] I imply this statement for for-profit organizations.

of performance measures. Performance measures serve managers for control or evaluation of the underlying business. A second purpose is communication, both internally and externally, whereas the third purpose, improvement, helps to close the identified performance gap. Van Veen-Dirks (2010) even pins the roles of performance measures down to two, a decision facilitating role and a decision-influencing role (similar Grafton, Lillis & Widener, 2010). The former targets the provision of information about the current problems and challenges whereas the latter aims at congruence of desired intentions and conducted behaviour between managers and subordinates. In that sense they play a vital role in facilitating strategy execution and monitoring the course of action towards achieving the intended strategies (Lillis, 2002; van der Stede, Chow & Lin, 2006).

Franco-Santos, Lucianetti and Bourne (2012) portrayed various consequences for people's behaviour, for organizational capabilities and for performance of using performance measurement[15]. Through carefully screening the literature, they found many aspects that were impacted by performance measurement. On the individual layer, they found mixed findings for motivational aspects. On the organizational layer, they found both positive and negative results for management practices due to organizational culture, user and system specificities, beneficial effects for the whole strategy process and mostly positive effects for communication. The consequences on performance were inconclusive. Rather obvious, it is not the mere existence of specific measures that has a positive influence on performance but the design, implementation and handling as well as the influence of contextual factors.

2.3.1.2 *Categories of performance measures*

In the literature there is no consensus on what to subsume to organizational performance and how to determine it (Carton & Hofer, 2006). One conventional classification splits organizational performance into a financial and a non-financial part (Cardinaels & van Veen-

---

[15] In particular, the authors focused on whole performance measurement systems.

Dirks, 2010; Venkatraman & Ramanujam, 1986) with multiple forms of financial, non-financial and hybrid performance measures (Henri, 2006b).[16]

The financial dimensions include foremost profitability and growth indicators, efficiency, liquidity, size or leverage (Carton & Hofer, 2006). Measures of profitability are derived by dividing profits by assets (ROA) or equity used (ROE) or sales achieved (ROS) to generate the return. ROS or also called EBIT is a rather popular measure of firm profitability. The limitations comprise different use of accounting methods with some scope of judgment (e.g. different depreciation methods or creative accounting are buzz words here), risk exclusion or unaffectedness by financing policy. Additionally these figures only represent past performance and give no indication of future prospects (Cornett, Marcus & Tehranian, 2008; Otley, 2007; Rappaport, 1998). Although there are limitations to profitability measures they are frequently used. The reason is partly the easy availability and reproducibility of the financial numbers and partly the results-based target of the bottom line of the business which is attractive for senior management.

Non-financial figures embrace the assessment of operational figures and operationally related figures as productivity, safety, product quality, cycle times, lead times, material handling, flexibility for production adjustments, inventory management or on-time delivery (Madapusi & D'Souza, 2012; Rho & Yu, 1998). Neely (2007) distinguished between quality, dependability, speed, flexibility and cost as the five objectives for measuring operational performance. In an earlier paper, Neely and colleagues (1995) listed quality, time, cost and flexibility as performance measures. These measures normally all aim at improving productivity and product quality, increasing speed, decreasing waste and streamlining processes. For example, reduced cycle times are one way to increase production output. In a similar vein, a good product quality reduces operational waste and minimizes customer enquiries and warranty calls. However, some of those operational measures are associated with trade-offs and have to be balanced. An obvious example would affect the trade-off between delivery cycles and inventory since short delivery cycles corresponds normally with

---

[16] Henry (2006b, p. 81) further distinguished between "drivers versus outcome measures, subjective versus objective measures, internal versus external measures". A further distinction can be made into qualitative and quantitative measures as well as in form of timing, i.e. lag or lead indicators (Kaplan & Norton, 1996a).

higher inventory (Skinner, 1974). High quality products, as another example, are more costly, since the material is probably more valuable and the production steps more difficult. Often operational figures supplement financial figures. They are also relevant when a project has not materialised any financial effect so far (Neely, 2007).

Other non-financial figures comprise internally related figures as innovativeness (e.g. generation of new products/services, new patents, spending of research and development cost) (Ittner, Larcker & Randall, 2003) and employee or team-related figures (employee satisfaction, meeting deadlines, managing time, delivering quality) (Choi, Lee & Yoo, 2010). Externally related figures subsume customer and market related figures (e.g. market share, customer complaints or customer satisfaction) (Grafton, Lillis & Widener, 2010; van Veen-Dirks, 2010), as well as social and environmental figures. Firms that incorporate these figures address more long-term oriented performance measures (Ittner, Larcker & Randall, 2003).

Next to the question whether financial measures, non-financial measures or a hybrid form containing a set of both measures should be used and besides closely related to this first deliberation is the question whether a range of performance measures should be applied or not. Proponents advocating the use of a broader range of performance measures argue that a single measure is too simplistic and cannot map the variety of actions that contribute to the overall organizational objectives whereas a diverse set of measures equips managers with more meaningful information to efficiently and effectively run the firm. Opponents reply that there are disadvantages as well, as managers could and some even will choose always different and for each situation the most beneficial performance measures. Additionally, manifold measures increase the complexity for evaluation and control (van Veen-Dirks, 2010). The purpose of a larger basket of performance measures certainly lies in the fact to enhance managerial decision making by incorporating measures from different angles (Lipe & Salterio, 2000, 2002). Otley (2007) adheres to a mixture of financial and non-financial performance measures since a sole focus on one or the other opens only one window into the organizational performance and thus provides only an incomplete picture of corporate success. In a similar fashion, Grafton, Lillis and Widener (2010, p. 689) argued for an integrated use of both financial and non-financial performance measures, in order to overcome the short-comings of either ones and to provide managers with a broader range of measures. This deliberation brings us to a vital instrument that exactly addresses this.

2.3.1.3 Performance measurement as an entity: The Balanced Scorecard

Johnson and Kaplan (1987) proposed that it is inappropriate to solely measure profits. Though profit is the central goal of an organization it should not be used as a stand-alone measure to steer companies. Profit, "the real bottom line for every organization" (Melnyk, Stewart & Swink, 2004, p. 209) is the final outcome after a long chain of single steps followed inside a corporation. It is more advisable that performance measures map all steps that are necessary for profit achievement (Kennerley & Neely, 2002). Managers should not only rely on financial measures but rather employ a selection of non-financial measures. A well-known instrument which uses a hybrid form of both financial and non-financial performance measures is the BSC (Hoque & James, 2000; Speckbacher, Bischof & Pfeiffer, 2003). The BSC, cited by the Harvard Business Review and other scholars as one of the most influential management tools (Atkinson et al., 1997; De Geuser, Mooraj & Oyon, 2009), had impressive diffusion rates[17] although critical voices raised the concern, whether the BSC resembles only 'old wine in new bottles' and brings existing concepts of performance measurement systems just with a new label (Anthony & Govindarajan, 2001; Burkert, Dávila & Oyon, 2010).

Kaplan and Norton (1992) addressed the inadequacies of the traditional sole focus on financial performance measures. The literature heavily criticized the short-termism (Bourne, 2005; Bourne et al., 2003; Kaplan, 1984) and the inward- and backward-looking concepts as well as their aggregate nature (Tan & Lau, 2012). Kaplan and Norton (1992) moved beyond this conventional thought. The concept of the BSC provided managers with tools to link long-term strategic objectives with short-term action plans (Kaplan & Norton, 1996c). The BSC comprises four perspectives. Apart from the financial dimension, they incorporated the customer perspective, the internal business process perspective, and the learning and growth perspective. The financial perspective addresses how the company wants to be seen by the shareholders. It encompasses a diverse set of profitability measures. The customer dimension

---

[17] One worldwide study showed an adoption rate of 51%, another study came to 62%. Figures for the largest companies in the US ranged from 20% to 43%, UK displayed a utilization of 55% (Matlachowsky, 2009). Germany exhibited a span width of 7% to 50% (Schäffer & Matlachowsky, 2008). In contrast to the other countries, France has a rare implementation rate that is due to a different method used in France (Bourguignon, Malleret & Nørreklit, 2004; Gehrke & Horváth, 2002). The Northern European countries also showed high adoption rates (Buhk & Malmi, 2005)

identifies how the company wants to be viewed by the customers. It comprises such measures as customer satisfaction, customer loyalty, customer retention, new customer acquisition, customer response time, market share, image, reputation and customer profitability. The internal business process perspective involves company specific series of action in terms of innovativeness, quality and speed it must excel at. The learning and growth area describes human resource practices to improve the skills of the employees and the information flows and to secure motivational climate (Kaplan & Norton, 1996b). The BSC provides detailed measures, targets and action steps for the selected strategic objectives in a cause-and-effect manner and hence builds a tool to communicate the strategic road map to the organizational subunits. The four perspectives are assumed to be causally linked to each other. Thus, a fundamental principle is that the financial success of the company is reached when the three other non-financial measures are satisfactory aligned (Kaplan & Norton, 1996b, 1996c).

Proponents of the BSC stress several benefits: Information is condensed in one document and can be approached from the management in one glance. Management is forced to develop a common understanding of the strategic course of action (Epstein & Manzoni, 1997) and effectively communicate this roadmap internally (Ittner & Larcker, 1998). The balanced view of performance areas allows a critical reflection of the crucial steps to bring the strategy to life with the help of quantifiable indicators and concrete action steps. The BSC goes beyond a mere checklist of financial and non-financial indicators (Kaplan & Norton, 2001b) and offers an aid for meticulously harmonizing a set of measures. Performance measures should display the organizational particularities and the specific strategy of each firm (Olve, Roy & Wetter, 1999). The BSC is a framework that targets the linkages between different management control elements. It ties various perspectives together and exemplifies the resulting causes and effects and thus presents an integrated whole of management control (Atkinson et al., 1997).

However, there are also weaknesses associated to the BSC. Malmi (2001) summarized the main criticism brought forward: Firstly, the model is seen as too vague and general. The BSC cannot be easily adapted to the organizational culture and specific company surroundings (Butler, Letza & Neale, 1997). A second claim is that the inter-relationship of the four perspectives is problematic. In practice it is very difficult to determine the exact outcome for a perspective. The cost-benefit ratio of an initiative cannot be easily derived. Nørreklit (2000) questioned the instant conclusion of the cause-and-effect chain. On the one hand there is a time lag, which makes a direct relation between two measures impossible because some results occur only after a few years. On the other hand there are no unidirectional linkages between the perspectives since the four areas are intertwined. In re-examining the cause-and-effect model and the criticism by Nørreklit (2000), Buhk and Malmi (2005) endorsed that the time dimension is implicitly integrated in the BSC.

To address the shortcomings of the cause-and-effect principle, the concept of the strategy map was developed (Kaplan & Norton, 2001a) and even deepened (Kaplan & Norton, 2004). Next to the description of the strategy comes the enabling element of the strategy implementation (De Geuser, Mooraj & Oyon, 2009). Since "the BSC translates the often-nebulous goals found in corporate mission statements into a strategic roadmap to be followed by employees" (Davis & Albright, 2004, p. 137), it acts nowadays primarily as a strategy implementation tool. Overall, it could be shown, that the BSC has a positive impact to the organizational performance and thus adds value (De Geuser, Mooraj & Oyon, 2009).

2.3.1.4 Benefits of a holistic use of performance measures

Some scholars pled for a broad set of measures since from their knowledge this increases performance.[18] This view is supported from agency theory (van der Stede, Chow & Lin, 2006) (see Chapter 2.4.4, p. 62) since placement of non-financial information into the measurement criteria, or even in the evaluation, promotion (Campbell, 2008; Gibbs, 2008) or rewarding scheme (Banker, Potter & Srinivasan, 2000) of the manager tightens the focus of managerial attention. Hoque and James (2000) also reported a positive effect on company performance with an inclusion of non-financial measures. Van der Stede, Chow and Lin (2006), relying both on financial and non-financial measures, found support for the positive effects of a diversified use on performance. Also Said, HassabElnaby and Wier (2003)

---

[18] Managers are keen on knowing the circumstances of effective performance measurement and the best selection of optimally designed, non-expensive and easy to implement performance measures from the myriad of factors available (Bourne, Kennerley & Franco-Santos, 2005; Shields, 1997). The thesis does not deal with the influence of performance measures on organizational effectiveness. Franco-Santos, Lucianetti and Bourne (2012) as well as Bourne, Kennerley and Franco-Santos (2005) provide more details on performance measurement effectiveness.

Implementation and change is not scope of this thesis. There are several investigations that address the evolution of performance measures or the multitude of drivers for changing those measures (e.g. Bourne et al., 2000; Bourne et al., 2003; Kennerley & Neely, 2002).

provided evidence that a combined use of financial and nonfinancial performance measures led to higher performance. Banker, Potter and Srinivasan (2000) investigated incentive plans in a large hotel chain that switched from a mere financially based reward plan to a new plan with non-financial measures too. The change of the incentive plan led to increased revenues and profit per room. Non-financial measures can increase comprehensiveness to assess the organizational performance because they focus on the current performance. More strategic aspects, as investments, negotiation with suppliers and pricing decisions are not reflected in the current or past performance (Dávila & Venkatachalam, 2004), but could be object to individual objectives that also fall within the area of the non-financial performance measures. However, other voices stated negative effects of a broader set of performance figures. This argumentation is based on increased complexity, bounded cognitive abilities and potentially contradictory measures (van der Stede, Chow & Lin, 2006).

The BSC approach (see Chapter 2.3.1.3, p. 39ff.) already indicated the beneficial effect of an integrated use of both kinds of performance measures. The literature stressed a higher feedback quality and quantity when non-financial measures and financial ones are used. Apart from this, non-financial measures are more easily available (Said, HassabElnaby & Wier, 2003). Groen, Wouters and Wilderom (2012) examined the stimulating behaviour of co-developing performance measures. Their implication was that the participation in designing and implementing performance measures improved the attitude (coming up with and executing new ideas for improvement), enlarged the social pressure (intensifying group influence for assiduous efforts, concretized workflows and responsibilities) and augmented the capability (through a chain of feedback mechanisms and mutual agreement between superiors and subordinates) to take initiatives. Van der Stede, Chow and Lin (2006) compiled a number of difficulties and problems associated to diverse measurements. These range from cognitive problems of the manager to grasp the complex business environment, over conflicting goals to tensions in human relations.

To choose the right performance measures certainly belongs to the imperative tasks organizations have to decide in order to monitor the execution of the strategy, to keep an eye on the organizational objectives and to judge the managerial ability (Ittner & Larcker, 1998). This is one of the underlying reasons why there is such a huge diversity in measures both conceptually and also specifically. In the past, there have been proclamations of innovations in performance measurement, e.g. the BSC concept. The BSC or any other integrated approach offers the opportunity to both balance a good mix of financial and non-financial performance information and to lay down a strategy implementation tool. Yet, a company still has to develop and specifically tailor performance measures in use to their needs. It is not the mere appearance of numbers, but the adequacy of the numbers that make a difference. Grafton, Lillis and Widener (2010, p. 689) stressed that a positive impact of performance measures is better reached when "performance evaluation schemes are also designed to reflect these measures. To the extent performance evaluation schemes do not reflect such decision-facilitating measures it is less likely managers will use these indicators to effectively manage performance". This statement provides the foundation for the transition to the next chapter on performance evaluation.

2.3.2 Performance evaluation

2.3.2.1 Nature and purpose of performance evaluation

Performance evaluation represents a central element of the MCS and is seen as a quite universal phenomenon for the management levels of corporations, although the level of dissatisfaction for carrying out a performance evaluation among both supervisors and the ones being monitored is often quite high.[19] Performance evaluation is characterized by Bourguignon (2004, p. 662) "as a process by which an authorized person formulates a judgment – producing various consequences – on the value of some attributes of another person, by the way of appropriate instrumentation". A different definition by the Advisory, Conciliation and Arbitration Service (cited in Armstrong, 2009, p. 18; Dransfield, 2000, p. 71) sees performance evaluation as a frequent "assessment of an employee's performance, potential, and development needs". The evaluation offers the chance to look on current performance, to look back on past achievements and agree future objectives. This view incorporates both the backward- and forward-looking character of the evaluation. On the one hand, the past achievements of the employee are dealt with and on the other hand the future prospects are addressed. In a nutshell, performance evaluation, often also named performance

---

[19] Executives feel often uncomfortable in conveying (negative) feedback and refer to executing this managerial instrument as a stressful situation (Aguinis, 2009; Nurse, 2005). Bol (2011) mentioned the psychological burden that lasts on managers and the possibility that the relationship between supervisors and subordinates could take harm.

appraisal[20], is about raters (mostly supervisors, seldom peers) judging and assessing the achievements of their ratees (mostly subordinates, seldom peers) to differentiate the efficiency levels of the employees and to determine how well employees fulfil organizational objectives. The term judging is important here, since it expresses that the same personal achievements can be seen completely different, depending on the raters and their individual perception (DeNisi & Pritchard, 2006; Murphy & Cleveland, 1995). Performance evaluation is one of the best devices which help to understand the employee and visualize his concerns, preferences, reservations and needs (Cardy, 2004). Particularly important is the sensitivity, the abilities and skills of the supervisor, both to "listen to subordinates' suggestions and provide important path-clearing resources … [and] information about what it takes to be successful in the organization" (Nathan, Mohrman Jr. & Milliman, 1991, p. 366).

The psychological literature (e.g. Jordan & Nasis, 1992, p. 963) lists "compensation, career development, promotion, layoff, and training and development" as evaluation purposes. Milliman and his three co-authors (2002) from the human resource side came up with a list of eleven items which they grouped to five areas (documentation, development, pay, promotion and subordinate expression). Cleveland, Murphy and Williams (1989, p. 132) compiled a list of different purposes of performance evaluation, such as between-person decisions (salary administration, retention/termination, identification of poor performance, promotion, recognition of individual performance, and layoffs), within-person decisions (identification of individual training needs, performance feedbacks, determination of transfers and assignments, and identification of individual strengths and weaknesses), systems maintenance (determination of organizational training needs, identification of organizational development needs, evaluation of personnel systems, manpower planning, evaluation of goal achievement,

---

[20] In human resource management, performance evaluation is only a subset of performance appraisal, mostly "synonymous with performance ratings" (Brutus, 2010, p. 145). However, in management journals "performance appraisal is conventionally equated with performance evaluation" (Kane & Freeman, 1997, p. 38). Becker (1994, p. 142) synonymously lists even more terms next to performance evaluation and performance appraisal, in particular "performance rating, performance review, performance assessment, … personal evaluation, personal rating, efficiency rating, merit rating, employ rating, employ evaluation". In this publication, I see performance evaluation in a broader way than the human resource area and not limited to rating. Looking to the management control area, Merchant and van der Stede (2007), Flamholtz (1979; 1983; 1996) or Flamholtz, Das and Tsui (1985) support this broader understanding of performance evaluation as well.

and assistance in goal identification) and documentation.[21] In a similar vein, Dorfman, Walter and Loveland (1986), Boswell and Boudreau (2000), as well as Youngcourt, Leiva and Jones (2007)[22] argued for both an evaluative or administrative purpose, similar to the between-person decisions, and a developmental function, similar to the within-person decisions, stated above.

As one can infer from the statements, there is a big overlap for the purposes of performance evaluation between the management, human resource and psychology literature. In my sense, the most important purposes are congruent with the ones by Cleveland, Murphy and Williams (1989) and comprise the provision of feedback on individual strengths and weaknesses for learning and development issues. A further purpose serves to determine compensation which is tightly coupled to promotion and layoff. A third purpose deals with administrative tasks such as documentation and overall human resource planning and development. According to DeNisi and Pritchard (2006) the reason why firms carry out performance evaluations is to raise the future performance of their employees which then leverages into better task fulfilment and an improved attainment of the organizational objectives. Thus by reviewing the performance and discussing the potential, performance evaluation educates employees "to meet the future work force requirement of an organization" (Ikramullah et al., 2012, p. 144). The multitude of purposes of the evaluation shows the conflict potential and the managerial intuition, tact and skill that is required (Becker, 1994).

2.3.2.2 Features and process of performance evaluation

Firms want employees to behave in a certain manner. Employees should perform to fulfil or contribute to the fulfilment of the organizational goals. In order to assess whether the employees engage themselves to the best use of the firm or whether there is some form of corrective need, performance evaluation comes into play. Performance evaluation helps to identify strengths and weaknesses, personal and team accomplishments as well as possible frictions of the employee.

---

[21] Purposes with factor loadings of <0.5 are suppressed.
[22] Next to this traditional understanding, Youngcourt, Leiva and Jones (2007) add the purpose of role definition, which indicates how to best allocate human resources over the different positions.

In performance evaluation the actual achievement of the employees are compared with the expectations of their supervisor, the imposed targets, standards or agreements by some sort of assessment criteria (Ferris et al., 2008). The frequency of formal[23] performance evaluations which are characterized by a specific incident or meeting ranges from quarterly to every second year, but is mostly executed annually (Achouri, 2011).

The assessment criteria comprise both judgmental/subjective and non-judgmental/objective measures. Objective measures are based on real outcomes independent of a behavioural component (Bommer et al., 1995). Examples for objective data include sales, profitability, or asset figures. In case of objective measures, "performance evaluation is based upon some system of measurement and the measures of performance commonly used are accounting measures such as budgets and standard costs. The evaluation process determines how rewards shall be administered to people" (Flamholtz, 1996, p. 601). Subjective measures that are derived by direct observations or informal sources (Rajan & Reichelstein, 2009) are based on "personal impressions, feelings, and opinions, rather than on external facts" (Bol, 2008, p. 2), and thus require judgment from the evaluator. Subjectivity comes into play in three ways: "(i) by using subjective performance measures, (ii) by allowing for (ex post) flexibility in the weighting of objective performance measures, and (iii) by allowing for ex post discretional adjustments based on factors other than the performance measures specified ex ante" (Bol, 2008, p. 2). The evaluator must consider specific circumstances for the evaluation which impacted the results. Prior research showed that, when subjectivity is incorporated in the performance evaluation context, it has both positive and detrimental effects. On the one hand, subjective measures are said to be more extensive than objective measures, which only cover a small fraction of performance requirements. Additionally, not foreseen events can be accounted for when specifying the consequences after the evaluation period. Furthermore, subjectivity may mitigate incentive distortion, reduce risk, and limit the vulnerability towards dishonest behaviour. On the other hand, cognitive limitations, systematic biases[24] of the

---

[23] Informal meetings can take place all the time.

[24] The main biases that occur are the outcome effect (knowledge of the outcome (good or bad) impacts the evaluation) (Ghosh & Lusch, 2000), leniency or upward bias (employees are rated higher than their actual performance ; an example is given by Bretz, Milkovich and Read (1992) that the majority of the ratees are placed among the best 60-70%), and centrality bias (ratings do not differ much from the median (Bol, 2011; Golman & Bhatia, 2012; Moers, 2005)).

human evaluators, lower accuracy and reliability interfere with the advantages (Baker, 1990; Bol, 2008, 2011; Bol & Smith, 2011; Ghosh & Lusch, 2000; Ittner, Larcker & Meyer, 2003). Bommer and his four co-authors (1995) warned not to exclusively rely on objective measures but to rather follow an integrated approach of both subjective and objective mechanisms.

The literature differentiates between different forms of evaluation. The most common form is the evaluation from the supervisor in which the recipient is evaluated from the ones who are a hierarchy above. Peer appraisals are pursued on the same hierarchical level. An upward looking appraisal is conducted from the subordinates who judge their managers. The 360 degree appraisal combines both upward and downward looking forms as well as peer appraisals and even more far reaching voices as the customer's or supplier's point of view. A further characteristic comprises the subject of evaluation, e.g. whether solely employees are assessed or whether both employees and their supervisors are in the focus of the assessment (Achouri, 2011; Kressler, 2001).

The evaluation itself is carried out in form of ratings the manager assigns to the employee and narrative comments they exchange during the appraisal interview. The ratings come in diverse ways. The performance can be assessed by quantitative, i.e. financial or non-financial information. Examinations on employing financial and non-financial measures are inconclusive and there is rare analysis in the performance evaluation context (Cardinaels & van Veen-Dirks, 2010; Ittner, Larcker & Meyer, 2003). Schiff and Hoffman (1996) found a greater reliance on financial measures for the departmental performance and a greater emphasis of non-financial measures for judging the managers performance. Cardinaels and van Veen-Dirks (2010) demonstrated that the arrangement of performance measures influenced the weighting of financial and non-financial measures for the evaluation purpose.

Evaluation may occur in relation to fixed and pre-set outcomes or numbers, alternatively the standard may be adapted after the evaluation period. Above, the evaluation can be subject to internal and external comparisons (Murphy & Cleveland, 1995).[25] Next to the quantitative components of ratings, managers also employ qualitative parts in their evaluation process by shifting numbers to words (Brutus, 2010).

Within the performance evaluation, communication between these two parties is a central theme since information should be conveyed to the rater (e.g. the manager) in order to enable them to make the best use of the skills of their subordinates, advance their capabilities and progress the whole performance of their employees (DeNisi & Pritchard, 2006; Murphy & Cleveland, 1995). This communication facilitates at the same time feedback mechanisms that fortify satisfactory work and address insufficient work performance (Vance et al., 1992). Regardless, of whether one looks at the manager or the employee anecdotal and empirical evidence suggests that both parties prefer qualitative evaluation over quantitative feedback, i.e. a preference for verbalized feedback (Brutus, 2010).

Summing up, it is obvious that performance evaluation is a core element of management control whose purposes are manifold. Notwithstanding the various classification purposes, the evaluation aims at managers determining the achievements of their employees and utilizing this information for pay, promotion and further people development. Companies need to devote time to the performance evaluation in order to secure an accurate, complete and fair process. Then, "clearly, performance evaluations have the potential to positively influence employee performance" (Milliman et al., 2002, p. 97).[26]

---

[25] I do not concentrate on the various other dimensions of performance evaluation as cognitive processing of information, specific rater/rate characteristics, errors, biases and problems, rating accuracy, formats and scales, sources in form of peer, self or supervisory, training, reactions, legal implications or social and political aspects and let this field to the human resource side. A thorough overview of the practices and topics involved in performance evaluation is provided by Murphy and Cleveland (1995), Bretz, Milkovich and Read (1992) and Levy and Williams (2004).

[26] Again, I do not touch the effectiveness of performance evaluation. Performance evaluations should deliver effective results. Otherwise, organizations waste resources and demotivate employees. The effectiveness heavily depends on setting up the right measures, on assessing accurate and fair, and on conveying the evaluation result in a timely and comprehensible manner through a feedback mechanism (Dorfman, Stephan & Loveland, 1986). Levy and Williams (2004) provide a detailed review. Another useful study is the paper by Ferris et al. (2008).

2.3.3 Rewards

2.3.3.1 Nature and purpose of rewards

The remark by Lawler, Mohrman Jr. and Resnik (1984, p. 21) "it is often noted that performance appraisal needs to be very clearly related to the pay system" provides a link to rewards. "Rewards are important because they inform or remind employees what result areas are desired and motivate them to achieve and exceed the performance targets" and "[p]erformance-dependent rewards provide the impetus for the alignment of employees' natural self-interests with the organization's objectives" (Merchant & van der Stede, 2003, p. 367). A fundamental objective of rewards is the motivational aspect to bundle the individual efforts to improve performance and to reach the organizational objectives. With rewards, companies strive to differentiate the poor from the average and the high-class performers (Meyer, 1975).

Rewards come in diverse ways with both positive and negative connotations. Punishments or penalties are negative rewards or, sometimes, "the absence of positive rewards" (Emmanuel, Otley & Merchant, 1990, p. 266), that come in form of non-promotion, lower demanding tasks or humiliation culminating to demotion or dismissal. Autonomy, power, recognition or special job assignments are among the positive non-monetary rewards whereas salary increases, bonuses and promotion are among the positive rewards with a financial impact (Merchant & van der Stede, 2003).

There are two different approaches to managing the topic of monetary rewards[27]. The proponents of a performance pay[28] believe that the functioning of rewards is only a matter of balancing targets and incentives. Opponents of this view emphasize that managers are not primarily incentivized by monetary awards and thus do not work harder (Anthony & Govindarajan, 2007). Future prospects, power, recognition, challenging tasks or participation in crucial projects are seen to be much more effective from a motivational point of view

---

[27] In the following, the thesis refers mainly to the financial aspect of rewards.
[28] There are two basic relationships between pay and performance, one looking at the influence of performance on pay and the other addressing the influence of pay on performance (Devers et al., 2007). This thesis focuses on the latter because of interest is the way to direct the behaviour of employees and thus look at the consequences of pay on performance. In a seminal contribution, Jensen and Murphy (1990b) target the first relationship and addressed the only marginal link of performance on pay.

(Emmanuel, Otley & Merchant, 1990). Those who advocate a fixed pay system also believe that an organization and their managers do not need rewards as this approach only binds time and resources and harms the natural flow of activities of the employees (Hope & Fraser, 2003). The difference of these two approaches lies in the treatment of performance and pay. The first system emphasizes pay which results from good performance, the second approach makes good performance a prerequisite for additional pay (Anthony & Govindarajan, 2007).[29]

There are different purposes or benefits associated to rewards, specifically informationally, motivationally and personally related. Informational benefits comprise a signalling effect. Rewards provide a signal to address important issues. Monetary effects remind employees to watch the agreed targets (Merchant & van der Stede, 2003). Furthermore, rewards incentivize employees to go the extra mile and work hard on their assignments because activities which lead to a reward are more in the focus of the recipient of the reward than those not being incentivized. This underlines the motivational advantages. Employees can get additional income which could encourage them to repeat and sustain a decent performance. It could withhold employees to leave the company and tie them stronger to the organization (Pepper, Gore & Crossman, 2013). Thus it helps to captivate and retain high quality employees (Aguinis, Joo & Gottfredson, 2013). A third benefit relates to the plain compensation and payment to the employees stressing the personnel component (Merchant & van der Stede, 2003). Extra pay gives more financial freedom for leisure activities, housing and education for the children (Aguinis, Joo & Gottfredson, 2013). The financial effect conveys also prestige and status (Jenkins Jr. et al., 1998). Monetary rewards hence serve as a symbol for the individual social standing and appreciation of the accomplishment. These purposes may be more important for senior persons and managers who fill crucial positions in the firms.

---

[29] The question of reward effectiveness is not subject to this thesis. Whether rewards have a positive or detrimental effect is fiercely debated among scholars and executives (Eisenberger & Cameron, 1996). There is some saying that there are ambiguous findings in literature (Bonner et al., 2000; Chong & Eggleton, 2007; Jenkins Jr. et al., 1998). Bonner and Sprinkle (2002) theoretically addressed the positive effects of incentives on effort and task performance. Aguinis, Joo and Gottfredson (2002b) provided some recommendations to facilitate the effectiveness of monetary rewards.

2.3.3.2 Categories of rewards

	EXAMPLES	REWARD ELEMENTS	DEFINITION
INTRINSIC REWARDS	Quality of Work and Life Status Development opportunities	Other Noncash Rewards	TOTAL REWARDS
EXTRINSIC REWARDS	Company Cars Club Memberships Financial and Legal Counselling	Perquisites	TOTAL REMUNERATION
	Retirement and Savings Plans Health Care Plans Paid Time Off Legally Required Benefits	Benefits	
	Stock/Equity Incentive Plans (Long-Term)	Long-term Variable	TOTAL DIRECT CASH
	Incentive plans (Short-Term) Bonuses/Spot Awards	Short-term Variable	TOTAL CASH
	Base Salary/Base Wage	Base Cash	

Table 3: Total rewards

Festing et al. (2012, p. 141) based on Manas and Graham (2003, p. 2) have laid out the whole spectrum of rewards which comprises every portion an employee receives from the company (see Table 3). They can be broadly classified into intrinsic and extrinsic rewards. Intrinsic rewards comprise non-financial components. Extrinsic rewards are part of the remuneration package with direct and indirect focus and short- and long-term components. All remunerations bear an equivalence to a financial value (e.g. in the area of perquisites bearing most of the cost for a company car has a certain monetary advantage for the employee).

Perquisites and benefits such as company cars, health care plans or retirement contracts are either not directly cash related or range into the very far future and thus are not part of the management control focus of this thesis. Acknowledging the classic categorization of direct monetary rewards – performance-based salary increases, short-and long-term incentive plans – this thesis mainly concentrates on the direct monetary aspect of rewards in particular those rewards in form of annual bonuses. This is based on the following reasons. Firstly, base salary and corresponding salary increases are excluded. Base salary, which is a fixed amount and not dependent on performance, should secure the living standard. In a strict sense, it is no management control element since there is no link to performance. Salary increases both compensate for inflation and higher cost-of-living and reward for merit (Lynch & Perry, 2003; Merchant & van der Stede, 2003). But salary increases, though annually recurring, have been rather small in Europe (Tanning & Tanning, 2013) and the US (Avalos & Cohen, 2011). Due to the small overall fraction of the total compensation they are of minor concern for management control. Additionally, according to a study by Ittner, Larcker and Rajan (1997), firms rarely have explicit rules to determine salary increases. Secondly, although promotion-based incentives are also a main source of rewards (Baker, Jensen & Murphy, 1988) and are normally accompanied by "an immediate and largely permanent increase in salary" (Gibbs, 1995, p. 249), which in turn provides the foundation for even higher rewards in the future, this thesis concentrates on the direct monetary aspect of rewards in particular those rewards in form of annual bonuses. Normally, promotions are not occurring each period as bonuses generally are. That is why bonuses[30] are a more on-going device whereas the chance for promotion depends on many circumstances, e.g. vacant positions, subordinate-superior relationship, mentoring, networking, reliance on internal promotion or external recruitment (Mayrhofer et al., 2002; Zimmermann, 2009). Thirdly, long-term incentive plans mainly serve the top management of companies. However, in this thesis, rewards are targeted for the subordinates of top management, who rarely have this kind of incentive scheme. Although, Park and Sturman (2012) state that long-term incentives are getting used more frequently in general and also at lower hierarchies, they mainly remain a tool for senior executives. Furthermore they are more out-of-sight with a loose connection to activities during the observed year (Pepper, Gore & Crossman, 2013). Finally, bonuses in form of cash payments, which are mainly based on the delivered performance of individuals, groups or the whole organization, often serve as "the main component of incentive pay for mid-level executives" (Indjejikian & Nanda, 2002, p. 794) and therefore are closely tied to management controls (Anthony & Govindarajan, 2007).

---

[30] The typical annual bonus plan consists of a bonus that is paid after reaching a certain threshold. When the bonus reaches the hurdle or floor, it increases with higher performance. The increases generally follow a linear path, but can also be convex or concave. Firms normally cap the bonus at an agreed maximum. The thresholds, performance standards and caps determining the incentive zone create room for rewards manipulation (for a graphical illustration see Hope & Fraser, 2003; Indjejikian & Nanda, 2002; Merchant & Otley, 2007)). Despite the difficulties associated with these bonus plans – (1) holding back profits, (2) pulling profits forward and (3) moving profits into next year that depend on where recipients are located in their performance outcome – these typical plans are widely used.

Summing up, rewards form a crucial part of the whole MCS. They are closely tied to performance evaluation since in the logical chain of activities rewards are provided after the evaluation. And, they are closely tied to the performance measurement area, since performance measures build the yardstick in determining the amount of rewards. Monetary rewards, in form of annual bonuses, are the object of observation. They are the most crucial devices for the level of investigation, namely middle managers.

2.4 Theories

2.4.1 Contingency-based approach

Contingency thoughts have its roots in the writing of Burns and Stalker (1961) who introduced the notion of different management systems (mechanistic and organic) depending on the level of environmental change. Lawrence and Lorsch (1967a; 1967b) introduced the term contingency theory and stated that the amount of differentiation and integration has to be fine-tuned according to the level of environmental change, while Chandler (1962) elaborated on the strategy and structure paradigm (Donaldson, 1996). Contingency theory is placed between two extreme situations. The situation specific approach is characterized by complete uniqueness and singularity of a company's MCS, whereas the universalistic approach is characterized by the appropriateness of one control design setting for all firms (Fisher, 1995, 1998). Conflicting empirical results with the universalistic framework, and the obvious fact that a universal view for all companies seemed to offer no valid characterization, stimulated thoughts of the contingency theory (Otley, 1980).

"The essence of the contingency paradigm is that organizational effectiveness results from fitting characteristics of the organization, such as its structure, to contingencies that reflect the situation of the organization" (Donaldson, 2001, p. 1). Scott and Davis (2007, p. 108) view the central paradigm of contingency theory that "there is no one best organizational form but many, and their suitability is determined by the goodness of fit between organizational form and the diverse environments to which they relate". The core premise of the contingency theory posits that no universal MCS exists that fits all organizations in all contextual surroundings. Within contingency thinking, researchers agree that the use and design of MCS are conditional on the specific circumstances a company is facing. Generalizations for the design and use of MCS can be inferred depending on certain categories or contingency factors. Thus, the contingency approach delivers the criteria of circumstances an MCS must match in order to be effective. Fit corresponds to matching at least two organizational features. The higher the fit between organizational contextual factors, and the design and use of MCS, the greater the effectiveness of the organization (Fisher, 1995, 1998; Merchant & Simons, 1986). "This fit-performance relationship is the heart of the contingency theory paradigm" (Donaldson, 2001, p. 7).

Contingency theory has been severely criticized. The main limitations can be summarized as follows. First, a full list of contingency factors leads to a tremendous amount of variables. Hofer (1975) identified 54 environmental and organizational variables. Schmid and Kretschmer (2010) listed 49 contingency factors attributed to strategy and management, structure and integration, market and technology, environment and general ones. The authors even stressed the non-exhaustiveness of their list. This explains why the full amount of potential contingency factors was barely elaborated and explored in empirical studies. Logically, it is nearly impossible to capture the full amount of contingency factors in one study, which is why only a small fraction have been researched (Fisher, 1995, 1998). A second point targets the definition of organizational effectiveness. Often, it is equated with higher firm performance. The effect of matching the particularities of contingent factors and MCS should then lead to higher effectiveness in the sense of higher performance; however, this may not be the only understanding. Other forms such as long-term firm survival, market share, customer or employee satisfaction, or consistent innovation could also be goals. More generally, organizational effectiveness could be described by attaining the pre-set goals, whatever they are. If researchers only apply the notion of a high annual performance, it might be short-sighted (Fisher, 1998). Third, contingency factors are ill-defined and differ across the studies, contributing only to rare cumulative knowledge (Merchant & Otley, 2007; Otley, 1980). Fourth, often, it is also the case that there are conflicting goals. For instance, while pursuing performance maximization, customer or employee satisfaction may decrease (Fisher, 1998). All possible interactions have been rudimentarily specified and tested. Fifth, since there is no single variable, but a multitude of variables encompassing the moderating effect of an MCS on effectiveness, it is difficult to extract the influence of one factor. "Given the fairly obvious proposition that most events and the outcomes of those events are likely to depend on the contextual settings, an important issue is whether ... insights from alternate theoretical perspectives" can be integrated (Chenhall, 2003, p. 157; 2007, p. 191).

Contingency theory entails variables in the areas of external environment (uncertainty, turbulence, hostility, diversity, and complexity), organizational strategy, organizational structure, organizational size, technology (complexity, task uncertainty, and interdependence), demographic factors, type of competition or management style, and national culture. These key elements determine the choice and design of MCS (Chenhall, 2003, 2007; Fisher, 1998).[31] Chenhall (2003, p. 152; 2007, p. 186) accentuates the deliberation to combine cultural phenomena with contingency thoughts: "the relationship between the design of MCS and national culture represents an extension of contingency-based research from its organizational foundations into more sociological concerns". Also van der Stede (2003, p. 264) provides evidence "that favourable managerial responses to MCISs *[management control and incentive systems – note of the author]* are likely to accrue from careful tailoring of these systems to specific national cultures on the basis of their cultural appropriateness." These statements justify seeing national culture as one contingency factor incorporated in managers' decision making.

2.4.2 New institutionalism

Among the organizational theories, new institutional theory[32, 33] has probably gained the most attention (Greenwood et al., 2008; Palmer, Biggart & Dick, 2008; Sturdy, 2004).[34] New institutionalism arose out of inconsistent observations of rational behaviour and structural contingency thoughts (Ribeiro & Scapens, 2006). "Institutional theory is ... usually an

---

[31] Chenhall (2003; 2007) provided a thorough overview of contingency-based research findings. The primary research method within contingency research has been questionnaire data (Merchant & Simons, 1986).

[32] The authors do not always explicitly state the whole term 'new institutionalism' in their work but rather 'institutionalism'. However, from reading it is rather clear that they refer to 'new institutionalism'. For example Greenwood et al. (2008) clearly label the starting point of new institutionalism with the works of Meyer and Rowan (1977) and Zucker (1977) which is consistent with the work of DiMaggio and Powell (1991).

[33] New institutionalism can be distinguished from old institutionalism. Walgenbach and Meyer (2008) provide a short summary about the two strands. DiMaggio and Powell (1991) also summarized the differences. Further papers to this distinction are Selznick (1996) or Abrutyn and Turner (2011).

[34] The following discussion is focusing on the social and organizational approach, particularly from a macro level point of view. New institutionalism also knows the micro foundation that was grounded by Zucker (1977). Micro-level understanding deals with the transfer of practices and procedures within organizations. The main difference between the micro- and macro-level is that from a macro perspective expectations are grounded in the environment of the institution, whereas the micro- point of view sees the expectations embedded in individuals' thoughts.

explanation of the similarity ("isomorphism") and stability of organizational arrangements" (Greenwood & Hinings, 1996, p. 1023). New institutional theory deals with organization-environment relationships. Organizations with similar surroundings will embody similar management practices. The managerial actions are formed by cultural rules, social values and expectations of the surrounding environment and their respective stakeholders (DiMaggio & Powell, 1983). Institutional theory is interested in questions about how preferences and actions are formed, influenced and bundled (Wooten & Hoffmann, 2008). The institutional thinking is not about competitive processes, but about social fitness (Scott, 2001). Organizations are affected "by their institutional context, i.e. by widespread social understandings" (Greenwood et al., 2008, p. 3), which corresponds to the "rationality myths of appropriate conduct" (Greenwood et al., 2008, p. 6). Rationality myths are "deeply ingrained in … social reality", incorporate manifold characterizations of societies as laws, traditions, public opinions or general beliefs and thus "are manifestations of powerful institutional rules" (Meyer & Rowan, 1977, p. 343). Meyer and Rowan (1977) explicate that organizations will use rationally rooted practices and procedures for their legitimate action.

Organizations strive for social acceptance and credibility in order to gain legitimacy and access to resources that ultimately secures business survival (see Figure 5). Organizations gain legitimacy by conforming to their cultural setting. They incorporate the expectations of their surrounding environment (Dowling & Pfeffer, 1975; Meyer & Rowan, 1977).

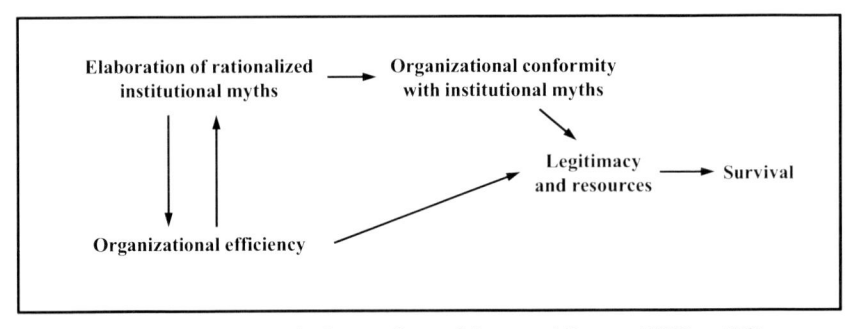

```
Elaboration of rationalized  ────▶  Organizational conformity
  institutional myths                with institutional myths
        │  ▲                                   │
        │  │                                   ▼
        │  │                              Legitimacy      ────▶  Survival
        ▼  │                            and resources
  Organizational efficiency  ─────────────▶
```

Figure 5: Organizational survival according to Meyer and Rowan (1977, p. 353)

Suchman (1995, p. 574) derived the following definition: "Legitimacy is a generalized perception or assumption that the actions of an entity are desirable, proper, or appropriate within some socially constructed system of norms, values, beliefs, and definitions". Thus, legitimacy is a social phenomenon of shared beliefs, which is subjectively constructed by social actors. Baxter and Chua (2003) declare management accounting practices as rationality myths that show compliance with their social world. As such, management control elements and systems can also be seen in this way.

Organizations utilize isomorphic measures to signal their social proof and to gain legitimacy. Isomorphism imposes convergence processes for organizations to resemble other organizations. According to DiMaggio and Powell (1983), organizations are affected by three types of isomorphism: coercive, mimetic and normative mechanisms. Coercive isomorphism is explicated by mandate, persuasion, force and pressure, but it can also derive from governmental regulations and policies. Rules and standards can be both subtle and directly imposed on the organization. Mimetic isomorphism is the orientation towards perceived successful models of other organizations. Especially in cases with high uncertainty, firms mimick other organizations. By ascribing to the flourishing business concepts of actors within the same organizational field (see below), firms copy well-proven business approaches and models to reduce risk. Normative pressure arises from increasing professionalism. Professional groups and bodies rely on similar networks, follow similar education paths, and thus exhibit a similar mind-set and orientation. This transfer of shared norms has a normative character.

Scott (1995) derived his three dimensions of legitimacy, regulative, normative and cognitive, which he connected with his three institutional pillars (see Figure 6).

	Regulative	Normative	Cultural-Cognitive
Basis of compliance	Expedience	Social obligation	Taken-for-grantedness Shared understanding
Basis of order	Regulative rules	Binding expectations	Constitutive schema
Mechanisms	Coercive	Normative	Mimetic
Logic	Instrumentality	Appropriateness	Orthodoxy
Indicators	Rules Laws Sanctions	Certification Accreditation	Common beliefs Shared logics of action
Basis of legitimacy	Legally sanctioned	Morally governed	Comprehensible Recognizable Culturally supported

Figure 6: Pillars of institutions according to Scott (2001, p. 52)

Scott's (1995) three pillars of institutions, regulative (similar to DiMaggio and Powell's coercive), cultural-cognitive (similar to DiMaggio and Powell's mimetic) and normative processes place the different elements of institutions along a continuum from regulative rules to taken-for-granted character. The elements and characteristics of the three pillars help to explain the behaviour of institutions and the basis of legitimacy. The three pillars also incorporate the notion of culture in the meaning of a shared understanding. Legitimacy in this sense is neither legally sanctioned nor morally enforced, but comprises a common frame and shared conceptions. All of the organizational actions of institutional players are based on the internal and cognitive evaluation of the environment (Scott, 1995; 2001; 2008).[35]

Since isomorphism increases legitimacy, firms are eager to adhere to managerial actions that foster legitimate thoughts. An apparently legitimate organization improves its prospect for business survival. So, the basic rationale, to behave in a legitimate way, is incorporated in managerial practice (Deephouse, 1996). Many managerial practices are institutionalized and, as such, compulsory for organizations; they continue to exist as rationality myths. Organizations that pursue managerial practices and address the variety of rationality myths are signalling their willingness for collective institutionalized efforts. Once organizations leave the normal path of socially embedded norms to secure legitimacy, they soon have to return to that path. Otherwise, once departures from this ideal path are discovered, legitimacy vanishes and organizations will be sanctioned (Suchman, 1995). This threat urges organizations to utilize measures to either ensure consistent legitimacy, or, if deviations are detected, recover to the former state, or take initiatives to alter the common understanding of the legitimacy concept (Dowling & Pfeffer, 1975).

Another important construct of the new institutional theory is the organizational field. Scott (1995; 2001) saw the field as an organizational fellowship that has a common understanding of the environment and has a higher and more intense interaction with in-field actors than with players from the outside. Among those actors are relevant business partners, govern-

---

[35] Lounsbury (1997) presented a two dimensional matrix of ideal types of new institutional approaches. The two axes are based on the different level of analysis and theories of action. The level of analysis dichotomizes the micro and macro level, whereas the theory of action distinguishes between routines or habits and interests and values. Quadrant four targets the macro-level and habitual and routine based thoughts. Lounsbury (1997) declares this cell, which he labelled cultural system, as the predominant understanding of new institutionalism. This viewpoint is similar to the dominant cognitive-cultural pillar of Scott.

ments and authorities, the public or other organizations. DiMaggio and Powell (1977, p. 148) speak of "a recognized area of institutional life". This former understanding of the organizational field comprised a homogenous and stable collection of actors within a field, and was orientated towards similar technology, markets or sectors. However, organizational fields also comprise competing organizations. Critical voices encountered the homogenous thought. The notion of change and dynamics within the organizational field brought up the issue of debate, contestation, conflict, and struggle between organizations, rather than isomorphism. Thus, the idea of the organizational field targets "the domain within which a particular institution operates" (Palmer, Biggart & Dick, 2008, p. 742). The common denominator is the interaction element and the same exposure to the institutional boundaries. Both understandings, the one of homogeneity and heterogeneity emphasize that organizational fields produce identical outcomes. Firms operating in the same institutional field will exhibit a common approach in dealing with and shaping the institutional context, as they face similar pressure to create harmony with their institutional environment (Wooten & Hoffmann, 2008).

Organizations have a series of alternatives to approach inconsistent expectations of their environment. These only partially effective solutions comprise resistance, rejection, concession, and promise of improvement (Meyer & Rowan, 1977), which mainly correspond to the strategic responses to institutional processes laid out by Oliver (1991) in form of defiance, avoidance, compromise and acquiescence.[36] A much more advanced way in institutionalized thinking is the method of decoupling where inefficiencies and inconsistencies between the institutionalized practices are maintained within the close area of the organization, but communication towards the outside world is rather positive. Decoupling in the sense of window-dressing is a way to uphold legitimacy, while organizational activities deviate from actual implementations. Decoupling occurs when there is a deviation between formal rules and standards and displayed handling, or in other words a gap between adopted policies and actual practices. When firms incorporate the multitude of institutionalized concepts the whole composition of these procedures could be inefficient. Companies might then decouple institutionalized practices from their normal business in distinguishing

---

[36] A fifth form of response is that of manipulation (Oliver, 1991).

between formal rules, guidelines, standards and actual habits. Companies would pretend to fulfil organizational structural adaptation, while at the same time pursuing their actions differently. Thus, effort is directed to making official statements and longing for ceremonial adoption, which gives credibility to the institutionalized concepts, affects legitimacy and exploits resources (Meyer & Rowan, 1977).

A second and different type of decoupling concerns the gap between means and ends. This is explicated by uncertainty about the usefulness of management control elements on the intended results, meaning that practices are implemented, but it is not clear what impact they have. So this explains why organizations waste time and resources on practices that do not contribute to the organizational goals. Whereas the former type of decoupling resembles a 'symbolic adoption', the latter can be characterized by 'symbolic implementation' (Bromley & Powell, 2012).

Returning to the concept of legitimacy, one could ask who assesses the level of legitimacy and challenges legitimacy, and who sets existing standards? The answer is provided by the organizational field; other actors in the organizational field value the level of legitimacy. Some argue that institutional entrepreneurs set the targets and norms. Although some firms might have the possibility to jiggle the rules of the game, they still do not have the power to bring in new standards in the field on their own. They might form coalitions, build networks and lobby for their intentions, but in the end, other actors in the field have to accept the new norms, too. If actions are deemed appropriate they will be reinforced in further interactions. Other voices argue that disruptive events in the form of mergers and acquisitions, regulatory changes and environmental catastrophes create leeway to changes in the field (Wooten & Hoffmann, 2008). In order to sustain legitimacy, the cognitive and socio-political expectations of key stakeholders have to be accounted for by building knowledge and developing trust and reputation (Aldrich & Fiol, 1994). The stakeholder approach addresses this element.

2.4.3 Stakeholder theory

Stakeholder theory brings a further lens to the context of this thesis. Organizations are embedded in their organizational surroundings and live in relationships with different stakeholders. It is the main responsibility of managers to govern and steer these relationships, and to create value for each stakeholder (Freeman, Harrison & Wicks, 2007; Freeman et al., 2010). In order to assess the process of value creation, managers employ a variety of control elements. The main elements are performance measurement, performance evaluation and reward systems.

The basic idea of the stakeholder approach ingrains in businesses a "set of relationships among groups that have a stake in the activities that make up the business. Business is about how customers, suppliers, employees, financiers ..., communities, and managers interact and create value" (Freeman et al., 2010, p. 3). Stakeholders are seen as "any group or individual who can affect or is affected by the achievement of the organization's objectives" (Freeman, 1984, p. 46). Donaldson and Preston (1995) presented a model with eight stakeholder groups around the organization, namely government, investors, political groups, customers, communities, employees, trade associations and suppliers.[37] The broad understanding and the universal definition of the term stakeholder was heavily critized, as all entities belong to the mentioned criteria. However, for managers, it is more important to know their respective core stakeholders (Laplume, Sonpar & Litz, 2008).[38] Laplume, Sonpar and Litz (2008, p. 1163) showed how organizations are influenced by stakeholders: answers range from "direct and indirect withholding and conditional usage strategies", "influence is determined by the power and legitimacy of a stakeholder" over "by forming coalitions and networks" to "influence depends on relationship structure, contractual forms, and institutional supports".

Stakeholder theory has been sparingly applied within the management control context. Arora and Alam (2005) found that CEO compensation is tied to the claims of stakeholders, especially shareholders, customers and employees. In their investigation, firms incorporated long-term incentive plans to their reward scheme. One contribution in the area of human resource management is by Colakoglu, Lepak and Hong (2006). They plead for a more holistic stakeholder perspective in evaluating human resource management practices.

---

[37] Investors (both owners and creditors) provide funds and expect an adequate return. Managers and employees devote time and personal resources to the organization and expect a fair compensation. Suppliers deliver resources and expect a return. Customers purchase the output of the organization and expect these products or services to deliver value. The government provides infrastructure and expects taxes and improvements in the quality of life for their citizens (Hill & Jones, 1992).

[38] Laplume, Sonpar and Litz (2008) presented a more tangible list of the various stakeholders that managers particularly care about. Mitchell, Agle and Wood (1997) developed various stakeholder classes based on the degree of power, legitimacy and urgency.

2.4.4 Agency theory

Top managers have a unique role within the stakeholder groups. They interact with all actors and exert direct decision-making control in the organization. Top management "balances the interests of various constituencies and manages responsibilities to various stakeholder groups" (Arora & Alam, 2005, p. 522). In doing so, the strategic and operational decisions should be "most consistent with the claims of the other stakeholder groups" (Hill & Jones, 1992, p. 134). In their role, top managers enter into a contract with the other stakeholders (Eisenhardt, 1989).

A theoretical perspective that addresses these contractual relationships is the agency theory (Arrow, 1985; Baiman, 1990; Eisenhardt, 1989; Holmstrom & Tirole, 1989; Jensen & Meckling, 1976; Lambert, 2001; Ross, 1973), which is the dominant theoretical paradigm for examining reward situations (Pepper, Gore & Crossman, 2013; Prendergast, 1999). Agency theory targets the relationship in which there are conflicting goals between principals and agents, in which compensation and incentives are key features in aligning the interests of principals and agents. The principal assigns a contract that links the performance and pay of the agent. The performance-tied compensation contract tries to balance information asymmetries between the two parties involved (i.e. a favourable information base of the agent that is very costly and difficult to observe) with a corresponding risk transfer (Banker, Lee & Potter, 1996; Bol, 2008). In light of the agency theory, the promise for rewards serves as a

> "contract under which one or more persons (the principal(s)) engage another person (the agent) to perform some service on their behalf which involves delegating some decision making authority to the agent ... [and] the principal can limit divergences from his interest by establishing appropriate incentives for the agent" (Jensen & Meckling, 1976, p. 308)[39]

The pecuniary reward is one piece of this incentive system between part of the stakeholders and the executives on the one side, and the executives and lower ranked managers on the

---

[39] Moral hazard is a post-contractual problem that is rooted in information asymmetries and divergent objectives of the principal and the agents (see Arrow, 1985; Baiman, 1990). Remedies to solve the problem of moral hazard, i.e. the agent reacts divergently from the intentions of the principal, are monitoring, which can be difficult and costly to achieve, and establishing incentives that seek to achieve goal congruence in aligning the interest of the principal and the agent (Eisenhardt, 1989; Holmstrom, 1979). Stevens and Thevaranjan (2010) have lately postulated an improved agency model in adding moral phenomena.

other side. Incentives help to reduce the assumed conflicting preferences of the principal and the agents. From an agency perspective, performance-dependent rewards are a tool to increase an individual's motivation (Bonner & Sprinkle, 2002) and overcome agency problems in harmonizing the preferences of organizations and individuals (Cadsby, Song & Tapon, 2007). Holmstrom and Milgrom (1991) showed that the inclusion of factors into performance evaluation and rewards affects the behaviour of employees. They provided reasoning that employees might solely turn their attention to the measured and rewarded activities. However, Anthony and Govindarajan (2007) remarked that the theory oversimplifies business reality and has not shown to impact managers in designing the management control element.

2.4.5 Synthesis of theoretical approaches

In conclusion, there is a considerable amount of literature on linking the context of MCS with the various contingency factors, among them culture (Chenhall, 2003, 2007). Given particular situations there are different assumed patterns of MCS, which corresponds to the idea that "it all depends" (Otley, 1980, p. 414f.). The claim "it all depends" equally shows that the term contingency-based approach is much more appropriate than speaking of a theory (Merchant & Otley, 2007). Thus, in the following I refer to the contingency-based approach. Also Chenhall (2003; 2007) noted that it is not appropriate to refer to one theory rather than a stream of theories. Particularly important is the integration of alternative theories to the contingency thoughts. Chenhall (2003, p. 160; 2007, p. 194) furthermore suggests that "many of the insights concerning the role of institutions within society on the adoption of MCS can be combined readily with contingency concepts" and national culture is a logical extension of the organizational contingency idea towards a wider sociological view. A contrasting element between the contingency-based approach and new institutionalism is the treatment of efficiency. The former approach wants to maximize efficiency in "achieving some 'fit' between environment and structure, while institutional theorists recognize that efficiency in a more objective sense may actually suffer as a result of the organization's need to legitimate itself to dominant constituencies" (Brignall & Modell, 2000, p. 285).

From the reading of the institutional literature I can clearly see an overlap with the national cultural acumen. There are many common elements in the definitions and concepts, which range from institutions as cultural themes or cultural and symbolic patterns (Caprar & Neville, 2012). Scott (1995) labelled his third column of institutions as cultural-cognitive, which underlines the congruence between the two notions. His third pillar incorporates the cultural element. The shared understanding and the taken-for-granted mentality incorporates a strong stability (Kara & Peterson, 2012). Since societal members are exposed to similar real-world influences, they are shaped by the same reality. Consequently, they develop a common cultural-cognitive understanding (Nisbett et al., 2001). "Values, beliefs, norms, taken-for-granted traditions, and routines" are cornerstones to institutions and culture (Caprar & Neville, 2012, p. 237) because "values, beliefs, ideas, attitudes, and morals ... are ingrained in the national culture" (Parboteeah, Addae & Cullen, 2012, p. 404).

According to the new-institutional understanding, which is also incorporated in the GLOBE project (Dickson, BeShears & Gupta, 2004), it is a "good reason to believe that the world came to be organized into distinctive, differentiated cultural groups that provide quite different contexts for work organizations" (Kara & Peterson, 2012, p. 351). Tempel and Walgenbach (2007) explicate that the new institutionalism sets the boundaries of the organizational field at national borders. Thus, cross-national variation of management control practices is well grounded in the institutionalized ends and means. From this view one would analyze variances in management control practices "based on political-cultural distinctions across nation-states such as whether societal systems are corporatist or individualist" (Lounsbury, 1997, p. 474).

Stakeholder theory deals with the question, which "'sticks' become 'stakes', that is, how potential claims (sticks) become actualized and legitimated claims (stakes), ... the latter being sustainably institutionalized in the organization's landscape" (Laplume, Sonpar & Litz, 2008, p. 1175). Stakeholder theory embraces a far-reaching understanding of the various mechanisms affecting organizations. Therefore, this theory can be readily combined with the institutional thinking, which also deals with mechanisms from the organizational surroundings that influence organizational actions (Brühl & Osann, 2010). Freeman et al. (2010, p. 151) also state "the conceptual similarities of stakeholder theory to institutional theory". A common denominator between the institutional thoughts and stakeholder theory is the legitimacy concept, which is exemplified by the intermingling of legitimacy and stakeholder classes (Mitchell, Agle & Wood, 1997).

Taking the cultural acumen into consideration, and treating society as a high-level construct of the organizational field, organizations will configure management control elements increasingly similar within a society or culture, and increasingly dissimilar across societies or cultures. Giacobbe-Miller, Miller and Zhang (2003, p. 402) express this idea because "from a theoretical standpoint, the intersection of culture and institutional theory suggests that cultures will vary in their adaptive responses based on cultural characteristics, but that enterprises will vary within cultures based on institutional characteristics". Hence, the cultural viewpoint is crucial in determining the causes and effects of organizational behaviour executed at the management level. The distinction of cultural manifestations enables the researcher to draw differences due to national context. Related to the MCS context, the institutional theory brings the following deliberations. Organizations will garner information with respect to the social expectations about norms and standards, incorporate this information in their decision-making process, and implement and further develop those management control elements towards a homogenous use that occurs in their respective organizational field. In conclusion, firms are heavily influenced by the local environment, which affects organizational practices, and hence MCS. If one exemplarily looks at human resource practices, firms are affected by legislation, law or market characteristics, which arise from regulatory, cognitive or normative processes (Björkman, Fey & Park, 2007).

The central claim of how culture manifests itself into organizational and managerial mechanisms and decisions has been answered. Managers and other organizational members live in a cultural context. They are exposed to the norms, standards and mechanisms that are ingrained in their cultural surrounding similar to an iron cage. They align all their behaviour, decisions and actions to those cultural values. The same principle applies to the organization's other stakeholders. They are also exposed to the same cultural values, thus their expectations towards design and use of control systems are influenced by this cultural context. Organizations rely on those control mechanisms, which match their respective organizational surrounding, with the consequence that the control mechanisms are influenced by culture. This writing gives credibility in using new institutionalism as the main theory for the explication of cross-cultural differences. Stakeholder theory helps to explain the relationships of managers and other social actors, while the contingency-based approach also weaves in culture as an explanatory variable.

3 Research overview and hypotheses

3.1 Methodology of literature review

An important step in discovering novel insights is to systematically and transparently consolidate existing knowledge. A thorough literature review makes scholars familiar with the topic and hence stimulates research into new avenues. A comprehensive and structured literature search on the interplay of cross-cultural issues and MCS was conducted to highlight the major research done in academia and to develop the hypotheses. A previous literature review on the bespoken interplay dates back to the article of Harrison and McKinnon (1999), who searched corresponding literature until 1997. However, while acknowledging their substantial contribution in cross-cultural research, the methodology section in their article is rather weak.[40]

The methodology I follow in the literature search is based on a synthesis of various broad and comprehensive literature reviews (Ennen & Richter, 2009; Euske, Hesford & Malina, 2011; Franco-Santos, Lucianetti & Bourne, 2012; Glock & Hochrein, 2011; Hesford et al., 2007; Maschke & Knyphausen-Aufseß, 2012), and advice given in methodological textbooks (Cooper, 2010; Cooper, Hedges & Valentine, 2009; Hair Jr. et al., 2011). The literature review is executed in six main steps (Appendix 3, p. 187ff., provides the detailed procedure).

First, I selected the relevant journals by combining the publication lists of Rosenstreich and Wooliscraft (2009) for accounting issues, Podsakoff (2005) for the area of management, and Kirkman et al. (2006) for further business and psychological areas. To secure high quality journals, which are well recognized in the scientific community, the target journals were restricted to the three mentioned sources. This process revealed a total list of 83 journals (see Appendix 4, p. 191).

Second, I compiled a broad set of appropriate search terms (Reed & Baxter, 2009). With reference to the topic, keywords were selected under each umbrella term both for the subject

---

[40] They do not state any criteria for their search, which would be important for replication. They presented twenty articles that were published in Accounting, Organizations & Society (10), Administrative Science Quarterly (3), Journal of International Business Studies (2), and five other journals (one article each).

of performance measurement, performance evaluation, rewards and culture. The search terms for performance measurement, performance evaluation and rewards followed the main elements of the framework of Malmi and Brown (2008) and the questionnaire used in the research project. The keywords for culture comprised: culture itself, cultural aspects and denotations, as well as notable representatives of cultural research. There was no upfront exclusion of specific study features in terms of method, design, sample features, statistical analysis or geographical focus (Wilson, 2009).

In a third step I searched various databases with reference to accessing the identified 84 target journals. Among the databases accessed were Ebsco, Emerald, Informs, Jstor, Sage, Science Direct, Springer, Swetswise, World Scientific, Taylor and Francis, websites[41], Wiley and Wiso. I decided to follow the mode of searching in subject indexes (White, 2009) and conducted a computer aided search in the title, keywords and abstract for the complete journal list over the years 1980-2013[42]. The date of retrieval was a two week period from June 18 to June 29, 2012 and February 5, 2014 for the latest articles. Papers had to match the combination of keywords from both major search terms: MCS (performance measurement, performance evaluation, rewards) and culture.

Fourth, I initially screened all articles for context relevance, i.e. related to the research focus, by reading the abstract. If a study met the selection criteria, i.e. treated national culture and performance evaluation or rewards, the article was added to the sample. Otherwise, articles were excluded from categorization. I assume that the very detailed search indicates a comprehensive far-reaching review. Although great effort was undertaken to achieve a thorough analysis, it is possible that I unintentionally overlooked some articles. I hope that any omissions will not affect the conclusions of the review (Tsui, Nifadkar & Ou, 2007).

In the fifth step, and to finally select the relevant articles, I reviewed the sample of previously identified articles. I read the abstract, the hypotheses and the method section – in some cases the entire article – to probe the applicability to the research context. Articles that portrayed

---

[41] Industrial Relations provides a search mechanism and free website access with a two-year delay.
[42] The timespan chronologically followed the years of the study from Harrison and McKinnon (1999). Of further interest has been a replication of their data period.

mere country comparisons, without specifying any cultural acumen in the whole text, were excluded from the analysis.

As a last step, I coded all relevant articles based on categories I derived from former literature (Chow, Shields & Wu, 1999; Harrison & McKinnon, 1999; Tsui, Nifadkar & Ou, 2007) and complemented by my own ideas. The final categories considered many different criteria of information not found in any prior literature review related to the context of MCS.

3.2 Research overview

Appendix 5 (p. 192ff.) provides more extensive information and lists all 50 studies I extracted from the review within the area of performance evaluation and rewards. One large block in the studies from the literature review deals with the topic of reward allocation. Only non-accounting studies targeted this theme, though I will not provide the diverse findings here, as this topic is of minor interest in the thesis. Only one subcomponent in the questionnaire targets the amount of equal sharing of rewards. Fischer and Smith (2003) provided a good overview of this topic by means of a meta-study that included 25 psychological publications. The survey studies mainly concentrated on the individual level, asking for preferences or personal choices of specific performance evaluation and reward practices. Studies with the organization as the level of analysis are quite rare among the identified studies. Among them are Bonache et al. (2012), Chiang and Birtch (2010), Jansen et al. (2009), Lowe et al. (2002), Merchant et al. (2011) and Van der Stede (2003). In the following, I limit my presentation to the main findings from the identified articles with respect to the research methodology and the hypotheses. I present the previous findings analogue to the variables and measures from the questionnaire.

Subjective evaluation/performance standards objectivity: Chow, Kato and Shields (1994) found no differences in the use of controllability filters in performance evaluation between Japanese and US MBA students. Controllability filters take exogenous effects into consideration and safeguard against uncontrollable events. This corresponds to subjective evaluation elements. By means of a field study, Merchant, Chow and Wu (1995) could not verify higher subjectivity in performance evaluation settings in Taiwan, which represents a culture with high uncertainty avoidance. Chow, Shields and Wu (1999) also found no such differences. It should be noted however that all firms investigated were Taiwanese companies with part-foreign ownership from Japan and the US. Thus, in the area of performance evaluation and reward, the national Taiwanese setting probably dominated the use of management controls, and this was the reason why no such differences were found.

Performance evaluation purpose: According to Chiang and Birtch (2010), the short-term focus of performance evaluation is more pronounced in low uncertainty avoidance and high individualistic and power distance cultures. Peretz and Fried (2012) found a positive correlation between the cultural dimension future orientation and the future purposes of performance evaluation related to organizational development.

Performance evaluation frequency: Early on, Vance et al. (1992) addressed the question of the transferability of the principles of performance evaluation (i.e. frequency of feedback). They examined this question in terms of the US and three Asian-Pacific countries. Since they found significant differences for the frequency of feedback, they sensitized managers to pay attention to a mere transferability of these practices. Chiang and Birtch (2010) found a higher frequency of feedback when assertiveness and individualism was high and uncertainty avoidance low.

Performance measures for rewarding (components): Awasthi, Chow and Wu (1998) found a higher preference for team-based performance measures on the part of US students compared to Chinese students. This finding was counterintuitive to the individualistic culture of the US. The authors attributed the behaviour of the US subject to deliberately counterbalancing their individualistic cultural setting. Chow, Kato and Shields (1994) investigated, among other controls, team-based rewards in an experimental setting. They found that Japanese students relied more on team-based rewards, though the differences for rewards connected to team performance among Japanese and US students were not significant. Chow, Shields and Wu (1999) found no differences for the perceived design of performance-oriented financial rewards for the Taiwanese companies mentioned above. Chiang and Birtch examined reward preferences and practices with a sample that focused on two or four countries from Canada, Finland, Hong Kong or the UK over a variety of papers. Chiang and Birtch (2005; 2007) found differences in terms of reward system preferences in the area of performance-oriented reward systems. Chiang and Birtch (2007) found differences with regard to individual-based and performance-oriented performance reward systems.

Jansen, Merchant and van der Stede (2009) replicated the study by Gibbs et al. (2004) and compared their findings in The Netherlands with earlier findings in the US. They analyzed the incentive compensation of general and departmental managers in car dealerships. They distinguished between different components of the managers' compensation package such as base salary, formula bonuses, discretionary bonuses which are based on subjective evaluation, and other rewards. Controlling for many situational variables, they posited significant differences between countries which they attributed to institutional factors and vaguely to the cultural traits of masculinity and long-term orientation. In particular, they found significant differences in the bases for assigning bonuses. US car dealerships employ more performance-based measures than did Dutch ones. Merchant et al. (2011), who extended the two country setting by including a Chinese aspect, showed significant differences in terms of financial and non-financial performance indicators between China and the US, and a low use of performance-dependent rewards in China. Schuler and Rogovsky (1998) found a higher incidence of individual components in reward schemes in cultures with higher levels of uncertainty avoidance and individualism.

Performance evaluation and rewarding objectivity: Jansen, Merchant and van der Stede (2009) found lower discretionary bonuses which are based on subjective judgments on the part of superiors, in terms of incidence and average size for Dutch managers compared to US managers. Merchant et al. (2011) used the cultural dimension of masculinity as an explanation for the differences in the incidence of rewards, and power distance as a predictor of the amount of discretionary bonuses.

Equality reward criteria: Fischer (2004), who compared Germany and the UK with a survey sample of 84% non-managerial employees, found no sizeable difference in terms of an equal sharing of rewards. Giacobbe-Miller, Miller and Zhang (2003), who used a fairly widespread and purely managerial sample, compared China, Russia and the US. They mainly found significant differences in the treatment of equality. Collectivistic cultures were found to be more equal than individualistic cultures.

Rewarding nature: Vance et al. (1992) also addressed the question of transferability of financial vs. non-financial rewards. They found significant differences between the US and three Asian-Pacific countries with regard to the nature of rewarding. Chiang and Birtch (2005) found that preferences for reward types (i.e. financial vs. non-financial rewards) differ between Canada, the UK, Hong Kong and Finland. Depending on the cultural dimension, they found mixed support for their hypotheses. Masculine cultures exhibited a stronger preference for monetary rewards, while individualistic and collectivistic cultures showed similar reward type preferences for financial rewards. Chiang and Birtch (2007) also showed significant differences in the preference for financial over non-financial rewards across the four countries. However, in terms of cultural effects, they found mixed support for their hypotheses. To incentivize performance, Hong Kong residents who are representatives of assertive cultures, were found to value financial rewards more than non-financial rewards (Chiang & Birtch, 2012).

3.3 Research hypotheses

3.3.1 Hypotheses development

Few earlier studies have broadened the horizon on the use and design of elements of management control across the different cultures under study. Thus, I will theoretically derive many new hypotheses for subject areas, without the ability to rely on previous empirical studies. For those newly derived hypotheses I will provide argumentation based on theory. In consequence, one half of the hypotheses I derive, and present in Chapters 3.3.2 – 3.3.6 is theoretically deduced from the subject matter; the remaining half of the hypotheses can be replicated from previous studies. For the replication category, I rely on the insights of previous studies that also have implications for my analysis. The reasoning to include replication elements in my hypotheses is because "replication is a pillar of normal scientific investigation. Through replication scientists learn whether findings hold again and this provides a basis for establishing empirical generalizations" (Uncles & Kwok, 2013, p. 1398). Many authors in the business context explicate the central role of replication research (Evanschitzky & Armstrong, 2013). Nevertheless, replication often displays low prestige and is "regarded as a pedestrian and uninspiring pursuit" (Bryman, 2008, p. 158). However, scientific progress builds upon replication, and the discovery of consistency is only made possible by continuing replication research and testing falsification (Popper, 2002) in the form of conjectures and refutations (Popper, 1972). Lindsay (1995, p. 35) states the need for replications since "replication provides the crucial test of the reliability and validity of facts, hypotheses and theories. It leads, when successful, to generalizable and predictable results".

I want to emphasize that this research is not about "'merely checking' others' results" (Evanschitzky et al., 2007, p. 413) but to further develop the research field. Studies show that there is often conflict between the original and the succession study (Evanschitzky et al.,

2007). Hubbard and Armstrong (1994) reported that up to 60% of replication studies conflict with the original results. This shows the need to re-test former hypotheses and reinforce a debate about causes and implications. That is why I have included hypotheses that have found support for their testing, and hypotheses that have only found partial support, or were not supported at all.

In terms of classification I followed the differentiated replication with an extension that is "a duplication of a previously published empirical research project that serves to investigate the generalizability of earlier research findings" (Hubbard & Armstrong, 1994, p. 236), with varying facets in terms of concept, methodology and content (Uncles & Kwok, 2013). I added additional variables for both performance evaluation and rewarding. I used a different approach to measure culture. Additionally, I used different populations and samples. The origins of the ideas for replication comprise the work of Newman and Nollen (1996), Schuler and Rogovsky (1998), Giacobbe-Miller, Miller and Zhang (2003), Fischer (2004), and a series of publications from Chiang and Birtch (2005; 2006; 2007; 2010; 2012) as well as Merchant et al. (2011). I will denote the replicated hypotheses and, especially, the newly developed ones. However, as stated, the hypotheses are not repeated as literal replications.

Many studies stress that only the most relevant cultural dimensions should be applied in the research context (Tsui, 2001). As the literature review demonstrated (see Chapter 3.2, p. 69f.), most cultural studies concentrate on just a few dimensions to illustrate the cross-cultural influence on MCS. On the other hand, a multiple approach of cultural dimensions only becomes necessary if the research context requires it. Only some cultural dimensions mostly impact single MCS elements. For this study, I evaluated what type of cultural dimensions best suit my research design. I used five of the nine GLOBE dimensions to derive the hypotheses and execute the analysis. I limited the study to the five dimensions of power distance, future orientation, assertiveness, individualism/collectivism [43] and uncertainty avoidance for the distinction of performance measures, performance evaluation and rewards.

From the five dimensions I use, assertiveness offers a relatively unchartered area (Den Hartog, 2004). The same applies to future orientation. Collectivism and individualism has

---

[43] In the following, individualism/collectivism replaces the wording of institutional collectivism.

been thoroughly researched and debated (Gelfand et al., 2004) although less known phenomena still exist. Power distance is of interest as two levels, one with top management and one with their subordinates, are addressed. Uncertainty avoidance is at the very core of organizational life and thus subject to investigation. I used the intersection of dimensions that were found to exhibit high relevance to performance evaluation (Chiang & Birtch, 2010; Myloni, Harzing & Mirza, 2004), performance measures and rewards. Chiang and Birtch (2010) chose assertiveness, uncertainty avoidance, in-group collectivism, and power distance. Peretz and Fried (2012) relied on power distance, individualism/collectivism, uncertainty avoidance and future orientation. I used individualism/collectivism instead of in-group collectivism, since the latter refers more to families and family lives. According to Chiang and Birtch (2010, p. 1374), these dimensions "reflect how individuals view themselves (assertiveness), their relationships with peers (in-group collectivism) and superiors (power distance), and company rules and procedures (uncertainty avoidance)". Gender egalitarianism is not applied as the hypotheses do not target gender issues and their involvement in decision-making. Human orientation is not used because I do not concentrate on social support and caring. Performance orientation is neglected as this dimension mainly aims at performance improvements (Javidan, 2004), which is not the focus of this thesis.

There are various links between the GLOBE construct and the MCS questionnaire. As a consequence, the following research hypotheses will be addressed.

3.3.2 Hypotheses related to power distance

The power distance concept is equated with "the degree to which members of an organization or society expect and agree that power should be shared unequally" (Carl, Gupta & Javidan, 2004, p. 517). A higher power distance stands for higher disparity in power. In high power distance cultures, power is concentrated at the top; subordinates rather react passively, respect hierarchy and tolerate solutions, rather than pro-actively engage in a dialogue with their superiors, express contrary views and refuse obedience. Higher participation in decision-making is preferred in low power distance cultures (Carl, Gupta & Javidan, 2004).

A flat hierarchy understanding facilitates an easier exchange between superiors and subordinates in low power distance cultures, and the participation of employees in the evaluation process is more likely. Sensitive issues can be brought up in a more personal environment. Managers probably care more about their subordinates in low power distance cultures, so it is more important for them to advance the capabilities and skills of their employees. Prior literature indicates (Chiang & Birtch, 2010) this negative relationship for power distance as well as learning and development needs, meaning that low power distance cultures emphasized learning and improvement. Therefore, I propose the following hypothesis:

Hypothesis 1 (r^{44}): Performance evaluation will be used more for feedback purposes in low power distance cultures. [C5a][45]

In high power distance cultures, employees more easily accept their positions within the firm and tie rewards to the respective level within the hierarchy. Since participation and delegation of authority is lower in high power distance cultures, managers will align rewarding on the same objectives that are normally valid for themselves. As a consequence, in high power distance cultures, top management will orient performance indicators towards the top. The arguments put forward lead me to assume the following:

Hypothesis 2 (n^{46}): The calculation of reward systems is orientated more towards a higher hierarchical level in cultures with high power distance, than in cultures with low power distance. [D1c]

3.3.3 Hypotheses related to future orientation

Future orientation comprises a sensitive handling with unfolding events. High future oriented cultures put more emphasis on forecasts. They want to ensure that plans evolve in the right direction. These cultures value long-term success and give more priority towards achieving the priorities in a longer time horizon (Ashkanasy et al., 2004).

In terms of performance evaluation, high future orientation cultures want to plan ahead, and seek more information and feedback to cope with the requirements to fulfil the organizational objectives. High future-oriented cultures are said to be more flexible and adaptive (Ashkanasy et al., 2004), Thus, they will pursue performance evaluation more often. With the

---

[44] In the remaining chapter, 'r' refers to replicated hypotheses.
[45] Questionnaire items (see Appendix 8, p. 200ff.) are always placed in brackets.
[46] In the remaining chapter 'n' refers to newly derived hypotheses.

higher frequency these cultures want to sustain an adaptive behaviour. Peretz and Fried (2012) found support for a positive relationship between future orientation and future purposes of performance evaluation related to organizational development (i.e. training and development). Hence, I postulate the following:

Hypothesis 3 (r): Performance evaluation will be used more for feedback purposes in high future-oriented cultures. [C5a]

Hypothesis 4 (n): Performance evaluation will take place more frequently in high future-oriented cultures. [C6]

Non-financial indicators are said to be future-oriented and to reflect a longer time horizon (Widener, 2006), which is valued in high future orientation cultures. In addition, the inclusion of individual components in the reward scheme also targets the future. Individual components could include projects, as well as smaller and very personalized steps of employees, towards the achievement of specific aspects of the strategic course of action. In contrast to this assumption, performance indicators are a reflection of the past and in turn backwards oriented. A very personalized approach in the setting of performance evaluation, which considers action, activities, leadership behaviour and individual effort, is going in the same direction. The BSC approach (see Chapter 2.3.1.3, p. 39ff.) considers broad-based performance criteria. A higher use of a balanced approach of financial, customer, process and human learning steps, in the rewarding scheme, indicates forward-looking behaviour. Thus, a stronger appearance of BSC criteria in the rewarding scheme indicates future-oriented behaviour. The preceding discussion provides the basis for the following:

Hypothesis 5 (n): In high future-oriented cultures rewards will be based more on non-financial performance indicators than in low future-oriented cultures, where financial performance indicators will be preferred. [D1a+b]

Hypothesis 6 (n): Individual-oriented performance evaluation will be preferred more in high future-oriented cultures than in low future-oriented cultures. [C3e-g]

Hypothesis 7 (n): Reward systems with individual components will be more prevalent in cultures with higher levels of future orientation. [D1a+b]

Hypothesis 8 (n): Reward systems with a performance orientation will be more prevalent in cultures with lower levels of future orientation. [D1a+b]

Hypothesis 9 (n): Multiple balanced scorecard perspectives will be more prevalent in reward settings in cultures with higher levels of future orientation. [D1a]

Generally speaking, the appetite for short-term thinking and financial rewards is more accentuated in low future-oriented cultures. Low future-oriented cultures prefer to receive rewards more instantaneously and thus value rewards to a higher extent. High future-oriented cultures value future prospects instead of rewards; hence,

Hypothesis 10 (n): In low future-oriented cultures the importance of rewards will be higher than in high future-oriented cultures. [D5b]

3.3.4 Hypotheses related to assertiveness

Assertiveness explicates the degree to which individuals behave in a tough, dominant, aggressive and confrontational manner. This cultural trait is linked with a 'can-do' mentality. Assertive persons like to take the initiative. High assertive cultures put emphasis on competition, success, self-achievement and admiration, but assertiveness does not bear the negative connotations of aggressiveness that comes with a violent and hostile character (Den Hartog, 2004).

Since assertive cultures behave more strongly in non-cooperative manner, one would assume that stronger training needs to compensate for the missing sensitivity in human relationships and concern for others. In order to evaluate the exact training needs, performance evaluation is executed in a faster cycle. Frequent feedback enables superiors to provide a quick response to tasks and projects that subordinates undertake. High assertive cultures proactively seek immediate feedback to discuss progress, and do not classify instant feedback as threatening. Consistent with the assumption of active feedback seeking behaviour (Luque & Sommer, 2000), Chiang and Birch (2010) found evidence that the frequency of performance evaluation is positively linked to higher assertiveness. This leads me to expect that:

Hypothesis 11 (r): Performance evaluation will take place more frequently in high assertive cultures. [C6]

Hypothesis 12 (n): Performance evaluation will be used more for feedback purposes in high assertive cultures. [C5a]

Assertive cultures reward performance. A high assertive culture values capabilities and likes to excel in things. Due to the positive influence of rewards and achievements, and the impulse to excel, reward allocation should be based on performance when assertiveness is high. Financial performance indicators most easily transport the message of success and failure. Chiang and Birtch (2005), who referred in their hypothesis to the very close form of Hofstede's masculinity dimension for assertiveness, found a preference for performance-oriented reward systems in masculine cultures. However, this relationship did not manifest for the references in the performance criteria. Still, I postulate:

Hypothesis 13 (r): Reward systems with a performance orientation will be more prevalent in cultures with high assertiveness. [D1a+b]

Chiang and Birtch (2006) outlined that residents from Hong Kong, who expressed one of the highest assertiveness scores in the GLOBE project, (see Den Hartog, 2004, p. 410) are monetary driven. Chang and Birtch (2012) repeated this finding of a higher perception of financial rewards in masculine (can be compared to high assertive) cultures. Money is seen as a facilitator to collect greater wealth and social status, which in turn leads to a stronger desire for rewards. I hypothesize the following:

Hypothesis 14 (r): In high assertive cultures financial rewards will be used more than in low assertive cultures, where non-financial rewards will be preferred. [D3d+e]

3.3.5 Hypotheses related to individualism/collectivism

The GLOBE project suggested that individualism and collectivism reflect the extent to which societies place emphasis on either autonomous practice and singular behaviour (individualism) or common practices and cooperative behaviour (collectivism). Individualism exhibits a loose integration of persons. Individuals emphasize their own achievements and personal needs. People strive for competition and boast a more aggressive and confrontational behaviour. As a consequence, competitive behaviour diminishes human-oriented and socially-oriented relationships. In contrast, collectivists qualify for a tight social interaction so that others are more easily integrated, whereas the self is less important than in individualistic cultures. People tend to engage more in social interaction patterns and group activities (Gelfand et al., 2004).

Individualistic cultures more easily accept unequal and separate treatment, which leads to individual oriented performance measures for evaluation and rewarding. On the contrary, collectivists do not favour a personal approach for evaluation and rewarding. Instead they strive for teamwork and harmony. Accordingly, individual oriented performance measures may damage the relationship with the group and thus are less appreciated. Instead, collectivists prefer group-based or more aggregated performance measures. Employees in individualistic cultures want to keep control over the outcome of financial rewards. This position effectuates that this group prefers evaluation and rewards that are aligned to their particular behaviour (Chiang & Birtch, 2005). Newman and Nollen (1996), who analyzed the impact of a creative and productive environment on team performance within some European and Asian subsidiaries of one US corporation, found support that an emphasis on individual contributions improved the returns in individualistic cultures. Chiang and Birtch (2007) received only partial support for a more intense desire for the extent of individual components in individualistic cultures, whereas Schuler and Rogovsky (1998) could confirm a positive link of individual performance ingredients and the amount of rewards. Therefore the following hypotheses are considered:

Hypothesis 15 (r): Individual-oriented performance evaluation will be preferred more in individualistic cultures than in collectivist cultures, where collectivistic-oriented performance evaluation will be preferred. [C3e-g]

Hypothesis 16 (r): Reward systems with individual components will be more prevalent in cultures with high individualism than in cultures with high collectivism. [D1a+b]

Another aspect targets the level where performance indicators, which determine the financial rewards, are calculated. Individualistic cultures may encourage an orientation towards a more aggregated level of an organization for the distribution of rewards. The compilation pattern for a higher organizational level is more compatible with individualistic cultures because smaller and more personal organizational units (team, business unit) are rather suitable for collectivists. Smaller and more concrete working environments are more easily palpable for collectivists, and thus a more appropriate level for rewarding. This led me to the following hypothesis:

Hypothesis 17 (n): The calculation of reward systems is orientated more towards a higher hiearchical level in cultures with high individualism than in cultures with high collectivism. [D1c]

Chiang and Birtch (2005; 2007) found also partial support for the notion that non-financial rewards are valued more in collectivistic cultures, whereas a stronger financial rewarding is found in individualistic cultures. In the same vein, I assume that individualistic cultures will show a preference for the inclusion of financial performance indicators in the rewarding scheme. Consequently, I hypothesize:

Hypothesis 18 (r): In individualistic cultures financial rewards will be used more than in collectivistic cultures, where non-financial rewards will be preferred. [D3d+e]

Hypothesis 19 (n): In individualistic cultures financial rewards will be based more on financial performance indicators than in collectivistic cultures, where non-financial performance indicators will be preferred. [D1a+b]

As motivation and commitment of rewarding is dependent on the extent of collectivism, either individually or socially-oriented (Gelfand et al., 2004), I believe that motivation and commitment is achieved with financial rewards in individualistic cultures, and with non-financial rewards in collectivistic cultures. Collectivistic cultures show a strong moral commitment and long-term relationship with their organizations, thus bringing non-financial rewards to the fore. Thus, the following hypotheses are tested:

Hypothesis 20 (n): In individualistic cultures the motivation and commitment purpose of financial rewards will be higher than in collectivistic cultures. [D4a-c]

Hypothesis 21 (n): In collectivistic cultures the motivation and commitment purpose of non-financial rewards will be higher than in individualistic cultures. [D4d-f]

The extent of sharing rewards is also treated differently. Whereas the equity model of rewarding (where persons are rewarded in proportion to their direct contribution) stresses personal gains and is strongly rooted in individualistic cultures, the allocation principle based on equality (where persons are rewarded evenly) is prominent in collectivistic cultures (Gelfand et al., 2004). In collectivistic cultures equal treatment in a rewarding scheme sustains harmonious relationships and team solidarity, whereas an egocentric focus would undermine organizational cohesion. Giacobbe-Miller, Miller and Zhang (2003) found vast support for the cultural difference between collectivists and individualists. They found the pattern consistent for US and Chinese managers, but not fully consistent for Russian managers. Fischer (2004) found the expected direction for a higher equitable solution for British firms (more individualistic) compared to German firms (more collectivistic). Hence, I propose the following hypothesis:

Hypothesis 22 (r): Employees in collectivistic cultures will have more equal reward criteria (=sharing) than those in individualistic cultures. [D3b]

Since individualistic cultures are accustomed to rationality and direct communication (Gelfand et al., 2004), they more easily accept that compensation is determined on the evaluation result. For this reason, individualistic cultures should emphasize the negotiation of compensation within performance evaluation. Consistent with this saying, Chiang and Birtch (2010) found support for the prediction that evaluation, which stresses future pay and rewarding, is present to a higher degree in individualistic cultures. Additionally, a distinct treatment of employees' performance contracts calls for more customization and less standardization. Since these two aspects belong together, it is hypothesized:

Hypothesis 23 (r): Performance evaluation will be used more for determining compensation in individualistic cultures than in collectivist cultures. [C5b]

Hypothesis 24 (n): Employees in individualistic cultures will have more customization in their performance-pay contracts than employees in collectivistic cultures. [D3a]

As individualistic cultures are said to follow more, but less intimate and shorter interactions, formal feedback sessions should appear more frequently (Gelfand et al., 2004). In individualistic cultures more regular and more direct employee evaluation has a positive effect on motivation and performance. A high frequency of direct interaction in the feedback process increases potential areas for conflict. Collectivistic cultures want to avoid direct interaction on the sensible issue of performance appraisal, and hence substitute these formalized procedures with informal and indirect sources. Chiang and Birtch (2010) supported the view that the frequency of performance evaluation is positively linked to high individualism. The arguments led me to assume the following:

Hypothesis 25 (r): Performance evaluation will take place more frequently in individualistic cultures. [C6]

Generally speaking, the appetite for short-term thinking and financial rewards is more accentuated in individualistic cultures. Hence,

Hypothesis 26 (n): In individualistic cultures the importance of rewards will be higher than in collectivistic cultures. [D5b]

3.3.6 Hypotheses related to uncertainty avoidance

Uncertainty avoidance is the extent to which organizational members are willing to take risks and tolerate a state of ambiguity. High uncertainty avoidance cultures are said to avoid risks and accept unpredictability about future states to a lesser extent. Risk assessment is connected to the level of uncertainty that originates from the insecure future. Thus, the perception of risk determines the arrangement of reward systems. The appraisal of uncertainty avoidance suggests that unforeseen conditions are treated differently depending on the estimation of risk. Cultures with high uncertainty avoidance have laws and rules in place to safeguard against unpredictable events (Luque & Javidan, 2004).

Cultures with high uncertainty avoidance make it more difficult to install reward systems, which aim at performance measures and are contingent upon uncertainty (Chiang & Birtch, 2010). Cultures with a high uncertainty avoidance attitude do not want to jeopardize their rewards and rather install systems that place more value into stable and clear conditions (Chiang & Birtch, 2006). In contrast, low uncertainty avoidance cultures accept risks to a higher degree and tend to pursue more questionable and insecure projects. These low uncertainty avoidance cultures do not focus on guaranteed and pre-set rewards, but include performance measures with a performance orientation. Hence, performance-based criteria are more easily placed in reward systems. Chiang and Birtch (2005) found partial support for the preference of performance indicators as reward criteria in low uncertainty avoidance cultures. Schuler and Rogovsky (1998), who investigated the relationships between compensation practices and cultural dimensions, found support for practices that focus on personal performance in cultures with lower levels of uncertainty avoidance. Their results suggest that cultures with high uncertainty avoidance should offer more certainty in the variable reward systems and include less individual components in that scheme. However, I disagree with their conclusion. In cultures with high uncertainty avoidance, risk is lower. Therefore, employees will rely more on factors they can influence on their own, as individual performance indicators, than factors beyond their reach. Hence, I expect:

Hypothesis 27 (r): Reward systems with individual components will be more prevalent in cultures with higher levels of uncertainty avoidance. [D1a+b]

Hypothesis 28 (r): Reward systems with a performance orientation will be more prevalent in cultures with lower levels of uncertainty avoidance. [D1a+b]

Additionally, one can infer that a basket of different performance measures, which determines the evaluation and reward, may place the assessment and rewarding of the employee on a broader footing. The broader footing of performance measures decreases risk and unpredictability for those being evaluated and rewarded. More variables in the catalogue of criteria decrease an unsteady evaluation and rewarding state. On the other hand, the decision for multiple performance measures might increase complexity and hence uncertainty for those compiling this basket. The associated reduction in uncertainty seems to be more beneficial to cultures with high uncertainty avoidance. I state two hypotheses about the multiplicity of performance measures for the evaluation and rewarding scheme depending on the level of uncertainty.

Hypothesis 29 (n): Multiple performance measures will be more prevalent in performance evaluation in cultures with higher levels of uncertainty avoidance. [C3h]

Hypothesis 30 (n): Rewards will be based more on multiple performance measures in cultures with higher levels of uncertainty avoidance. [D1a]

The broader footing of performance measures is also assumed to be valid for the appearance of the perspectives of the BSC, i.e. number of BSC perspectives used, in the reward scheme. Thus, the hypothesis covers the balanced aspect of performance measures for rewarding schemes.

Hypothesis 31 (n): Multiple balanced scorecard perspectives will be more prevalent in reward settings in cultures with higher levels of uncertainty avoidance. [D1a]

Contrary to the mere appearance of such a balanced approach in the rewarding scheme, the propensity to execute a rather symmetrical state for the whole operational course of action is expected to be reversed. Cultures that face stronger uncertainty avoidance will concentrate on specific performance areas (e.g. financials, customers, employees, internal processes and operations) and relatively neglect other performance areas. Hence, these cultures will classify the importance of their performance areas in a more dissimilar fashion, and organizations in these cultures will adopt a less balanced approach in the importance of their performance areas.

Hypothesis 32 (n): The propensity to adopt a balanced approach in executing different performance areas is less prevalent in cultures with higher levels of uncertainty avoidance. [G2]

Jansen, Merchant and van der Stede (2009), who compared incentive compensation schemes of automotive retailers between the Netherlands and the USA in an explorative manner, found evidence for their expectation that the USA, which has a lower uncertainty avoidance score according to GLOBE, relies compared to the Netherlands more on subjective and discretionary criteria, rather than predetermined formulas in the handling of rewards. However, the findings from Merchant et al. (2011), who extended the two country setting by a Chinese aspect, show the highest discretionary criteria for China, which has the highest uncertainty avoidance score of the three cultures according to GLOBE. They provide reasoning that the high Chinese score for subjective evaluation can be attributed to the less developed performance evaluation scheme. Still, one can assume that a higher level of objectivity, which reduces uncertainty, is also prevalent in the performance evaluation schemes of companies in high uncertainty avoidance cultures. Thus, pre-set rules, procedures and practices go hand-in-hand with more objective and less subjective behaviour. Hence, the following hypotheses are tested:

Hypothesis 33 (r): Objective performance standards will be used more for performance evaluation in cultures with high uncertainty avoidance. [C4b-d]

Hypothesis 34 (r): Performance evaluation and compensation schemes used in organizations would be, on average, more objective in cultures with high uncertainty avoidance than in cultures with low uncertainty avoidance. [D2+C4a]

In order to reduce uncertainty, individuals seek to get feedback sooner rather than later. In high uncertainty settings, employees strive for more frequent feedback to promptly know whether their individual performance deviates from the expectations; this frequent feedback reduces anxiety (Luque & Javidan, 2004). The study by Chiang and Birtch (2010) confirmed that high uncertainty avoidance cultures had a higher frequency of feedback. Hence, I investigate the following:

Hypothesis 35 (r): Performance evaluation will take place more frequently in cultures with high uncertainty avoidance. [C6]

4 Research methodology

4.1 Sample

The level of analysis is equivalent to the SBUs of corporations. While the term of SBU is more or less abstract, we[47] subsumed entities and independent units (Kotha & Orne, 1989) with a clear product-market boundary (Day, Shocker & Srivastava, 1979) which face unique (with regard to other parts of the organization) competitive situations and follow a distinct competitive strategy. Larger firms are often more diversified (Gupta, 1984) and consequently have different SBUs, whereas small and medium corporations more often possess a homogenous product portfolio and exhibit only one SBU. For many companies with one core business the SBU resembles the stand-alone company. The intended respondents were CEOs, CFOs, COOs or managing directors of SBUs. The reliance on top management as key respondents for this study is deemed appropriate for the main reason that these senior executives are knowledgeable about the whole range of MCS, often playing an active role in executing and orchestrating them. This implies that a mechanic approach cannot be applied in choosing the interviewee. Of particular interest is the question of how top management guides and directs the behaviour of their operative subordinates.

We decided against a mere convenience sampling in terms of simply approaching companies in the reach and cognizance of the researchers (Bryman, 2008). With this approach we surpass the sampling frame of those management accounting researchers who do not aim at a very generalizable sample selection (van der Stede, Young & Chen, 2005). We followed a proportionate stratified random sampling procedure (Daniel, 2012; Ember & Ember, 2009; Hair Jr. et al., 2011; Singh, 2007) to come up with a representative and unbiased sample that allows empirical generalizations (Handfield & Melnyk, 1998; van der Stede, Young & Chen, 2005). This approach separates the population into mutually exclusive and collectively exhaustive sub-groups. This allows more precise and generalizable conclusions. This approach was possible since we had the necessary information on size and industry available to stratify the data (Bryman, 2008). The sampling process for Belgium, Germany and Poland

---

[47] The method section deals with many steps that have been agreed within the project group or that arose out of collective efforts. That is why I often use the collective 'we'.

comprises all companies from the same database ORBIS[48]. Scott's Directories[49] was chosen for Canada.

Firms were selected given the following criteria. Firstly, companies with various subsidiaries are condensed to one parent or holding company. Secondly, a size criterion was applied. The literature assumes that size affects the degree of control and thus MCS (Chenhall, 2003, 2007; Henri, 2006a; Lau & Eggleton, 2004). There are expectations that size of the company alters the MCS instruments towards more sophisticated configurations (Dávila & Foster, 2005). The research group set 250 employees as the minimum size criterion in order to reflect useful relationships of the top management in guiding and directing the behaviour of their operative subordinates. Firms of this minimum size are expected to implement some sort of formalized MCS. With this size criterion it was ensured that the firms showed the whole range of topics studied in a decent and complex manner. The research group applied the size criterion of 1,000 employees to divide the population into subpopulations of small and large companies. Thirdly, industry focus is also seen as a differentiating factor for MCS configuration (Williams & Seaman, 2001). The research group used broad industry categories of manufacturing, services and trade (retail and wholesale) because a more detailed classification would have complicated the sampling unnecessarily. The industry classification and the size characteristic define the six individual strata.

According to this procedure the target population for Germany consisted of 2,075 firms, Belgium contributed 444 firms. The Canadian sample incorporated 300 firms. Poland had a sample of 389 firms. All firms were allocated to the six clusters. Random sampling[50] was performed in each country in each of the six categories in order to give all companies the same chance of being picked for the initiation of contact (Flick, 2011). The combined

---

[48] ORBIS is a database from the Bureau van Dijk that provides comprehensive information including industry segmentation, ownership structures and financial information on companies on a global scale. We chose the database since it covered all European countries that participated in the large research project. Further information about the database can be found here: http://www.bvdinfo.com/en-gb/products/company-information/international/orbis. Retrieved June 21, 2014.

[49] Scott's Directories offers similar information for Canadian companies. Further information about the database can be found here: https://secure.scottsdirectories.com. Retrieved June 21, 2014.

[50] The process of the random sampling was done in the Excel-file. We complemented a blank column with the function "=RAND()", freezed these randomly set numbers and then sorted the whole column with either the sequence ascending or descending.

procedure of proportionate stratified and random sampling aimed at securing a reasonable and real random representation of the whole organizational population (Handfield & Melnyk, 1998).

Belgium, Canada, Germany and Poland have been primarily chosen as research subjects for the cross-cultural comparison as they belong to different cultural clusters and therefore show many cultural differences.[51] The mean scores of the original GLOBE study show enough disparity but also similarity for the four countries. GLOBE classified 61 societal cultures[52] into ten regional clusters mainly based on geographic proximity, linguistic commonality, religion and historical facts (Gupta & Hanges, 2004). Appendix 6 (p. 201) that is based on Gupta and Hanges (2004, p. 193) features the cultural clusters. Germany belongs to the Germanic Europe cluster (Szabo et al., 2002), the English speaking part of Canada is part of the Anglo cluster (Ashkanasy, Trevor-Roberts & Earnshaw, 2002; Egri et al., 2012),[53] Belgium is said to belong to the Latin Europe cluster (Brodbeck et al., 2000; Jesuino, 2002; Zeng et al., 2013) or when looking at the split between Wallonians (French-speaking) and Flemings (Dutch-speaking) features both characteristics of the Latin Europe and Germanic Europe cluster. Belgium is said to comprise two diverging regions, Flanders and Wallonia. From a political standpoint, these differences are also stated. However, looking at cultural values[54], "the differences between Flemings and Walloons are not so large after all" (Billiet, Maddens & Frognier, 2006, p. 929) and thus I assume Belgium as a whole as a fair representation.[55] Poland advances our understanding of Eastern Europe (Bakacsi et al., 2002). Although West and East Germany due to the division after World War II have been separated in the GLOBE study and showed some small deviations in their scores, I did not differentiate between the two. Reunification has been 25 years apart which brought the two states together. Additionally, there has been migration within Germany so that new employees are

---

[51] Within the research group of the management control configurations' project, I launched an additional enquiry and won the collaboration of partners doing research in Belgium (Sophie Hoozée, although she is associated with a different institution, is of Belgian nationality), Canada (Maurice Gosselin) and Poland (Piotr Bednarek) to learn about the interplay of MCS and national cultures.

[52] The Czech Republic was excluded due to response bias (Gupta & Hanges, 2004).

[53] I will test possible differences between French and English speaking parts in Chapter 5.1.5 (p. 124).

[54] Billiet, Maddens and Frognier (2006) compare seven universal values from the Schwartz value scores across these two entities.

[55] I will test possible differences between Flanders and Wallonia in Chapter 5.1.5 (p. 124).

also bringing their mind-set and background into the organization. Hence the two former German parts are thought to be comparable. Thus, these four countries combine both cultural consonance and cultural distance across the cultural dimensions. This stresses sufficient variation, distinct separation and the appropriateness for further hypotheses testing (Gupta & Hanges, 2004; Gupta, Hanges & Dorfman, 2002).

A recent editorial (Tung & Verbeke, 2010) of the Journal of International Business Studies (JIBS) brought forward a minimum postulation of seven to ten countries for cross-cultural research. With this four country participation I am not yet at this mark. But, four countries are much better than the numerous studies which covered only two countries. Since the vast majority of previous cross-cultural MCS research targeted Anglo and Asian firms, this study with a focus on Europe supplemented by Canada is a fruitful extension since "Europe is generally considered as culturally diverse and interesting to study national culture differences" (van der Stede, 2003, p. 280). Additionally, Poland brings in new insights into a country from the Eastern European emerging markets.

4.2 Questionnaire design

4.2.1 Management control systems' questionnaire

I used the entire MCS questionnaire agreed by the international research collaboration group.[56] The structure of the questionnaire follows Malmi and Brown's (2008) framework, from strategic and short-term planning via performance measurement and evaluation to administrative structures and cultural controls. The English questionnaire that was compiled by the Finnish scholar Mikko Sandelin has been modified, streamlined and improved by the whole international research group.[57]

---

[56] As previously mentioned, the thesis is part of an international research project. Part of the entire questionnaire, section C and D, explicitly deals with the content of the thesis.

[57] The research proposal of the Finnish team outlined the reasoning of the main sections of the questionnaire. The scholars repeated the argumentation in the first international project meeting in December 2010. Between January and March 2011, scholars of the whole research group addressed numerous comments in several rounds in order to improve the quality of the questionnaire. Many suggestions were incorporated.

The final MCS questionnaire is structured as follows (variables and measures follow in Chapter 4.4, p. 101f.):

Section	Management control element
A	Strategic planning
B	Short-term planning
C	Performance measurement and evaluation
D	Rewards and compensation
E	Organizational structure and management processes
F	Organization culture and values
G	Organization and environment

Table 4: Sections of the MCS questionnaire

The German speaking teams of Berlin, Münster[58] and Vienna translated the questionnaire on 'MCS as a package' into German. The main purpose of the translation into the native language is for the interviewed person to better understand the survey. We aimed at minimizing the systematic bias which would occur if respondents answer a questionnaire which is not in their native language (Harkness & Schoua-Glusberg, 1998). We did not aim at the most strict or literal translation based on the lexical denotation of survey items (Chidlow, Plakoyiannaki & Welch, 2014; Harkness, 2002). However, we were more concerned with the accuracy and adequacy of the translated MCS concepts. The interview itself offered an additional benefit since any construct item could be verbally explained.

In a second step we applied a back-translation process. The core idea of back-translation is to compare the original and the back-translated version in meaning and assess in this way the quality of the translation. Based on the outcome, similarities and differences determine the quality of the translation procedures. If necessary, several rounds should follow until the semantic equivalence can be secured (Brislin, 1986). Two independent teams in Münster and Vienna translated the German version back into the original language source English. A thorough comparison of the original English questionnaire version with the two back-

---

[58] Researchers from University of Münster participated until December 2011.

translated surveys was made by the primary German and Austrian researchers. Any discrepancies between the two versions were discussed in telephone meetings between the three researchers of Berlin, Münster and Vienna. Any necessary revisions were made.

The questionnaire was pre-tested prior to usage with a small group of management consultants, academics, and executives. The pre-test also aimed at securing the right terminology used in the business acumen (van der Stede, Young & Chen, 2005). This process led to some minor changes of the wording. Additionally, the three group members exchanged reasoning of critical phrasing, additional verbal information needed and further thoughts on the questionnaire.

The translation, independent back-translation and pre-testing approach secured the cross-cultural comparability, established linguistic equivalence, conceptual and functional equivalence (Cascio, 2012; Harkness & Schoua-Glusberg, 1998).

4.2.2   GLOBE questionnaire

The cultural dimensions, which are used as the explanatory variables in this study, should be directly measured to supply solid rational as being related to the MCS. It is useful "to measure the concept that is hypothesized to produce the observed cultural differences" (Leung & Iwawaki, 1988, p. 47) when drawing cross-cultural inferences. The use of a cultural dummy variable, as is most often done in the cross-cultural area, can only result to exploratory findings since there is no measuring of the explanatory cultural variables (Merchant et al., 2011). Taras, Kirkman and Steel (2010) acknowledge that collecting a new score for the cultural construct has more explanatory power. Some authors, often in the limitation section of their study, acknowledge that retesting the cultural dimensions would have been helpful (e.g. Tsui, 2001).

The new measurement of the cultural scores also provides updated and novel data since changes and drifts can occur in the cultural dimensions. It has been shown that culture is subject to change over time (Taras, Kirkman & Steel, 2010). The GLOBE data was obtained almost 20 years ago. Although culture is expected to slowly alter, it is not clear that the scores are still valid. An indication for such a change was given by Mączyński et al. (2010) who found significant changes in the Polish cultural scores of power distance (higher) and future orientation, individualism/collectivism, human orientation and gender egalitarianism (lower) between 1996/1997 and 2008/2009. Second, the cultural data scores originate from the same sample (i.e. set of organizations) and thus provide more evidence for a close link to the MCS elements. Third, cultural scores for Belgium were not collected in the original GLOBE study. Therefore, we followed the suggestion from literature and collected the current cultural practice scores of our respondents in all four countries.

We used the existing GLOBE questionnaires to collect the cultural practices. These questionnaires are available in different languages and are well proven in terms of statistical requirements (validity and reliability). Contact has been made with principal researchers who conducted the original GLOBE survey in Germany (Felix Brodbeck), France (Marc Deneire), the Netherlands (Celeste Wilderom) and Poland (Jerzy Mączyński) to obtain the original questionnaires that were used in the GLOBE survey during the 1990s. The English version could be found on the GLOBE website.[59] The German, Dutch and Polish questionnaires were provided by electronic documents while the French one was sent by post and transcribed to a Word file.

Since the GLOBE questionnaires have been handed out to the interviewee and distributed to different persons within the respective organization, we put additional effort into the professional format of the questionnaires. The Belgian researcher applied Dillman's (2007) principles of tailored design to polish the GLOBE questionnaires up. Based in social exchange theory, the likelihood of responding to the request to complete a self-administered questionnaire, and doing so accurately, is greater when the respondent trusts that the expected rewards of responding will outweigh the anticipated costs. Institutional logos added on the cover page and researchers' names on the next pages establish trust. Contact information is showing positive regard and saying thank you is rewarding too. The opportunity for feedback is a positive signal. Several visual navigational guides reduce social costs. Guidelines for survey addressees and data collection has been provided from the German researchers for the teams in Belgium, Canada and Poland.

---

[59] At the time of questionnaire preparation, there was only the English version available on the GLOBE website: http://business.nmsu.edu/programs-centers/globe/instruments. The Spanish and French versions are also available. Retrieved June 21, 2014.

4.3 Data collection

4.3.1 Methods of data collection

There are different forms of survey administrations that can be distinguished by written and oral formats. In an oral interrogation researchers mainly sit face-to-face with the respondent and record the interview or take notes of the answers (Flick, 2011). Bryman and Bell (2011, p. 175) and Hair et al. (2011, p. 187) illustrate the main forms of survey administration which are depicted in Figure 7.

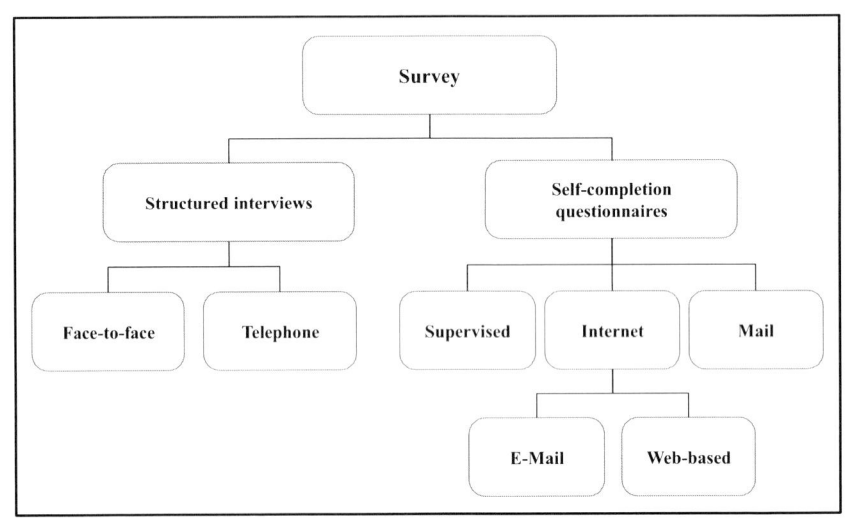

Figure 7: Modes of survey administration

The obvious but fundamental difference between the structured interview and the self-administered questionnaire is the absence of the interviewer in the second approach. In the interview setting, the interviewer reads questions and interacts with the respondent which is especially important for long questionnaires. The main advantages of the interview approach lie in the facts of helping respondents to truly understand the questions so that the level of complexity and difficulty can be much higher, to secure that the questionnaire has been answered by the right person and to minimize missing data. Face-to-face conversation allows a comprehensive run through the questionnaire whereas the telephone data collection method allows only limited time resources. Besides, many persons are not inclined to share personal and sensitive information over the telephone when they are not acquainted with the other person (Czaja & Blair, 2005). On the other hand, the advantages of the self-administered questionnaire in form of mail and web surveys are much lower cost because of the omission of travel cost and much faster time for data collection because all questionnaires can be distributed at the same time by mail or for the web and E-mail survey administered online. Any possible interviewer effects that might bias the respondent are absent in the self-completion approach for mail, E-mail and web survey. A greater sense of anonymity may be more credible and create more serious responses. The respondents can also answer a self-completed questionnaire at their timely convenience. The supervised self-completion questionnaire combines the face-to-face interaction of the structured interview and the self-completed questionnaires and thus bears the same advantages and drawbacks (Bryman & Bell, 2011; Hair Jr. et al., 2011).

The multiple forms of surveys enable researchers to collect large data sets. Surveys are frequently used for testing, refining and explaining the theories' use, and rarely for exploring unknown phenomena. Furthermore, management control phenomena have been tremendously studied with survey research (Merchant & Otley, 2007).

4.3.2 Acquisition process

Many companies in the German sample derived from the ORBIS database were classified to either the wrong industry category or they were grouped wrongly as either small or large companies (e.g. small and large service companies belonged often to manufacturing, vice versa small manufacturing companies were in fact service related). In order to uphold the pre-defined proportionate sampling both wrong industry category and size were corrected in a two-step approach.[60]

The acquisition of the interview appointments for the MCS questionnaire was done in a step by step approach. The randomized companies in each of the six strata were complemented

---

[60] To improve the correct matching of the firms, I addressed the top 100-200 German companies of each of the six strata and classified the companies in a first step to the broad industry categories according to the information on their website. From this information firms could be clearly attached to the three sections. In a second step, the wrong size related classification was accounted for after 50 interviews were held. The percentage of wrong size classifications, which could be verified during the personal interviews, was adapted to the whole sample. This procedure was repeated after 80 interviews. This procedure led to the final percentage points for the number of firms to be interviewed in each stratum. Due to much lower mistakes in other countries, scholars did not reclassify the percentage points of their strata.

upfront by important information (potential interviewees, contact data, address, website, telephone number, further comments). To facilitate the acquisition process I compiled a research project outline, which stated the essential features of the topic, the interview process and the benefits for the company. I addressed companies based on the randomized numbering and tried to speak to members of the top management team by telephone. The probability to acquire an interview appointment was high when talking on the phone to the executives directly because I could provide immediate feedback to open questions and provide a convincing and personal argumentation. Consistent with the recommendations to increase co-operation (Huber & Power, 1985) I explained the purpose and nature of the study on the phone, stressed the usefulness of the research results to the manager and his organization, ensured anonymity and confidentiality of the results, disclosed candid information for the length of the interviewing and offered much freedom to place the interview in their crowded schedule. When I could not directly contact the executives, I sent E-mails and attached the research project outline (see Appendix 7, p. 202) to explain the purpose, nature and benefits of the study. In that case, I made constantly and consistently follow-up calls to get the targeted interviewee on the phone. Alternatively, further E-mails were sent a second and third time.

Once the manager was willing to participate, interview appointments were made. Because of the extensive travelling across Germany, I undertook efforts to bundle interview appointments in near geographic areas to save time and budget. While I agreed an interview appointment I also mentioned the additional cultural aspect of the research project. I explained that I will bring additional paper-based GLOBE questionnaires to the interview appointment. The intention was that the managers handed out the cultural questionnaires within the organization and send it back by mail. To encounter threats of reduced cognitive efforts of the participants filling out the GLOBE questionnaire we shortened the time span for each respondent to 15 minutes (Lindell & Whitney, 2001).

4.3.3 Interview process

Data was collected by face-to face interviews with top management for five reasons. The first reason captures the sufficient knowledge of the top management to answer the whole variety of the MCS questionnaire and to deliver the answers in a very truthful and conscientious manner. The next rationale relates to the typical threats of surveys, validity and reliability. Respondents might interpret the questions in a different way than intended by the researchers.

Therefore it is useful to assure the meanings of each question in the interview situation. Uncertainties with single questions can be more easily ruled out. Further elaboration of specific items facilitates the understanding. "The issue of the validity of self-assessment is often raised as a concern" (Chenhall, 2003, p. 134; 2007, p. 170). To minimize the interviewer bias and the misinterpretation of the researcher, a construct document has been provided both explaining the origin and the essential components of the different questions. To prepare for the interviews, I informally exchanged the understanding of the whole questionnaire with five other researchers among them, the initiator of the questionnaire. The third reason hinted at ideally excluding any missing data since the questionnaires were filled out during personal appointments. The personal setting was also chosen to foster a proper survey completion to all questions and to ensure that we had the correct respondent. The fourth reason concerns the length of the questionnaire. Response rates would be very low when sending the questionnaire by mail. In a personal interview setting it can be ensured to a great extent that respondents take their time and devote concentration and effort to the questionnaire. Fifth, additional insights on qualitative argumentation can be won during the interviews. The executives are thinking out aloud and provide much more information in the interview about their actual practices of MCS. This information substantiates the qualitative underlying of the single constructs (Dávila & Foster, 2005). Qualitative data was collected through tape recordings. This secured to listen to specific passages of the interview again.

A multiple respondent strategy that improves accuracy and minimizes potential respondent bias was not pursued mainly because it was difficult enough to address one respondent. The high amount of single respondents inevitably raises the concern of whether I am reliably capturing the management control practices of the firm, or rather the respondents' wrong perceptions of those practices. I assume the single response to be reliable for one main reason. We approached only top managers, who act as key persons and consequently are the most qualified persons in the organization. Homburg et al. (2012) remarked that informants with a high hierarchical position and a longer tenure (see Chapter 5.1.2, p. 122ff.) are more reliable. Therefore, our respondents should be well informed and knowledgeable about their control elements. Additionally, we always asked about the practices, i.e. the way things are done, within the organizations rather than the perceptions of the top managers about how things could be done. The random sampling approach and the joint approach to target respondents from the top management team only secured internal validity. Since we are relying on executives their view on the use and design of MCS gives a truthful and realistic picture and thus improves external validity and generalizability.

In the beginning of the interview, I introduced myself and outlined the main parts of the project. This was done to familiarize the respondents again with the topic (there was often a longer period between consent to interview and interview itself). Strict confidentiality of the content and anonymity of the person and organization were guaranteed by signing a confidentiality agreement (Flick, 2011). This helped to ensure that managers felt more comfortable when providing confidential and sensitive information. My experience during the interviews was that respondents felt more comfortable with the questions in the personal atmosphere than having them addressed by a mail survey or telephone interview. Most interviews have been tape recorded to have verbal explanations as well.

Response rates that address the extent of participation are always a matter of the research subject, the respondent and his status, the effort undertaken to convince the respondent and other general facts (Bryman, 2008). The response rates[61] are higher than anticipated despite the lengthy questionnaire and the large amount of time needed for the interview. The response rates were 22.2% for Germany, 44.2% for Belgium, and 32.7% for Poland.[62] If the response rate for mature firms is compared to other studies which target top management team, these rates are far better than the range of 15%-25% for mailed-survey questionnaires (Henri, 2006a). Cycyota and Harrison (2006) identified a median top manager response rate of 32%. They also highlighted that topical salience was the only variable that led to higher response rates (they did not include timing in their analysis). Our response rates are at the outer edge for Germany and even above for Belgium and Poland. The overwhelming reason for the companies, which did not participate, was, that managers were too busy to devote two hours of their time to an interview, or that they lacked interest in the topic, or that companies are frequently approached by many universities, research institutions and consultancies, or that companies had bad experiences in the past and do not participate in any study at all (compare with Egelhoff and Frese (2009)).

---

[61] The response rate is calculated as the percentage of interviews in relation to the number of targeted companies irrespective of a communicated rejection.

[62] The Canadian researcher did not provide this data.

Chapter 4 – Research methodology

Non-response bias affects the generalizability of the results. Non-response bias "occurs in a statistical survey if those who respond to the survey differ in important respects from those who do not respond" (Cascio, 2012, p. 2541). A high response rate is one good indicator for non-response bias. Even low response rates can contribute to generalizable findings. I tackled passive non-response by a thorough acquisition process. So the main concern is active non-response, i.e. an intentional judgment of withholding participation (Thompson & Surface, 2007). A crucial indicator for the generalizability is the commonality of the respondents and the non-respondents by means of the non-response bias. A common technique is to compare early and late interviews (van der Stede, Young & Chen, 2005). A second practice is to compare firms which were interviewed with firms that were contacted but refused to participate in an interview.

A three-step analysis addresses non-response bias. Although the interview process was structured very different across the four countries – some researchers started with either small or large companies, some others began with a specific industry focus – this method is applied too. In a first and second step, I analyzed data across two financial accounts (sales, number of employees) from early and late respondents as well as for interviewed and not-interviewed firms by analyzing the mean scores of each variable given in the original database. Third, the firms' industry specific NACE[63] codes were compared to approach any industry bias (Fullerton and McWatters (2002), Henry (2006a) or Widener (2007) chose a similar approach).

Analysis showed no significant differences in the means for interviewed and non-interviewed but contacted firms on a country specific level. The values were as follows: Germany (for sales: $F=0.353$, $p=0.553$; for employees: $F(Welch)^{64}=0.705$, $p=0.403$), Belgium (for sales: $F=0.461$, $p=0.499$; for employees: $F=0.970$, $p=0.327$) and Poland (for sales: $F=0.330$,

---

[63] NACE stands for Nomenclature générale des Activités Économiques dans les Communautés Européennes (General Industrial Classification of Economic Activities within the European Communities). Further information with a link to the publication of the NACE classification scheme can be found here: http://epp.eurostat.ec.europa.eu/statistics_explained/index.php/NACE_backgrounds. Retrieved June 21, 2014.

[64] Chapter 4.5.3 (p. 107) provides explanation for the Welch test.

p=0.567; for employees: F=0.865, p=0.354).[65] Analysis also showed no significant differences in the means for early, medium and late[66] interviewed firms on a country specific level. The values were as follows: Germany (for sales: F(Welch)=1.299, p=0.285; for employees: F=1.165, p=0.321), Belgium (for sales: F(Welch)=3.396, p=0.053; for employees: F(Welch)=3.082, p=0.065) and Poland (for sales: F(Welch)=0.455, p=0.639; for employees: F=2.186, p=0.135). The data showed that in Belgium larger firms have been mainly interviewed in the first and second third of all interviews. Different analysis of group variance (ANOVA) tests for each industry type and per country showed no statistical differences in the industry means (represented by the first two digits of the NACE code) between the responding and non-responding firms. The p-values for Belgium, Germany and Poland were all above 0.05. More importantly, the industries based on the NACE codes spanned 61 of 74 two-digit (the second highest level) NACE industry codes.[67] This suggests that any bias is minimized because a very broad classification of sub-industries, which was intended by the sampling approach, is among the respondents already.[68] Thus, I assume that the mean differences for both size and industry are not statistically significant and that the interview approach did not create a response bias.

---

[65] The Canadian researcher did not provide this data.

[66] A differentiation was made for early (first third of interviews), medium (second third of interviews) and late (last third of interviews).

[67] There are 81 different two-digit NACE codes. Seven codes comprise categories that are not in our target list (e.g. non-profit organizations, trade unions, state- or community-owned libraries or museums).

[68] As an example, the two-digit codes most frequently used are 10 (Food products: 17x, 7.1%), 28 (Industrial machinery: 15x, 6.3%), 20 (Chemicals and chemical product: 10x, 4.2%), 43 (Specialised construction activities: 10x, 4.2%), 46 (Wholesale trade, except of motor vehicles and motorcycles: 9x, 3.8%), 25 (Fabricated metal products, except machinery and equipment: 8x, 3.3%), 23 (Other non-metallic mineral products (glass, porcelain, ceramics, cement, concrete, clay building materials): 8x, 3.3%), 47 (Retail trade, except of motor vehicles and motorcycles: 8x, 3.3%), 41 (Construction of buildings, 7x, 2.9%), 24 (Primary metal product and processing: 7x, 2.9%) and 22 (Rubber and plastic products: 7x, 2.9%). Chapter 5.1.3, p. 120f. presents more details on the industry composition. Many wrong classifications of NACE codes in the original database (more than half of the cases showed deviations) gives some caution to the numbers presented. The logic of the inquiry from the database required that firms were bundled at the highest hierarchical level. Therefore, the database often labels the wrong NACE code "Activities of head offices" which did not resemble the operational engagement of the whole company.

Chapter 4 – Research methodology 101

4.4 Variables and measures

4.4.1 Management control variables

The MCS questionnaire contains multiple questions, which were mainly taken from previous literature. The holistic approach of the MCS package project to capture a full range of management control elements led to many single-item measures in the questionnaire in the performance evaluation and reward section, particularly for those variables we felt to be easily understandable in that fashion. Multi-item scales have been also asked. Loo (2002) pled for using single-item measures only for concrete and homogenous scales ("i.e. perceived in a similar way by all respondents, and/or can be easily and clearly covered by one question" (Speckbacher & Wentges, 2012, p. 39)) whereas for heterogeneous scales multi-item measures are favourable. Bergkvist and Rossiter (2007, p. 175) compared multiple and single-item measures too and concluded that for "a concrete singular object and a concrete attribute … single-item measures should be used" which acknowledges the fact that "practitioners seem to favor single-item measures". Hansen and van der Stede (2004) followed a similar approach of combining single-item measures and multi-item scales. Thus this mixture is considered useful for the research context. Since we were relying on many single-item scales, we exchanged our understanding of the questionnaire items and formulations used, inside the project group. Experience from the Finnish scholar team who had already held some interviews and the joint approach with the research group to finalise the questionnaire gave confidence to establish content validity.

The original questionnaire construct overview has been provided by Mikko Sandelin and complemented by the author. Table 5 – Table 7 provide an overview of the representation of all questionnaire items, the nature of construct and the original source from which the items have been derived and used as is or taken in a modified form. The first table presents the section on performance evaluation and corresponding performance measures. The second table shows the measures on rewards. The third table concerns performance areas. Responses are mainly measured with a seven point Likert scale[69] which is a very popular format in the

---

[69] There is a wide debate on the amount of response categories, e.g. five or seven point Likert scales. Some scholars even pled for more categories to increase the granularity of responses (Pearse, 2011). Dawes (2008) found no difference for the five point and seven point formats which are most frequently used.

social science. Likert scales follow an interval format. If the intervals bear equidistance they are treated as quasi-metric scales. In a strict sense it is not valid to assume equal intervals between the codings of the different scales although this the common approach (Hair Jr. et al., 2011). Two anchor points exemplified responses ranging from 1 = not at all up to 7 = very high extent/very important. Questions C6 and D1c were asked in the form of alternatives. In question D1a, performance measures could be answered with free text which was later on categorized based on a detailed scheme. The full part of the questionnaire with explanations for the coding procedure can be found in Appendix 8 (p. 203ff.).

Section C	Item	Nature of construct	Source (m= modified, u=used as is)
C3. Performance measure nature	a,b	Single items	Grafton, Lillis & Widener, 2010; Ibrahim & Lloyd, 2011; Ittner, Larcker & Randall, 2003; Kaplan & Norton, 1996b (m)
C3. Performance measure specificity	c,d	Single items	Simons, 2005 (m)
C3. Subjective evaluation	e-g	Reflective	Simons, 2005 (m)
C3. Number of measures	h	Single item	Simons, 2005 (m)
C4. Performance standards objectivity	a-d	Reflective	Bogsnes, 2009 (m)
C5. Performance evaluation purpose	a-c	Single items	Merchant & van der Stede, 2007 (m)
C6. Performance evaluation frequency	a,b	Single items	Achouri, 2011; Merchant & van der Stede, 2007 (m)
C7. Performance measurement and performance evaluation importance		Single item	

Table 5: Questionnaire constructs on performance evaluation

Section D	Item	Nature of construct	Source (m= modified, u=used as is)
D1. Performance measures for rewarding	a-c	Single items Categories	Grafton, Lillis & Widener, 2010; Ibrahim & Lloyd, 2011; Ittner, Larcker & Randall, 2003; Kaplan & Norton, 1996b (m)
D2. Performance evaluation and rewarding objectivity	a-d	Reflective	Bol & Smith, 2011; Gibbs et al., 2004; Ittner, Larcker & Meyer, 2003 (m)
D3. Customization of contracts	a	Single item	Simons, 2005 (m)
D3. Equality reward criteria	b	Single item	Deutsch, 1985; Giacobbe-Miller, Miller & Zhang, 2003 (m)
D3. Rewarding nature	e,f	Single items	Ittner, Larcker & Meyer, 2003 (m)
D4. Rewarding purpose	a-c; d-f	Reflective	Jensen, Murphy & Wruck, 2004 (m)
D5. Rewarding importance		Single item	

Table 6: Questionnaire constructs on rewards

Section G	Item	Nature of construct	Source (m= modified, u=used as is)
G2. Performance areas	a-i	Single items/ Reflective	Grafton, Lillis & Widener, 2010; Ibrahim & Lloyd, 2011; Ittner, Larcker & Randall, 2003; Kaplan & Norton, 1996b (m)

Table 7: Questionnaire constructs on performance areas

4.4.2 Cultural dimensions

Looking at the quartet structure of the GLOBE questionnaires (Organization 'As Is' and 'Should Be' as well as Society 'As Is' and 'Should Be'), I decided whether to apply the whole quartet structure or whether to concentrate on single paths of the quartet. House, Quigley and de Luque (2010) stressed that the research question should guide the decision between cultural practices or values. If the primary focus lies on cultural differences in the way a society is acting, and not on values, desires or the way a society wants to act, the societal practices should be applied. The major focus of my thesis is the organization. I want to explain country specific differences in the MCS practices. Thus, I aim at societal cultural distinctions. Since I also control (see Chapter 4.4.3, p. 104ff.) for organizational culture, organization was included too. In the current thesis I focus on practice scores to analyze national cultural differences for the MCS configurations. For instance, Chui and Kwok (2009), Sarala and Vaara (2010) and Peretz and Fried (2012) dealt with cross-cultural variations and used the GLOBE practice scores as well.

Many studies stress that solely the most relevant cultural dimensions should be applied in the research context (Tsui, 2001). As the literature review demonstrated (see Chapter 3.2, p. 69f.), most cultural studies concentrate on just a few dimensions to illustrate the cross-cultural influence on MCS. On the other hand, a multiple approach of cultural dimensions becomes only a necessity if the research context requires it. Single MCS elements are mostly impacted by only some cultural dimensions. I evaluated which kind of GLOBE dimensions best suit my research design. I still collected data for all dimensions because skipping some of the dimensions upfront is not useful as later research might require particular dimensions intentionally disregarded in the beginning. Since the hypotheses required no holistic approach, I limited the analysis on five GLOBE dimensions for the distinction of performance measures, performance evaluation and rewards. I relied on power distance, future orientation, assertiveness, individualism/collectivism, and uncertainty avoidance (the argumentation is provided in Chapter 3.3.1, p. 72ff.).

GLOBE comprised the following measures for the construct of power distance: basis of influence, degree of obedience, behaviour of powerful people, specific power privileges, and the concentration of power. GLOBE measured societal practices for uncertainty avoidance by questions on orderliness and consistency, the frequency of structured lives, the extent of details for job requirements and instructions as well as the amount of rules and laws. Future orientation deals with the degree of forward planning for social and business lives in contrast to the focus on the status quo, the propensity for present living and the preference for spontaneity. GLOBE measured societal practices in terms of individualism/collectivism by asking its respondents about group loyalty, individual or collectivistic interests, group cohesion and group acceptance. Assertiveness asks respondents about the degree of aggressiveness, assertiveness, dominance, toughness and physical behaviour. The GLOBE scales were all asked using a seven-point Likert scale with many reverse coded items (see Appendix 9, p. 211ff.).

4.4.3 Control variables

Multiple control variables are involved in the analysis: industry type, headcount, sales, degree of internationalization, ownership structure/public listing, country of origin effect, environment, strategic flexibility, organizational culture and tenure.

I considered institutional, organizational and demographic variables to control for any confounding effects. The list is derived by incorporating those control variables that had a significant impact on performance evaluation and reward systems. I included covariates related to an organizational background (Peretz & Fried, 2012) rather than demographic characteristics (e.g. gender, position, age, education) that have been found not to alter the significant influence of culture on reward preferences and practices (Chiang and Birtch 2005; 2006, 2007; 2010; 2012).[70] Within the demographic variables I incorporated tenure. Institutional theory supports the notion of organizational background variables since "industries develop along particular trajectories" and "size ... tends to influence the methods used for controlling and coordinating employees" (Gooderham, Nordhaug & Ringdal, 2006, p. 1502). Schuler and Rogovsky (1998) explicitly state industry type, size and ownership as

---

[70] Similar findings were made by Douglas et al. (2007) on the topic of budgets.

control variables which should be included in research. Jansen, Merchant and van der Stede (2009) state the necessity to integrate many of the following variables in robustness checks in order to better infer cross-cultural variances and in order to highlight confounding effects.

Industry type: I distinguish between manufacturing, trade and service firms (further argumentation is provided in Chapter 4.1, p. 87f.).

Size: Few studies have looked at size as a contingent variable (Chenhall, 2003, 2007). The contingency-based approach names a variety of measures, among them sales and the number of employees which is the preferred criterion. Jansen, Merchant and van der Stede (2009) found significant differences in the amount of sales for a Dutch and US sample. Complemented with Chinese data, Merchant et al. (2011) found these differences too. I control for size with the number of employees and latest sales numbers (additional argumentation is provided in Chapter 4.1, p. 87f.)

Internationalization: The more far-reaching the internationalization, the more societal cultures are involved. I therefore controlled for internationalization by the number of countries in which an organization has operations, an operational footing or service functions. Number of countries is a single question with integer response possibilities (1, 2, 3, etc.).

Ownership structure: The measure is split in an indicator variable of whether the firm has an investor in the background or not and whether the firm is owned by a family or any other source. Cornett, Marcus and Tehranian (2008, p. 359) state that "large institutional investors have the opportunity, resources, and ability to monitor, discipline, and influence managers". Speckbacher and Wentges (2012, p. 42-43) "found strong evidence that firms in which members of the founding family assume an executive role in the TMT *[top management team – note of the author]* differ from other firms in their use of formal control mechanisms". Since many family firms have members in the top management team, it is possible that family firms apply management control elements differently. La Porta (1999) showed huge differences for the amount of family-owned firms in Canada, Belgium and Germany. Chakrabarty (2009) found that the cultural influence of individualism/collectivism has an effect on the number of family-owned firms, leading to the fact that those firms could attribute a different approach in exercising control.

Country of origin: The study of Björkman et al. (2007) revealed home country or country of origin effects. They found vast support for anticipated differences across different host countries and interpret their findings in the context of new institutionalism. They indicate that host country influence is probably stronger. Van der Stede (2003) examined national cultural differences at 37 Belgian firms and corresponding business-units. He used the responses from these subsidiaries and assumed a constant level of Belgian national culture at the corporate layer. He found a dominance of parental effects that overrule cultural facts. Cooke and Huang (2011) presented findings from a field study of four Chinese firms acquired by American companies. They stated strong resistance to adapt to the parent norms of performance evaluation and reward schemes. These conflicting findings still led me to include country of origin as a control variable. I compare organizational headquarters with country of investigation to determine whether home country or host country is present.

Environmental uncertainty: Studies normally used a measure of uncertainty (stability and predictability) (Gordon & Narayanan, 1984) over various aspects of competitive, supplier and customer environment as well as the technological and regulatory background (see Hansen and van der Stede (2004)). Collins, Almer and Mendoza (1999) showed many differences in the area of environmental turbulence and instability between the US and Latin America. I used an average score of the amount of material changes and the respective predictability for environmental uncertainty split to customer, supplier, competitor, and technology as well as regulatory and economic uncertainty. Former research also highlighted the influence of competition on a variety of management controls which was confirmed by a study of Hoque (2011) who found positive effect of competition on the number of changes in MAS. I therefore included competition and used a single-item measure on competitiveness.

Flexibility of strategic ends and means: Chiang and Birtch (2010) outlined that strategic priorities and the interval of a strategic revision could influence the frequency or purpose of evaluation feedback. Additionally, one might think that the purpose of rewards could be influenced too. Therefore, I include the frequency of the revision of strategic objectives and their corresponding action plans connated by strategic ends and means flexibility (Brews & Hunt, 1999) as covariates. A faster revolving strategic review and revision cycle might for instance go along with a higher feedback frequency and a stronger reliance for feedback.

Organizational culture: Webster and White (2010) found an influence of national culture on organizational culture. Gerhart (2009b) addresses caution to the relationship of national culture on organizational culture. He concludes that national culture does not constrain organizational culture to a larger extent. In fact, I could image that the organizational level of culture has an influence on MCS design. In consequence, the interplay has to be controlled for. I used an average score of the respondents for each firm to the organizational cultural questions.

Tenure: I measured tenure with an open-ended question about the years in the firm or SBU. Tenure of the top management team may also influence the decisions of the executives "because it takes time to gain an adequate understanding of the company" (Cornett, Marcus & Tehranian, 2008, p. 360). Studies highlight that managers with a short tenure tend to apply new practices whereas long-tenured managers rely on their instituted practices. Burkert and Lueg (2013) found mixed results for the influence of CEO and CFO tenure on the sophistication of Value-based Management.

4.5 Tests of and remedies for measurement error

4.5.1 Missing data

To ensure the quality of the coded data, I did a variety of consistency checks with data from all team members and asked all team members for data check or correction if applicable. In order to facilitate the right data entry, the Excel coding template has been programmed in such a way to only allow data entries of "1-7". Missing data was labelled by an "x" and not applicable data was labelled by "0". Nevertheless, manual overwriting could occur as well as wrong entries. Additionally I executed some consistency checks on the sum of certain variables (e.g. if the sum should equal 100) or the consistent number of data entries for section D1. In SPSS, I checked all minimum and maximum scores for each variable in order to find wrong data entries.

Missing data for the MCS questionnaire was very limited since all interviews have been done by the interviewers and data quality was assured during the interview. Only five missing values occurred for 17.679 data entries which result to a rate of 0.03%[71]. One case did not answer question D1b and thus contributed with four missing values. One missing value occurred for question C5b. I decided to leave the missing values because only two questions were targeted. Zero was not considered a missing value as such since the respondents declared that the respective practice was not applicable or was not performed. Although there are voices that heavily discourage the use of a pairwise deletion (drops only cases in which an answer for the particular variable in the analysis is missing, opposite to listwise deletion which retains only complete data sets (Harrington, 2009)), I applied this method for the MCS items and excluded the respective case for any particular analysis if missing values occurred. Pairwise deletion only applied to two variables (C5b; D1b) with five missing values.

Missing data for the GLOBE questionnaires was also very limited. Although these questionnaires have been distributed by the managers, only 36 out of 14.284 values were missing for the societal practice scores which correspond to a rate of 0.25%. One case with ten missing values did overlook a whole page and was excluded. For the remaining cases I examined whether the data were completely missing at random (MCAR) and performed the Little MCAR-Test for each country (Little, 1988) in the R package lavaan (Rosseel, 2012). The data are missing completely at random, hence are "randomly distributed throughout the matrix" (Acock, 2005, p. 1014), if the p-value of the χ^2-Test is significant (p > 0.05) (Little & Rubin, 2002).[72] The significance level holds for the data (see Table 8).

Country	X^2	df	p-value	Missing values
Belgium	215.62	195	0.148	5
Canada	122.43	115	0.300	5
Germany	69.76	78	0.736	2
Poland	317.25	308	0.346	14

Table 8: Little MCAR-Test for GLOBE data

---

[71] A rule of thumb declares missing values below 1% as "trivial" (Schendera, 2007, p. 120).
[72] The null hypothesis for Little's MCAR test is that the data are missing completely at random.

Due to single missing values spread over the cultural constructs, I followed a casewise mean imputation method for each individual construct[73] by averaging the remaining items and placing this value for the missing one (e.g. a four item construct with one missing value and three scores of 5.00, 6.00 and 7.00 results to 6.00 as the imputed value). This method is different to a plain mean imputation technique based on the variable mean, which is a practice to be avoided. Still, there occurs a bias for the variance that is presumably smaller after imputation. Despite this effect, this method can be reasonably applied (Schafer & Graham, 2002).

4.5.2 Outlier analysis

Outliers will distort analysis since erroneous values contaminate the other data. According to Barnett and Lewis (1994, p. 7), an outlier in a data set "is an observation (or subset of observations) which appears to be inconsistent with the remainder of that set of data". There are various forms to deal with outliers. The techniques range from removing entire cases, transforming the whole data and replacing the score (Field, 2013). In order to detect outliers, a very common method relies on the interval which covers the mean plus/minus three standard deviations. Another method is the interquartile approach. Leys et al. (2013, p. 764) pled for the median absolute deviation (MAD) as a much more robust procedure which is independent of sample size, as "the mean and standard deviation are strongly impacted by outliers". The MAD figure is calculated as follows:

$$MAD = b\, M_i \left(|x_i - M_j(x_j)| \right)$$

In case of normal distributed data, "b" denotes a constant of 1.4826. M_i denotes the median of the series, x_j stands for the n original responses and M_j is the median of the construct. In moderately conservative terms the decision to label a value as an outlier should serve the following threshold:

$$\frac{x_i - M}{MAD} > |\pm 2.5|$$

---

[73] The five missing values of the MCS questionnaire do not belong to a construct and thus were not corrected.

I applied the steps suggested by Leys et al. (2013) for each established construct of my data analysis. Therefore the outlier detection was only applied to the GLOBE dimensions. First, I calculated the median of the observations for each construct in each country. I then calculated the median of all absolute values which were the differences between each construct item x_i with the median of the construct M_j. The MAD was then derived by multiplying this value for each culture construct by the constant factor b=1.4826. The figure for the MAD was then placed into the formula to determine the lower and upper bound. All values that were beyond these two demarcating lines were marked. All individual responses in the four countries which showed more than one violation of this conservative threshold (again a conservative approach) were finally labelled as an outlier. In this way 13 cases were removed from the data base.

4.5.3 Test of normality, homogeneity, skew and kurtosis

I run several tests to address the normality assumption, the homogeneity of the data as well as skew and kurtosis. For the MCS items I performed the Kolmogorow-Smirnoff test to evaluate the normality of the data. This test showed a violation of the normal distribution assumption for all but one tested variable. Assessing the skew and kurtosis, I ran the SPSS command and converted the values to z-scores. It resulted to three significant variable scores for each the skew and kurtosis. However, as Field (2013, p. 184) states, "we don't need to worry about normality" for large data sets. The homogeneity of variance is assessed each time by the Levene's test. If the test shows a significant result ($p<0.05$), i.e. the assumption of homogeneity is violated, I use the Welch test which corrects for this violation (Bacher, 2004).

I assessed skew and kurtosis for the GLOBE items within R. Five of twenty-one items showed skewness above 3.0. The highest kurtosis showed 3.5 which is far below the threshold of 10.0 (Kline, 2011). The GLOBE items show no severe violation of non-normality which allows Maximum-Likelihood estimation to assess the cultural constructs.

4.5.4 Common-method bias

Increasingly reviewers of journals ask authors how they deal with common method bias or common method variance (CMV). Especially studies, which rely on one questionnaire with one key informant, are potential candidates for CMV. Although there is much controversy whether common method variance is overstated and an 'urban legend' (Spector, 2006) or a serious problem to be dealt with (Podsakoff et al., 2003), in some fields of management research authors have to report on appropriate actions on that issue. For instance, a recent JIBS editorial highlighted CMV as a frequent concern (Chang, van Witteloostuijn & Eden, 2010). CMV is a "variance that is attributable to the measurement method rather than to the constructs the measures represent" (Podsakoff et al., 2003, p. 879).

There are both ex ante and ex post measures to address CMV. CMV can be avoided upfront when measures of both predictor and criterion variables are retrieved from different sources. Dependent variables (i.e. MCS items) should have a different source than independent variables (i.e. national culture) (Cascio, 2012). Up-front I try to avoid CMV by having different persons responding to the MCS questionnaire (top management team of the SBU) and the measures of culture (different persons within the organization spread over hierarchical levels). A different approach targets the design and administration of the study. I also assured anonymity and confidentiality of the responses, and ensured that there is no best way of answering, and that honesty is essential (Chang, van Witteloostuijn & Eden, 2010).[74]

4.5.5 Construct analysis

4.5.5.1 *General remarks on construct validity*

Adcock and Collier (2010, p. 529) state that "validity is specifically concerned with whether operationalization and the scoring of cases adequately reflect the concept the researcher seeks to measure". Validity concerns the idea whether we are really measuring what we would like to measure (Nunnally & Bernstein, 1994). Sometimes it is difficult to directly measure what we would like to measure, e.g. a latent variable as culture. That is why we introduce so called manifest variables which represent an underlying construct, the latent variable. The challenge

---

[74] Ex-post remedies include a set of statistical measures such as multitrait-multimethod procedures, Harman's single-factor test, and a marker-variable technique (Lindell & Whitney, 2001; Malhotra, Kim & Patil, 2006; Podsakoff et al., 2003; Richardson, Simmering & Sturman, 2009; Williams, Hartman & Cavazotte, 2010). I ran Harman's one-factor test to analyze the presence of CMV. I entered all MCS variables into an EFA, used the unrotated principal component method and restricted the number of factors to one. 46 distinct factors emerged. Of those 15 factors showed an eigenvalue greater than 1.0 and accounted for 63.9% of the total variance. The largest factor accounted for 14.4% of the total variance. In conclusion, no single factor is apparent. Hence, I expect CMV is not present.

Lindell and Whitney (2001) introduced a particular marker-variable technique to overcome the problems of the Harman's test. The marker is defined as "theoretically unrelated to at least one other scale in the questionnaire" (Lindell & Whitney, 2001, p. 115). An ideal marker variable is expected to have no correlation with the other variables. Their approach has received substantial notice among organizational researches after publication (Richardson, Simmering & Sturman, 2009).

is to find the right manifest variables that indicate the latent concept. Construct validity "is involved whenever a test is to be interpreted as a measure of some attribute or quality which is not 'operationally defined'" (Cronbach & Meehl, 1955, p. 282). It should show whether a construct is represented by the measures and not by other elements.

Constructs are measured via exploratory and confirmatory factor analyses. When there is sufficient knowledge on the constructs, confirmatory factor analysis (CFA) is the most appropriate method. For explorative constructs, i.e. when there is only preliminary knowledge about the constructs, exploratory factor analysis (EFA) should be applied. The main objective of factor analysis "is to reduce a number of observed variables to less factors in order to enhance interpretability and detect hidden structures in the data" (Treiblmaier & Filzmoser, 2010, p. 198). The constructs for performance evaluation and reward items are dealt with an EFA, the cultural constructs for the GLOBE dimensions are dealt with a CFA.

4.5.5.2 Performance evaluation and reward constructs

EFA is a statistical tool to discover constructs that are inhibited in a multitude of different items. It is a useful approach to decide on new scales or to validate the measurement model or to explore latent structures. EFA serves as a data reduction technique. It is a purely explorative fashion and resembles data mining. Its purpose is to find factors that share a high degree of variance. With the exploratory factors, the analysis finds variables that combine a maximum amount of variance. Data reduction is a practical tool to replace a large number of variables with a few number of factors that have the same underlying idea (Field, 2013). An EFA is used when the researcher has a-priori no idea about the emerging factors. If one had, one would have to choose a confirmatory approach instead (see Chapter 4.5.5.3, p. 115ff.). There is a wide range of techniques and decisions to take. First, the researcher has to decide on factor extraction methods (determines the amount of factors or criteria to stop the appearance of factors), the type of rotation assuming either correlation of the factors (oblique rotation) or not (orthogonal rotations) as well as the post-hoc test of Cronbach's α (Field, 2013).

Cronbach's α is the main reliability measure. It shows the degree of consistency of measures and relates to stability (low changes over time) (Bryman, 2008). If a measure is reliable, one can say with confidence that repeated administrations would lead to the same results (Hammersley, 1987). The minimum value of 0.70 is usually considered as an acceptable level, although Nunnally and Bernstein (1994) refer to this cut-off point for the early stages of research. The survey questionnaire contained many single item measures and only a few constructs. For the five constructs, performance standards objectivity, subjective evaluation, financial and non-financial rewarding purpose and internal business processes I performed exploratory factor analyses. I used principal component analysis for data reduction purpose with varimax rotation to determine factor loadings and decided to apply the Eigenvalue criterion greater than 1 to identify the number of factors. I also performed the Bartlett's test of sphericity and calculated the Kaiser–Meyer–Olkin (KMO) measure to determine the suitability of the data (Treiblmaier & Filzmoser, 2010).

Table 9 reports the results of the Kaiser–Meyer–Olkin measure, Bartlett's test of sphericity, factor loadings and Cronbach Alphas. Factor loadings range between 0.51 and 0.88. Cronbach Alpha exceeds the 0.7 threshold in only two of five cases, one time reliability gets very close. Still I adhere to these constructs.[75]

---

[75] Due to missing alternatives, Groen, Wouters and Wilderom (2012) also used a scale despite a very low Cronbach's alpha of 0.36.

Performance evaluation and reward scale items[a]	Factor loadings
C3: Subjectivity of performance evaluation SBU top management bases subordinates' performance evaluation on: (3 items, KMO=0.639, Bartlett's test: $p<0.01$, $\alpha=0.60$)	
Achievements in leadership behaviour	0.738
Actions and activities taken	0.765
Individual effort	0.738
C4: Objectivity of performance standards SBU top management evaluates subordinates' performance in relation to: (3 items, KMO=0.682, Bartlett's test: $p<0.01$, $\alpha=0.68$)	
Internal benchmarks (league table position)	0.750
External benchmarks (league table position)	0.745
Past performance (trend-based evaluation)	0.641
C4/D2: Objectivity of rewarding How is the way of evaluating and compensating subordinates' performance in your SBU? (5 items, KMO=0.682, Bartlett's test: $p<0.01$, $\alpha=0.58$)	
We use absolute, preset numbers (euros, time, %)	0.667
We determine weights of performance measures as the evaluation takes place (**R**)	0.521
We evaluate performance on the basis of quantitative metrics	0.514
We adjust the amount of bonus based on actual circumstances (**R**)	0.552
We use predetermined criteria in evaluation and rewarding	0.726
D4: Purpose of financial rewards How important are the following purposes of financial rewarding in your SBU? (3 items, KMO=0.666, Bartlett's test: $p<0.01$, $\alpha=0.75$)	
Committing subordinates	0.861
Motivating subordinates	0.838
Directing subordinates' attention	0.727
D4: Purpose of non-financial rewards How important are the following purposes of non-financial rewarding in your SBU? (3 items, KMO=0.666, Bartlett's test: $p<0.01$, $\alpha=0.81$)	
Committing subordinates	0.841
Motivating subordinates	0.883
Directing subordinates' attention	0.807
G2: Balance of performance areas: Internal business processes How important are the following performance areas for your SBU right now? (5 items, KMO=0.712, Bartlett's test: $p<0.01$, $\alpha=0.60$)	
Operational performance	0.600
Quality	0.665
Supplier relations	0.657
Environmental performance	0.625
Innovation	0.578
[a] Items were coded on a seven-point Likert scale (Not at all - Very high extent/Very important). Reverse coding (indicated by '**R**') was applied when necessary.	

Table 9: Performance evaluation and reward scale items

4.5.5.3 GLOBE constructs

CFA "deals specifically with measurement models, that is, the relationships between observed measures or *indicators* (e.g., test items, test scores, behavioural observation ratings) and latent variables or *factors*" (Brown, 2006, p. 1; Brown & Moore, 2012, p. 361). CFA enables the researcher "every aspect of the model specifications" (Brown, 2006, p. 88). CFA evaluates new measures and allows to "test an existing theory" (Matsunaga, 2010, p. 98). Or in other words it is a valuable tool for testing instruments and validating pre-existing constructs. Thus, the specification of the underlying model must be based on theoretical deliberations and former research (Brown, 2006). CFA is a sound approach if one relies on existing measures (Harrington, 2009). The objective of the factor analysis is to specify the "number and nature of factors that account for the variation and covariation among a set of indicators" (Brown & Moore, 2012, p. 361). CFA enables researchers to set relationships among factor and indicators by content related thoughts. A further advantage is that CFA can be used on a stand-alone basis and also accounts for measurement error (Harrington, 2009). CFA requires that missing data is either non-existing or handled with great care (see Chapter 4.5.1, p. 107f.), and that data is multivariate normally distributed (Harrington, 2009). To assess normality, Kline (2011) suggests upper limits for skewness of 3.0 and 10.0 for kurtosis as well as using a sample size above 150 as an acceptable level for most models and a minimum of three measures for each variable.

Different fit statistics exist in order to assess the match between the underlying CFA model and the real data. There is a plethora of model fits available which can be grouped to absolute and incremental fit indices and all researchers tend to favour a specific basket (Bagozzi & Yi, 2012). The χ^2 statistic is considered the most fundamental one (Barrett, 2007). The recommendations for the cut-off values are presented in Table 10. It is useful to take both type of fit indices into consideration and report the χ^2 and its p-value, χ^2/df, RMSEA, its p-value and its confidence interval, the Standardized Root Mean Square Residual (SRMR), the Goodness-of-fit Index (GFI), the Adjusted Goodness-of-Fit Index (AGFI), the Comparative Fit Index (CFI) as well as the Tucker-Lewis Index (TLI) (Jackson, Gillaspy & Purc-Stephenson, 2009; Mueller & Hancock, 2001). Overall, it is advisable to rely on different fit indices and report them all "because they provide different information about model fit" (Brown & Moore, 2012, p. 369-371). All the indices should be interpreted together with sample size and the complexity of the overall model (Miles & Shevlin, 2007).

Fit measure	Cut-off values	Source
Absolute fit indices		
p-value of χ^2	> 0.05	Barrett, 2007, p. 816; Kline, 2011, p. 199f.
χ^2 / degrees of freedom	< 2.0	Schermelleh-Engel & Moosbrugger, 2003, p. 52
Root Mean Square Error of Approximation (RMSEA)	≤ 0.05 close approximate fit ≤ 0.08 reasonable fit ≥ 0.10 poor fit	Kline, 2005, p. 139
p-value	> 0.05	Brown, 2006, p. 84
Standardized Root Mean Square Residual (SRMR)	≤ 0.10 ≤ 0.08 ≤ 0.07	Kline, 2005, p. 141 Hu & Bentler, 1998, p. 449; Hu & Bentler, 1999, p. 27 Bagozzi & Yi, 2012, p. 29
Goodness-of-Fit Index (GFI)	≥ 0.95	Schermelleh-Engel & Moosbrugger, 2003, p. 52
Adjusted Goodness-of-Fit Index (AGFI)	≥ 0.90	Schermelleh-Engel & Moosbrugger, 2003, p. 52
Incremental fit indices		
Comparative Fit Index (CFI)	≥0.95	Hu & Bentler, 1998, p. 449; Hu & Bentler, 1999, p. 27
Tucker-Lewis Index (TLI)	≥0.95	Hu & Bentler, 1998, p. 449; Hu & Bentler, 1999, p. 27

Table 10: Cut-off criteria for fit indices

Although the GLOBE constructs are well-established I wanted to verify the cultural constructs I use for hypotheses testing. I applied a one-dimensional CFA to the five GLOBE dimensions[76] to verify the model fit.

To deal with the CFA I chose the open-source software R. This statistic tool was chosen over AMOS, which has a graphics user interface, because of its free use, a multitude of additional software packages and good documentation. I used the software R package lavaan (Rosseel, 2012). I ran the CFA for the GLOBE societal practice data set corrected for outliers. Based on recommendations to inspect the residuals (Brown & Moore, 2012), I eliminated four variables (QS31 (future orientation); QS5 (power distance); QS6R/QS14R (assertiveness)

---

[76] Hanges and Dickson (2004) only provided an average CFI of 0.89 for the societal practice scores.

Chapter 4 – Research methodology

which showed poor fit to the construct. Table 11 presents the overview of the various fit measures for societal practices scores. I got excellent fit results for the four factors and remaining indicators that belong to the cultural dimensions uncertainty avoidance, future orientation, power distance and assertiveness.[77] The model did not converge for the dimension individualism/collectivism. Nevertheless, the four indicators that comprise the factor individualism/collectivism are still assumed to hold.[78, 79]

Fit measures	Cut-off value	Uncertainty avoidance	Future orientation	Power distance	Assertiveness
χ^2	report	0.17	1.15	0.90	4.35
df	report	2	2	2	2
p-value	(> 0.05)	0.92	0.56	0.64	0.11
χ^2 / df	< 2.0	0.1	0.6	0.5	2.2
RMSEA	< 0.05-0.08	0.00	0.00	0.00	0.06
p-value	(> 0.05)	0.96	0.77	0.82	0.33
CI [MIN]	< 5%	0.00	0.00	0.00	0.00
CI [MAX]	> 95%	0.04	0.09	0.09	0.14
SRMR	< 0.10	0.01	0.02	0.01	0.03
GFI	> 0.95	1.00	1.00	1.00	1.00
AGFI	> 0.90	1.01	1.01	1.01	0.98
CFI	> 0.95	1.00	1.00	1.00	0.96
TLI	> 0.95	1.06	1.02	1.02	0.88
Residuals	Max < 0.1	0.01	0.04	0.03	0.09
N		344	344	344	344

Table 11: CFA reports on GLOBE dimensions

---

[77] Only two scores for assertiveness slightly besides the proposed cut-off values (χ^2 / df and the TLI).

[78] The scores for Cronbach Alpha are rather mediocre. Power distance exhibits 0.62, future orientation results to 0.53, uncertainty avoidance lies at 0.52 and assertiveness scores 0.45. The Cronbach Alpha for individualism/collectivism is truly bad with 0.28. Kreyer (2011) received very similar Cronbach Alpha scores for her German and French GLOBE sample of 205 students. Taras, Rowney and Steel (2009) report an average Cronbach's alpha of 0.72 and a range from 0.41-0.94 in their meta-study on instruments for measuring culture. The average internal reliability figure in the original Hofstede study was 0.68.

[79] Fit measures are in the same range for organizational practices scores. The Cronbach Alphas are rather mediocre as well: Power distance exhibits 0.47, future orientation results to 0.41, uncertainty avoidance lies at 0.58, assertiveness scores 0.41 and individualism/collectivism results to 0.42.

ANOVA-tests "share an important assumption: that the scores from each group are comparable (i.e., equivalent)" (Sharma, Durvasula & Ployhart, 2011, p. 76). Cross-cultural studies, with cultures as the relevant groups, need to show data equivalence "to ensure that any differences found between cultures truly reflect the phenomena of interest" (Hult et al., 2008, p. 1028). Measurement invariance indicates the extent of generalizability and transportability across different groups. Therefore, it is a prerequisite for making legitimate comparisons based on testing mean differences (Sharma, Durvasula & Ployhart, 2011). For the cultural setting, the data equivalence test targets whether the GLOBE constructs are comparable across cultures. "If not tested, violations of measurement equivalence assumptions are as threatening to substantive interpretations as is an inability to demonstrate reliability and validity" (Vandenberg & Lance, 2000, p. 6). The assurance of measurement invariance allows researchers to proceed with testing the means of different groups. Table 12 lists the three relevant steps to assess measurement invariance (Sharma, Durvasula & Ployhart, 2011, p. 76; Steinmetz et al., 2009, p. 603).

(1)	Configural invariance:	Do people in different groups interpret the construct in a conceptually similar manner?
(2)	Metric invariance:	Are the items of the measure calibrated to the latent construct similarly across groups? Do items have the same relative importance or meaning across groups?
(3)	Scalar invariance:	Do respondents in different groups use response scales of items in a similar way?

Table 12: Steps to assess measurement invariance

First, the overall or baseline model that corresponds to Table 11 (p. 117) has to show that the measurement model is appropriate for the whole sample (Byrne, Shavelson & Muthén, 1989; Dimitrov, 2006). Each additional and subsequent model bears more constraints (van de Schoot, Lugtig & Hox, 2012; Vandenberg & Lance, 2000). Configural invariance is established if there are identical patterns of factor loadings. Configural invariance uses a non-restrained model (model 1). Metric invariance requires equal factor loadings across groups (model 2). Scalar invariance (model 3) postulates the same "degree of up- or downward bias of the manifest variable" across groups (Steinmetz et al., 2009, p. 603). I tested scalar invariances by adding the constraint of equal intercepts to the constraint of equal factor loadings (Sharma, Durvasula & Ployhart, 2011; Steinmetz et al., 2009). The χ^2 statistic is a useful method to assess the goodness-of-fit of multi-group data (Dimitrov, 2006). If the χ^2 test is significant, modification is required. With a successful modification (in technical terms the intercept of the manifest variable is freed), partial invariance is established (Byrne, Shavelson & Muthén, 1989).

Two of the five GLOBE dimensions showed measurement non-invariance (individualism/collectivism and uncertainty avoidance). The other three dimensions showed partial measurement invariance.[80] Violation of measurement invariance precludes caution with regard to the comparison of the different cultural groups (Steinmetz et al., 2009). As an important comment with regard to the measurement invariance tests, the GLOBE researchers (Hanges & Dickson, 2004, p. 147) note that "the similarity of any within-group factor structure is not the critical issue. The important issue … is the appropriateness of a factor structure that accounts for between organization or societal variation". A test of societal differences in the within-society factor structure was not possible for the GLOBE team. Taking this objection into consideration, I am aware of potential biases in the GLOBE data, but proceeded in taking the sum scores for my hypotheses (see Chapter 5.1.5, p. 128ff.).

---

[80] For future orientation, I freed the intercept of the manifest variables QS30, QS8R, QS3R; for power distance, I freed the intercept of the manifest variables QS13R; for assertiveness, I freed the intercept of the manifest variables QS2R, QS6R for all but the Canadian data.

5 Results

5.1 Descriptive statistics

5.1.1 Report on interviews

239 interviews have been held in total. This figure exactly hits the mean sample size and outnumbers the median sample size of survey studies in management accounting research. More important this figure is within the range of justifiable research with a decent extent of face validity (van der Stede, Young & Chen, 2005). Of the 239 interviews, 87 interviews have been executed by the author in Germany. Formal interviewing and completion of the questionnaire in the German firms took on average two hours which confirmed the pre-test observation. Similar experience was made in the other countries as well.

Country	# of interviews	First interview	Last interview	Total period
Belgium	50	23.05.2011	13.08.2012	448 days
Canada	52	07.10.2011	27.09.2012	356 days
Germany	87	20.07.2011	30.03.2012	254 days
Poland	50	22.06.2012	02.11.2012	133 days

Table 13: Period of interviews

Interviews were mainly held personally (88.3%), the remaining by telephone (11.7%). The interviewers were mainly members of the core project team (93.3%). The high amount of telephone talks in Canada is certainly attributed to the long distances across the continent. However, the Canadian researcher is well experienced and has a decent reputation among executives so that the problems ascribed in Chapter 4.3.1 (p. 94f.) are of minor concern. In addition to this qualitative argumentation, I tested whether the Canadian data differs between personal talks and telephone interviews. Only the two variables 'purposes of performance evaluation' showed a significant difference ($p<0.05$) for the form of interview. Thus, I do not see major differences that would inhibit to use the full Canadian data set. In minor cases (6.7%), Master students who were closely involved in the project collected data in Canada and Poland as well.

Country	Form of interview		Interviewer	
	Personally	Telephone	Researcher	Student only
Belgium	49	1	50	
Canada	27	25	43	9
Germany	86	1	87	
Poland	49	1	43	7
Total	211	28	223	16

Table 14: Form of interview and interviewers

5.1.2 Respondent demographics

Respondents were mainly situated in top management. CEOs and CFOs were interviewed in two third of the cases whereas other top management team members were approached in one third of the cases. Belgium stands out in addressing merely CEOs in 90% of the interviews, whereas Canada approached other top management team members in more than half of the interviews. 90% were male, 10% female respondents. Female managers were more frequently addressed in Poland (18%). On average, the respondents showed a higher education background. Almost all (97.1%) respondents had a university degree, 79.9% obtained a Master degree or higher. Nearly 60% of those with a bachelor degree and higher had a management, business or economics background. One fifth of this group studied engineering.

Tenure ranged between 3 months and 39 years with an average of 12 years those managers worked for their company. I observed equally distributed tenure among managers to a large extent. Overall, Table 15 and Table 16 summarize the information on the executives of the interviewed firms. The figures on education are similar to the findings of Burkert and Lueg (2013) who examined CEO and CFO characteristics whereas tenure is even much higher in our sample. The figures show that the respondents are well experienced and were thus qualified to answer the questions.

Function	BEL	CAN	GER	POL	TOTAL	in %
CEO	45	9	38	21	113	47.3
CFO	3	16	17	9	45	18.8
Other management	2	27	32	20	81	33.9
	50	52	87	50	239	
Highest degree						
High school	1	0	6	0	7	2.9
Bachelor	3	34	1	3	41	17.2
Master	46	18	62	41	167	69.9
Ph.D.	0	0	18	6	24	10.0
	50	52	87	50	239	
Field of study (for bachelor or higher)						
Business/Management/Economics	23	27	58	31	139	58.2
Law	3	12	1	0	16	6.7
Engineering	17	7	14	11	49	20.5
Humanities	2	0	3	2	7	2.9
Natural sciences	4	1	3	0	8	3.3
Others	0	5	2	6	13	5.6
	49	52	81	50	232	
BEL = Belgium; CAN = Canada; GER = Germany; POL = Poland[81]						

Table 15: Demographic data (part 1)

---

[81] I partly use these abbreviations in the following tables too.

Gender	BEL	CAN	GER	POL	TOTAL	in %
Male	45	48	80	41	214	89.5
Female	5	4	7	9	25	10.5
Tenure in the current firm (in years)						
Up to five	12		35	22	69	28.9
> 5 - 10	10	10	18	10	48	20.1
> 10 - 15	5	23	12	6	46	19.2
> 15 - 20	5	9	5	7	26	10.9
> 20 - 25	13	10	9	2	34	14.2
> 25	5		8	3	16	6.7
MIN	1	6	1	0	0	
MAX	35	24	39	37	39	
MEAN	14	14	11	10	12	
MEDIAN	14	13	6	6	11	
SD	10	5	10	9	9	

Table 16: Demographic data (part 2)

5.1.3 Industry composition

Table 17 presents the industrial composition of the 239 firms in the sample. Overall, there is a broad heterogeneity which can be ascribed to the random sampling approach and the broad background of the population. The core of the firms is concentrated in manufacturing (63%), followed by services (29%) and trade (8%). In manufacturing, construction (8.4%), chemical and pharmaceutical products (7.9%), food, beverages and tobacco (7.9%), metallic products (6.3%), machinery and equipment (6.3%) as well as other manufacturing (8.4%) have the highest share. All wholesale and trade activities comprise 8.4%. The service sector is heterogeneous as well. Here, firms operate mainly in administrative and support service activities (5.0%), finance and insurance (4.2%), transportation and storage (3.8%), as well as telecommunications and IT (3.3%).

Chapter 5 – Results

	Industry	BEL	CAN	GER	POL	TOTAL	in %
1	Agriculture, forestry and fishing		2			2	0.8%
2	Mining and quarrying	1	4	1	2	8	3.3%
3	Manufacturing of food, beverages and tobacco	7	7	2	3	19	7.9%
4	Manufacturing of textile and apparel	3		2	1	6	2.5%
5	Manufacturing of chemical and pharmaceutical products	6	2	5	6	19	7.9%
6	Manufacturing of non-metallic products	3	2	2	1	8	3.3%
7	Manufacturing of metallic products	2	7	6		15	6.3%
8	Manufacturing of electrical and electronic products	1	4	7		12	5.0%
9	Manufacturing of machinery and equipment	1	5	6	3	15	6.3%
10	Manufacturing of vehicles and other transport		5	2	2	9	3.8%
11	Manufacturing of other products	2	9	5	4	20	8.4%
12	Electricity, gas, steam and air conditioning supply			2	2	4	1.7%
13	Water supply, sewerage, waste management and remediation activities			2	1	3	1.3%
14	Construction	6	3	7	4	20	8.4%
15	Wholesale and retail trade, repair of motor vehicles and motorcycles	3	1	8	8	20	8.4%
16	Transportation and storage	2	1	4	2	9	3.8%
17	Accommodation and food service activities	2		1	1	4	1.7%
18	Entertainment	1		2		3	1.3%
19	Telecommunications and IT	3		5		8	3.3%
20	Finance and insurance	2		6	2	10	4.2%
22	Professional, scientific and technical activities	2		2	3	7	2.9%
23	Administrative and support service activities	3		6	3	12	5.0%
26	Human health and social work activities			4	2	6	2.5%
	Total	50	52	87	50	239	100%

Overall N = 239. The table provides industry compositions of the sample. The industry categories are classified on two-digit NACE codes for Belgium, Germany and Poland. Original six-digit Standard Industrial Classification (SIC) codes for Canada are reclassified to the NACE scheme. The industries comprise (1) 01 – 03; (2) 05 – 09; (3) 10 - 12; (4) 13 - 14; (5) 20 - 22; (6) 23; (7) 24 - 25; (8) 26 – 27; (9) 28; (10) 29 - 30; (11) 15 - 19; 31 - 33; (12) 35; (13) 36 – 39; (14) 41 – 43; (15) 45 – 47; (16) 49 – 53; (17) 55 – 56; (18) 58 – 60; (19) 61 - 63; (20) 64 – 66; (21) 68; (22) 69 – 75; (23) 77 – 82; (24) 84; (25) 85; (26) 86 – 88; (27) 90 – 93. The following industry categories do not appear in the sample: (21) – Real estate activities, (24) – Public administration and defence, compulsory social security, (25) – Education, and (27) – Arts, entertainment and recreation.

Table 17: Industry composition

5.1.4   Firms' characteristics

The plurality of the organizations is not publicly traded (59.8%). Hence, publicly quoted firms comprise 40.2%. The most substantial group of ownership structure are family firms (42.3%). Large institutional investors have also a high fraction (20.1%) whereas small individual investors comprise 7.5%. Companies are owned by members of cooperative societies in 9.2% of the cases. Governments are the most significant owner in 7.5% of the firms. Venture capitalist firms play a minor role (5.0%). All other stakeholder groups (municipalities, partners, trust funds, others) contribute with 8.4%. On a per country comparison, Belgium has a much higher percentage of family firms (56.0%) and lower institutional investors (18.0%). The same picture emerges for Germany. Family firms play the major role (49.4%), followed by investors (21.8%). On contrast, Canada has a low representation of family firms (25.0%) and a much higher portion of investors (46.2%). Poland is something in between. The figure for family firms is 34.0% and the one for investors is 28.0%.

Firms were mainly headquartered in their respective country of investigation (see Table 18). Belgian, German and Polish firms have headquarters from either eight or nine foreign countries whereas Canada which also shows the highest in-country fraction has only headquarters in four foreign countries. It is interesting to note that non-European headquarter origins almost fail to appear in the firms from Europe. The same pattern is valid for Canada. In the Canadian sample there is also only a small fraction from outside Canada or the US.

Headquarter	BEL	CAN	GER	POL	TOTAL	in %
Austria	1		1	1	3	1.3
Belgium	40				40	16.7
Canada		44			44	18.4
Denmark				1	1	0.4
Finland				1	1	0.4
France	1		2	1	4	1.7
Germany	1		72	4	77	32.2
Great Britain	1	3	3		7	2.9
India		1			1	0.4
Ireland	1				1	0.4
Italy			1		1	0.4
Luxembourg	1				1	0.4
Netherlands	2		1		3	1.3
Poland				37	37	15.5
Spain			1	1	2	0.8
Sweden		1	2	1	4	1.7
Switzerland	1		2		3	1.3
USA	1	3	2	3	9	3.8
Total	**50**	**52**	**87**	**50**	**239**	**100%**
Headquarter = country of investigation	80%	85%	83%	74%	83%	

Table 18: Firms' headquarters

Table 19 provides descriptive statistics of financial information and size for the sample. The corporate firms or SBUs under investigation ranged from EUR 2.1 million to EUR 20.8 billion EUR in sales. Total Assets had a range of EUR 1.7 million to EUR 46.7 billion. Employees were within the range of 40 and 80.000. The corporates with the highest employees (top five) came from Poland, followed by Germany (six, eight to ten). The five large Polish companies were four times SBUs with foreign headquarters.

	Mean	Median	SD	MIN	MAX	Q1	Q3	N
Employees	2,370	700	7,376	40	80,057	410	1,600	239
Sales 2010	704	147	2,025	2	20,794	64	481	231
Total Assets 2010	1,512	117	5,722	2	46,725	42	579	216
EBIT 2010	60	7	215	-187	1,619	2	25	227
Sales 2009	612	131	1,808	1	19,693	57	394	232
Total Assets 2009	1,370	99	5,272	1	40,838	39	481	218
EBIT 2009	48	4	193	-385	1,374	1	20	228
ROA 2010	7.3%	5.9%	9.2%	-24.9%	56.3%	2.4%	10.1%	213
ROS 2010	5.1%	5.1%	12.4%	-120.2%	39.1%	2.1%	8.5%	227
ROA 2009	5.4%	4.5%	10.5%	-42.9%	79.2%	1.0%	7.9%	215
ROS 2009	3.9%	4.2%	15.3%	-168.5%	61.5%	1.1%	7.4%	228

Overall N = 239. Descriptive statistics include the mean, median, standard deviation (SD), the range (MIN and MAX), the 25% and 75% quartile (Q1 and Q3) and the valid sample size (N). Sales, EBIT figures and Total Assets are listed in Million €. If applicable, Canadian $ and Polish złoty have been converted with the corresponding exchange rates of year-end figures for Total Assets and annual average rates for sales and EBIT. ROA (return on assets) is obtained by dividing EBIT by Total Assets. ROS (return on sales) is obtained by dividing EBIT by sales. Valid answers (N) vary for sales, EBIT, Total Assets, ROA and ROS because companies did not always provide these financial figures nor was it possible to get these figures for some SBUs from other legal documents. For calculation of ROS and ROA both numerator and denominator must be available.

Table 19: Employees and financial indicators of sample firms

5.1.5 GLOBE scores

GLOBE scores for the five dimensions were calculated based on new data collection. For statistical analysis I derived the aggregated mean national score by averaging the scores of the individuals in the respective society. In order to derive the score of each factor, I followed the unit weighting approach. With this simple technique each indicator has the same weight and the final score is the average for all indicator items (Kline, 2011). I did not calculate factor scores since I wanted to maintain the original scaling format. In addition to the excluded outliers in the CFA, all those cases were eliminated for the calculation of the country score for which the citizenship and the country of birth did not match to the country of investigation. This expelled further seven cases and left a total of 337 valid answers[82].

Table 20 shows the GLOBE scores for the dimensions uncertainty avoidance, future orientation, power distance, individualism/collectivism and assertiveness and lists the historical GLOBE values as a reference.[83]

Country		Uncertainty Avoidance	Future Orientation	Power Distance	Individualism /Collectivism	Assertiveness
Belgium	Mean	4.63	4.70	4.89	4.28	3.52
(N=72)	SD	0.73	0.79	0.83	0.67	0.77
Canada	Mean	4.17	3.95	4.03	3.89	3.87
(N=79)	SD	0.61	0.65	0.68	0.56	0.56
	Mean (2004)	4.58	4.44	4.82	4.38	4.05
Germany	Mean	5.12	4.78	5.10	4.06	4.24
(N=101)	SD	0.63	0.77	0.73	0.69	0.71
	Mean (2004)	5.21	4.21	5.31	3.74	4.59
Poland	Mean	3.84	3.38	5.00	4.48	4.28
(N=85)	SD	0.74	0.74	0.97	0.76	0.59
	Mean (2004)	3.62	3.11	5.10	4.53	4.06
Legend		Low level	Low level	Low level	Low level	Low level
		High level	High level	High level	High level	High level

Table 20: GLOBE scores for the dimensions of national culture

Compared to the original GLOBE study, Canada substantially deviates from the numbers published in 2004. The scores are lower for all five cultural dimensions. The highest deviation can be found for power distance.

---

[82] The CFA remained stable.
[83] Belgium was not part of the original GLOBE study.

Country		Uncertainty Avoidance	Future Orientation	Power Distance	Individualism /Collectivism	Assertiveness
Belgium	Delta	n.a.	n.a.	n.a.	n.a.	n.a.
Canada	Delta	-0.41	-0.49	-0.79	-0.49	-0.18
Germany	Delta	-0.09	0.57	-0.21	0.32	-0.35
Poland	Delta	0.22	0.27	-0.10	-0.05	0.22

Table 21: Deviations of GLOBE scores to the original study

I checked whether the difference in Canada may be attributed to French vs. English speaking parts because the original GLOBE study focused on the English speaking part of Canada. I found no significant differences for this assumption.[84] I tested whether the Flemish data deviates from the Wallonian data in Belgium. With the exception of assertiveness, I found no significant differences for this assumption.[85] I verified whether the cultural differences are significantly different for the hierarchical level of the respondents or the age of the respondents. I found no significant differences ($p<0.10$) for all five cultural dimensions in all four countries. Thus, a reason for these large differences can be attributed to differences that occurred over time or sampling differences based on the narrower industry composition of the original GLOBE study. Germany shows a more heterogeneous picture in terms of movements in the cultural dimension over time. Germany seems to be more future oriented and more collectivistic compared to the original GLOBE findings, whereas assertiveness and power distance is now lower. There is only a minimal change for uncertainty avoidance. Kreyer (2011) who recently collected GLOBE scales in Germany by means of a student sample found nearly identical scores for uncertainty avoidance (5.10 vs. 5.12), power

---

[84] In Canada, 16 persons are French speaking, among those only six respondents have no English literacy. Among the respondents who do not speak French (=63), 61 speak English. I performed an ANOVA by literacy of French vs. no literacy of French. The results are as follows: uncertainty avoidance ($F=0.515$, $p =0.475$), future orientation ($F=0.751$, $p=0.389$), power distance ($F=1.350$, $p=0.249$), individualism/collectivism ($F=0.579$, $p=0.449$) and assertiveness ($F=0.004$, $p=0.950$). The same patterns arise when I compare the six persons who speak only French with all the remaining ones. The p-values of the ANOVA are all non-significant.

[85] In Belgium, seven of the 72 persons have answered the French speaking questionnaire. I performed an ANOVA. The results are as follows: uncertainty avoidance ($F=1.467$, $p =0.269$), future orientation ($F=0.973$, $p=0.359$), power distance ($F=0.968$, $p=0.329$), individualism/collectivism ($F=0.011$, $p=0.915$) and assertiveness ($F=5.479$, $p=0.022$). The same patterns arise when I compare the persons in the companies in the South of Belgium (Wallonia) with all other companies. The p-values of the ANOVA are all non-significant with the exception of assertiveness.

distance (4.95 vs. 5.10) and future orientation (5.03 vs. 4.78) compared to my sample. Her scores are much higher for assertiveness (4.92) and more inclined towards individualism (3.37) which could be attributed to the student sampling of a business school. Contrary to my assumptions, that Poland might have undergone major shifts in the national culture scores due to the fall of communism, the opening of Eastern Europe, the Solidarność movement, upcoming privatisation and the membership in the European Union, Poland exhibits only very slight deviations for all five cultural dimensions. Thus, there seems to be no dramatic shifts in the cultural dimensions in Poland. The results for the GLOBE data sets provide confidence in the validity of the cultural data.

I used the GLOBE scores for each cultural dimension as theoretical indication to hypothesize the direction of the various performance evaluation and reward elements. A similar procedure for the rare occasion of retesting cultural scales can be found in O'Connor (1995). Based on the GLOBE scores for each cultural dimension, countries have been grouped to either low cultural level or high cultural level. I dichotomized the four countries into two classes, a low and a high group, to simplify interpretation and presentation of results and because of prior usage of this approach (DeCoster, Iselin & Gallucci, 2009; Iselin, Gallucci & DeCoster, 2013). Basically, the four dichotomous mean variables for each cultural dimension are attributed to the low and high groups based on a cut-off decision. I did not follow a mere mean nor median split of the data. Rather I applied the highest distance criterion between the four individual country scores to separate low from high level cultures. For instance, the highest distance for future orientation is between Belgium and Canada (distance = 0.75). This decision criterion works well for future orientation and power distance. For uncertainty avoidance and assertiveness two scores are very similar (distances: 0.49 and 0.47; 0.38 and 0.35), for individualism/collectivism all three scores are very similar (distance: 0.20, 0.22 and 0.17). For these dimensions I made the decision to allocate the two highest countries to high level and the two lowest countries to low level cultures.

There is heavy critique in recent editorials (Beckstead, 2012; Dawson & Weiss, 2012) and empirical examinations (DeCoster, Iselin & Gallucci, 2009; Iselin, Gallucci & DeCoster, 2013) on the practice of dichotomization of variables because "most causes and effects are continuous and not discrete" (Dawson & Weiss, 2012, p. 225) and thus dichotomization conceals the fine nuances in between. Negative consequences comprise loss of information, loss of effect size and loss of statistical power (Cohen, 1983; MacCallum et al., 2002). I want to follow good practice to provide reasoning for the use of dichotomization.[86] To encounter these threats I justify my approach because I can provide "clear evidence for the existence of distinct groups" (MacCallum et al., 2002, p. 38). First, "misclassification tends to be most extreme near the split" (Dawson & Weiss, 2012, p. 225) of the two groups. This means that the highest distance criterion I apply softens this statistical threat. To further support this point Shim and Steers (2012) stressed that a GLOBE score which is one-half a point above another score indicates 'relative strength'. The GLOBE project introduced a bandwidth to express true differentiation of cultural groups. The bandwidth is calculated by multiplying the standard error of the difference (SED) with a standardized normal difference (C). The normal distance is set to 1.96 and corresponds to the 95% confidence interval (Hanges, Dickson & Sipe, 2004, p. 219-221). The group distances I reached with my method were for three dimensions far above the 0.5 threshold and the bandwidth threshold, one time roughly equal and one time slightly below these thresholds.

	Uncertainty Avoidance	Future Orientation	Power Distance	Individualism /Collectivism	Assertiveness
SED	0.32	0.31	0.27	0.32	0.32
Bandwidth	0.63	0.61	0.53	0.63	0.63
Group distance	0.92	1.10	0.97	0.41	0.61

Table 22: Bandwidth and group distance of GLOBE scores

First, Table 23 shows highly significant differences (t-values) for all five dimensions between low and high level cultural groups. Second, the 25% and 75% percentile for the low and high level groups imply cut-off points that are clearly distinctive for uncertainty avoidance (<4.50 and >4.50), future orientation (<4.00 and > 4.25) and power distance (<4.50 and >4.50) and only show minor overlaps for collectivism (<4.25 and >4.00) and assertiveness (<4.25 and >3.75).

---

[86] 80% of studies do not provide any justification for the use of dichotomization (MacCallum et al., 2002).

	Uncertainty Avoidance		Future Orientation		Power Distance		Individualism /Collectivism		Assertiveness	
	Low	High	Low	High	Low	High	Low	High	Low	High
N	164	173	164	173	79	258	180	157	151	186
Mean	4.00	4.92	3.65	4.75	4.03	5.01	3.98	4.39	3.70	4.26
SD	0.70	0.71	0.75	0.78	0.68	0.85	0.64	0.72	0.69	0.66
Q1	3.50	4.50	3.25	4.25	3.50	4.50	3.50	4.00	3.25	3.75
Q3	4.50	5.25	4.00	5.25	4.50	5.50	4.25	5.00	4.25	4.75
T-value	11.949 ***		13.125 ***		9.333 ***		5.487 ***		7.577 ***	
Significance levels: *** p<0.001.										

Table 23: GLOBE scores for low and high level

Third, the dichotomization of the cultural values targets the national level whereas the management control practices cover the organizational level. Normal regression methods, which attribute the same cultural mean score in each country to each organization, would be simplistic. Hierarchical linear models, which analyze multi-level phenomena of cross-cultural research, require richer data sets with a rule of thumb of 20 cases for each level (Snijders, 2004).

The independent variables (four countries) are made categorical (low and high) for each cultural dimension in order to test group differences "in the mean of the dependent variable *[management control elements – note of the author]* for the two groups *[for each of the cultural dimensions – note of the author]* represented by the dichotomized independent variable" (MacCallum et al., 2002, p. 19). For each hypothesis the management control variables of the respective countries are consolidated based on the premise of either low or high cultural classification. For example, a hypothesis testing differences according to the cultural dimension of uncertainty avoidance leads to management control data of Germany and Belgium in the high level group and data of Canada and Poland in the low level group. The classification scheme of consolidating data of the four countries consequently changes for each cultural dimension (compare with Table 20 (p. 129) to see low and high level countries). Overall, I believe the GLOBE scores provide enough disparity to test the hypotheses based on the aggregation of low level and high level culture and their MCS data.

5.2   Multivariate analysis

The underlying research agenda used several ANOVAs of the various management control elements across the four countries, and the low and high cultural groups. ANOVAs are superior to normal t-tests if the assumption of homogeneity of variance is broken. In addition, the t-test and the ANOVA for two groups show the same results (Field, 2013).[87] The direction of the differences is hypothesized by theoretical thoughts based on the corresponding type of cultural dimensions and their respective scores (see Chapter 3.3, p. 72f.). I have derived specific hypotheses that are firmly ingrained in theory and are partly rooted in previous research.

Table 24 (p. 135) and Table 25 (p. 136) provide the figures of the hypotheses testing. For each hypothesis, means and standard deviations are shown for high and low level cultural data. The F-value and η^2 provide information on significance levels and effect sizes of the ANOVA. To provide an even richer picture of the results, the same type of information is also given for the four participating countries in Appendix 10 (p. 220f.).

For power distance the findings reveal the opposite picture of the stated hypotheses. The findings refute Hypothesis 1 ($p<0.01$), which proposed that performance evaluation would be used more for feedback purposes in low power distance cultures. In contrast to Hypothesis 2, high power distance cultures tend to base ($p<0.001$) the calculation of reward systems more towards lower levels.

Hypothesis 3 stated that performance evaluation would be used more for feedback purposes in high future-oriented cultures. The result confirmed the proposed direction, but it was only marginally significant ($p<0.1$). The frequency of performance evaluation, as stated in Hypothesis 4, was not different ($^{a)}$ $p=0.991$, $^{b)}$ $p=0.868$) for the cultural dimension of future orientation for both leadership and business performance. In fact, the mean scores were similar for both high and low levels. Hypothesis 5, which predicts that future orientation and non-financial performance indicators are positively related in low future-oriented cultures, whereas financial performance indicators are positively related in high future-oriented

---

[87]   Post-hoc tests in the two case (low vs. high level) scenarios are not performed.

cultures, is supported (p<0.01). Hypothesis 6 is not supported. Both low and high future-oriented cultures demonstrated an equal use of individual-oriented performance evaluation. Lending support to Hypothesis 7, a higher use of individual components was found in cultures with higher levels of future orientation (p<0.001). Hypothesis 8 predicted that reward systems with a performance orientation show higher scores in cultures with lower levels of future orientation; this was not found. Hypothesis 9 is confirmed. Multiple balanced scorecard perspectives were more prevalent in reward settings in cultures with higher levels of future orientation. Consistent with Hypothesis 10, the importance of rewards was found to be higher in low future-oriented cultures than in high future-oriented cultures (p<0.001).

	Culture	MCS item	High		Low		F	η^2
			Mean	SD	Mean	SD		
H1	PD	C5a	5.72	1.11	5.08	1.34	10.10 **	0.050
H2a	PD	D1c	2.95	0.60	2.03	0.18	175.47***	0.359
H2b	PD	D1c	2.79	0.60	1.61	0.51	67.15***	0.419
H3	FO	C5a	5.69	1.15	5.43	1.23	2.85 †	0.012
H4a	FO	C6	1.49	1.51	1.49	1.77	0.00	0.000
H4b	FO	C6	3.53	4.14	3.44	4.02	0.03	0.000
H5	FO	D1a+b	63.30	31.68	76.39	33.56	8.92**	0.039
H6	FO	C3e-g	4.96	1.10	4.90	1.04	0.19	0.001
H7	FO	D1a+b	25.11	30.30	7.94	20.20	25.29***	0.097
H8	FO	D1a+b	41.20	33.15	42.63	42.01	0.08	0.000
H9	FO	D1a	1.84	0.71	1.46	0.66	17.03***	0.072
H10	FO	D5b	4.85	1.40	5.67	1.05	26.77***	0.094
H11a	ASS	C6	1.49	1.57	1.50	1.70	0.00	0.000
H11b	ASS	C6	3.51	4.08	3.45	4.11	0.01	0.000
H12	ASS	C5a	5.69	1.18	5.43	1.20	2.85 †	0.012
H13	ASS	D1a+b	34.28	33.78	52.76	39.79	13.07***	0.059
H14	ASS	D3d-D3e	1.08	2.16	0.70	1.89	1.77	0.008

1) PD: power distance, FO: future orientation, ASS: assertiveness.
2) The possible range for mean scores is [1; 7] for H1, H3, H6, H10 and H12. For "C6" in H4 and H11, the figure states the yearly frequency, for D1a in H9 the range is [1; 4], for "D1a+b" in H5, H7, H8 and H13 the range is [0; 100], for "D1c" in H2 the range is [1; 4] (lower scores indicate more top level focus), and for "D3d-D3e" in H14 the range is [-6; 6].
3) For MCS items in Section D of the questionnaire, data is limited to all those organizations that use a rewarding scheme.
4) H2 was split (a, b) for the distinction of stand-alone company (a) vs. several SBUs (b).
5) H4 and H11 were split (a, b) for the distinction of leadership issues (a) and business performance (b).
6) According to Cohen (1988, p. 286-287) η^2 (eta squared) shows a small effect for values above 0.0099, a medium effect for values above 0.0588 and a large effect for values above 0.1379.
7) The homogeneity of variance is tested using Levene's test. If applicable, Welch's F is taken.
8) Significance levels: † p<0.10, * p<0.05, ** p<0.01, *** p<0.001.

Table 24: Means, SD, ANOVA, and effect size for high and low cultural levels (1)

	Culture	MCS item	High		Low		F	η^2
			Mean	SD	Mean	SD		
H15	IND/COLL	C3e-g	4.84	1.15	5.01	1.01	1.52	0.006
H16	IND/COLL	D1a+b	16.08	24.16	17.99	29.54	0.28	0.001
H17a	IND/COLL	D1c	2.81	0.50	2.66	0.74	1.73	0.012
H17b	IND/COLL	D1c	2.65	0.42	2.46	0.91	1.92	0.015
H18	IND/COLL	D3d-D3e	1.92	1.88	0.26	1.90	41.11***	0.157
H19	IND/COLL	D1a+b	64.39	30.71	72.61	34.38	3.31 †	0.015
H20	IND/COLL	D4a-c	5.28	1.00	5.27	1.10	0.01	0.000
H21	IND/COLL	D4d-f	4.91	1.51	5.21	1.23	2.65	0.012
H22	IND/COLL	D3b	2.67	1.99	4.37	2.14	35.35***	0.138
H23	IND/COLL	C5b	4.80	1.51	5.21	1.42	4.58*	0.019
H24	IND/COLL	D3a	3.78	1.89	4.05	2.21	1.00	0.004
H25a	IND/COLL	C6	1.94	2.30	1.17	0.72	10.29**	0.054
H25b	IND/COLL	C6	5.63	4.82	1.95	2.52	48.59***	0.198
H26	IND/COLL	D5b	5.07	1.29	5.29	1.35	1.58	0.007
H27	UA	D1a+b	25.11	30.30	7.94	20.20	25.29***	0.097
H28	UA	D1a+b	41.20	33.15	42.63	42.01	0.08	0.000
H29	UA	C3h	4.93	3.22	5.58	4.18	1.81	0.008
H30	UA	D1a	2.93	1.43	2.22	1.57	12.42***	0.053
H31	UA	D1a	1.84	0.71	1.46	0.66	17.03***	0.072
H32	UA	G2	2.65	1.41	2.17	1.20	7.61**	0.031
H33	UA	C4b-d	3.42	1.30	4.87	1.21	76.67***	0.244
H34	UA	D2+C4a	5.47	1.07	4.74	0.97	27.95***	0.112
H35a	UA	C6	1.49	1.51	1.49	1.77	0.00	0.000
H35b	UA	C6	3.53	4.14	3.44	4.02	0.03	0.000

1) IND/COLL: individualism/collectivism, UA: uncertainty avoidance.
2) The possible range for mean scores is [1; 7] for H15, H20-H24, H26, H33 and H34. For "C3h" in H29 and for "D1a" in H30 there is no theoretical upper limit, for D1a in H31 the range is [1; 4], for "C6" in H25 and H35 the figure states the yearly frequency, for "D1a+b" in H16, H19, H27 and H28 the range is [0; 100], for "D1c" in H17 the range is [1; 4] (lower scores indicate more top level focus), for "D3d-D3e" in H18 the range is [-6; 6], and for G2 in H32 the range is [0; 12].
3) For MCS items in Section D of the questionnaire, data is limited to all those organizations that use a rewarding scheme.
4) H17 was split (a, b) for the distinction of stand-alone company (a) vs. several SBUs (b).
5) H25 and H35 were split (a, b) for the distinction of leadership issues (a) and business performance (b).
6) According to Cohen (1988, p. 286-287) η^2 (eta squared) shows a small effect for values above 0.0099, a medium effect for values above 0.0588 and a large effect for values above 0.1379.
7) The homogeneity of variance is tested using Levene's test. If applicable, Welch's F is taken.
8) Significance levels: † p<0.10, * p<0.05, ** p<0.01, *** p<0.001.

Table 25: Means, SD, ANOVA, and effect size for high and low cultural levels (2)

The frequency of performance evaluation for both leadership and business performance based on the level of assertiveness, as stated in Hypothesis 11, was not significant. In fact, high and low levels exhibited similar scores. Hypothesis 12 stated that performance evaluation would be used more for feedback purposes in high assertive cultures. The results confirmed the proposed direction, but with only marginal significance ($p<0.1$). Hypothesis 13 predicted the performance orientation of reward systems would be higher in cultures with high assertiveness, but this practice was significantly ($p<0.001$) lower in these cultures. Hence, Hypothesis 13 had to be rejected. Since financial rewards were hypothesized to a higher degree in high assertiveness cultures, Hypothesis 14 receives no support.

Hypothesis 15 is not supported. While individualistic cultures demonstrated greater use of individual-oriented performance evaluation, the differences were not statistically significant ($p=0.220$). I observed similar scores for reward systems with individual components in individualistic and collectivistic cultures, which rejects Hypotheses 16. As predicted by Hypothesis 17, the calculation of reward systems is slightly orientated more towards a higher level in cultures with high individualism than in cultures with high collectivism. However, distinguishing the amount of SBUs (single entity vs. several SBUs), non-significant differences were found for stand-alone companies ($p=0.191$) and for several SBUs ($p=0.169$). The findings contradict Hypothesis 18, i.e. individualistic cultures use financial rewards to a higher degree than collectivistic cultures; the opposite picture holds ($p<0.001$). The mean scores for the financial rewards in high and low individualistic cultures indicate that in collectivistic cultures non-financial performance indicators will be preferred ($p<0.1$). Thus, Hypothesis 19 is supported. The relationship between the motivation and commitment purpose of financial and non-financial rewards, and the degree of individualism, led to the rejection of Hypotheses 20 and 21. While the motivation and commitment purpose of non-financial rewards in collectivistic cultures was marginally higher ($p=0.105$) than in individualistic cultures, the one for financial rewards was not significantly different ($p=0.933$). The present study showed that employees in collectivistic cultures depart from the equality norm and do not elicit a stronger use ($p<0.001$) of equality reward criteria (=sharing) than those in individualistic cultures. Thus, Hypothesis 22, which stated the opposite, has to be rejected. Testing cross-cultural differences for the use of performance evaluation for determining compensation (Hypothesis 23), I found a higher score for individualistic cultures ($p<0.05$). This finding lends credence to the hypothesis that performance evaluation will be used more for determining compensation in individualistic cultures than in collectivist cultures. Hypothesis 24 is not supported. Employees in individualistic cultures did not exhibit more customization in their performance-pay contracts ($p=0.319$). The extent of individualism had an impact on the frequency of performance evaluation for leadership

($p<0.01$) and business performance ($p<0.001$), but these findings reject Hypothesis 25 as collectivistic cultures tend to show a higher frequency. The contention that the importance of rewards will be higher in individualistic cultures was in the hypothesized direction of Hypothesis 26, but not significant ($p=0.211$).

The results suggest that there was a large difference between high and low level towards the extent of individual components and the level of uncertainty avoidance. This finding supports ($p<0.001$) the notion of Hypothesis 27, that reward systems with individual components will be more prevalent in cultures with higher levels of uncertainty avoidance. Hypothesis 28 predicted that reward systems with a performance orientation show higher scores in cultures with lower levels of uncertainty avoidance; this was not found ($p=0.778$). While multiple performance measures were more prevalent in performance evaluation settings in cultures with lower levels of uncertainty avoidance, the difference was not statistically significant ($p=0.180$); hence, Hypothesis 29 was not supported. Hypothesis 30 proposes that rewards will be based more on multiple performance measures in cultures with higher levels of uncertainty avoidance. The findings reveal this direction ($p<0.001$). Hence, Hypothesis 30 is supported. Hypothesis 31 shows a similar picture and is supported ($p<0.001$). Multiple balanced scorecard perspectives were more prevalent in reward settings in cultures with higher levels of uncertainty avoidance. Hypothesis 32 examined whether a balanced approach in executing different performance areas is followed less in cultures with higher levels of uncertainty avoidance. The results support Hypothesis 32 ($p<0.01$). Hypothesis 33 predicted that objective performance standards will be used more for performance evaluation in cultures with high uncertainty avoidance; this dimension had a significant effect ($p<0.001$), but the sign was opposite to the prediction. Hypothesis 33 has to be rejected. Hypothesis 34, which examined the relationships between the level of objectivity in performance evaluation and uncertainty avoidance, was supported ($p<0.001$). Objectivity occurred in cultures with higher uncertainty avoidance. The frequency of performance evaluation, as covered by Hypothesis 35, was not different for uncertainty avoidance and leadership ($p=0.991$), as well as for business performance ($p=0.868$). In fact, the mean scores were equal for both high and low levels.

In terms of effect sizes (η^2) and following the classification from Cohen (1988, p. 286-287) (small effect for values above 0.0099, medium effect for values above 0.0588 and large effect for values above 0.1379), the supported hypotheses exhibit a medium effect for Hypotheses 7,

9, 10, 27, 31 and 34 and a small effect for Hypotheses 3, 5, 12, 19, 23 and 32. The directional support indicated a small effect for Hypothesis 17a, b. The rejected hypotheses showed no effect, with the exception of Hypothesis 21, which exhibited a small effect. What is interesting to note is that the hypotheses, which were opposite to the prediction, showed six times a large effect for Hypotheses 2a, 2b, 18, 22, 25b and 33, and one time a medium effect for Hypothesis 13. Hypothesis 25a was close to a medium effect. Hypothesis 1 showed a small effect.

Overall, the results suggest that almost all performance evaluation and reward characteristics show significant differences for at least one cultural dimension.

5.3 Robustness tests

Cultural dimensions may not solely determine the researched management control practices. There are a variety of factors with the potential to influence performance evaluation and rewards practices translating to the fact that the revealed differences may stem from influences independent of culture. Or in other words, the relationship between management control practices and cultural dimensions may not be a 'true' relationship; the difference between low and high level data is rather driven by other variables, e.g. the ones stated as control variables in Chapter 4.4.3 (p. 104ff.).

I conduct several robustness checks to validate the cultural findings. My approach primarily follows the procedure from Jansen, Merchant and van der Stede (2009). I began the robustness checks by first investigating the differences of the control variables between the low and high manifestation of the cultural dimensions. This gives an indication of whether to include the control variables in further tests. Secondly, correlation tables for the MCS items and control variables provide the final selection for the analysis of covariates (ANCOVA). The ANCOVA includes further variables, i.e. the covariates, in the analysis of variances that may influence the dependent variables (i.e. the various MCS items) (Field, 2013). In particular, as outlined in Chapter 4.4.3 (p. 104ff.), I controlled for industry type, size (logarithm of sales, number of employees), internationalization, ownership structure, environmental uncertainty split to customer, supplier, competitor, technology, regulation and economic uncertainty, competition, flexibility of strategic ends and means, tenure, home country, as well as organizational cultural variables.

	Belgium		Canada		Germany		Poland		F-value
	Mean	SD	Mean	SD	Mean	SD	Mean	SD	
Sales (log)	2.16	0.52	2.77	0.40	2.21	0.62	1.88	0.87	24.81***
No. of employees	1,275	2,457	1,321	1,101	1,682	2,909	5,754	15,073	1.77
Industry type	1.46	0.61	1.13	0.34	1.56	0.66	1.58	0.76	11.63***
Ownership[a]	0.74	0.44	0.54	0.50	0.69	0.47	0.72	0.45	1.80
Ownership[b]	0.44	0.50	0.75	0.44	0.51	0.50	0.66	0.48	4.93**
Internationalization	5.46	6.57	17.23	30.48	5.67	11.73	7.32	17.57	2.55 †
Envir. uncert. - customer	3.64	1.16	3.99	0.70	3.96	1.42	3.90	0.83	1.16
Envir. uncert. - supplier	3.39	1.33	3.92	0.86	3.24	1.32	3.78	1.07	5.34**
Envir. uncert. - competitor	3.65	1.16	3.91	0.76	3.21	1.22	3.91	1.18	6.58***
Envir. uncert. - technology	3.53	1.24	3.90	0.86	3.11	1.15	3.32	0.94	7.61***
Envir. uncert. - regulation	4.03	1.31	4.03	0.76	3.85	1.57	4.25	1.26	0.87
Envir. uncert. - economic	5.33	0.91	3.88	0.88	4.63	1.44	4.73	1.22	21.99***
Intensity of competition	5.64	1.16	4.62	1.11	5.49	1.11	5.36	1.51	7.63***
Interval of strategic revision[c]	1.81	2.68	1.05	0.61	1.59	1.51	1.98	1.83	6.70***
Interval of strategic revision[d]	2.08	2.33	1.03	0.51	2.65	2.66	2.17	1.83	17.29***
Tenure	14.36	9.70	14.23	5.00	10.84	9.77	9.71	8.62	5.10**
Home country	0.80	0.40	0.85	0.36	0.83	0.38	0.74	0.44	0.65
Organizational culture:									
Uncertainty Avoidance	3.83	0.85	4.04	0.65	4.08	0.88	4.81	0.90	11.29***
Future Orientation	4.85	0.92	4.14	0.57	4.76	0.71	4.49	0.65	9.52***
Power Distance	3.63	0.76	3.82	0.53	3.64	0.77	3.93	0.84	1.73
Individualism/Collectivism	4.36	0.80	4.04	0.61	4.41	0.64	4.31	0.63	2.59 †
Assertiveness	3.82	0.59	3.95	0.62	3.82	0.48	4.06	0.49	2.02

[a] Investor-owned firm vs. remaining ones.
[b] Family-owned firms vs. remaining ones.
[c] Strategic ends.
[d] Strategic means/actions.
Significance levels: † p<0.10, * p<0.05, ** p<0.01, *** p<0.001.

Table 26: Variable definitions and descriptive statistics

Table 26 illustrates the descriptive statistics for the diverse control variables – institutional, organizational culture and demographic factors – of the four countries. The four-country comparison already shows many significant differences. Ten control variables are highly significant (p<0.001), three are significant (p<0.01), two are marginally significant (p=0.054 and p=0.059) and seven variables show no significant difference.

Chapter 5 – Results 141

	F-values for low and high level cultural characteristics'				
	Uncertainty Avoidance	Future Orientation	Power Distance	Individualism/ Collectivism	Assertiveness
Sales (log)	1.48	1.48	72.52***	19.06***	16.43***
No. of employees	3.23	3.23	4.59*	3.11	5.00*
Industry type	4.33*	4.33*	34.89***	1.87	12.30***
Ownership[a]	1.69	1.69	4.99*	2.56	1.05
Ownership[b]	12.91***	12.91***	9.70**	0.53	0.31
Internationalization	6.51*	6.51*	6.68*	2.21	4.66*
Envir. uncert. - customer	0.56	0.56	1.00	1.85	0.70
Envir. uncert. - supplier	14.15***	14.15***	10.80**	0.31	2.00
Envir. uncert. - competitor	14.62***	14.62***	8.39**	4.25*	4.95*
Envir. uncert. - technology	6.56*	6.56*	18.49***	0.02	14.38***
Envir. uncert. - regulation	1.84	1.84	0.02	1.68	0.04
Envir. uncert. - economic	12.93***	12.93***	38.40***	17.82***	0.18
Intensity of competition	12.38***	12.38***	21.61***	4.14*	3.99*
Interval of strategic revision[c]	0.51	0.51	17.93***	4.01*	1.86
Interval of strategic revision[d]	10.61**	10.61**	50.78***	0.10	12.00***
Tenure	0.01	0.01	7.79**	0.00	11.65***
Home country	0.20	0.20	0.63	1.49	0.29
Organizational culture:					
Uncertainty Avoidance	12.64***	12.64***	2.31	4.18*	12.90***
Future Orientation	18.78***	18.78***	18.32***	2.07	1.65
Power Distance	4.76*	4.76*	0.67	0.42	0.16
Individualism/Collectivism	4.05*	4.05*	7.34**	0.64	2.82
Assertiveness	5.32*	5.32*	0.34	0.77	0.17

[a] Investor-owned firm vs. remaining ones.
[b] Family-owned firms vs. remaining ones.
[c] Strategic ends.
[d] Strategic means/actions.
Significance levels: * p<0.05, ** p<0.01, *** p<0.001.

Table 27: F-values of control variables for low and high level cultural dimensions'

In order to show a more distinct analysis, Table 27 shows the analysis for the five cultural dimensions. For simplicity, it only depicts the F-values for the same control variables. The F-value is derived by testing group differences between low and high level cultural characteristics. More specifically, and tied to the hypotheses, the low level characteristics compared to the high level attributes show many differences across all five cultural dimensions. Only environmental uncertainties for customers and regulations, as well as country of origin, show no significant differences in any of the five cultural dimensions. The 19 other control variables show differences for at least one cultural dimension. The intensity of competition even differed across all five dimensions. This undermines the necessity to include these variables in further statistical analysis (for the sake of completeness environmental uncertainties for customers and regulations as well as home country are also included in the correlations).

The findings in Table 28 (p. 143) show significant correlations for all of the covariates on the various performance evaluation and reward items.[88] Many of the signs of the correlations are not surprising. To name a few covariates with many impacts, size (measured by sales) had a deeper impact on many items and corresponded with greater objectivity of performance standards, a lower performance evaluation frequency, more financial indicators, a top-level oriented reward calculation base, more equal sharing of rewards and a higher importance of rewards. The degree of internationalization goes along with more objectivity of performance standards, more financial indicators, less balanced performance measures, more customization of variable pay contracts and more equal sharing of rewards. Technological uncertainty is correlated with a higher number of performance measures, more objectivity of performance standards, but contrary to this, a lower objectivity of rewarding; further, a lower performance evaluation frequency, more customization of variable pay contracts, less balanced performance areas and a higher importance of rewards. The correlation between the intensity of competition and the number of performance measures for evaluation and rewarding, as well as the objectivity of performance evaluation and rewarding, is also significant. Competition is also connected to more non-egalitarian rewarding. A longer tenure is associated with a higher subjectivity of performance evaluation, less performance measures, less balanced performance measures, a higher percentage of financial indicators and more equality of rewards. As an example from the organizational cultural variables, a higher organizational future orientation is connected to more performance measures, more objectivity of performance evaluation and rewarding, less customization of variable pay contracts, less equality of rewards and a higher extent of financial rewards.

Table 28 (p. 143) and Table 29 (p. 144) show the selection of covariates that might influence or alter the tested hypotheses. Only significant correlations are tested in the ANCOVAs.

---

[88] For reasons of simplicity, the table only depicts significant correlations. Non-significant correlations, which range between -0.16 and 0.16, are not shown.

MCS items	1	2	3	4	5	6	7	8	9	10	11	12	13	14	15	16	17
PE subjectivity													-0.17**			0.18**	
Number of performance measures											0.15*		0.13*				
Objectivity of performance standards	0.21**				0.16*	0.18**		0.19**	0.13*	0.25**		-0.20**		-0.19**	-0.20**		
PE purpose (a)[a]											0.16*		0.17**				
PE purpose (b)[a]	0.22**	0.14*					0.14*			0.22**							
PE frequency (a)[b]													-0.14*	0.15*			
PE frequency (b)[b]	-0.22**									-0.16*		0.19**	0.13**	-0.16**		-0.15**	-0.14**
No. of performance measures																	
% of financial indicators	0.16*					0.19**						-0.14*		-0.16**		0.16**	
% of individual indicators														0.14**	0.17**		
% of profit indicators																0.15*	
Level of reward (a)[c]	-0.21*		0.28**											0.22**			
Level of reward (b)[c]	-0.40**		0.20*			-0.31**				-0.26*							
Objectivity of rewarding		0.24**							0.19**	-0.22**					0.14*		
Customization of contracts			-0.12*			0.19**				0.15*			0.19**				-0.17*
Equality of reward criteria	0.26**	-0.16*	-0.20**			0.16*							-0.25**	-0.20**		0.13*	
Extent of financial rewards	-0.18**											0.16*					
Purpose of financial rewards																	
Purpose of non-financial rewards	0.22**						0.23**	0.16*		0.18**							
Importance of rewards	0.21**	0.17*															
Balance of performance measures						-0.24**						0.15**				0.15*	-0.16**
Balance of performance areas										-0.26**		0.14*			0.17**		

1) Pairwise correlations (mainly Pearson, for industry type: Kendall's Tau; for ownership: point-biserial correlations).
2) Smallest N = 213 (data in reward section is limited to companies that use a rewarding scheme).
3) Only significant results are shown. Non-significant correlations range within [-0.16; 0.16].
4) Two-tail significance: * p≤0.05, ** p≤0.01.
5) Legend: (1) Sales (log), (2) Number of employees, (3) Industry type, (4) Ownership: Investor-owned firm vs. remaining, (5) Ownership: Family-owned firms vs. remaining, (6) Internationalization, (7) Environmental uncertainty – customer, (8) Environmental uncertainty – supplier, (9) Environmental uncertainty - competitor, (10) Environmental uncertainty - technology, (11) Environmental uncertainty - regulation, (12) Environmental uncertainty – economic, (13) Intensity of competition, (14) Interval of strategic revision, (15) Interval of strategic action revision, (16) Tenure, (17) Home country.
6) [a] PE purpose (a): Provide feedback, PE purpose (b): Determine compensation, [b] PE frequency (a): for leadership, PE frequency (b): for business performance, [c] Level of reward (a): stand-alone companies, Level of reward (b): companies with several SBUs.

Table 28: Correlations of covariates, performance evaluation and reward variables (1)

MCS items	Uncertainty Avoidance	Future Orientation	Power Distance	Individualism/ Collectivism	Assertiveness
PE subjectivity			-0.15*		-0.17*
Number of performance measures					
Objectivity of performance standards	0.17*				
PE purpose (a)[a]					
PE purpose (b)[a]					
PE frequency (a)[b]				0.17*	
PE frequency (b)[b]		0.17*	0.17*		
No. of performance measures					
% of financial indicators					
% of individual indicators					
% of profit indicators					
Level of reward (a)[c]	-0.24*	0.43**		0.30**	
Level of reward (b)[c]		0.29**			
Objectivity of rewarding		-0.20**			
Customization of contracts					
Equality of reward criteria	-0.23**	-0.21**		-0.20**	
Extent of financial rewards		0.16*			0.18*
Purpose of financial rewards					
Purpose of non-financial rewards					
Importance of rewards					
Balance of performance measures					
Balance of performance areas					

1) Pairwise correlations (Pearson).
2) Smallest N = 169 (only companies for which organizational cultural data is available).
3) Only significant results are shown. Non-significant correlations range within [-0.18; 0.17].
4) Two-tail significance: * p<0.05, ** p<0.01.
5) [a] PE purpose (a): Provide feedback. PE purpose (b): Determine compensation. [b] PE frequency (a): for leadership. PE frequency (b): for business performance. [c] Level of reward (a): stand-alone companies. Level of reward (b): companies with several SBUs.

Table 29: Correlations of covariates, performance evaluation and reward variables (2)

One important presumption of the ANCOVA is the homogeneity of the regression slopes. In graphical terms this refers to parallel regression slopes, i.e. the slopes for the relationship between the dependent variable and the covariate is similar for the categories of low and high level cultural data. To control for the homogeneity of the regression slopes, one has to monitor the p-value of the interaction term of the covariate and the dependent variable. If there is an interaction, the groups of the dependent variable differ significantly for the covariate (Field, 2013). D'Alonzo (2004), who suggests that a p-value of less than 0.10 reveals a significant interaction, illustrates a simple procedure to distinguish the groups of the covariate for which the dependent variable differs. In order to approach the problem of the homogeneity of the regression slopes D'Alonzo (2004) proposes a grouping of the covariate into a high and low category. I used the median split of the covariate variables for this differentiation.

I performed ANCOVAs for all MCS items with a significant ($p<0.05$) correlation between the covariate and the MCS items (all details are shown in Appendix 11, p. 222ff.; all details for heterogenous regression slopes are shown in Table 59 - Table 61, p. 232 - 234). All hypotheses, with the exception of Hypothesis 20, were affected. For all of these hypotheses, I first tested whether the covariates have a significant impact on the MCS item alone, and second, whether the result of the ANOVA was confounded by the covariate (i.e. changed significance levels). I identified 135 cases in total, 94 cases with homogenous regression slopes, and 41 cases with heterogeneous regression slopes. I performed additional tests for those 41 cases. Running these procedures for all possible confounding factors, I found a significant impact ($p<0.05$) of the diverse covariates in 67 of the 94 cases, and a marginal significant impact ($p<0.10$) for 13 further cases. The effect size of those 94 cases with homogenous regression slopes (a non-significant p-value for the covariate) was, for the overall majority, small. Only five cases exhibited a medium effect and only one case a large effect. This lends support that the covariates have an influence, but not a major one.

Only 23 of the 135 cases deserve specific attention for particular control variables. They either showed significant interaction effects, which translates to the fact that the hypotheses are valid only for specific characteristics of the covariates, or have to be rejected for specific characteristics of the covariates. In some cases the marginal significance of the cultural variable disappeared when controlling for the effect of the covariate. Hypotheses 3 and 12, which investigated the feedback purposes of performance evaluation, showed a drop in significance levels beyond the marginal significance cut-off point, when controlling for the intensity of competition. Hypothesis 5 was controlled for sales, ownership, degree of internationalization, economic uncertainty, frequency of strategic reviews and tenure. The ANCOVA showed that the hypothesis that high future-oriented cultures will use more non-financial performance indicators for rewarding is contrary to the prediction for small companies. Small companies use more financial criteria in high future oriented cultures. The hypothesis is also not confirmed for companies that are in a turbulent economic environment. Hypothesis 6, which was not significant in the ANOVA, can be confirmed in high competitive situations. This refers to the fact that individual-oriented performance evaluations more often take place in high future oriented cultures, when there is a high degree of competition. Hypothesis 14, which stated that rewards are more financially oriented in high assertive cultures, is confirmed in a less turbulent economic environment. Hypothesis 16, which ties individual components in reward setting to high individualistic cultures, can be confirmed for companies that frequently review their strategic actions. Hypothesis 17, which related the calculation criteria for reward systems to individualism, also showed significant interaction effects in the ANCOVA. For stand-alone companies the hypothesis is valid for manufacturing firms and is contrary for service firms. For firms with several SBUs the hypothesis can be confirmed for high sales' situations, but is contrary to the hypothesized direction for companies with low sales. Firms with low organizational future orientation showed the hypothesized effect. The cultural effect of Hypothesis 19, which tested whether financial rewards are based on financial performance indicators in individualistic cultures, is no longer significant when controlling for sales, degree of internationalization, economic uncertainty and frequency of strategic revision. Only non-family firms tend to use more financial indicators in individualistic cultures. Hypothesis 21, which sees the motivation and commitment purposes of non-financial rewards stronger in collectivistic cultures, is no longer marginally significant when controlling for sales. As stated in Hypothesis 23, the higher importance for individualistic cultures to determine the compensation in performance evaluation is no longer significant when controlling for sales. Hypothesis 24, which stated that employees in individualistic cultures will have more customization in their performance-pay contracts, is significant for firms with low organizational future orientation. Hypothesis 26 investigates the higher importance of rewards in individualistic cultures. The hypothesis finds support for firms with higher sales. Hypothesis 30, which bases rewards more on multiple performance measures in cultures with high levels of uncertainty avoidance, has to be rejected for the low tenure of the top management respondents. Additionally, Hypothesis 30 has to be rejected for firms with a high degree of organizational future orientation. Hypothesis 31, which sees multiple balanced scorecard perspectives as more prevalent in reward settings in cultures with higher levels of uncertainty avoidance, is not valid in economic turbulence and when there is a low tenure of the top management respondent. Hypothesis 32 postulated a lower propensity to adopt a balanced approach in executing different performance areas in cultures with higher levels of uncertainty avoidance. This is not valid in times of economic turbulence.

5.4 Summary of hypotheses

These robustness tests confirm the results presented in Table 24 and Table 25 (p. 135 – 136). Thus, culture has a significant impact by itself. Table 30 – Table 32 provide the final summary of the results. The tables structure the results according to the subcomponents and topics of the performance evaluation and rewarding sections (see Table 5 – Table 7, p. 102f.). The tables list whether the hypotheses have been significant or not, and whether the proposed directions have been confirmed or not in the statistical analyses. There are three possible outcomes. The combination "Yes" (sign.) / "Yes" (confirmed) gives credit to the support of the hypothesis. The combination "Yes" (sign.) / "No" (confirmed) indicates that the opposed direction of the hypothesis is supported. The combination "No" (sign.) / "No" (confirmed) expresses no support of the hypothesis.[89]

---

[89] The combination of "No" (sign.) / "Yes" (confirmed) is no valid alternative.

Hypotheses		Sign.	Confirmed
C3. Subjective evaluation			
H6 [N]	Individual-oriented performance evaluation will be preferred more in high future-oriented cultures than in low future-oriented cultures.	No	No
H15	Individual-oriented performance evaluation will be preferred more in individualistic cultures than in collectivist cultures, where collectivistic-oriented performance evaluation will be preferred.	No	No
C3. Number of performance measures			
H29 [N]	Multiple performance measures will be more prevalent in performance evaluation in cultures with higher levels of uncertainty avoidance.	No	No
C4. Performance standards objectivity			
H33	Objective performance standards will be used more for performance evaluation in cultures with high uncertainty avoidance.	Yes	No
C5. Performance evaluation purpose			
H1	Performance evaluation will be used more for feedback purposes in low power distance cultures.	Yes	No
H3	Performance evaluation will be used more for feedback purposes in high future-oriented cultures.	No	No
H12 [N]	Performance evaluation will be used more for feedback purposes in high assertive cultures.	No	No
H23	Performance evaluation will be used more for determining compensation in individualistic cultures than in collectivist cultures.	No	No
C6. Performance evaluation frequency			
H4 [N]	Performance evaluation will take place more frequently in high future-oriented cultures.	No	No
H11	Performance evaluation will take place more frequently in high assertive cultures.	No	No
H25	Performance evaluation will take place more frequently in individualistic cultures.	Yes	No
H35	Performance evaluation will take place more frequently in cultures with high uncertainty avoidance.	No	No
New hypotheses are indicated with [N]. Significance level: $p<0.01$.			

Table 30: Summary of hypotheses' testing on performance evaluation

Chapter 5 – Results

Hypotheses		Sign.	Confirmed
D1. Performance measures for rewarding (number)			
H30 [N]	Rewards will be based more on multiple performance measures in cultures with higher levels of uncertainty avoidance.	Yes	Yes
H9 [N]	Multiple balanced scorecard perspectives will be more prevalent in reward settings in cultures with higher levels of future orientation.	Yes	Yes
H31 [N]	Multiple balanced scorecard perspectives will be more prevalent in reward settings in cultures with higher levels of uncertainty avoidance.	Yes	Yes
D1. Performance measures for rewarding (components)			
H5 [N]	In high future-oriented cultures rewards will be based more on non-financial performance indicators than in low future-oriented cultures, where financial performance indicators will be preferred.	Yes	Yes
H19 [N]	In individualistic cultures financial rewards will be based more on financial performance indicators than in collectivistic cultures, where non-financial performance indicators will be preferred.	No	No
H7 [N]	Reward systems with individual components will be more prevalent in cultures with higher levels of future orientation.	Yes	Yes
H16	Reward systems with individual components will be more prevalent in cultures with high individualism than in cultures with high collectivism.	No	No
H27	Reward systems with individual components will be more prevalent in cultures with higher levels of uncertainty avoidance.	Yes	Yes
H8 [N]	Reward systems with a performance orientation will be more prevalent in cultures with lower levels of future orientation.	No	No
H13	Reward systems with a performance orientation will be more prevalent in cultures with high assertiveness.	Yes	No
H28	Reward systems with a performance orientation will be more prevalent in cultures with lower levels of uncertainty avoidance.	No	No
D1. Performance measures for rewarding (level)			
H2 [N]	The calculation of reward systems is orientated more towards a higher hierarchical level in cultures with high power distance, than in cultures with low power distance.	Yes	No
H17 [N]	The calculation of reward systems is orientated more towards a higher hierarchical level in cultures with high individualism than in cultures with high collectivism.	No	No
D2. Performance evaluation and rewarding objectivity			
H34	Performance evaluation and compensation schemes used in organizations would be, on average, more objective in cultures with high uncertainty avoidance than in cultures with low uncertainty avoidance.	Yes	Yes
D3. Customization of contracts			
H24 [N]	Employees in individualistic cultures will have more customization in their performance-pay contracts than employees in collectivistic cultures.	No	No
D3. Equality reward criteria			
H22	Employees in collectivistic cultures will have more equal reward criteria (=sharing) than those in individualistic cultures.	Yes	No
New hypotheses are indicated with [N]. Significance level: p<0.01.			

Table 31: Summary of hypotheses' testing on rewards (1)

Hypotheses	Sign.	Confirmed
D3. Rewarding nature		
H14 In high assertive cultures financial rewards will be used more than in low assertive cultures, where non-financial rewards will be preferred.	No	No
H18 In individualistic cultures financial rewards will be used more than in collectivistic cultures, where non-financial rewards will be preferred.	Yes	No
D4. Rewarding purpose		
H20 [N] In individualistic cultures the motivation and commitment purpose of financial rewards will be higher than in collectivistic cultures.	No	No
H21 [N] In collectivistic cultures the motivation and commitment purpose of non-financial rewards will be higher than in individualistic cultures.	No	No
D5. Rewarding importance		
H10 [N] In low future-oriented cultures the importance of rewards will be higher than in high future-oriented cultures.	Yes	Yes
H26 [N] In individualistic cultures the importance of rewards will be higher than in collectivistic cultures.	No	No
G2. Balance of performance areas		
H32 [N] The propensity to adopt a balanced approach in executing different performance areas is less prevalent in cultures with higher levels of uncertainty avoidance.	Yes	Yes
New hypotheses are indicated with [N]. Significance level: p<0.01.		

Table 32: Summary of hypotheses' testing on rewards (2)

6 Discussion and conclusion

6.1 Discussion of results

A review of the hypotheses on performance evaluation and rewards reveals an interesting picture of the proposed predictions. Overall, the most crucial finding is that a variety of differences are apparent in the practice of performance evaluation and reward systems. Thus, national culture has an influence on these MCS items, albeit the hypothesized differences are in the expected direction in less than half of the cases. In total, 35 hypotheses were tested.[90] As a restriction, not all hypotheses could be confirmed in the proposed direction. After controlling for the covariates, nine hypotheses were significant ($p<0.01$) and in the proposed direction (Hypotheses 5, 7, 9, 10, 27, 30, 31, 32 and 34), two hypotheses were marginally significant (Hypothesis 3 and 12), and 17 hypotheses found no support. Seven hypotheses were significant ($p<0.01$) and contrary to the initial thoughts (Hypotheses 1, 2, 13, 18, 22, 25, and 33).

My findings indicate that for the majority of the MCS items (performance standards objectivity; purpose and frequency of performance evaluation; number, components and level of performance measures for rewarding; performance evaluation and rewarding objectivity; equity, nature and importance of rewarding; balance of performance areas) at least one cultural dimension has a significant influence. Three areas of MCS items showed no difference for the cultural dimensions under investigation (subjective evaluation; number of performance measures; purpose of rewarding); therefore, the overall pattern is not clear-cut. There are many performance measures, performance evaluation and reward instruments for which culture matters, but, for a large part, are contrary to the hypothesized directions. With respect to the hypotheses tested for the first time, I reach both expected and contrary outcomes. The thesis confirms the findings of previous investigations and theoretical deductions for those hypotheses tested for the first time. My findings shed new light on hypotheses in the area of future orientation. High future-oriented cultures relied more on non-financial performance indicators (Hypothesis 5) and individual components (Hypothesis 7) in

---

[90] Six of the hypotheses had slight variations, but showed a similar picture in each case.

their reward scheme. High future-oriented cultures use a balanced approach in reward settings (Hypothesis 9) and also de-emphasize the importance of rewards (Hypothesis 10). However, I also obtained conflicting results with earlier studies and opposing findings for some newly derived hypotheses.

I explored cultural differences among organizations in their respective control practices, in particular in performance evaluation and reward schemes. The results provide strong evidence that culture matters. The fact that I found many statistically significant findings for previously untested hypotheses is encouraging. In the following, I will provide a discussion and comparison to former research for each of the replicated control instruments. I will also provide a discussion for the newly derived hypotheses. I would like to follow Bromwich's (2014, p. 3) advice for the discussion that "not too much should be claimed in the conclusions. Any generalisations from the results need to be justified".

Number of performance measures: I predicted that the number performance measures will be more prevalent in performance evaluation in cultures with higher levels of uncertainty avoidance. Hypothesis 29 found no support. A possible explanation might be found in an effect for the superiors. The argument that a broader footing of performance measures decreases risk and unpredictability, for those being evaluated and rewarded, could be counterbalanced by the increase in risk and unpredictability for those doing the evaluation. The choice to include many measures in the performance evaluation increases complexity for the managers. Thus, they might use fewer performance measures as criteria to hold subordinates accountable.

Subjective evaluation/performance standards objectivity: I found no cultural influence on the subjectivity of the evaluation style (Hypotheses 6 and 15), but did on the level of objectivity (Hypothesis 33). I found the opposite for the hypothesized objective standards in performance evaluation settings for cultures with high uncertainty avoidance (Hypothesis 33). I found objective performance standards in cultures with low uncertainty avoidance. A possible answer could be as follows: a cultural influence on the level of subjectivity in performance evaluation and rewarding arises for procedures (tested for objectivity), but not for elements (tested for subjectivity). The degree of subjective evaluation in the form of personalized achievements and individual effort is executed more uniformly across cultures. In terms of elements, all countries place more emphasis on financial measures in performance evaluation compared to subjective evaluation (three companies even show a significant higher use). Hence, the element 'subjective evaluation' could be of minor importance. On the other hand, subjective performance standards in procedural terms will be used more for performance evaluation in cultures with high uncertainty avoidance. In case of high uncertainty avoidance, managers might want to maintain a certain level of manoeuvrability in their assessment of subordinates' performance. That is why they could employ fewer objective criteria in performance evaluation.

My findings confirm prior research with regard to subjective evaluation in individualistic and collectivistic cultures (Hypothesis 15). Although Chow, Kato and Shields (1994) expected a preference for subjective evaluation elements in high collectivistic cultures – I provided arguments for those elements in high individualistic cultures – they also found no support. My findings complement prior research for performance standards objectivity in high uncertainty avoidance cultures (Hypothesis 33). Chow, Kato and Shields (1994) and Merchant, Chow and Wu (1995) expected a preference for subjective standards in high uncertainty avoidance cultures. Although they did not find such support, I could confirm their conjecture.

Performance evaluation purpose: Contrary to the findings of Morrison, Chen and Salgado (2004), who reported lower feedback seeking behaviour of new employees in high power distance cultures, and opposed to the hypothesized differences for the performance evaluation purposes, I found only support for the higher feedback purpose in high power distance cultures. De Luque and Sommer (2000) mentioned that the cultural context matters in the way feedback is obtained. In addition to propositions about feedback-seeking behaviour, they illustrated arguments on how feedback is given (e.g. individual vs. group-based, top-down vs. interactive, indirect vs. direct). Compared to the results of Morrison, Chen and Salgado (2004), feedback seeking behaviour and feedback provision is apparently different. This is not surprising since the roles in performance evaluation are clear-cut between supervisors and subordinates. Differences in the act of feedback provision, which I did not cover in my analysis, could be a reason why the two purposes under investigation (provision of feedback on individual strengths and weaknesses for learning and development issues, determination of compensation) show a cultural effect for the feedback purpose for power distance only. I found that feedback is more often conveyed in high power distance cultures. I offer the following explanation: although there is an easier interaction between hierarchy levels in low power distance cultures, feedback is an area with the potential for conflict. Thus, feedback is more easily transported when there is a clear-cut hierarchy gap. Additionally, the sensitive issue of feedback provision to address learning potentials cannot be advocated in a comprehensive way when there is a very egalitarian relationship between supervisors and subordinates. Thus, a higher power distance could facilitate feedback.

Prior research indicated the influence of culture on the purpose of performance evaluation. Peretz and Fried (2012) found a positive relationship between future orientation and an organizational development purpose of performance evaluation. I did only find a marginal significant effect for a higher feedback purpose in future-oriented cultures (Hypothesis 3). Chiang and Birtch (2010) found that performance evaluation is used for evaluative feedback (short-term perspective) in individualistic cultures to a higher degree (Hypothesis 23). Chiang and Birtch (2010) found a negative relationship between power distance and evaluative feedback (e.g. low power distance favoured training and development) (Hypothesis 1). The short-term perspective is used for determining compensation, whereas in contrast the long-term perspective fosters learning and development. After controlling for sales, I did not find a significant impact on the short-term perspective of performance evaluation in individualistic cultures (Hypothesis 23), although the direction of the effect is sustained. Looking from the angle of power distance, performance evaluation was used for feedback purposes to a higher degree in high power distance cultures (Hypothesis 1). This is in contrast to the finding of Chiang and Birtch (2010).

Performance evaluation frequency: My findings complement the prior research of Vance et al. (1992). They found significant differences with regard to the frequency of feedback. However, they did not propose any direction. Previous research (Chiang & Birtch, 2010) has noted that performance evaluation will take place more frequently in high assertive (Hypothesis 11) and individualistic cultures (Hypothesis 25), and cultures with high uncertainty avoidance (Hypothesis 35). My results for the cultural dimension of individualism/collectivism indicate that performance evaluation occurs more often in collectivistic cultures. Collectivistic cultures meet much more frequently in my investigation. Hence, the frequency of performance evaluation (Hypothesis 25) is in the opposite direction as found by Chiang and Birtch (2010).

The two other cultural dimensions seem not to affect feedback frequency. I want to examine three explanations. First, Chiang and Birtch (2010) provided a possible explanation by stressing the different strategic priorities of firms. According to them, organizations that pursue strategic priorities such as service quality convey more frequent feedback. I tested this proposition, but found a highly non-significant relationship in my sample. A further explanation might be found in the higher need for social interaction in collective-oriented cultures, which goes along with a higher frequency of feedback (Gelfand et al., 2004). More frequent feedback enables "supervisors and sub-ordinates to interact, exchange ideas, and discuss performance expectations" (Chiang & Birtch, 2010, p. 1384-1385) to a greater extent. Despite potential areas of conflict between subordinates and supervisors, employees in cultures with a higher collective manifestation want to express their ongoing commitment towards the firm and in return receive feedback about their actions in a more timely fashion. The greater interaction element is more feasible with more frequent feedback.

Performance measures for rewarding (number): The findings presented appear to match the hypotheses reasonably well. I expected that firms rely on multiple performance measures in their reward scheme in cultures with higher levels of uncertainty avoidance to reduce complexity and uncertainty from the managerial point of view (Hypothesis 30). I also expected that multiple balanced scorecard perspectives are more prevalent in reward settings in cultures with higher levels of future orientation (Hypothesis 9) and uncertainty avoidance (Hypothesis 31). A stronger appearance of BSC criteria in the rewarding scheme would indicate future-oriented behaviour and a broader footing of performance measures decreases risk and unpredictability for the one being evaluated and rewarded. I found support for all three hypotheses.

Performance measures for rewarding (components): My findings shed new light on hypotheses in the area of future orientation. High future-oriented cultures relied more on non-financial performance indicators (Hypothesis 5). The extent of financial vs. non-financial performance indicators is not corrobated for collectivism (Hypothesis 19). Merchant et al. (2011) showed significant differences with regard to financial and non-financial performance indicators between China and the US and, correspondingly, a lower use of performance-dependent rewards.

Additionally, reward systems with individual components are more prevalent in cultures with higher levels of future orientation (Hypothesis 7) and uncertainty avoidance (Hypothesis 27). I found no relationship to collectivism. My findings support prior research in the area of individual components in reward schemes. Contrary to the findings of Schuler and Rogovsky (1998), but consistent to my inferences, I found individual components in reward schemes more prevalent in cultures with higher levels of uncertainty avoidance (Hypothesis 27). Previous research has noted that reward systems with individual components will show a preference (Chiang & Birtch, 2005; 2007) or be more prevalent (Schuler & Rogovsky, 1998) in cultures with high individualism (Hypothesis 16). In contrast to this, Awasthi, Chow and Wu (1998) showed a lower preference for team-based performance measures of Chinese students compared to US students. This finding was counterintuitive to the collectivistic culture of the Chinese. The authors attributed the behaviour of the US subject to deliberately counterbalance their individualistic cultural setting. US students wanted to encourage teamwork among their fellow students. Chow, Kato and Shields (1994) found Japanese students to rely more on team-based rewards though the differences for rewards connected to team performance among Japanese and US students were not significant. My findings are positioned in between. I could not find any differences in the amount of individual-based performance measures in reward contracts. I want to offer some possible interpretations. I have no information to what extent the individual subordinates' reward settings implicitly comprise teamwork settings. Individual-based performance measures will certainly depend on other organizational members work as well. The findings of Schuler and Rogovsky (1998) concentrated only on a small industry segment, i.e. consultancy-based survey data from 18 countries, which affects generalizations as well.

Despite differences in the reward practices on non-financial and individual indicators, performance-oriented indicators did not differ (Hypothesis 8). Previous research has noted that reward systems with a performance orientation will show a preference (Chiang & Birtch, 2005; 2006; 2007) or will be more prevalent (Schuler & Rogovsky, 1998) in cultures with lower levels of uncertainty avoidance (Hypothesis 28). However, Chow, Shields and Wu (1999) found no differences for the perceived design of performance oriented financial rewards for Taiwanese companies with foreign ownership. I found no such relationship for future orientation and uncertainty avoidance too. I even found the opposite of the hypothesized direction for reward systems with a performance orientation in assertive cultures. I found a stark contrast to the findings of Chiang and Birtch (2005) with respect to reward systems and performance orientation based on the level of assertiveness (Hypothesis 13). While Chiang and Birtch (2005) found evidence for a preference of performance-based reward system in high assertive cultures, I found that the practices were more prevalent in cultures with low assertiveness. A possible answer could be attributed to the reference of masculinity instead of assertiveness in the paper of Chiang and Birtch (2005). But the GLOBE project clearly attributes the dimension of assertiveness to the former masculinity/femininity dimension of Hofstede, which was also acknowledged from Hofstede (2006). A different explanation relates to fundamental differences between the studies of Chiang and Birtch and mine. The differences pertain to the distinction of practices and preferences. The scholars reported on reward type preferences and asked for the desired policies. In contrast to this, I inquired about practices. I expect preferences and practices to differ, which would explain the opposite findings in my results. Chow, Shields and Wu (1999) reported large differences between practices and preferences for a larger set of management controls.

Performance measures for rewarding (level): Opposed to the hypothesis I found that the calculation of reward systems is orientated more towards a lower hierarchical level in cultures with high power distance (Hypothesis 2). This surprising finding invites explanation. Since participation and delegation of authority is lower in high power distance cultures, managers in those cultures might want to bridge the gap towards their employees. Thus, they could base the calculation of reward systems more towards a lower hierarchical level in cultures with high power distance. Second, managers in high power distance cultures are aware of the power concentration and therefore align the reward level of their subordinates more towards a lower level (e.g. business unit).

Performance evaluation and rewarding objectivity: My findings support prior research in the area of objectivity of rewards. In line with the findings of Jansen, Merchant and van der Stede (2009), uncertainty avoidance is positively related to the use of objective standards in reward schemes (Hypothesis 34). Jansen, Merchant and van der Stede (2009) used a managerial sample of Dutch car dealerships and compared their findings to a US-based study by Gibbs et al. (2004). However, my findings contradict the findings of Merchant et al. (2011). They provided an extension of the study from Jansen, Merchant and van der Stede (2009) and extended the US and Dutch data by a Chinese set-up. Since they found the highest discretionary criteria for China, which has the highest uncertainty avoidance score of the three cultures according to GLOBE, subjectivity is associated with high uncertainty avoidance in their sample. They provided reasoning that the high Chinese score for subjective evaluation can be attributed to the less developed performance evaluation scheme. One has to remark that these three studies narrowly focused on a small industry segment with very different incentive structures. Thus, my findings partly corroborate previous research and enhance the generalizability for the topic objectivity of rewards.

Customization of rewards: As a surprising finding, there is no difference in the customization of performance-pay contracts between individualistic and collectivistic cultures. Possibly, the contracts are country-specific, tailored to legal requirements, without close influence from national culture. Choi (1994) illustrated differences in contract enforcement across cultures. More specifically, Huang (2013, p. 836) mentioned that "a collective-oriented culture, which (in contrast to an individualistic culture) seems inherently prone to the usage of relational contracts" would underline customization behaviour. A second reason targets a more nuanced view on customization. Germany, as a representative of an individual culture, exhibits the lowest customization (see Appendix 10, p. 220f.) of all countries. A reason could be the long lasting tradition of coordinated tariff wages in Germany (Alda, Bellmann & Gartner, 2008).

Equality reward criteria: As a quite surprising finding, employees have less equal reward criteria (=sharing) in collectivistic cultures than employees in individualistic cultures (Hypothesis 22). My findings, which indicate that employees in individualistic cultures share rewards more equally, have also to be contrasted to the findings of Fischer (2004) and Giacobbe-Miller, Miller and Zhang (2003). In contrast to Fischer (2004), who compared non-managerial employees in Germany and the UK, I found sizeable difference for an equal sharing of rewards. In contrast to Giacobbe-Miller, Miller and Zhang (2003), who found collectivistic cultures to be more equal than individualistic cultures in the treatment of equality, I found the opposite.

I want to offer a possible methodological explanation. The question "to what extent are rewards shared evenly to subordinates" could be simplified since it does not concretize two components of rewards. Rewards can be stated in absolute amounts which are independent of individual salaries and in relative terms which are dependent on individual salaries. Above, the question offers no answer to display the non-egalitarian character across different subordinates (e.g. department heads). This simplification could have altered the response behaviour.

Rewarding nature: I found that collective cultures employ more financial rewards (Hypothesis 18). My findings complement previous research by Vance et al. (1992). They found significant differences in terms of the nature of rewarding. However, they did not propose any direction. Whereas Chiang and Birtch (2005) found mixed results for the preference in the degree of financial rewards in individualistic cultures, I found that collectivistic cultures rely more on financial rewards. I found no difference for the use of financial rewards for the degree of assertiveness (Hypothesis 14). This finding is inconsistent to prior research. Chiang and Birtch (2012) found a financial rewards' orientation in masculine cultures and higher non-financial rewards in feminine cultures. Two possible explanations occur to me: first, I have not measured financial rewards in absolute terms. I concentrated on the relative amount compared to non-financial rewards. The absolute amount of financial rewards in individualistic and assertive cultures could still outweigh the one in collectivistic and non-assertive cultures. Second, the different finding compared to Chiang and Birtch (2005) could also be explained by the difference between preferences and practices.

Rewarding purpose: I found no influence of cultural factors for the rewarding purposes under investigation (Hypotheses 20 and 21). The purposes to commit, motivate and direct subordinates' attention by means of either financial or non-financial rewards seem to be universally dealt with in different cultures.

Rewarding importance: Whereas the importance of rewards was higher in individualistic cultures than in collectivistic cultures the difference was not significant (Hypothesis 26). Apparently, the appetite for financial rewards and short-term thinking is not so much accentuated in individualistic cultures. Rewarding importance is rather tied to the future-oriented dimension. As hypothesized in this study, low future-oriented cultures value the importance of rewards to a higher degree (Hypothesis 10).

Balance of performance areas: The findings presented appear to match the hypotheses that cultures with higher levels of uncertainty avoidance have a lower propensity to adopt a balanced approach in executing different performance areas reasonably well.

Control variables: The findings of the ANCOVA mainly confirm that the significant differences in the ANOVA are not merely attributable to the control variables but to the cultural dimensions. No control variable affected the MCS items to a larger extent. There are only some cases in which the covariates affect my results of the cross-cultural differences. Economic turbulence might be a variable that has a larger impact. High turbulence in the economic conditions affects Hypotheses 5, 31 and 32, and offsets the imbalance of performance indicators for rewarding. Economic turbulence has far-reaching implications.

Firms are faced with declining sales and environmental instability. This could lead to a concentration process that is also reflected in reward systems. Tenure might be another variable. A low tenure offsets multiple performance measures (Hypothesis 30) and BSC perspectives (Hypothesis 31) for rewarding. Lower tenure might exhibit a balanced use since it requires knowledge about the right balance of performance measures. Acquiring this knowledge requires some time. However, the ANCOVA provides assurance as to the robustness of my cultural findings. With one exception (Hypothesis 23) the findings of testing the hypotheses remained stable when controlling for confounding factors. Thus, culture has a significant impact by itself.

6.2 Contributions to theory and former research

In conclusion, I have addressed the relevance and necessity to investigate MCS from a cross-cultural perspective. Fast changing business surroundings and increasing international activities require a better understanding of the design and use of MCS across various countries and cultures. There were various calls to study cross-cultural MCS. The broad-based literature review for performance measurement, performance evaluation and rewards over a 30-year period revealed only a truly astonishing low number of articles per year. Thus, the literature of management, accounting and organizations has paid little empirical attention to the role of culture on MCS. Researchers in the management control area are just beginning to recognize that culture matters. The findings of previous cross-cultural studies suggest that researching MCS from the traditional viewpoint restricted to one-country settings needs to encompass a broader cross-cultural view. More research of cross-cultural phenomena is needed. Another lesson of the literature review is that researchers should aim at qualitatively improving their cross-cultural research.

The aim of this thesis was to explore the question of whether there are differences among organizations across different cultures in their respective MCS, in particular in performance measurement, performance evaluation and reward schemes. In combining these control elements, the study reinforces a broader view of the cross-cultural MCS topic. I addressed several MCS characteristics at a time, unlike most previous research. In particular, I believe this study contributes to the extant literature on cross-cultural differences. This thesis, to the best of my knowledge, is the first to highlight such cultural differences for a broader set of characteristics of performance evaluation and rewards in one study.

I showed variations in management control elements based on cultural characteristics. From an institutional point of view I stated that firms within an institutional field will exhibit a common approach in setting up management control elements. I explained that the new institutionalism sets the boundaries of the organizational field at national borders. I demonstrated through various results that the institutional boundary can be extended to the cultural manifestations of low and high context.

The quality of the research relies heavily on a variety of conditions within and outside the control of the researchers, but at least orientates itself on the weakest part of the whole survey process (van der Stede, Young & Chen, 2005). The cross-cultural work brings along barriers and specific challenges. To address these, we[91] generally followed the recommendations from the checklist provided by Hult et al. (2008) and encountered specific methodological challenges raised by Cascio (2012). We relied on existing and well-tested scales for the GLOBE construct. We addressed unidimensionality of the constructs in the MCS questionnaire by means of explorative factor analysis. We ensured linguistic equivalence through a translation and back-translation process for the MCS questionnaire. We followed the same approach in sampling and data collection, secured honest and reliable answers in the personal interview setting and protected respondent anonymity. We separated measurement of dependent and independent variables. We undertook further remedies to minimize measurement error.

One of the major methodological strengths of the study is the generalizability of the results beyond a particular organization or a narrow industry focus. In one quarter of the previous cross-cultural studies, data were almost exclusively collected in only one country. These studies often focused on subsidiaries of foreign firms in the host country, or merely compared their one-country findings with another study. The quality and authenticity of this data collection method is certainly questionable. To achieve sample equivalence in a cross-cultural study is a further important methodological step and can be achieved by using random samples (Tsui, Nifadkar & Ou, 2007). Since my research setting followed a stratified random sampling approach in all four countries and thus targeted a very broad industry background

---

[91] The method section deals with many steps that have been agreed within the project group or that arose out of collective efforts. That is why I often use the collective 'we'.

spanning the whole spectrum of industries over manufacturing, services and trade firms, I strongly believe that my conclusions are generalizable. I used companies that truly differ in terms of organizational boundaries, but are at the same time representative of their country. Next, the target respondents were exclusively from the top management level, often CEOs or CFOs. These senior executives are well aware of the issues of investigation. Another methodological strength of the thesis is the independence of the data sources of management control variables and cultural items. A top management member has answered the MCS questionnaire, whereas the answers for the cultural data have been generated from different employees within the same organization. The approach to have different respondents for dependent and independent variables facilitates high validity.

The theoretical foundations are grounded in the cultural framework of the GLOBE study. In the past, the theoretical underpinning was rarely addressed explicitly. More than half of the studies presented a "culture theory" for their subject matter. These studies relied on the national culture construct as the major explanation for the theoretical underpinning. The quotation by Harrison (1992, p. 12) exemplifies this: "This paper has drawn on Hofstede's (1980) dimensions of culture as a theoretical framework within which the cross-national or cross-cultural generalizability of research results in MAS design may be examined". My study also makes a contribution to theory by accompanying the cultural explanations by institutional, stakeholder and contingency thoughts. In so doing, my thesis delivers an additional contribution. First, I clarify additional underlying theoretical conditions that facilitate cross-cultural explanations. Prior literature did not necessarily take an explanation besides merely stating the cultural framework. I identify three theories: the contingency-based approach, new institutionalism and stakeholder theory, which provide a sound grounding for cultural thoughts. I also highlight several contingency factors that might affect organizational control practices. Jansen, Merchant and van der Stede (2009, p. 82) suggested to modify individual-related theories, explicitly agency thoughts, "to make them situationally contingent". This deliberation is worthwhile since I presented many findings that national culture matters for a variety of management control elements. I am far from neglecting the validity of these theories. In fact I want to raise the awareness that organizational and national effects superimpose these individual-related theories.

The study provides empirical evidence that, as theory and cultural acumen predicted, the five cultural dimensions are related to the design and use of MCS. In particular, my study contributes to the literature by extending our cultural understanding of performance evaluation and rewards. A major contribution relates to the methods used for measuring culture. Despite some findings of the interplay between MCS and national culture, the existing literature has not systematically conceptualized nor empirically studied these links with the GLOBE framework. I did not follow the tradition of many researchers in using the Hofstede model. To analyze cross-cultural effects, this piece of work built upon the GLOBE study (House et al., 2004). I emphasized that GLOBE is the most recent (Drogendijk & Holm, 2012) and most appropriate culture-specific research construct for our analysis to explain national differences for management control elements. GLOBE builds on Hofstede, and tackles many of the weaknesses (Chui & Kwok, 2009; Scandura & Dorfman, 2004) addressed to the influential Dutch researcher. The five cultural dimensions of GLOBE show a more fine-grained analysis of the cultural influence on MCS. In employing GLOBE, I followed the admonitory assertion to use other cultural models to capture a fuller cultural understanding (Chow, Shields & Wu, 1999). Boyacigiller et al. (2004, p. 111) accentuated that the GLOBE project offers "one important step" in widening the toolbox of methods used. As there is evidence for change in the national culture scores, the collection of up-to-date cultural data encounters the risk of artefacts. The frequent call to directly measure the cultural dimensions gives more credibility to the appropriateness of the cultural values. I went beyond using culture dummies (e.g. scores from the original GLOBE study) and thus provide more specification. Adopting GLOBE's typology still allows me to compare my results with prior research, as the major understanding of the cultural dimensions is similar to the one from Hofstede, which most prior research builds upon. A novelty was the inclusion of a culture from Eastern Europe as well as the new data collection for Belgium. My findings also offer new insights into new cultural factors (future orientation) that have not been taken to explain cross-cultural differences. Other cultures could benefit from this study. Based on original GLOBE scores they could place themselves into either a high or low cultural level.

I extended the scope of investigation and included many possible confounding factors that have not been rigorously carried out in previous research. My finding of significant effects for institutional, organizational and demographic covariates has several consequences for cross-cultural research. First, I provided evidence that these factors matter. Institutional variables might help to explain why former researchers found both significant and non-significant cultural differences for a specific dependent variable (e.g. MCS item) in their study since those studies often did not control for these variables. Second, it is important to integrate these controls in any analysis, as I showed some significant effects of these variables, although they do not confound my cross-cultural results.

Contrasting the findings from ANOVA and ANCOVA methodology has interesting implications for the analysis of my data. The ANOVA tests compared the mean values of performance evaluation and reward items, as reported by respondent managers in four different countries, based on a culture specific group to either a low or high category. ANCOVA provided robustness tests, as these findings remain stable when controlling for possible confounding effects. Through these methods it has been found that differences clearly exist for a variety of performance evaluation and reward items.

6.3 Managerial and practical implications

It is tempting to unfold the same kind of practices when going abroad, since it creates less coordination problems in the first instance. However, the transfer of organizational control practices to different cultural environments is unlikely to succeed since culture matters in many specific control instruments. Firms need a holistic understanding when transferring practices (Le Thang et al., 2007). "Employees who assume jobs in cultural contexts different from their own ... should learn about and adapt to different behavioral orientations and expectations" (Morrison, Chen & Salgado, 2004, p. 17).

There are myriads of companies that operate internationally. Thus, employees in those companies are exposed to cross-cultural issues. I believe my findings will be of importance to them. My study has several important implications for practitioners. From a practical perspective, my findings could be of special interest to managers of internationally operating firms with respect to performance evaluation of their subordinates and corresponding reward systems. Firms have to decide whether to transfer their policies to foreign countries or whether they should locally adapt these policies, as the wrong practices could counteract the intended purpose. Subordinates also profit from an understanding of the cultural impact on performance evaluation and rewards. It is irrespective whether managers or any other employees are affected by the cultural contexts.

This study has highlighted many areas that are dealt differently across cultures. In particular, I showed which performance evaluation and reward areas differ for the low and high level groups of five cultural dimensions. Culture is an important differentiation mechanism for companies. My findings empirically corroborate this assumption for performance evaluation and reward settings. Uncovering the existing differences across a multitude of performance evaluation and rewards, my analysis reveals that a mere homogenous effort may not be enough to deploy successful MCS. Under certain circumstances, firms need to specify their control systems in foreign operations. A more effective approach for managers willing to acknowledge cultural diversity is to carefully adapt these control variables according to the cultural footing. Managers who change location are likely to engage the same behaviour than in their home culture. However, it is more advisable to take cultural differences into consideration.

Accordingly, my findings demonstrate areas for which management control practices should be adapted and areas for which management control practices could be harmonized in the whole company. Some specific managerial recommendations comprise the distinction in the objectivity of performance standards, in performance evaluation purpose and frequency, as well as in the design, objectivity, equality, nature and importance of rewards. Organizations should in this way think globally, act locally and truly customize their policies based on the similarity of the foreign culture to their own national culture, and more precisely, based on the similarity of the respective cultural dimension involved.

Practical implications indicate that managers have to be aware of the arrangement of performance standards in performance evaluation. High uncertainty avoidance cultures seek more subjective criteria. I found that organizations stress the feedback purpose of performance evaluation in high power distance cultures. Additionally, performance evaluations occur less frequently in individualistic cultures. If managers have to provide feedback in collectivistic cultures they have to adapt to the different expectations in those cultures and increase the frequency of performance evaluation. Employees should be aware of the higher focus on feedback provision for learning and development. As another example, the component structure of rewards systems should acknowledge the individual component to a higher degree in high future-oriented and high uncertainty avoidance cultures. Non-financial performance indicators are more relevant in high future-oriented cultures. Cultures with a higher level of uncertainty avoidance give credit to a higher level of objectivity in the rewarding scheme. Future orientation addresses the general importance of rewards. Low future-oriented cultures value rewards to a higher degree.

From a managerial point of view the takeaway of this study is to provide practically relevant results, i.e. topical cross-cultural insights into performance evaluation and rewards, as well as to draw up specific recommendations for the design and further development. Concluding, my thesis has strong managerial implications.

6.4 Limitations

I want to address some words of caution related to the potential limitations of the study. Some limitations relate to methodology, others to the cultural instrument and others to theory.

First, and related to methodology, the hypotheses are tested using survey data and thus are subject to the usual limitations associated with such data (i.e. perceptual measurement, response bias, truthfulness of self-reports). The cross-cultural aspects complicate methodological issues (Leung, 2008). In terms of survey development, the linguistic fidelity is only one way to address this problem. Questions may be understood completely differently. The thesis could have a potential bias linked to the instrument design; in case our respondents exhibit a different answer pattern across cultures and nations. This would be the case when cultures have a different predisposition to answer the questions and, for example, tend to tick a higher or lower score more easily than other cultures, or when, instead of extreme positions, respondents tend to cluster their scores towards the middle of the scales. In short, responses could tend towards different answering patterns. Jong et al. (2008) found differences in the response styles towards extreme positions across countries and cultures. Roster, Albaum and Rogers (2006) also found differences in the responses of extreme positions. I collected data on the control elements only from one organizational member, which might raise common method bias. However, I followed several steps to limit concerns with the reliability and validity of the data. I used a stratified random sampling approach, collaborated abroad with local scholars, performed back-translation techniques, pilot-tested the survey, assured anonymity and confidentiality, and provided evidence on the construct validity, and reliability of the measures. Therefore, I believe that the careful sampling approach, in line with the best practice recommendations by Schaffer and Riordan (2003) as well as by Harzing, Reiche and Pudelko (2013), minimize systematic measurement error. Some caution has to be addressed to the GLOBE data that arises of the measurement invariance tests (compare with Chapter 4.5.5.3, p. 115ff.).

The study's limitations include the nature of the questionnaire data available. These items represent many single item scales and thus less established multi-item factors. The data do not include information on the instrumentation (e.g. who participates in defining and choosing the measures), nor the consequences (perceived satisfaction, motivation, achieved performance) of performance evaluation and rewarding. This study, with small exceptions, examined only one form of rewards, i.e. financial incentives.

A further limitation connotes to the sampling approach. First, the study was limited to four countries. Advice for a minimum number of countries in comparative studies is higher. Second, these countries could have substantial within-country differences. These inherent cultural differences would undermine the allocation of the whole country to either low or high level cultural grouping. For instance, Canada is said to comprise both English and French traits, whereas Belgium has both Flemish and Wallonian influence. Also, Germany could still have differences between its former western and eastern states, but also between its northern and southern regions. I could only run tests with small sub-samples for Canada and Belgium. The Polish economy is still rapidly developing. As Merchant et al. (2011) have laid down for their sample of Chinese managers, Polish executives might also face lower experience with reward systems. This might result in different outcomes in the use and design irrespective of the cultural footing for Poland. Third, the unit of analysis is the top management and their view on guiding and directing subordinates' behaviour. Conclusions for the top management hierarchical level may not be valid.

Cultural limitations that warrant careful consideration are as follows. The five cultural dimensions cannot be assumed to exhibit the whole sphere of differences between national cultures. Taras, Rowney and Steel (2009, p. 362) state that "despite the great variety of dimensions, it is still too early to claim that every aspect of culture is captured by any single model or even by all existing models taken together". In reality, cultural relationships will display even more variety than I was able to test in my empirical study. Taras, Kirkman and Steel (2010) remark that there can be different subcultures within a nation. One has to admit that the qualitative approach provides a more solid base to explore the causes and consequences, compared to only the values and practices, of cultural behaviour. In this vein, also falls the much criticized equation of country and culture (Gerhart, 2008). However, the qualitative approach rarely contributes to generalizations of organizational behaviour across cultures. Boyacigiller et al. (2004) pointed out that those thick descriptions of culture play a minor role in cross-cultural comparisons. Reliance on the cultural approach of GLOBE locates my work in the quantitative paradigm, which is the dominant school of thought for cross-cultural comparison in the management context (Boyacigiller et al., 2004). The understanding of culture in the sense of the quantitative management paradigm is in a way an oversimplification of the nature of culture. There are voices that stress the inadequacy of the mere cultural dimensions' approach (Leung, 2008). However, the cultural dimensions used in this study can provide useful estimations and are the only means in a large-scale quantitative study.

Within-country differences have been argued to be even greater than between-country differences. This comes as no surprise since national scores are aggregated average scores of the individuals in the respective society. Assuming that all individuals exhibit the same cultural trait is oversimplifying the complex nature of culture. Organizations incorporate many individuals and thus many cultural practices. Gerhart and Fang (2005) found that organizational differences might be even larger than national differences. However, they acknowledge that country differences are meaningful for organization level research when many individuals are involved. GLOBE, in contrast to Hofstede, minimized this effect by framing their questioning (Gerhart, 2009a).

The line of analysis builds upon the dichotomization of the four countries to two cultural groups. Culture is a complex phenomenon and therefore a sharp contrast into high and low categories is difficult. Javidan (2004, p. 246) explains that "most cultures do not neatly fit into the extremes in any typology stereotype". Although the four participating countries neatly fall into low or high categories, the allocation towards high and low levels leaves out fine-grained nuances. The dichotomization process is sharply attacked in the literature and warrants careful consideration. Consistently, there have been highly significant differences ($p<0.01$) between the four countries under investigation. However, the cohesiveness of the exact rank order of the cultural dimensions and the management control elements is rarely achieved. These countries may not be representative of such a classification. The decision to treat different cultural levels by means of separating them on a 0.5 level (see Chapter 5.1.5, p. 128f.) may be questioned as well. However, I only hypothesize about the degree based on the level of culture. That is why I allocated the cultures to either low or high level.

The institutional paradigm also serves as an explanation, as the institutional environment restricts the organizational actors and the managerial degrees of freedom within the organizational field that was shown to equal national boundaries. Harris and Carr (2008, p. 103) emphasize that "different institutional arrangements are a clear reason why management behaviour varies between countries". I have not addressed societal variables as regulatory concerns (e.g. degree of employees' participation in firm governance, tightness of labour market, restraints for layoffs, political pressure), institutional factors (e.g. shareholder influence, education system, labour union strength) or macroeconomic variables (e.g. gross domestic product, tax rates). For instance, Crossland and Hambrick (2007) showed and reinforced (2011) country specific differences in managerial discretion and attributed these to the interrelation of culture, dispersion of firms' ownership structure and board governance. Aguilera and Jackson (2003) illustrated from an institutional standpoint different organizational corporate governance practices across countries.

Further theoretical concepts in the literature of comparative international business are the approaches "national business system" (Whitley, 1991, 1992) and "varieties of capitalism" (Hall & Soskice, 2001). The former uses a comparative framework to classify how specific firm-market relationships have historically developed and how the institutional context has shaped business systems and vice versa (Redding, Bond & Witt, 2014). The latter sees organizations as the central players in the economy. The organizational actors have to efficiently interact with other players to sustain their competitiveness. Cultural elements grow out of shared accumulated experience, which influences the organizational actions (Hall & Soskice, 2001).

And finally, the theoretical deduction of the hypotheses is based on causal arguments that cannot be tested by my data. In cross-cultural research, causality cannot be established. Causal arguments can infer indirect evidences (Leung, 2008). I cannot solve this causality problem and thus the reader may assess the theoretical arguments that were developed. It is not clear whether the differences I obtained in the various MCS practices are truly attributable to the hypothesized cultural variables. I only verbalize why such differences can be linked to culture, but I cannot give causal explanations. I cannot preclude factors other than the cultural dimensions and the included covariates being relevant for arising differences.

6.5 Avenues for future research

For the area of cultural management, Taras et al. (2014, p. 238) argued for "more sophisticated research designs, collaboration across fields of studies, and more complex conceptualizations [*restricting cultural research not just to one dimension – note of the author*] ... to fully understand the fascinating and important phenomenon of culture."

My findings suggest many avenues for further research. After being trapped for years in the Hofstede paradigm, my study shines light on the cultural acumen by applying the GLOBE study with the chosen cultural dimensions. Rather than relying on the Hofstede framework, which looks like normal science in the Kuhnian sense, the more recent GLOBE study could help. In the past, scholars often did not even justify the paramount use of Hofstede, as if no other framework existed for cross-cultural studies. In those cases, where authors provide arguments, they mostly state that Hofstede is the most widely used and well-established framework. One may wish that authors list criticisms of Hofstede and are aware of pitfalls in his typology. As an example Chiang and Birtch (2012) have listed the short-comings of Hofstede. The research community can only advance our knowledge "if we question and reassess established paradigms" (Kostova, Roth & Dacin, 2008, p. 1003).

A valuable investigation would be to repeat this kind of study in other cultural settings. This study focused on four countries that have been grouped to either a low or a high level for five cultural dimensions. Of beneficial interest would be whether the hypotheses hold in further cultures. Those cultures could be culturally similar to the ones in this study. Cultures could be also situated at more extreme levels based on the cultural dimensions. In other words, the design and use of performance evaluation and reward from other countries is worthy of investigation. I especially think of other European countries, such as those in Scandinavia and Southern Europe, the middle East (Kabasakal et al., 2012) as well as other emerging countries such as China, India, Brazil or Russia (Luo, Sun & Wang, 2011) or Africa (Walumbwa, Avolio & Aryee, 2011). Future research could also target within-country differences. Hofstede et al. (2010) found strong within-country differences in Brazil and thus argued for more nuanced research in this area. Yamawaki (2012) derived very strong differences in the degree of collectivism over all Japanese prefectures. Vandello and Cohen (1999) found the same pattern of differences for the US.

Chapter 6 – Discussion and conclusion

Next, my findings warrant future research on organizational influences. We need further clarification of whether there is an influence of organizational cultural variables as well. Webster and White (2010) found the dominance of national over organizational culture, but Gerhart (2009b) remarked the higher discretion for organizational culture. I measured organizational culture by the GLOBE questionnaire. However, there are other and more distinct organizational measures such as the 'Organizational Culture Profile' (O'Reilly III, Chatman & Caldwell, 1991). Further research may fruitfully adopt other organizational culture practice scores as well.

More research is needed to shed light on the design and use of MCS. I studied performance evaluation and rewards in close collaboration with performance measures. I identified a mismatch in the degree of objectivity for performance evaluation and rewards. Future research could address the reasons for this behaviour. Further, we combined a variety of factors management uses for rewarding into the performance measure variable of individual objectives. Abernethy, Bouwens and van Lent (2013) distinguished between project and personal measures. Individual factors could be classified in the rewarding scheme too. Future research is needed to address other management control elements as well. The MCS frameworks clearly outline several other control elements, such as strategic and short-term planning as well as mere performance measurement. Studies on strategic planning in cross-cultural settings are fairly non-existent. Exceptions comprise a recent study by Shim and Steers (2012), an operations study (Flynn & Saladin, 2006) with a tiny section on strategic planning, or the one by Joshi (2001) on the diffusion of accounting practices. Mere short-term planning, besides the often-studied financial aspect of the budget, has also been rarely addressed so far. Future research could provide additional aspects of management control elements. Future analysis could expand on a sole focus on financial rewards to include other rewards as well. Among the monetary forms, studies could focus on salary levels, salary increases and long-term oriented financial benefits. Among the non-monetary forms, further different elements could be targeted (e.g. promotion, ambitious tasks, office equipment, and managerial responsibility). A more extensive replication of how firms design, structure and use their performance evaluation and reward settings could complement research projects.

This study also takes a static perspective on management control elements. I am not addressing cultural propensity for change. Chanegrih (2008) showed the heterogeneity of changes in MCS and provided some cultural explanation for the nature of change. Some scholars show that the design of MCS can change over time as a result of uncertainty (e.g. Dye (2004)), learning (e.g. Bol and Moers (2010)), or personal factors (e.g. Stergiou, Ashraf and Uddin (2013)). This implies that future research could focus on a more dynamic approach and incorporate the impact of change.

Another field of investigation could target international non-profit organizations (Fenwick, 2005). These organizations are very powerful and rarely researched (Angelé-Halgand et al., 2010). O'Sullivan (2010) stakes out challenges for the HRM. Fenwick (2005) states that these organizations have no variable pay system. Research could target the reasons for this in a qualitative fashion and assess the benefit of implementing such systems based on non-financial indicators for non-governmental organizations as well. Performance evaluation is a further challenge for these organizations since real feedback is sparse. Thus, these organizations are worthy of investigation for the kind of managerial practices targeted in this thesis.

The debate on convergence or divergence of management practices has reached little consensus (Pudelko et al., 2006). Proponents of convergence see an increasing homogenization of management practices, often towards the business model of the industrialized Western hemisphere. Competitiveness is the driving force behind this mechanism (Ogbor & Williams, 2003). Management practices are "irrespective of national culture or institutional context" (Pudelko & Harzing, 2007, p. 536). These voices speak of universal management principles, independent of national cultural differences. From an institutional point of view, these can be attributed to isomorphistic pressures (Jansen, Merchant & van der Stede, 2009). Opponents of this view, as I would position the line of my thesis, favour the divergence approach. By contrast, divergence is characterized by the national cultural context that works as a demarcation line for business practices (Pudelko & Harzing, 2007). The forces from within a cultural domain dominate outside influences. Thus, management practices from the outside hardly affect the particular cultural dimensions. With the intent to balance these two extreme position, convergence and divergence, Ralston et al. (1993) introduced the crossvergence concept, which combines national culture and economic thoughts (Ralston et al., 2008). In a way, Festing (2012, p. 48-49) has stated the "puzzle on convergence and divergence", which could be attributed to the concept of crossvergence. Bonache, Trullen and Sanchez (2012) also offered a position they call 'culturally-animated' that acknowledges universally valid human resources principles while at the same time culture reconciles their effectiveness. These concepts might help to enrich the theoretical underpinning.

A central claim of new institutionalism is the decoupling of organizational practices and structure (Meyer & Rowan, 1977). One could investigate how firms, which need to incorporate the rational myths of their environment, differ in their day-to-day activities across cultures. One could compare official documents, registered reports and press releases and the way managerial practices are really dealt with. One might suspect differences in the adherence to the official statements, policies and ceremonies across different cultures. On the national level it would be a fruitful endeavour to investigate what kind of influence organizations have on the institutional structure of different nation-states (Geppert, Matten & Schmidt, 2004).

I assume that the empirical research agenda, which I exemplified, is demanding, particularly when applying the same broad scaled sampling approach. However, I am confident that such research will be worth the effort, as it will enrich cross-cultural research.

6.6 Conclusion

Chow and Harrison (2002) have nicely outlined insights into meaningful research. In reflecting about the significance of my own publication, I believe I have addressed a real world problem, namely the question whether management control practices, and in particular, whether performance evaluation and rewards that are tightly coupled with performance measures are configured similarly or differently across different cultures. Secondly, I am confident that I placed my study in a large research gap by using a fine-grained cultural framework on a little studied phenomenon with a unique and generalizable sample. I further tried to advance theory by integrating contingency thoughts, institutional ideas and the stakeholder approach into the cross-cultural paradigm. I am optimistic at having achieved new and striking results. I also tentatively hope that I have introduced the GLOBE framework as a new and helpful tool in the area of management control to address cross-cultural issues.

Questions regarding the cultural influence on MCS are of continuing interest for the scientific community and business world. Given the meagre state of the literature in management control with a cross-cultural emphasis, which I aimed to contribute, my effort was to look for cultural differences. In this thesis, I sought to shed light on one of the more intriguing questions within this domain: whether there are differences among organizations across different cultures in their respective MCS, particularly in performance measurement, performance evaluation and reward schemes. I posited that there are cultural factors that determine the degree of variance between countries. While prior research primarily focused on one MCS element in one study, often contrasted only two countries, and used secondary cultural data, I augmented this methodology. In the present study, I extended the current state of cultural investigation in the domain of performance evaluation and rewards, and stressed some areas in which future empirical cross-cultural research can benefit, and some areas where conceptual thoughts could be advanced.

First, I illustrated the main assumptions concerning the cultural influence on MCS. Subsequently, I presented the theoretical framework in form of the GLOBE study and extended this by a contingency-based approach and new institutionalism. I derived a variety of hypotheses that comprised both new phenomena and were partly borrowed from previous research. I tested these by means of several ANOVAs, complemented by thorough robustness tests. Consistent with my initial research question, the results indicate, at least for particular subcomponents of the cultural acumen, that there are national-specific differences across cultures. My findings provide a useful confirmation but also extension of the previous line of inquiry. A simple rule to incorporate homogenous management control practices across firms' geographic boundaries is precarious. This study sheds light on several differences. It is imperative for managers to be sensitive to the cultural context in which a firm operates. An awareness of the management control preferences helps to successfully install globally universal and locally adaptable performance evaluation and reward systems. In this, organizations maximize the degree of certainty for the transferability of these management practices across cultures. I examined inherent limitations of the study, assessed my contribution and proposed several ideas that could contribute to the future development of cross-cultural research.

I posit that my findings opened some further interesting research avenues and some intellectual stimuli for new theoretical insights. Further studies illuminating the design and use of other management control elements, are a promising direction for future research. Additional empirical evidence, which repeats this line of research with different samples in other cultural areas, and a substantiation of the theoretical concepts are a prerequisite to progress in this research field. There is still a lot more to learn about the interplay of culture and MCS. This thesis is just a further step in the advancement of knowledge about MCS and cultural implications. There remains much unchartered territory.

Appendix

Appendix 1: Definitions of management control systems 176

Appendix 2: Major management control systems' frameworks 179

Appendix 3: Steps of literature review 187

Appendix 4: Journals included in the literature review 191

Appendix 5: Results of literature review 192

Appendix 6: GLOBE regional clusters 201

Appendix 7: Project outline 202

Appendix 8: Excerpt of MCS questionnaire and coding instructions 203

Appendix 9: GLOBE questionnaire and coding instructions 211

Appendix 10: Means, SD, ANOVA, and effect size by country 220

Appendix 11: ANCOVA tests 222

Appendix 1: Definitions of management control systems

Author	Definition of Management Control Systems
Anthony (1965, p. 5)	A planning and control system, then, consists of diverse parts that serve a common purpose, this purpose having to do with planning and control.
Lowe (1971, p. 5)	A system of organizational information seeking and gathering, accountability, and feedback designed to ensure that the enterprise adapts to changes in its substantial environment and that the work behavior of its employees is measured by reference to a set of operational sub-goals (which conform with overall objectives) so that the discrepancy between the two can be reconciled and corrected for.
Bhattacharyya (1973, p. 45)	A planning and control system would have the following subsystems as integral parts of the total system: a) planning; b) measuring; c) recording; d) appraising; e) reporting; and f) remedial action (where recorded performance is at variance with planned goals).
Lorange and Scott Morton (1974, p. 42)	We propose that the fundamental purpose for management control systems is to help management accomplish an organization's objectives by providing a formalized framework for (1) the identification of pertinent control variables, (2) the development of good short-term plans, (3) the recording of the degree of actual fulfillment of short-term plans along the set of control variables, and (4) the diagnosis of deviations.
Flamholtz, Das and Tsui (1985, p. 36)	Control systems are techniques and processes to achieve goal congruence and may be designed for all levels of behavioral influence: individuals, small groups, formal subunits and the organizational as a whole.
Simons (1987, p. 358)	Management control systems are the formal, information-based routines and procedures managers use to maintain or alter patterns in organizational activities.
Birnberg and Snodgrass (1988, p. 447)	A management control system (MCS) is a mechanism designed to limit the decision space of individuals within an organization so as to affect their behavior. Its purpose is to coordinate the decisions which they make so as to increase the probability of achieving the organization's goals. A control system performs its function by controlling the flow of information, establishing criteria for evaluation and designing appropriate rewards and punishments.
Cunningham (1992, p. 86)	Management control systems embody the techniques and mechanisms which companies employ to pursue objectives, accomplish goals and successfully pursue strategies. MCS integrate, motivate, assist decision making, communicate objectives, provide feedback, etc.
Otley, Broadbent and Berry (1995, p. 32)	A broad set of control mechanisms designed to assist organizations to regulate themselves.
Abernethy and Chua (1996, p. 573)	A system that comprises a combination of control mechanisms designed and implemented by management to increase the probability that organizational actors will behave in ways consistent with the objectives of the dominant organizational coalition.
Flamholtz (1996, p. 598)	A set of mechanisms - both processes and techniques - which are designed to increase the probability that people will behave in ways that lead to the attainment of organizational objectives. The ultimate objective of a control system is not to control the specific behavior of people *per se*, but, rather, to influence people to take actions and make decisions which in their judgement are consistent with organizational goals.

Author	Definition of Management Control Systems
Otley (1999, p. 364)	Management control systems provide information that is intended to be useful to managers in performing their jobs and to assist organizations in developing and maintaining viable patterns of behaviour.
Chenhall (2003, p. 129; 2007, p. 164-165)	Management accounting refers to a collection of practices such as budgeting or product costing, while management accounting systems refers to the systematic use of management accounting to achieve some goal. Management control system is a broader term that encompasses management accounting systems and also includes other controls such as personal or clan controls.
Bisbe and Otley (2004, p. 709)	The term MCS refers to the set of procedures and processes that managers and other organizational participants use in order to help ensure the achievement of their goals and the goals of their organizations, and it encompasses formal control systems as well as informal personal and social controls.
Anthony and Govindarajan (2007, p. 17)	The system used by management to control the activities of an organization is called the management control system. Management control is the process by which managers influence other members of the organization to implement the organization's strategies.
Merchant and Otley (2007, p. 785)	In broad terms, a management control system is designed to help an organization adapt to the environment in which it is set and to deliver the key results desired by stakeholder groups, most frequently concentrating upon shareholders in commercial enterprises. Managers implement controls, or sets of controls, to help attain these results and to protect against the threats to the achievement of good performance.
Merchant and van der Stede (2007, p. 5)	All the devices managers use to ensure that the behaviors and decisions of their employees are consistent with the organization's objectives and strategies.
Malmi and Brown (2008, p. 290)	Those systems, rules, practices, values and other activities management put in place in order to direct employee behavior should be called management controls. If these are complete systems, as opposed to a simple rule (for example not to travel in business class), then they should be called management control systems.
Carenys (2010, p. 49)	The management control system seeks to orient in the decision-making process and influence the behaviour of the organisation members so that their performance increases its chances of achieving its objectives.
Kallunki, Laitinen and Silvola (2011, p. 21)	The main purpose of management control systems (MCS) is to monitor decisions throughout the organization and to guide employee behavior in desirable ways in order to increase the chances that an organization's objectives, including organizational performance, will be achieved.
Ho, Wu and Wu (2014, p. 38)	An important role of management control systems is to help managers successfully implement strategies within the organization.

Table 33: Definition of management control systems

Ansari (1977) differentiates between a structural and a behavioural view of MCS. The former focuses on communication and information whereas the behavioural perspective deals with ensuring that subordinates achieve organizational goals. The behavioural approach embodies the importance of social and human aspects and incorporates ideas of motivation (Carenys, 2010). The structural way goes along with information on performance targets, actual data and corresponding variances that are measured, collected, processed and then communicated. This is closely connected to cybernetic thoughts (Ansari, 1977). The definitions of Lowe (1971), Bhattacharyya (1973) and Lorange and Scott (1974) are proponents of this view. The cybernetic thinking is portrayed in Merchant and Otley's (2007, p. 785) understanding of the "generic management process, which involves (1) setting objectives, (2) deciding on preferred strategies for achieving those objectives, and then (3) implementing those strategies while (4) making sure that nothing, or as little as possible, goes wrong". This conceptualization of management control includes strategy formulation, strategic control processes and learning.

Merchant and van der Stede (2007) follow a narrower view of the constituents of MCS. They distinguish between management control and strategic control. According to Ansari's (1977) categorization they can be placed in the behavioural camp. Management control addresses ways to influence employees' behaviour. Cunningham's (1992) definition may be interpreted as partly fulfilling the behavioural idea. Although he does not explicitly state a behavioural term, he weaves in motivation, communication and provision of feedback. Otley (1999) speaks of behaviour patterns that will be affected. Simons (1995b) sees a variety of formal routines and procedures to become MCS when their use affects patterns in organizational life. In recent works, authors tend to emphasize the behavioural perspective (Carenys, 2010; Kallunki, Laitinen & Silvola, 2011).

Flamholtz, Das and Tsui (1985) expand the understanding beyond the behavioural view towards achieving goal congruence for the whole organization. In later years Flamholtz (1996) repeated his idea of consistency of organizational objectives and subordinates' actions and decisions. Even in his early understanding, Flamholtz (1979) viewed the ultimate intent not in controlling employees' conduct but in influencing them towards aligning their actions with goal attainment of the organization. Abernethy and Chua (1996) take into account the same deliberations of consistency or goal congruence. Birnberg and Snodgrass' (1988) combine both information elements and behavioural aspects. This broad understanding they already depict major elements of the later MCS concept of Malmi and Brown (2008).

Appendix 2: Major management control systems' frameworks

Selection of management control frameworks

The most influential MCS frameworks were derived from various sources. Bredmar (2011) examined the most important references for management control literature during 1977 to 2003. I extracted all those authors who contributed with an MCS framework on their own from the list of the 50 most cited references (articles, books). Among those are Otley, Merchant & van der Stede[92], Flamholtz and Simons. Since this list is biased towards appearance in one journal (Accounting, Organizations and Society) and neglects newer work (from 2003 onwards), additional frameworks were captured by analyzing valuable literature reviews of MCS research (Berry et al., 2009; Chenhall, 2003, 2007; Merchant & Otley, 2007) as well as a thorough screening of the most important management accounting journals (Bonner et al., 2006), namely Accounting, Organizations and Society (AOS), Journal of Accounting Research (JAR), The Accounting Review (TAR), Contemporary Accounting Research (CAR) supplemented by Journal of Management Accounting Research (JMAR), Management Accounting Research (MAR) and European Accounting Review (EAR).

The common overlap of the major contributions in the field of MCS typologies include the following control frameworks[93] which will be presented in the following: Anthony (1965), Anthony and Govindarajan (2007), Ansari (1977), Flamholtz (1979; 1983; 1996; 1985), Otley (1980; 1999) with extensions by Ferreira and Otley (2009), Daft and Macintosh (1984), Simons (1995b) with a conceptual advancement of Tessier and Otley (2012), Fisher (1995), Merchant and van der Stede (2007) as well as Malmi and Brown (2008).

This list is partly overlapping with the landscape identified in a review of MCS by Strauß and Zecher (2013). Their work included textbooks, syllabi and research papers. They identified the top three main textbooks on MCS. They approached accounting faculty members worldwide by E-mail and additionally analyzed syllabi with a specific focus on MCS. They

---

[92] Merchant was listed five times individually. However, a real framework was developed in his book with van der Stede.

[93] According to the Cambridge online dictionary (http://dictionary.cambridge.org), a framework is "a system of rules, ideas, or beliefs that is used to plan or decide something". The Oxford online dictionary (http://oxforddictionaries.com) depicts framework as "a basic structure underlying a system, concept, or text". Retrieved June 21, 2014.

supplemented this list by relevant paper-based contributions to MCS frameworks. But their list is much shorter. Additionally, I disagree with their decision to exclude Flamholtz from the major frameworks. They distinguish between different categories, i.e. types and frameworks. In doing so, they classify Flamholtz as a MCS type.[94] However, in my opinion and from the reading of various other literature reviews, the contributions of Flamholtz have to be categorized as a framework.

Publications which only contain the name framework or concept in its headline or abstract, but later present something different, are neglected. Some authors have developed methodologies or types rather than frameworks. Machin (1979) labelled his contribution 'expectation approach' providing managers with a guideline what to incorporate into the MCS and what to leave out. Many researchers who concentrated on rather single MCS elements have also been left out. For example, Gordon and Miller (1976) depict a so-called contingency framework for accounting information systems limited to accounting information (reporting, cost allocation, performance evaluation). Ouchi's (Ouchi, 1979) conceptual framework for the design of organizational control mechanisms depicts markets, bureaucracies and clans[95] as different mechanisms to handle the challenge of performance evaluation and control. These four authors are exemplarily listed for the frameworks which were not considered.

Framework Anthony (1965), Anthony and Govindarajan (2007)

Anthony (1965) was the first representative of MCS since he dealt with management control from a system's perspective (Giglioni & Bedeian, 1974). He separated management control from strategic planning (in later works strategy formulation), which is the least systematic process of the three, and operational control, which is the most systematic process. Management control has the purpose to implement and execute strategies. The operational control focuses on the short-term assurance that individual tasks are dealt with efficiently and effectively. With these three categories he came up with a control taxonomy that uncovered

---

[94] A framework is a typology or an overarching instrument for analysis whereas a type only provides characteristics of specific elements within an organizational anchoring. Whereas several MCS elements are part of a MCS framework, elements already form a specific relationship within a type.

[95] More in Ouchi's (1990) publication on markets, bureaucracies, and clans.

the control devices from strategic planning, operating budgets, performance measurement and evaluation to compensation plans (Anthony & Govindarajan, 2007).

The approach of Anthony and Govindarajan (2007), which is an extension of the early works and comparable to the ideas, places all controls in a feedback process to take corrective actions. They "focus primarily on the systematic, (i.e., formal) aspects of the management control function" (Anthony & Govindarajan, 2007, p. 6). This framework disconnects these formal control elements from the informal ones, such as organization's structure (roles, reporting lines, decision-making guidelines), organizational culture (values, norms and spirit) and human resource management (nomination, training, appraisal, promotion and dismissal). Summing up, Anthony's and Govindarajan's understanding of management controls see them as one way for the implementation of strategy.

Framework Ansari (1977)

Ansari's (1977) framework considers information and communication aspects as well as social relationships. The core of this system is the controlled variable, i.e. the objective of the company. The four essential components, which gather around the core, namely leadership style, information structure, subordinate personality and rewards are equally influencing each other. He indicates various interrelationships of these four components and outlined the interaction of managers and subordinates as the main criterion for effective integration. In his thinking he combines two different perspectives of MCS, namely the structural view and the behavioural view. In addition he emphasizes that studying effective combinations of the different elements will be a useful research approach.

Framework Flamholtz (1979/1983/1985/1996)

In an early publication, Flamholtz (1979) presented his core ideas of an organizational control system. The model whose fundamentals were quite stable over time (Flamholtz, 1983, 1996; Flamholtz, Das & Tsui, 1985) consists of a core control system. In its latest version it comprises four subsystems or control mechanism, (1) planning, (2) operations, (3) measurement and (4) evaluation and reward which are linked with two types of feedback mechanisms, both corrective and evaluative.

The planning elements contain broad scale qualitative objectives and quantitative goals. The operational subsystem is for on-going day-to-day activities. The measurement elements aim at both monitoring and measuring the achievement of goals since this also works as a stimulus to alter people's behaviour. Evaluation and rewards represent ex ante control in terms of initial motivation and ex post control in terms of actual rewards and compensation. This core control system which bears cybernetic thoughts is surrounded by the control context which subsumes the external environment and societal context, organizational culture and organizational structure. Flamholtz directs further research towards elaborating the circumstances of the system's effectiveness. He also proposes that there are different configurations and combinations of control elements in one organizational setting (Flamholtz, 1983, 1996; Flamholtz, Das & Tsui, 1985). Although Flamholtz does not explicitly state a holistic idea of MCS, his core control system and different configurations of elements support this view.

Framework Otley (1980/1999)

Otley (1980) introduced a framework on organizational control with reference to contingency theory. Briefly, contingency theory states there is no universal applicable control system with universal validity to all organizations in all settings (see Chapter 2.4, p. 53f.). In contrast, the specific surroundings and external factors an organization is exposed to shape the system (Otley, 1980). Even more surprising about this fact is that he is conflating accounting and management information with organizational design and other control elements to an organizational control package. He argues that this holistic thinking of control systems is a requirement to determine equally promising control combinations. For him the collection of control elements "form a package which can only be evaluated as a whole" and "act as a package and must be assessed jointly" (Otley, 1980, p. 422). This call raises the first noise for alternative configurations of control systems that may be equally effective. He senses that his framework is over-simplified since dependencies and interrelationships between control package ingredients are not stated.

Almost twenty years later, Otley (1999, p. 365-366) proposed another model for the operation of MCS in which he highlighted a checklist of five questions to improve the picture of control systems. This set of questions refers to the definition of objectives and the assessment of their achievement, to strategies and plans, to targets and benchmarking, to rewards and punishments and to feedback. He compares three major control techniques – budgetary control, economic value added and the BSC – based on these central issues. He shows that answers to all relevant control matters are addressed by only the variety of control elements which again supports the holistic idea.

Framework Daft and Macintosh (1984)

Research findings from a qualitative study performed by Daft and Macintosh (1984) about the viewpoint of middle managers resulted in the following MCS characteristics. Two management control subsystems are responsible for formulating business strategy whereas four subsystems which they as well call MCS package qualify for implementing business strategy. The four formal subsystems (budget, statistical reports, policies/procedures and performance appraisal) build the MCS package. The authors could not find the approach of a specifically designed and coordinated control package. All MCS had an initiator on their own, but still the various sub-systems supplemented each other.

Framework Simons (1995/2000)

Simons' (1995b) levers of control framework copes with the most effective way to implement firms' strategies. It arose of the question how executives deal with balancing the need for innovation with the need for control. Simons' framework resulted from qualitative data collected in more than one hundred companies over a period of ten years. Business strategy along with competitiveness and interaction with competitors is the core of his thinking. Four key concepts are built around this core: core values, risks to be avoided, critical performance variables and strategic uncertainties. Each of these is controlled by a system or lever of control. "These four levers create the opposing forces – the yin and the yang – of effective strategy implementation" (Simons, 1995b, p. 7). Belief systems set the core values and establish mission, vision and purpose of an organization. This serves for guidance, motivation and inspiration of employees. Boundary systems are the delineating factor to demarcate the room for opportunities and define limits for inappropriate activities. Diagnostic control systems are feedback systems to guarantee goal attainment. This thermostat-like thinking serves for measuring, monitoring and assessing performance variables and then incentivizes their achievement. Interactive control systems stimulate the search for out-of-the-box thinking. They focus attention to strategic uncertainties and induce forward-looking dialogues to improve organizational learning and to generate new ideas for sustainable success (Simons, 1994, 1995a, 1995b).

The framework introduced by Simons has a number of strengths. Simon's framework provides a more solid ground "to the use of MCS to manage behavior and effect strategic change" (Langfield-Smith, 2007, p. 778). A valuable contribution of the levers of control framework is Simons' useful categorization and broader foundation for the study of MCS

(Berry et al., 2009; Ferreira & Otley, 2009; Otley, 2003). He includes a wide range of controls and shows ways to balance organizational tensions necessary to execute business strategy. However, his framework also has a number of weaknesses. Scholars have criticized the vagueness and ambiguity of concepts. Some authors remark that the levers of the control framework are lacking the issues of "how" and "why" organizations are pursuing a control mix (Abernethy & Chua, 1996; Ahrens & Chapman, 2004). Linked to this argument, some authors stress unclear relations among the different control levers (Bisbe & Otley, 2004), respectively an unambiguous assignment of control elements to one lever of control (Ferreira & Otley, 2009). In addition, many informal control processes (group norms, socialization, and culture) which are a crucial part of MCS too, are left out of his conceptualization (Collier, 2005). Berry et al. (2009) criticize that the target group is limited to the senior management team. Despite the critics, Simons' framework has been frequently used. Empirical work of Henry (2006a) supports most of Simons' propositions, the study of Widener (2007) also found evidence for his framework.

Framework Fisher (1995/1998)
Fisher (1995; 1998) developed a MCS framework based on contingency ideas. He therefore referred to his model as contingent control framework. The whole process follows a feedback loop which represents an iterative process. There are both exogenous and endogenous contingency variables involved. Some contingent factors are in the sphere of the organization, but over time may get out of control. This is exemplified by a product decision which is the result of a decision based on strategic orientation and market competitiveness. The product increasingly gets out of the firm's direct control after official product launch. Fisher uses the term organizational control package which covers cybernetic control elements and other parts. He stresses that the different components of the control package have to be configured in the sense that they carry on to the aspiration of the desired organizational outcomes. Interrelationships of control elements have to be taken into account when it comes to arranging them appropriately. For instance, a lesser extent of cybernetic control systems can be compensated by reliance on a strong organizational culture.

Framework Merchant and van der Stede (2003/2007)
According to Merchant and van der Stede (2003; 2007), the need for management control grounds on three main causes: lack of direction, motivational issues and personal limitations. In their comprehensive textbook they refine the object-of-control framework and distinguish

between the control alternatives results, actions, and personnel/culture (Merchant & Otley, 2007). They want to provide an exhaustive but still understandable framework with distinct categories. Results controls centre around the cybernetic principle of defining performance categories, measuring performance, setting appropriate targets and finally providing rewards. There is a high autonomy associated with this category which is seen as a beneficial element for innovation. Employees are held accountable for the results they realize and not the action steps they follow. Action controls involve any of the following forms, behavioural constraints, pre-action reviews, action accountability, and redundancy. The behavioural constraints function as a negative form of control and make undesirable actions harder to accomplish, either physically or by means of administrative issues. Reviews come in formal and informal ways and require a close monitoring. Employees are held accountable for their action steps. Redundancy although rarely used builds some form of slack to enhance chances of task fulfilment with the additional buffer. Personnel controls concern mechanisms to clarify the organization's objective to employees, to secure appropriate skills and capabilities for the activities and to rely on self-measurement. This comes along with the right job placement, trainings, mutual trust, allegiance, self-motivation and self-control. Cultural controls encourage group dynamics and specific social norms that apply to the working environment. Formal documents and informal communication help to shape the corporate culture towards the desired state (Merchant & van der Stede, 2003, 2007). The main strength of their framework lies in the wide coverage of MCS elements (Roush & Mohammed, 2008).

Framework Ferreira and Otley (2008)

To overcome the weaknesses – omission of vision and mission, focus on diagnostic control systems, lack of exact use of accounting and control information, static perspective that ignores dynamism and no focus on interconnections – raised in the paper by Ferreira and Otley (2009), both authors extend Otley's five points to 12 questions. The core of their framework is built on questions that cover (1,2) strategy formulation („What is the vision and mission of the organization", „How to transport these ideas to the stakeholders", „What are the key success factors"), (3,4) strategy implementation („What is the organization structure", „What strategies and plans has the organization") (5) key performance measures and (6) the respective targets as well as (7) processes for performance evaluation and (8) the design of rewards. Furthermore, the authors address further questions on (9) information flows, (10) use of information and control mechanisms, (11) change processes and (12) the strengths and coherence of links between the components. They also add the system element to the name of the framework, which they label the performance management systems (PMS) framework. In this, they bring in a broad understanding of control.[96]

Framework Tessier and Otley (2012)

Tessier and Otley (2012) extended Simons' framework incorporating various criticism brought up in literature. In particular the authors deconstruct the original framework and rearrange it in a new form. They reclassify the belief system to a social form of control that builds with technical controls part of an overall control system. The inner circle of the revised framework consists of social and technical controls that steer daily business. The second level contains a strategic and an operational level, namely strategic performance, strategic boundaries, operations performance and operational boundaries. The original three remaining levers of control have vanished from the illustration but are still included in the framework. Part of the diagnostic control systems belongs to the operational performance; part of the interactive controls is reflected in the strategic performance whereas the boundary controls are split into two components. The remaining portions of the diagnostic and interactive systems as well as the positive and negative forces, introduced by the yin and yang principle, are placed in the outer level of managerial intentions. This third level maps the managerial intentions subsumes "the choices managers can make regarding the control systems" (Tessier & Otley, 2012, p. 181). Managers decide whether controls will be used for initiating discussions and fostering learning (interactive use) or whether controls are used for corrective actions (diagnostic use). Additionally, intentions include decisions on fostering creativity (enabling) or focussing on predictability (constraining). A third decision stream targets the consequences of the subordinates' actions (rewards or punishments). The presentation and communication of the designed controls determine the perceptions of controls towards the employees. Managers should be conscious about their power to intentionally configure the control system, the perception of it remains dependent on the addressee (Tessier & Otley, 2012).

---

[96] A further twist is done by Broadbent and Laughlin (2009) who concentrate on the outer circle of the Ferreira and Otley (2009) framework. They extend the contextual questions 9-12 with a special focus on questions 9 and 10. Building on work of Weber and Habermas, they place the MCS into a continuum from relational (stakeholders debate about and have to agree on the right strategic ends and means) to transactional (precise and clear idea of strategic means to reach the organizational ends) with underlying principles of instrumental rationality (based on rational thoughts) versus communicative rationality (based on mutual understanding and systematic discourse among various stakeholders).

Appendix 3: Steps of literature review

1. Selection of relevant journals
2. Compilation of search terms
3. Search of articles
4. Evaluation of articles
5. Selection of articles
6. Coding of articles

Table 34: Six steps of literature review

(1) Since the object of investigation is placed in various disciplines (management control, management accounting, general management, international business, organization science and cross-cultural management), I included a variety of journals for the literature review. A first source was the list of 34 major accounting journals which can be found in the publication of Rosenstreich and Wooliscraft (2009). Four tax and audit related journals[97] were excluded due to the completely different content they provide. A second source was the comprehensive list of Podsakoff (2005) which contributed the most relevant journals in all areas of management. This list includes 28 journals in the field of "strategic management, human resources/personnel, leadership, general management, industrial and labour relations, entrepreneurship, organizational behaviour, organizational theory, organizational decision making, international business, and management science" (Podsakoff et al., 2005, p. 475). The MIT Sloan Management Review was excluded since it is a practitioner-oriented journal. In order to further convey cultural aspects these two steps have been supplemented by a third source which adds all business related journals used in a meta-literature review by Kirkman et al. (2006).[98] This source led to additional 36 journals[99]. To secure high quality journals, which are well recognized in the scientific community, the target journals were restricted to the three

---

[97] Auditing: A Journal of Practice & Theory, Journal of the American Taxation Association, Managerial Auditing Journal, National Tax Journal.

[98] Kirkman et al. (2006) investigated the empirical usage of the Hofstede framework over 25 years. They analyzed 180 studies in 40 both top-tier management and applied psychology journals.

[99] Journals from the field of Psychology or Sociology that did not contribute any article among the 180 studies have been excluded from my list.

mentioned sources. Overall [100] this process revealed a total list of 83 journals (see Appendix 4, p. 191). This literature review does neither contain unpublished papers (e.g. conferences or working papers) nor textbooks, dissertations or book chapters. I believe that the focus on high-quality journal publications gives a thorough guide to the research conducted.

(2) After completing the journal list, I compiled a set of search terms to determine relevant articles. The search terms were specified in order to maximize the amount of relevant studies, to exclude the number of irrelevant studies (false positives) and to minimize the number of studies not identified (false negatives). To rule out as many false negatives as possible, the search had to be broadened to many appropriate terms (Reed & Baxter, 2009). With reference to the topic, keywords were selected under each umbrella term both for the subject of performance evaluation, rewards and culture. The search terms for performance measurement, performance evaluation and rewards followed the main elements of the framework of Malmi and Brown (2008) and the questionnaire used in the research project. The keywords for culture comprised: culture itself, cultural aspects and denotations, as well as notable representatives of cultural research. There was no upfront exclusion of specific study features in terms of method, design, sample features, statistical analysis or geographical focus (Wilson, 2009).

(3) In a third step I searched various databases with reference to accessing the identified 84 target journals. Among the databases accessed were Ebsco, Emerald, Informs, Jstor, Sage, Science Direct, Springer, Swetswise, World Scientific, Taylor and Francis, websites[101], Wiley and Wiso. I decided to follow the mode of searching in subject indexes (White, 2009) and conducted a computer aided search in the title, keywords and abstract for the complete journal list over the years 1980-2013[102]. The date of retrieval was a two week period from June 18 to June 29, 2012 and February 5, 2014 for the latest articles. Papers had to match the combination of keywords from both major search terms. Any of the search terms of the first

---

[100] There have been partial overlaps among the journals mentioned in Podsakoff et al. (2005) and Kirkman et al. (2006).

[101] Industrial Relations provides a search mechanism and free website access with a two-year delay.

[102] The timespan chronologically followed the years of the study from Harrison and McKinnon (1999). Of further interest has been a replication of their data period.

line in Table 35 had to appear in combination with any of the search terms of the second line. The operationalization looked as follows[103, 104, 105].

perform* or measur* or evaluat* or assessm* or feedback* or reward* or incentiv* or compens* or bonus*
AND
cultur* or Hofstede or GLOBE or Hall or Schwartz or Trompenaars or Hampden

Table 35: Search operationalization

(4) All articles were initially screened for context relevance (i.e. related to the research focus) by reading the abstract. If a study met the selection criteria, i.e. treated national culture and performance evaluation or rewards, the article was added to the sample. Otherwise, articles were excluded from categorization. This search has been enriched by appropriate articles from major reviews (i.e. Kirkman, Lowe and Gibson (2006) and Tsui, Nifadkar and Ou (2007)).[106]

Complementary searching strategies, often seen as a valuable tool to comprehensively grasp the relevant literature (Cooper, 2010) have not been used. Personal contact requests or mass solicitation to other researchers was not seen as reasonable due to the unfamiliarity among this research group, the high heterogeneity of principal researchers and the expected difficulty to establishing contacts. An additional search by Google scholar or by enlarging the journal list could not be followed without losing the quality criteria of the journals. A third option, screening additional articles from all authors identified, would have created unnecessary complexity. Overall, I assume that the very detailed search indicates a comprehensive far-reaching review. Although great effort was undertaken to achieve a thorough analysis, it is

---

[103] The Boolean 'AND' operator joins various concepts. It will narrow and confine the search. The Boolean 'OR' operator disjuncts the different search terms and retrieves outcomes that have one of the search terms included. 'OR' generally enlarges the search (Reed & Baxter, 2009).

[104] The asterisk function (*) lists a multitude of variations of the corresponding search term. For example, cultur* retrieves articles which comprise culture(s), cultural, cross-culture, cross-cultural, national culture or societal culture (Reed & Baxter, 2009).

[105] In cases where a title, keyword and abstract search was not available, only an abstract search was applied. For one journal a manual title search was complemented. Any promising article has been reviewed in full in a second step.

[106] All articles identified in these two reviews have been screened towards applicability to the MCS theme under investigation.

possible that I unintentionally overlooked some articles. I hope that any omissions will not affect the conclusions of the review (Tsui, Nifadkar & Ou, 2007).

(5) To finally select the relevant articles, I reviewed the sample of previously identified articles. A classification scheme was developed to facilitate the examination of the literature (see Table 36). I read the abstract, the hypotheses and the method section – in some cases the entire article – to probe the applicability to the research context.

— Articles should refer to (non-)financial measures, performance evaluation or reward.
— Each article has to involve a minimum of two countries/cultures to allow cross-cultural comparisons. Articles with one country focus should be excluded.
— Articles should be based on an empirical study (either quantitative or qualitative). Mere conceptual papers should be excluded.

Table 36: Classification scheme

Articles that portrayed mere country comparisons, without specifying any cultural acumen in the whole text, were excluded from the analysis. An example is a paper by Coates, Davis and Stacey (1995) who report findings of performance measurement and reward systems for UK, US and German multinational companies. They explicitly state that they have not integrated national culture into their study. There are also studies in the HRM area which do not fulfil the cultural criterion (e.g. Carr and Pudelko (2006), Pudelko and Harzing (2008)).

(6) Categories have been extracted from former literature to synthesize the essential information from each article in a similar manner. The reviews of Harrison and McKinnon (1999), Chow, Shields and Wu (1999) and Tsui, Nifadkar and Ou (2007) gave a solid foundation for the final categories. Complemented by my own ideas (labelled with *) this resulted to the final categories that are pictured in Table 37. This literature review considers many different criteria of information not found in any prior review related to the context of MCS.

Study (author(s) and year), countries involved, number of countries with data collection *, sample size, sample characteristics, research design, realization of random sampling *, pre-tests * and back-translation *, response rate *, cultural framework *, cultural dimensions, data collection of cultural values, MCS characteristic(s), primary statistical tool, control variables * and hypothesis.

Table 37: Coding categories literature review

Appendix 4: Journals included in the literature review

Abacus	Journal of Applied Behavioral Science
Academy of Management Journal	Journal of Applied Psychology
Academy of Management Review	Journal of Applied Social Psychology
Accounting and Business Research	Journal of Business Finance & Accounting
Accounting and Finance	Journal of Business Research
Accounting, Auditing & Accountability Journal	Journal of Business Venturing
Accounting Education: An International Journal	Journal of Cross-Cultural Psychology
Accounting Horizons	Journal of Economic Behavior and Organization
Accounting, Organizations and Society	Journal of Economics & Management Strategy
Administrative Science Quarterly	Journal of Experimental Social Psychology
Advances in Accounting	Journal of Human Resources
Advances in Global Leadership	Journal of International Accounting, Auditing and Taxation
Advances in International Comparative Management	Journal of International Business Studies
Behavioral Research in Accounting	Journal of International Management
British Accounting Review	Journal of Management
British Journal of Social Psychology	Journal of Management Accounting Research
California Management Review	Journal of Management Information Systems
Contemporary Accounting Research	Journal of Management Studies
Critical Perspectives on Accounting	Journal of Occupational & Organizational Psychology
Decision Sciences	Journal of Organizational Behavior
European Accounting Review	Journal of Personality and Social Psychology
European Journal of Social Psychology	Journal of Research in Personality
Financial Accountability & Management	Journal of Vocational Behavior
Group and Organization Management	Journal of World Business
Human Relations	Leadership Quarterly
Human Resource Management	Management Accounting Research
Industrial and Labor Relations Review	Management International Review
Industrial Relations	Management Science
Information Systems Research	MIS Quarterly
International Journal of Commerce and Management	Multinational Business Review
International Journal of Conflict Management	Operations Research
International Journal of Intercultural Relations	Organization Science
International Journal of Organizational Analysis	Organizational Behavior and Human Decision Processes
International Journal of Psychology	Personnel Psychology
International Journal of Research in Marketing	Production and Operations Management
International Studies of Management and Organization	Review of Accounting Studies
Journal of Accounting & Economics	Small Group Research
Journal of Accounting & Public Policy	Strategic Management Journal
Journal of Accounting Literature	The Accounting Historians Journal
Journal of Accounting Research	The Accounting Review
Journal of Accounting, Auditing & Finance	The International Journal of Accounting
Journal of Applied Accounting Research	

Table 38: Journals included in the literature review

Appendix 5: Results of literature review

Sample review

The extensive literature review resulted to 50 studies in 26 journals for the area of performance evaluation and rewards, among only twelve accounting journal articles and 38 non-accounting journals papers. Table 39 exhibits an overview of these journals and the number of publications with the first appearance in 1982. Strikingly, in the past ten years there appeared only five publications in accounting journals. The list shows the great heterogeneity of journals and thus the fragmented approach to cross-cultural MCS research. An explanation certainly lies in the interdisciplinary nature of this research. The publications in this research field started with Bond, Leung and Wan (1982), Leung and Bond (1984) and Leung and Park (1986) on the topic of reward allocation. There were five stronger years (1995, 1998, 2004, 2007 and 2012) in which more than two articles have been published. The average yearly publication output in the last thirty years amounts to 1.7 articles.

19 studies concentrated on a US vs. Non-US comparison. Adding the studies with an Australian, Canadian or UK context reveals the dominance of Anglo-American researchers. European samples appear more in the larger-scale surveys, in 18 cases. East European samples are almost non-existent (two studies listed the Czech Republic or Poland). 22 studies concentrated on a two-country comparison. Three studies are mono-cultural and compare their results with previous research. Ten studies examined seven or more countries and were in this sense 'real' cross-cultural studies, which fulfilled the minimum criterion of Franke and Richey (2010) required to draw convincing generalizations in international business. Tung and Verbeke (2010, p. 1259-1260) stress that "researchers should never formulate strong conclusions about the impact of cultural dimensions … based on samples that include only one or a few countries". A reason for the low number of countries investigated in each study is probably the difficulty of getting access to participants in various countries without an established research network of scholars in multiple countries.

A look at the sample sizes reveals a huge range. Respondents in the six field studies ranged from 15 to 92 interviews. The twelve experimental studies ranged from 93 to 484 respondents with an average of 229 respondents. While the largest survey study conducted by Peretz and Fried (2012) involved roughly 6.000 respondents, the smallest study from Chen, Romicki and Zuckerman (1997) included 66 respondents.

Appendix

Table 39: Publications of literature review by journal source and year

YEAR	ACCOUNTING					GENERAL MANAGEMENT					INTERNATIONAL BUSINESS					ORGANIZATION STUDIES				PSYCHOLOGY					OTHER		total
	AOS	EAR	IJA	AAAJ	MAR	AMJ	JMS	JBR	JSMO	JOM	JIBS	MIR	JWB	IJIR	JIM	HR	OBHDP	JOB	OS	JCCP	BJSP	JAP	JP&SP	PP	HRM	IJRM	
2013																				1		1					2
2012		1					1	1					1														4
2011							1									1											2
2010							1													1							2
2009	1																										1
2008													1				1					1					3
2007	1											1															2
2006																									1		1
2005																1			1								2
2004				1										1	1							1					4
2003		1									1																2
2002																	1	1									2
2001																								1			1
1999	1		1																								2
1998					1				1		1									1							4
1997			1																		1						2
1996	1					1																					2
1995	1					1												1									3
1994										1																	1
1993							1																				1
1992											1																1
1991																							1				1
1990	1																										1
1988																			1								1
1986																				1							1
1984																					1						1
1982																										1	1
Total	6	2	2	1	1	3	3	2	1	1	3	2	2	1	1	2	2	1	1	5	2	1	1	1	2	1	50

AOS — Accounting, Organizations and Society; EAR — European Accounting Review; IJA — The International Journal of Accounting; AAAJ — Accounting, Auditing & Accountability Journal; MAR — Management Accounting Research; AMJ — Academy of Management Journal; JMS — Journal of Management Studies; JBR — Journal of Business Research; JSMO — International Studies of Management and Organization; JOM — Journal of Management; JIBS — Journal of International Business Studies; MIR — Management International Review; JWB — Journal of World Business; IJIR — International Journal of Intercultural Relations; JIM — Journal of International Management; IIR — Human Relations; OBHDP — Organizational Behavior and Human Decision Processes; JOB — Journal of Organizational Behavior; OS — Organization Science; JCCP — Journal of Cross-Cultural Psychology; BJSP — British Journal of Social Psychology; JAP — Journal of Applied Psychology; JP&SP — Journal of Personality and Social Psychology; PP — Personnel Psychology; HRM — Human Resource Management; IJRM — International Journal of Research in Marketing

Note: The classification of journals is derived from the association of business schools and the international guide to academic journal quality (http://www.bizschooljournals.com)

The mean survey sample size amounts to 917 participants. A special remark is given to the sample of the managerial elites. Top management team is rarely targeted. Only three survey studies address the top-level hierarchy, one with the help of an international business news and financial information group (Pepper, Gore & Crossman, 2013), one study successfully approached 159 Taiwanese top two level managers (Chow, Shields & Wu, 1999), the third study reached 100 senior managers of foreign subsidiaries (Roth & O'Donnell, 1996). This translates to the fact that no study in this sample targeted so many senior executives (compare with next Chapter) in such a careful manner as the project group this thesis is rooted in.

The overwhelming majority of the studies relied on the Hofstede framework. Almost half of the studies used Hofstede as the single source of cultural explanation, eight studies simultaneously followed Hofstede and another framework. Scholars often do not argue why they use Hofstede, as if no other framework existed for cross-cultural studies. In those cases where authors provide arguments, they mostly state that Hofstede is the most widely used and well-established framework. However, from 2002 onwards, criticism has been raised against Hofstede and pitfalls and shortcomings of his typology have been noted, for example by Chiang and Birtch (2012). There is a larger fraction of studies that did not use any cultural framework at all, although all of them referred to cultural or cross-cultural issues in their abstract or key word list. Four studies examined cultural differences with the GLOBE framework (Bonache, Trullen & Sanchez, 2012; Chiang & Birtch, 2010; Chong, 2013; Peretz & Fried, 2012), the first in 2010. The late appearance is not surprising given that the GLOBE book was published in 2004. Interestingly, Chiang and Birtch, who used a very similar research design for their 2010 and 2012 papers published in the same journal, conducted their 2010 study with GLOBE and switched back to Hofstede for the 2012 paper.

Content review

Table 40 - Table 45 list the studies from the literature review. The tables provide information on many of the coding categories presented in Table 37 (p. 190), in particular study (author(s) and year), sample size, sample characteristics, research design, cultural framework, cultural dimensions and primary statistical tool.

Study	Geographical context (sample size)	Sample size	Primary research design	Respondents	Cultural framework	Cultural dimension(s)	Primary statistical tool
Awasthi, Chow & Wu (1998)	Taiwan (75), USA (75) * Collected in Taiwan	150	Experiment	Students (MBA & undergraduate)	Hofstede	I-C	Regression
Awasthi, Chow and Wu (2001)	Taiwan (75), USA (75) * Collected in Taiwan	150	Experiment	Students (MBA & undergraduate)	Hofstede	I-C, PD	Regression
Birnberg & Snodgrass (1988)	Japan (550), USA (501)	1,051	Survey	Mix (employees & others)	Kluckhohn & Strodtbeck	Human Nature	(M)AN(C)OVA/ t test
Bonache, Trullen & Sanchez (2012)	Mexico (25), Argentina (1), Puerto Rico (1), Peru (16), Costa Rica (26), Nicaragua (18), Panama (8), Ecuador (9), El Salvador (7), Paraguay (2), Honduras (10), Guatemala (10), Colombia (1), Bolivia (2), Uruguay (1), Chile (1)	138	Survey	Mix (TMT & others)	Hofstede & GLOBE	PO	HLM
Bond, Leung & Kwok (1982)	Hong Kong (108), USA (99)	207	Experiment	Students ((Under)graduate)	Hofstede	I-C	Regression
Chen (1995)	China (277), USA (205)	482	Survey	Mix (TMT & other employees)	Hofstede & Other	I-C	(M)AN(C)OVA/ t test
Chen, Romocki & Zuckerman (1997)	US-based Japanese affiliates (66 in total) * Collected in USA	66	Survey	Mix (TMT & other employees)	Hofstede	M-F, I-C, PD, UA	(M)AN(C)OVA/ t test
Chiang & Birtch (2005)	Canada(378), Finland (189), Hong Kong (252), United Kingdom (186)	1,005	Survey	Mix (TMT & other employees)	Hofstede	M-F, I-C, PD, UA	(M)AN(C)OVA/ t test
Chiang & Birtch (2006)	Finland (189), Hong Kong (252)	441	Survey	Mix (TMT & other employees)	Hofstede	M-F, I-C, PD, UA	(M)AN(C)OVA/ t test
Chiang & Birtch (2007)	Canada(378), Finland (189), Hong Kong (252), United Kingdom (186)	1,005	Survey	Mix (TMT & other employees)	Hofstede	M-F, I-C, PD, UA	(M)AN(C)OVA/ t test

Legend:
TMT: Top Management Team
M-F: Masculinity-Femininity; I-C: Individualism–Collectivism; PD: Power Distance; UA: Uncertainty Avoidance; PO: Performance Orientation

Table 40: Summary of articles from literature review (1)

Study	Geographical context (sample size)	Sample size	Primary research design	Respondents	Cultural framework	Cultural dimension(s)	Primary statistical tool
Chiang & Birtch (2010)	Canada (378), Finland (189), Hong Kong (252), Singapore (212), Sweden (175), United Kingdom (186), USA (357)	1,749	Survey	Mix (TMT & other employees)	GLOBE	ASS, UA, I-C, PD	Regression
Chiang & Birtch (2012)	Finland (232), Hong Kong (336)	568	Survey	Mix (TMT & other employees)	Hofstede	M-F, I-C, PD, UA	(M)AN(C)OVA/ t test
Chong (2013)	Singapore (120) * The results are compared with a study in Great Britain (58).	178	Survey	Mix (TMT & other employees)	Hofstede & GLOBE	None	Cluster Analysis
Chow, Kato & Shields (1994)	Japan (39), USA (54)	93	Experiment	Students (MBA)	Hofstede	I-C, PD, UA, M-F	(M)AN(C)OVA/ t test
Chow, Shields & Wu (1999)	Japan (56), Taiwan (59), USA (44) * Collected in Taiwan	159	Survey	TMT	Hofstede	M-F, I-C, PD, UA	(M)AN(C)OVA/ t test
Cooke & Huang (2011)	China, USA (92 in total) * Collected in China	92	Interview	Mix (TMT & other employees)	None	Egalitarianism	n.a.
DeVoe & Iyengar (2004)	Argentina (150), Brazil (235), Mexico (150), Philippines (86), Taiwan (175), USA (1.150)	1,945	Survey	Mix (TMT & other employees)	None	None	HLM
Efferin & Hopper (2007)	Chinese Indonesian (10) * Collected in Indonesia	15	Interview	Mix (TMT & other employees)	Others	Confucian values, Javanese	n.a.
Fischer (2004)	Germany (70), UK (87) / Germany (184), UK (130)	471	Survey	Other Employees	Hofstede & Schwartz	I-C, UA, Egalitarianism	(M)AN(C)OVA/ t test
Fischer et al. (2007)	Brazil (153), Germany (179), New Zealand (91), UK (106), US (131)	660	Survey	Mix (TMT & other employees)	Schwartz	Other	HLM

Legend:
TMT: Top Management Team
M-F: Masculinity-Femininity; I-C: Individualism–Collectivism; PD: Power Distance; UA: Uncertainty Avoidance; ASS: Assertiveness;
Other: Hierarchy-Egalitarianism, Embeddedness-Autonomy, Harmony-Mastery

Table 41: Summary of articles from literature review (2)

Study	Geographical context (sample size)	Sample size	Primary research design	Respondents	Cultural framework	Cultural dimension(s)	Primary statistical tool
Giacobbe-Miller, Miller & Victorov (1998)	Russia (120), US (81) / Russia (125), US (80)	406	Survey	Mix (employees & others)	Hofstede & Other	I-C	(M)AN(C)OVA/ t test
Giacobbe-Miller et al. (2003)	China (113), Russia (87), USA (66)	266	Survey	Middle Managers	Hofstede	I-C	(M)AN(C)OVA/ t test
Hui, Triandis & Yee (1991)	Hong Kong (72), USA (88)	160	Experiment	Students ((Under)graduate)	Others	I-C	(M)AN(C)OVA/ t test
Jackson, Amaeshi & Yavuz (2008)	Kenyan Africans, Asians, and British (in total 34) * Collected in Kenya	34	Interview	Mix (TMT & other employees)	Others	None	n.a.
Jansen, Merchant & van der Stede (2009)	The Netherlands (206) * The results are compared with a study in USA	206	Mix	Mix (TMT & other employees)	Hofstede & Other	M-F, LTO, Other	Regression
Kim, Park & Suzuki (1990)	Japan (117), Korea (140), USA (132)	389	Experiment	Students ((Under)graduate)	Hofstede	M-F, I-C	(M)AN(C)OVA/ t test
Kinglake Tower, Kelly & Richards (1997)	Russia (80), UK (80)	160	Experiment	Students ((Under)graduate)	Others	I-C	(M)AN(C)OVA/ t test
Leung & Bond (1984)	Hong Kong (96), USA (96) / Hong Kong (144), USA (128)	336	Experiment	Students ((Under)graduate)	Hofstede & Other	I-C	(M)AN(C)OVA/ t test
Leung & Iwawaki (1988)	Japan (160), South Korea (160), USA (164)	484	Experiment	Students ((Under)graduate)	Others	I-C	(M)AN(C)OVA/ t test
Leung & Park (1986)	Korea (88), USA (88)	186	Experiment	Students ((Under)graduate)	None	None	(M)AN(C)OVA/ t test
Leung et al. (2012)	China (141), USA (76)	217	Experiment	Students ((Under)graduate)	None	None	Regression

Legend:
TMT: Top Management Team
M-F: Masculinity–Femininity; I-C: Individualism–Collectivism; PD: Power Distance; UA: Uncertainty Avoidance; ASS: Assertiveness; Other: Belief about the role of corporate (shareholder vs. stakeholder)

Table 42: Summary of articles from literature review (3)

Study	Geographical context (sample size)	Sample size	Primary research design	Respondents	Cultural framework	Cultural dimension(s)	Primary statistical tool
Lindholm (1999)	China (270), Germany (246), India (86), Thailand (107), UK (843), USA (297)	1,849	Survey	Mix (TMT & other employees)	Hofstede	M-F, I-C, PD, UA	Regression
Lowe et al. (2002)	Australia (435), Canada (124), China (190), Indonesia (241), Japan (271), Korea (237), Mexico (179), Taiwan (241), USA (144), Costa Rica/Guatemala/Panama/Nicaragua/Venezuela (143)	2,205	Survey	Mix (TMT & other employees)	None	I-C	Descriptive
Merchant, Chow & Wu (1995)	Taiwan (32), USA (n.a.)	32	Interview	Mix (TMT & other employees)	Hofstede	M-F, I-C, PD, UA, LTO	Descriptive
Merchant et al. (2011)	China (260) * The results are compared with a study in the US and the Netherlands	260	Survey	Mix (TMT & other employees)	Hofstede	M-F, PD/ Egalitarianism	Regression
Murphy-Berman & Berman (2002)	Hong Kong (101), Indonesia (114)	215	Experiment	Students ((Under)graduate)	Schwartz & Triandis	I-C	(M)AN(C)OVA/ t test
Newman & Nollen (1996)	Australia (10), Austria (7), Belgium (3), Denmark (3), France (11), Germany (28), Hong Kong (6), Italy (9), Japan (15), Malaysia (5), Netherlands (10), New Zealand (7), Philippines (3), Singapore (4), Spain (14), Switzerland (15), Turkey (5), UK (21)	176	Survey	Other Employees	Hofstede	M-F, I-C, PD, UA, LTO	(M)AN(C)OVA/ t test
Palich, Horn & Griffeth (1995)	Austria (44), Belgium (71), the Netherlands (75), Spain (66), Portugal (11), Greece (23), Finland (36), Norway (47), Italy (224), England (371), Denmark (47), West Germany (383), German-speaking Switzerland (114), Sweden (90), British-Canada (166)	1,859	Survey	Mix (TMT & other employees)	Hofstede	M-F, I-C	SEM

Legend:
TMT: Top Management Team
M-F: Masculinity-Femininity; I-C: Individualism–Collectivism; PD: Power Distance; UA: Uncertainty Avoidance; LTO: Long-time Orientation

Table 43: Summary of articles from literature review (4)

Study	Geographical context (sample size)	Sample size	Primary research design	Respondents	Cultural framework	Cultural dimension(s)	Primary statistical tool
Peng & Peterson (2008)	Japan (204), USA (397)	601	Survey	Middle Managers	Others	I-C, PD	(M)AN(C)OVA/t test
Pennings (1993)	France (5), Netherlands (11), USA (51)	67	Interview	TMT	Hofstede	M-F, I-C, PD, UA	n.a.
Pepper & Gore (2013)	Australia (31), Argentina (14), Brazil (52), China (51), France (35), Germany (31), India (31), Mexico (28), Middle East (75), Netherlands (55), Poland (30), Russia (45), Spain (30), South Africa (31), Switzerland (40), United Kingdom (34), United States (123), Other (20)	756	Survey	TMT	Hofstede & Other	I-C, Uncertainty Aversion, LTO	Others
Peretz & Fried (2012)	Australia (259), Austria (270), Canada (464), Denmark (516), Finland (293), Germany (320), Greece (180), Hungary (59), Ireland (230), Israel (175), Italy (117), New Zealand (286), Philippines (56), Portugal (150), Slovenia (161), Sweden (383), Switzerland (311), The Netherlands (397), Turkey (171), United Kingdom (633), USA (560)	5,991	Survey	Mix (TMT & other employees)	GLOBE	I-C, UA, FO, PD	HLM
Roth & O'Donnell (1996)	Canada (14), Germany (12), Japan (12), UK (22), USA (40)	100	Survey	TMT	Hofstede	M-F, I-C, PD, UA	Regression
Schuler & Rogovsky (1998)	Argentina, Australia, Austria, Brazil, Canada, France, Germany, Ireland, Israel, Italy, Japan, Mexico, Norway, Spain, Sweden, UK, USA, The Netherlands (size n.a.)	n.a.	Survey	Other Employees	Hofstede	M-F, I-C, PD, UA	Correlation

Legend:
TMT: Top Management Team
M-F: Masculinity-Femininity; I-C: Individualism-Collectivism; PD: Power Distance; UA: Uncertainty Avoidance; LTO: Long-time Orientation; FO: Future Orientation

Table 44: Summary of articles from literature review (5)

Study	Geographical context (sample size)	Sample size	Primary research design	Respondents	Cultural framework	Cultural dimension(s)	Primary statistical tool
Segalla et al. (2006)	Austria (100), France (117), Germany (111), Italy (137), Spain (98), UK (89)	652	Survey	Middle Managers	Hofstede	I-C, UA	Regression
Tosi & Greckhamer (2004)	Argentina, Australia, Belgium, Brazil, Canada, France, Germany, Hong Kong, Italy, Japan, Malaysia, Mexico, the Netherlands, New Zealand, Singapore, South Africa, South Korea, Spain, Sweden, Switzerland, United Kingdom, United States, Venezuela	23	Archival data	TMT	Hofstede	M-F, I-C, PD, UA	Regression
Van der Stede (2003)	Belgium (115), Canada/Czech Republic/Denmark/France/Germany/Greece/Luxembourg/Netherlands/Norway/Portugal/UK (38 in total) * Collected in Belgium	153	Survey	Middle Managers	Hofstede	M-F, I-C, PD, UA	(M)AN(C)OVA/ t test
Vance et al. (1992)	Indonesia (177), Malaysia (192), Thailand (182), USA (156)	707	Survey	Middle Managers	Hofstede	I-C, PD, UA	(M)AN(C)OVA/ t test
Wickramasinghe, Hopper & Rathmasiri (2004)	Japan, Sri Lanka (48 in total) * Collected in Sri Lanka	48	Interview	Mix (TMT & other employees)	None	None	n.a.
Wilson (2010)	Different ethnic groups (White, Black, Asian, Other) * Collected in UK	667	Survey	Other Employees	None	None	(M)AN(C)OVA/ t test

Legend:
TMT: Top Management Team
M-F: Masculinity-Femininity; I-C: Individualism–Collectivism; PD: Power Distance; UA: Uncertainty Avoidance

Table 45: Summary of articles from literature review (6)

Appendix 6: GLOBE regional clusters

Cultural Dimension	High-Score Clusters	Mid-Score Clusters	Low-Score Clusters	Cluster Range
Performance Orientation	Confucian Asia Germanic Europe Anglo	Southern Asia Sub-Saharan Africa Latin Europe Nordic Europe Middle East	Latin America Eastern Europe	3.73 — 4.58
Assertiveness	Germanic Europe Eastern Europe	Sub-Saharan Africa Latin America Anglo Middle East Confucian Asia Latin Europe Southern Asia	Nordic Europe	3.66 — 4.55
Future Orientation	Germanic Europe Nordic Europe	Confucian Asia Anglo Southern Asia Sub-Saharan Africa Latin Europe	Middle East Latin America Eastern Europe	3.38 — 4.40
Humane Orientation	Southern Asia Sub-Saharan Africa	Middle East Anglo Nordic Europe Latin America Confucian Asia Eastern Europe	Latin Europe Germanic Europe	3.55 — 4.71
Institutional Collectivism	Nordic Europe Confucian Asia	Anglo Southern Asia Sub-Saharan Africa Middle East Eastern Europe	Germanic Europe Latin Europe Latin America	3.86 — 4.88
In-Group Collecitivism	Southern Asia Middle East Eastern Europe Latin America Confucian Asia	Sub-Saharan Africa Latin Europe	Anglo Germanic Europe Nordic Europe	3.75 — 5.87
Gender Egalitarianism	Eastern Europe Nordic Europe	Latin America Anglo Latin Europe Sub-Saharan Africa Southern Asia Confucian Asia Germanic Europe	Middle East	2.95 — 3.84
Power Distance		Southern Asia Latin America Eastern Europe Sub-Saharan Africa Middle East Latin Europe Confucian Asia Anglo Germanic Europe	Nordic Europe	4.54 — 5.39
Uncertainty Avoidance	Nordic Europe Germanic Europe	Confucian Asia Anglo Sub-Saharan Africa Latin Europe Southern Asia	Middle East Latin America Eastern Europe	3.56 — 5.19

Table 46: GLOBE cultural clusters on societal practices scores

Appendix 7: Project outline

ESCP EUROPE
PARIS LONDON BERLIN MADRID TORINO BUSINESS SCHOOL
Chair of Management Control
Prof. Dr. Rolf Brühl – Michael Hanzlick

RESEARCH PROJECT – EFFECTIVENESS OF MANAGEMENT CONTROL SYSTEMS

Topic
The **international research project** seeks to understand how organizations in different countries configure their **management control systems** and what impact the different configurations have on performance. Subsystems comprise strategic and operational planning, performance measurement and evaluation, rewards and compensation, organizational structure, processes and corporate culture. The specific aim is to conceptualize and empirically analyze the packages of management control systems and the linkages between control elements within a **cross-cultural context**. In a nutshell, the project aims to identify how top management is **guiding and directing subordinate behaviour**. The objective of this project is to provide **managerially and practically relevant results**, i.e. topical cross-cultural insights into management control systems, as well as to draw up **specific recommendations for the design and further development**.

Process – Your contribution
Several well-known universities and business schools from **11 countries** are participating in this international research project on management control systems (Northern- and Western Europe, Australia and Canada). In Germany, the research project is carried out from ESCP Europe Business School Berlin.

The German research team focuses the research agenda across various industry branches on the strategic business units of the largest 2.000 companies operating in Germany. Interview **respondents are executives from the management board, management directors or heads of strategic business units**. Data collection will be based on a formal **questionnaire** that is filled in during a personal. This procedure seeks to ensure that questions are understood correctly, but also to enable additional insights into challenges of management control. Answers will be handled and stored with the greatest care and a single organization will remain **anonymous** in the analysis. If a company wishes, we will sign a formal non-disclosure agreement. We will spend approximately **two hours per interview**. The supplementary cross-cultural questions, which have to be filled out individually by four other employees, who are working in the scope of the interview partner, require **15 minutes**.

Your benefits
There are **various benefits for your company** in participating:
- Invitation to a **seminar/workshop** to exchange experience with other firms
- **Exclusive report of research results**
- Possibility to give **tailored feedback** to an organization and to **critically reflect company's management control systems**

Appendix 8: Excerpt of MCS questionnaire and coding instructions

EFFECTIVE MANAGEMENT CONTROL SYSTEMS

Confidential International Survey Research
2011-2012

ESCP EUROPE
PARIS LONDON BERLIN MADRID TORINO BUSINESS SCHOOL

Contact Berlin

Michael Hanzlick
ESCP Europe Business School Berlin

Heubnerweg 8-10
14059 Berlin

Chair of Management Control
Tel: +49 (0) 30 - 320 07 186
Fax: +49 (0) 30 - 320 07 107
E-Mail: mhanzlick@escpeurope.eu
Internet: www.escpeurope.de/controlling

© Michael Hanzlick / Mikko Sandelin 2011

PURPOSE OF THE RESEARCH

This interview contributes to an international research project that seeks to understand what kind of management control arrangements exist, what arrangements are effective and in what kind of settings. This holistic approach to management control is addressed in this questionnaire. The questionnaire is structured as follows:

	Section A	Strategic planning
	Section B	Short-term planning
	Section C	Performance measurement and evaluation
	Section D	Rewards and compensation
	Section E	Organizational structure and management processes
	Section F	Organization culture and values
	Section G	Organization and environment

KEY TERMS

- → **SBU** refers to the strategic business unit or autonomous/standalone firm, which you are part of.
- → **SBU top management** refers to the top two levels in the SBU as a whole (e.g. CEO, CFO, COO and other personnel on the executive management team).
- → **Subordinates** refer to the direct reports of the top management team that typically are responsible for a business unit, department, profit center, or cost center performance.

ANSWERING PERSPECTIVE

The questions are to be answered from the perspective of the top management team of a strategic business unit (SBU) or autonomous/standalone firm, but not from the perspective of management of a head/corporate office of a group of firms.

Questions mainly focus on SBU top management – subordinate relationships. It is acceptable to focus on those managers who run the major business functions and have large number of subordinates of their own. This means that support and administrative managers can be excluded if necessary.

ANSWERING TECHNIQUE

- → Most questions are asked in the form of scales (e.g. 1-7). For these questions, please circle the single number that reflects your SBU practice.
- → Some questions are asked in the form of alternatives followed by boxes. For these questions, please check the box next to the relevant alternative. If there are more than one column of boxes, please check one alternative in each column.
- → There are no right or wrong responses. Not applicable (N/A) is always an option as well.

Please start here:

1. How many years have you worked for your current SBU?   Code years
2. What is the title of your position?   See instructions
3. What is your highest degree?   See instructions
4. What was your field of study?   See instructions

Appendix 205

Section C. Performance Measurement and Evaluation

C3. Please indicate to what extent SBU top management bases subordinates' performance evaluation on:

		Not at all						Very high extent
a	Financial measures	1	2	3	4	5	6	7
b	Non-financial measures	1	2	3	4	5	6	7
c	Detailed measures (e.g. budget line item, input volume, time, quality etc.)	1	2	3	4	5	6	7
d	Aggregate, summary measures (e.g. EBIT, Profit, ROI, ROCE, market share, brand value, brand image, total customer satisfaction, etc.)	1	2	3	4	5	6	7
e	Achievements in leadership behaviour	1	2	3	4	5	6	7
f	Actions and activities taken	1	2	3	4	5	6	7
g	Individual effort	1	2	3	4	5	6	7
h	For how many performance measures does SBU top management hold subordinates accountable?	_____ Code number						

C4. Please indicate to what extent SBU top management evaluates subordinates' performance in relation to…

		Not at all						Very high extent
a	Absolute, preset numbers (euros, time, %)	1	2	3	4	5	6	7
b	Internal benchmarks (league table position)	1	2	3	4	5	6	7
c	External benchmarks (league table position)	1	2	3	4	5	6	7
d	Past performance (trend-based evaluation)	1	2	3	4	5	6	7

C5. Please indicate how important the following purposes of performance evaluation are in your SBU:

		Not at all						Very important
a	Provide feedback for learning & continuous improvement	1	2	3	4	5	6	7
b	Determine subordinate compensation	1	2	3	4	5	6	7
c	Direct subordinates' attention to important issues	1	2	3	4	5	6	7

C6. Please indicate how often formalized performance evaluations (for determining compensation or providing individual feedback) are conducted in your SBU. (Please check one box in each column):

		a LEADERSHIP PERFORMANCE	b BUSINESS PERFORMANCE
1	Monthly		
2	Quarterly		
3	Three times a year		
4	Twice a year		
5	Once a year		
6	Less frequently than once a year		
0	Not applicable (N/A)		

		Not at all						Very important
C7.	How important is performance measurement and evaluation in guiding and directing subordinate behaviour?	1	2	3	4	5	6	7

Section D. Rewards and compensation

D1. a) Please name the most important performance measures for determining subordinates' financial rewards   **b)** Please indicate weight (%) of each measure in rewarding formula   **c)** Please indicate the level at which performance measure is calculated
C = Corporate = 1
S = SBU = 2
B = BU = 3
P = Personal (leadership) = 4

Measure 1: Code number (see above) ____   Code % _____   _____
Measure 2: _____   _____   _____
Measure 3: _____   _____   _____
Measure 4: _____   _____   _____
Measure 5: _____   _____   _____

D2. Please indicate to what extent the following statements describe the way of evaluating and compensating subordinates' performance in your SBU:

		Not at all						Very high extent
a	We determine weights of performance measures as the evaluation takes place	1	2	3	4	5	6	7
b	We evaluate performance on the basis of quantitative metrics	1	2	3	4	5	6	7
c	We adjust the amount of bonus based on actual circumstances	1	2	3	4	5	6	7
d	We use predetermined criteria in evaluation and rewarding	1	2	3	4	5	6	7

	D3. Please indicate to what extent…	Not at all						Very high extent
a	Performance-pay contracts are customized for each subordinate	1	2	3	4	5	6	7
b	Financial rewards are shared evenly to subordinates (e.g. profit sharing)	1	2	3	4	5	6	7
c	Financial rewards increase as subordinate's performance exceeds targets	1	2	3	4	5	6	7
d	Rewarding is financial (bonuses, share-based rewards)	1	2	3	4	5	6	7
e	Rewarding is non-financial (e.g. recognition, promotion, training)	1	2	3	4	5	6	7

Appendix

D4. How important are the following purposes of financial and non-financial rewarding in your SBU:

		Financial		Non-financial	
		Not at all Very important		Not at all Very important	
a	Committing subordinates	1 2 3 4 5 6 7		1 2 3 4 5 6 7	d
b	Motivating subordinates	1 2 3 4 5 6 7		1 2 3 4 5 6 7	e
c	Directing subordinates' attention	1 2 3 4 5 6 7		1 2 3 4 5 6 7	f

	Not at all Very important
D5. How important are rewards and compensation in guiding and directing subordinate behaviour?	1 2 3 4 5 6 7

Section G. Organization and Environment

G2. Please indicate how important the following performance areas are for your SBU right now:

		Not at all Very important
a	Financial results (e.g. annual earnings, return on assets, cost reduction)	1 2 3 4 5 6 7
b	Customer relations (e.g. market share, customer satisfaction, customer retention)	1 2 3 4 5 6 7
c	Employee relations (e.g. employee satisfaction, turnover, workforce capabilities)	1 2 3 4 5 6 7
d	Operational performance (e.g. productivity, safety, cycle-time)	1 2 3 4 5 6 7
e	Quality (e.g. defect rates, quality awards)	1 2 3 4 5 6 7
f	Alliances (e.g. joint marketing or product design, joint ventures, open technology platforms)	1 2 3 4 5 6 7
g	Supplier relations (e.g. on-time delivery, input into product/service design, supplier assistance)	1 2 3 4 5 6 7
h	Environmental performance (e.g. government citations, environmental compliance or certification)	1 2 3 4 5 6 7
i	Innovation (new product/ service development success, process innovation, business concept innovation)	1 2 3 4 5 6 7

G6. Please fill in the following financial and non-financial information

Annual sales	a	2010	_____	M€	2009	_____	M€	d
Total assets	b	2010	_____	M€	2009	_____	M€	e
Operating Profit (EBIT)	c	2010	_____	M€	2009	_____	M€	f

	Well below Industry average Well above
g. How does your organization perform in relation to industry average? (ROI in relation to industry average)	1 2 3 4 5 6 7

G7. This question is about competitive and operating environment of your SBU.
Over the past three years:

  i) How many changes have occurred that had a material impact on the nature of your business?
  ii) How predictable or unpredictable have changes in the external environment been?

	i) Number of changes		ii) Predictability	
	Very few changes → Very many changes		Very unpredictable → Very predictable	
a *Customers* (e.g. levels of demand, customer requirements)	1 2 3 4 5 6 7		1 2 3 4 5 6 7	g
b *Suppliers* (e.g. markets for key inputs, quality of resources)	1 2 3 4 5 6 7		1 2 3 4 5 6 7	h
c *Competitors* (e.g. competitors entering/leaving, tactics/strategies)	1 2 3 4 5 6 7		1 2 3 4 5 6 7	i
d *Technological* (e.g. R&D advances, process innovations)	1 2 3 4 5 6 7		1 2 3 4 5 6 7	j
e *Regulatory* (e.g. new initiatives for laws, regulations)	1 2 3 4 5 6 7		1 2 3 4 5 6 7	k
f *Economic* (e.g. interest and exchange rates)	1 2 3 4 5 6 7		1 2 3 4 5 6 7	l

G10. SBU/DIVISION INFORMATION

  a. What is the number of employees in your SBU?   Code number _____ employees
  b. In how many countries does your SBU have operations?   Code number _____ countries
  c. What is your SBU's main industry?
        1 = manufacturing
        2 = services
        3 = wholesale & trade
  d. In which country is your parent company registered?   Code verbally _____
  e. Is your SBU part of a publicly quoted company?   _____ (0 = No   1 = Yes)
  f. Who is the <u>most significant</u> owner of your organization? (Please tick one) Code number (1-11)

i. ____ Members of cooperative society		ii. ____ Large institutional investors
iii. ____ Small institutional investors		iv. ____ Municipalities
v. ____ Venture capitalist(s)		vi. ____ Families
vii. ____ Government		viii. ____ Partners
ix. ____ Trust Fund		x. ____ Company
xi. ____ Other			

Appendix

CODING INSTRUCTIONS (page 1):

Instructions are marked with blue colour on the questionnaire. Regarding Gutman-type scales, the letters are now replaced with numbers (i.e. score to be coded).

The parallel columns are marked with letters. Moreover, if there are two parallel columns with Likert scales, the columns on the right hand side have been given an own letter (i.e. they are to be coded as independent indicators). If the respondent has indicated n/a with respect to any question, please code zero value (n/a = 0). If there are missing values, please code the cell with an "x".

The coding template follows the structure of the questionnaire.

The following general information can be found in the beginning of the Excel template.

- General numbering
- Country of investigation
- Date of interview
- Form of interview (Personally = 1; Telephone = 2)
- Interviewer (Researcher = 1; Student only = 2)
- Financial data acquisition (objective documents = 1; subjective information = 2)
- Company name
- NACE Code
    - see NACE file on statistical classification of economic activities in the European Community, the detailed structure starts at p. 61
    - type four digit number as presented in column 'class' without a dot, or use three digit number as shown in column 'group' and add a zero (e.g. 42.1 → 4210, 42.91 → 4291)
- SBU vs. stand-alone company (separate SBU(s) = 1; stand-alone company = 2)

In the following find details for questions on p. 4

- Gender (Male = 1; Female = 2)
- Title of interviewee (CEO = 1; CFO = 2; COO = 3; Other = 4);
  If more than one person was present at an Interview (e.g. CEO and Controller), list only the most senior person
- Highest degree/education (High School = 1; Bachelor = 2; Master = 3; Ph.D. = 4)
- Field of study (Business/management/economics = 1; Law = 2; Engineering = 3; Humanities = 4; Natural sciences = 5; Others = 6)

Clarification for question A5: Participation in the formation of SBU's strategic ends and means

- A5: When SBU = Company, and only Top Management participates in the formation the SBU's strategic ends and means, then choose answer B (answer A is not applicable in this case since there is no corporate)

CODING INSTRUCTIONS (page 2):

D1a: The details for categorizing question D1a are based on performance evaluation metrics from a review of the literature (e.g. Grafton et al. 2010, Ittner, Larcker & Randall 2003, BSC literature)

1. Financial – Revenue (e.g. sales)
2. Financial – Profit (e.g. EBIT, profit margin, gross margin)
3. Financial – Cost (e.g. operating expenditures, capital expenditures)
4. Financial – ROI (e.g. ROA, ROS, ROCE)
5. Financial – Cash flow (e.g. free cash flow, working capital)
6. Customer / market (e.g. market share, market growth, customer satisfaction/retention)
7. Employee / team (e.g. employee satisfaction, individual & team performance, workforce capabilities, 360 evaluation, individual development)
8. Operational (e.g. productivity, safety, cycle time, health and safety compliance, inventory turnover, lead time)
9. Quality (e.g. defect rates, quality assessments)
10. Alliances / Supplier relations (e.g. on-time delivery, joint venture metrics)
11. Innovation (e.g. new product/service development, R&D spend)
12. Social and environmental (e.g. public image, community ratings, environmental compliance)
13. Individual objectives (e.g. fulfilment of specific projects)
14. Other

Appendix 9: GLOBE questionnaire and coding instructions

MANAGEMENT CONTROL SYSTEMS:
A CROSS-CULTURAL FRAMEWORK

Questionnaire Version Society

This questionnaire is based on the GLOBE (Global Leadership and Organizational Behavior Effectiveness) research program

Michael Hanzlick
ESCP Europe Business School Berlin
Chair of Management Control
Heubnerweg 8-10
14059 Berlin

Tel: +49 (0) 30 - 320 07 186
Fax: +49 (0) 30 - 320 07 107
E-Mail: mhanzlick@escpeurope.eu
Internet: www.escpeurope.de/controlling

The purpose of this questionnaire that is based on the GLOBE research program is to learn about the interplay of management control systems and national and organizational cultures and to explain cross-national differences. Within this research context 300 – 400 persons from four countries will answer this questionnaire. Participants in this study cover various industry sectors. The questionnaire that you are asked to complete consists of 52 questions and will take about 15 minutes of your time.

In the following pages, you are asked to choose a number of statements that reflect your observations of cultural practices, your beliefs, or your perceptions. This is not a test, and there are no right or wrong answers. We are mainly interested in learning about the beliefs in your society, and how various societal practices are perceived by you and the others participating in this research. Your responses will be kept completely confidential. Apart from the researchers engaged in this project, nobody will have access to your responses. Further, the name of your organization will not be publicly released.

If you have any questions or comments about this study, you can contact us at the address on the letterhead. We would also be very happy to send you a summary of the responses we get and a copy of any papers we produce.

Thank you very much for taking part in the survey.

Yours faithfully

Prof. Rolf Brühl (ESCP Europe, Berlin, Germany)
Michael Hanzlick (ESCP Europe, Berlin, Germany)
Dr. Piotr Bednarek (Wroclaw University of Economics, Poland)
Prof. Maurice Gosselin (Université Laval, Québec, Canada)
Prof. Sophie Hoozée (IESEG School of Management, Lille-Paris, France)

Appendix

Section 1 - The way things are in your society

Instructions

In this section, we are interested in your beliefs about the norms, values, and practices in your society. In other words, we are interested in the way your society is - not the way you think it should be.

There are no right or wrong answers, and answers do not indicate goodness or badness of the society.

Please respond to the questions by *circling* the number that most closely represents your observations about your society. Please reply to all questions.

Section 1 begins here.

1. **In this society, orderliness and consistency are stressed, even at the expense of experimentation and innovation.**

strongly agree			neither agree nor disagree			strongly disagree
1	2	3	4	5	6	7

2. **In this society, people are generally:**

aggressive						non-aggressive
1	2	3	4	5	6	7

3. **The way to be successful in this society is to:**

plan ahead						take life events as they occur
1	2	3	4	5	6	7

4. **In this society, the accepted norm is to:**

plan for the future						accept the status quo
1	2	3	4	5	6	7

5. **In this society, a person's influence is based primarily on:**

one's ability and contribution to the society						the authority of one's position
1	2	3	4	5	6	7

6. **In this society, people are generally:**

assertive						non-assertive
1	2	3	4	5	6	7

7. **In this society, leaders encourage group loyalty even if individual goals suffer.**

strongly agree			neither agree nor disagree			strongly disagree
1	2	3	4	5	6	7

8. **In this society, social gatherings are usually:**

planned well in advance						spontaneous (planned less
(2 or more weeks in advance)						than an hour in advance)
1	2	3	4	5	6	7

9. **In this society, people are generally:**

very concerned						not at all concerned
about others						about others
1	2	3	4	5	6	7

10. **In this society, people are generally:**

| dominant | | | | | | non-dominant |
| 1 | 2 | 3 | 4 | 5 | 6 | 7 |

11. **In this society, children take pride in the individual accomplishments of their parents.**

strongly			neither agree			strongly
agree			nor disagree			disagree
1	2	3	4	5	6	7

12. **The economic system in this society is designed to maximize:**

| individual interests | | | | | | collective interests |
| 1 | 2 | 3 | 4 | 5 | 6 | 7 |

13. **In this society, followers are expected to:**

obey their leaders						question their leaders
without question						when in disagreement
1	2	3	4	5	6	7

14. **In this society, people are generally:**

| tough | | | | | | tender |
| 1 | 2 | 3 | 4 | 5 | 6 | 7 |

15. **In this society, teen-aged students are encouraged to strive for continuously improved performance.**

strongly			neither agree			strongly
agree			nor disagree			disagree
1	2	3	4	5	6	7

16. **In this society, most people lead highly structured lives with few unexpected events.**

strongly			neither agree			strongly
agree			nor disagree			disagree
1	2	3	4	5	6	7

17. **In this society, boys are encouraged more than girls to attain a higher education.**

strongly			neither agree			strongly
agree			nor disagree			disagree
1	2	3	4	5	6	7

Appendix

18. In this society, major rewards are based on:

only performance effectiveness		performance effectiveness and other factors (for example, seniority or political connections)			only factors other than performance effectiveness (for example, seniority or political connections)	
1	2	3	4	5	6	7

19. In this society, job requirements and instructions are spelled out in detail so citizens know what they are expected to do.

strongly agree			neither agree nor disagree			strongly disagree
1	2	3	4	5	6	7

20. In this society, being innovative to improve performance is generally:

substantially rewarded			somewhat rewarded			not rewarded
1	2	3	4	5	6	7

21. In this society, people are generally:

very sensitive toward others						not at all sensitive toward others
1	2	3	4	5	6	7

22. In this society, there is more emphasis on athletic programs for:

boys						girls
1	2	3	4	5	6	7

23. In this society, parents take pride in the individual accomplishments of their children.

strongly agree			neither agree nor disagree			strongly disagree
1	2	3	4	5	6	7

24. This society has rules or laws to cover:

almost all situations			some situations			very few situations
1	2	3	4	5	6	7

25. In this society, people are generally:

very friendly						very unfriendly
1	2	3	4	5	6	7

26. In this society, people in positions of power try to:

increase their social distance from less powerful individuals						decrease their social distance from less powerful people
1	2	3	4	5	6	7

27. In this society, rank and position in the hierarchy have special privileges.

strongly agree			neither agree nor disagree			strongly disagree
1	2	3	4	5	6	7

28. In this society, aging parents generally live at home with their children.

strongly agree			neither agree nor disagree			strongly disagree
1	2	3	4	5	6	7

29. In this society, being accepted by the other members of a group is very important.

strongly agree			neither agree nor disagree			strongly disagree
1	2	3	4	5	6	7

30. In this society, more people:

live for the present than live for the future						live for the future than live for the present
1	2	3	4	5	6	7

31. In this society, people place more emphasis on:

solving current problems						planning for the future
1	2	3	4	5	6	7

32. In this society, people are generally:

very tolerant of mistakes						not at all tolerant with mistakes
1	2	3	4	5	6	7

33. In this society, people are generally:

very generous						not at all generous
1	2	3	4	5	6	7

34. In this society, power is:

concentrated at the top						shared throughout the society
1	2	3	4	5	6	7

35. In this society:

group cohesion is valued more than individualism			group cohesion and individualism are equally valued			individualism is valued more than group cohesion
1	2	3	4	5	6	7

36. In this society, it is worse for a boy to fail in school than for a girl to fail in school.

strongly agree			neither agree nor disagree			strongly disagree
1	2	3	4	5	6	7

37. In this society, people are generally:

physical						non-physical
1	2	3	4	5	6	7

38. In this society, who is more likely to serve in a position of high office?

men			men and women are equally likely to serve			women
1	2	3	4	5	6	7

39. In this society, children generally live at home with their parents until they get married.

strongly agree			neither agree nor disagree			strongly disagree
1	2	3	4	5	6	7

Section 2 on demographic data follows next page

Section 2 - Demographic questions

Instructions
Following are several questions about you, your background, and the place where you work. These questions are important because they help us to see if different types of people respond to the questions on this questionnaire in different ways. They are NOT used to identify any individual.

Section 2 begins here.

Questions about your personal background

40. How old are you? _____ years

41. What is your gender? *(check one)* ☐Male   ☐Female

42. What is your country of citizenship/passport? _____

43. What country were you born in? _____

44. How long have you lived in the country where you currently live? _____ years

45. Besides your country of birth, how many other countries have you lived in for longer than one year? _____ countries

Questions about your work background

46. How many years of full-time work experience have you had? _____ years

47. Since when have you worked for your current employer? ____ *(month)* ____ *(year)*

48. What is your job title? _____

Questions about your educational background

49. What is your highest degree (e.g., high school, BA, M.Sc.)? _____

50. What was your main field of study? _____

Appendix

Questions about this organization

51. Please indicate the kind of work primarily done by the unit you manage/work in:
- _____ Administration
- _____ Engineering, manufacturing, or production
- _____ Finance or accounting
- _____ Human resource management or personnel management
- _____ Marketing
- _____ Planning
- _____ Purchasing
- _____ Research and development
- _____ Sales
- _____ Support services (for example, plant and equipment maintenance)
- _____ Other *(please specify)* _____

52. What language(s) do you use at work?
- _____ English
- _____ Flemish/Dutch
- _____ French
- _____ German
- _____ Other *(please specify)* _____

This concludes the questionnaire.

Thank you for taking the time to complete this questionnaire. Your assistance in providing such information is very much appreciated. If there is anything else, you would like to tell us about this survey, please do so in the space provided below.

Appendix 10: Means, SD, ANOVA, and effect size by country

MCS items		N	Country								F-value[f]	η^2
			Belgium		Canada		Germany		Poland			
			Mean	SD	Mean	SD	Mean	SD	Mean	SD		
C3e_g	Subjectivity of performance evaluation[a]	239	5.19	0.92	5.31	0.54	4.83	1.18	4.48	1.25	8.23***	0.080
C3h	Number of performance measures	239	6.38	4.01	5.52	1.64	4.10	2.31	5.64	5.76	8.17***	0.059
C4b_d	Objectivity of performance standards[b]	239	3.82	1.24	5.50	0.77	3.19	1.28	4.21	1.24	64.48***	0.355
C5a	Purpose of performance evaluation	239	5.80	0.90	5.08	1.34	5.63	1.28	5.80	0.99	3.97**	0.054
C5b	Purpose of performance evaluation	239	4.42	1.54	5.69	1.12	4.93	1.51	5.18	1.40	7.06***	0.083
C6a	Frequency of performance evaluation[c]	239	1.94	2.25	1.07	0.69	1.24	0.73	1.93	2.36	4.01**	0.055
C6b	Frequency of performance evaluation[d]	239	5.64	4.91	1.35	1.00	2.31	3.04	5.61	4.78	24.84***	0.206
G2	Balance of performance areas[e]	239	2.41	1.55	1.65	0.73	2.78	1.32	2.70	1.35	17.63***	0.107

[a] Factor analysis (principal components) retains one factor (KMO=0.639, Bartlett's test: p<0.01; eigenvalue = 1.67) for subjectivity of performance evaluation (factor loadings: 0.74-0.77) that explains 55.80% of the variance. The composite scale's Cronbach Alpha is 0.60.
[b] Factor analysis (principal components) retains two factors (KMO=0.682, Bartlett's test: p<0.01; eigenvalues = 2.57 and 1.62) for objectivity of performance evaluation (factor loadings: 0.66-0.76) and objectivity of rewarding (factor loadings: 0.45-0.68) that explain 52.27% of the variance. The composite scale's Cronbach Alpha is 0.68 for evaluation and 0.55 for rewarding (see also Table 48).
[c] The figure states the yearly frequency for leadership issues.
[d] The figure states the yearly frequency for business performance.
[e] The score for 'Balance of performance areas' is derived in three steps. First, the scores related to three of the four BSC perspectives are taken as is: financial aspects [G2a], customer aspects [G2b], employee relation [G2c]. The score for internal business processes is calculated. This score is the mean of five variables: operational performance, quality, supplier relations, environmental performance and innovation (G2d, e, g, h, i). Second, the mean score of the four perspectives is calculated. In a third step, the final score is derived by adding the absolute differences for each of the four dimensions and the mean score of the four perspectives. Lower scores indicate more balance. Factor analysis (principal components) retains one factor (KMO=0.712, Bartlett's test: p<0.01; eigenvalue = 1.96) for internal business processes (factor loadings: 0.58-0.67) that explains 39.20% of the variance. The composite scale's Cronbach Alpha is 0.60.
[f] The homogeneity of variance is tested using Levene's test. If applicable, Welch's F is taken.
Significance levels: ** p<0.01, *** p<0.001.

Table 47: Means, SD, ANOVA, and effect size by country – performance evaluation

Appendix

MCS items		N	Country								F-value[g]	η^2
			Belgium		Canada		Germany		Poland			
			Mean	SD	Mean	SD	Mean	SD	Mean	SD		
D1a	Number of performance measures[a]	222	3.36	1.55	1.25	0.52	2.72	1.33	3.22	1.66	56.62***	0.265
D1a	Balance of performance measures[a]	222	2.03	0.78	1.08	0.27	1.75	0.66	1.86	0.70	45.69***	0.230
D1a+b	Percentage of financial indicators[a]	222	68.54	25.07	91.04	25.44	60.78	34.28	61.16	34.40	14.33***	0.139
D1a+b	Percentage of individual indicators[a]	222	15.92	21.06	0.00	0.00	29.53	33.08	16.20	26.55	34.61***	0.167
D1a+b	Percentage of profit indicators[a]	222	48.33	32.44	56.08	44.54	37.77	33.14	28.64	34.36	4.98***	0.072
D1c	Level of calculation base for rewards[a, b]	127	2.90	0.41	2.03	0.18	3.11	0.66	2.73	0.57	65.34***	0.406
D1c	Level of calculation base for rewards[a, c]	95	2.63	0.38	1.61	0.51	2.94	0.72	2.66	0.46	24.59***	0.448
D2+C4a	Objectivity of rewarding[d, e]	223	5.24	1.13	4.26	0.45	5.57	1.02	5.24	1.11	42.82***	0.216
D3a	Customization of contracts[d]	223	3.72	1.76	5.77	1.37	2.96	1.94	3.82	2.01	34.94***	0.263
D3b	Equality reward criteria[d]	223	3.62	2.18	6.02	1.08	3.32	1.98	1.94	1.46	94.46***	0.403
D3d-e	Extent of (non-)financial rewards[d]	223	1.85	1.83	-0.15	1.43	0.52	2.11	1.98	1.94	18.31***	0.173
D4a-c	Purpose of financial rewards[d, f]	223	5.15	1.10	5.85	0.57	4.90	1.19	5.39	0.91	14.59***	0.119
D4d-f	Purpose of non-financial rewards[d, f]	223	5.49	1.14	5.56	0.62	4.99	1.45	4.47	1.62	8.75***	0.094
D5b	Importance of rewards	239	4.64	1.31	5.83	0.94	4.97	1.45	5.50	1.13	11.54***	0.109

[a)] Data is limited to all those organizations that use a rewarding scheme. Five companies in Germany and eleven companies in Belgium do not have a financial rewarding scheme in place, one company in Germany did not reveal information for D1b. [b)] Focus is on stand-alone companies. [c)] Focus is on companies with several SBUs. [d)] Data is limited to all those organizations that use a rewarding scheme and includes one firm mentioned in (a). [c,d)] The score is derived by summing up the percentage values related to the four hierarchical levels (corporate, SBU, business unit, and individual) and multiplying them with a factor [1-4]. The theoretical range is between 0 and 4. Lower scores indicate more top level focus. [e)] Factor analysis (principal components) retains two factors (KMO=0.682, Bartlett's test: p<0.01; eigenvalues = 2.57 and 1.62) for objectivity of performance evaluation (factor loadings: 0.66-0.76) and objectivity of rewarding (factor loadings: 0.45-0.68) that explain 52.27% of the variance. The composite scale's Cronbach Alpha is 0.68 for evaluation and 0.55 for rewarding. [f)] Factor analysis (principal components) retains two factors (KMO=0.666, Bartlett's test: p<0.01; eigenvalues = 2.43 and 1.62) for the importance of non-financial (factor loadings: 0.82-0.88) and financial purposes (factor loadings: 0.66-0.84) of rewarding that explain 67.44% of the variance. The composite scale's Cronbach Alpha is 0.68 for financial and 0.81 for non-financial rewarding. [g)] The homogeneity of variance is tested using Levene's test. If applicable, Welch's F is taken. Significance levels: ** p<0.01, *** p<0.001.

Table 48: Means, SD, ANOVA, and effect size by country – rewards

Appendix 11: ANCOVA tests

H	MCS item	CD	Homo-geneity	Covariate	B	F-value	η^2 (value)	MCS →	Mean High	Mean Low	F-value	η^2 (value)
6	C3e-g	FO	RS*	13	0.02	7.54**	0.031		4.96	4.90	0.18	0.001
6	C3e-g	FO	✓	16	-0.14	6.32*	0.026		4.86	4.99	0.82	0.003
15	C3e-g	Coll	✓	13	0.02	7.56**	0.031		4.84	5.01	1.53	0.006
15	C3e-g	Coll	✓	16	0.38	3.17 †	0.013		4.99	5.50	1.11	0.005
29	C3h	UA	✓	10	0.40	4.98*	0.021		4.97	5.53	1.36	0.006
29	C3h	UA	✓	11	0.45	5.55*	0.023		4.83	5.73	3.42 †	0.014
29	C3h	UA	✓	13								
33	C4b-d	UA	RS*	1								
33	C4b-d	UA	✓	5	0.15	0.82	0.003		3.44	4.85	69.31***	0.227
33	C4b-d	UA	✓	6	0.01	2.88 †	0.012		3.44	4.84	69.50***	0.227
33	C4b-d	UA	✓	8	0.10	2.06	0.009		3.44	4.84	68.17***	0.225
33	C4b-d	UA	✓	9	0.02	0.08	0.000		3.43	4.86	71.08***	0.231
33	C4b-d	UA	RS*	10								
33	C4b-d	UA	RS***	12								

a) H: hypothesis
b) CD: cultural dimension (UA: uncertainty avoidance, FO: future orientation, PD: power distance, I/C: individualism/collectivism, Ass: assertiveness).
c) Homogeneity: homogeneity of regression slopes. This expresses whether "the relationship between the outcome (dependent variable) and the covariate is the same in each of our treatment groups" (Field, 2013, p. 486). Significance means non-homogenous regression slopes.
d) Covariates (compare with Chapter 4.4.3, p. 104ff., and Chapter 5.3, p. 139ff.): (1) Sales (log), (2) Number of employees, (3) Industry type, (4) Ownership (a), (5) Ownership (b), (6) Internationalisation, (7) EU - customer, (8) EU - supplier, (9) EU - competitor, (10) EU - technology, (11) EU - regulation, (12) EU - economy, (13) Intensity of competition, (14) Interval of strategic revision, (15) Interval of strategic action revision, (16) Tenure, (17) UA_Organization, (18) FO_Organization, (19) PD_Organization, (20) Coll1_Organization, (21) Ass_Organization, (22) Home country.
e) The sign of the B-value expresses "the direction of the relationship between the covariate and outcome variable" (Field, 2013, p. 497-498).
f) MCS -->: values to the right side of this column show the effect of the covariate on the outcome variable (i.e. means of high and low cultural group, F-values, p-values and η^2 with regard to the effect of the covariate).
g) Significance levels: † p<0.10, * p<0.05, ** p<0.01, *** p<0.001.

Table 49: ANCOVA tests (1)

H	MCS item	CD	Homo-geneity	Covariate	B	F-value	η² (value)	MCS →	Mean High	Mean Low	F-value	η² (value)
33	C4b-d	UA	RS †	14								0.052
33	C4b-d	UA	RS †	15								0.034
1	C5a	PD	✓	11	0.15	7.01**	0.029		5.72	5.07	12.94***	0.016
1	C5a	PD	✓	13	0.11	3.16 †	0.013		5.70	5.15	8.32**	0.005
3	C5a	FO	✓	11	0.16	7.43**	0.031		5.71	5.41	3.73 †	0.013
3	C5a	FO	✓	13	0.15	5.61*	0.023		5.66	5.48	1.28	0.008
12	C5a	Ass	✓	11	0.15	6.71*	0.028		5.70	5.43	3.03 †	0.004
12	C5a	Ass	✓	13	0.15	6.22*	0.026		5.67	5.46	1.88	0.025
23	C5b	Coll	✓	1	0.44	9.21**	0.039		4.89	5.09	0.90	0.016
23	C5b	Coll	✓	2	0.00	6.12*	0.025		4.76	5.24	6.09*	0.021
23	C5b	Coll	✓	7	0.16	3.84 †	0.016		4.82	5.20	3.90*	0.001
23	C5b	Coll	✓	10	0.29	11.93***	0.048		4.80	5.21	4.92*	
4a	C6a	FO	✓	13	-0.19	4.78*	0.020		1.54	1.43	0.25	
11a	C6a	Ass	RS †	13								

a) H: hypothesis
b) CD: cultural dimension (UA: uncertainty avoidance, FO: future orientation, PD: power distance, I/C: individualism/collectivism, Ass: assertiveness).
c) Homogeneity: homogeneity of regression slopes. This expresses whether "the relationship between the outcome (dependent variable) and the covariate is the same in each of our treatment groups" (Field, 2013, p. 486). Significance means non-homogenous regression slopes.
d) Covariates (compare with Chapter 4.4.3, p. 104ff., and Chapter 5.3, p. 139ff.): (1) Sales (log), (2) Number of employees, (3) Industry type, (4) Ownership (a), (5) Ownership (b), (6) Internationalisation, (7) EU - customer, (8) EU - supplier, (9) EU - competitor, (10) EU - technology, (11) EU - regulation, (12) EU - economy, (13) Intensity of competition, (14) Interval of strategic revision, (15) Interval of strategic action revision, (16) Tenure, (17) UA_Organization, (18) FO_Organization, (19) PD_Organization, (20) Coll1_Organization, (21) Ass_Organization, (22) Home country.
e) The sign of the B-value expresses "the direction of the relationship between the covariate and outcome variable" (Field, 2013, p. 497-498).
f) MCS -->: values to the right side of this column show the effect of the covariate on the outcome variable (i.e. means of high and low cultural group.
F-values, p-values and η² with regard to the effect of the covariate).
g) Significance levels: † p<0.10, * p<0.05, ** p<0.01, *** p<0.001.

Table 50: ANCOVA tests (2)

H	MCS item	CD	Homo-geneity	Covariate	B	F-value	η^2 (value)	MCS →	Mean High	Mean Low	F-value	η^2 (value)
25a	C6a	Coll	RS*	13								
35a	C6a	UA	✓	13	-0.19	4.78*	0.020		1.54	1.43	0.25	0.001
4b	C6b	FO	✓	1	-1.32	11.51***	0.048		3.46	3.68	0.16	0.001
4b	C6b	FO	✓	10	-0.60	6.22*	0.026		3.44	3.56	0.05	0.000
4b	C6b	FO	RS †	14								
11b	C6b	Ass	RS*	1								
11b	C6b	Ass	RS †	10								
11b	C6b	Ass	✓	14	0.33	5.13*	0.021		3.41	3.51	0.04	0.000
25b	C6b	Coll	✓	1	-0.61	2.77 †	0.012		5.55	2.07	46.34***	0.169
25b	C6b	Coll	RS**	10								
25b	C6b	Coll	✓	14	0.19	2.02	0.009		5.57	1.92	58.48***	0.199
35b	C6b	FO	✓	1	-1.32	11.51***	0.048		3.46	3.68	0.16	0.001
35b	C6b	FO	✓	10	-0.60	6.22*	0.026		3.44	3.56	0.05	0.000
35b	C6b	UA	RS †	14								

a) H: hypothesis
b) CD: cultural dimension (UA: uncertainty avoidance, FO: future orientation, PD: power distance, I/C: individualism/collectivism, Ass: assertiveness).
c) Homogeneity: homogeneity of regression slopes. This expresses whether "the relationship between the outcome (dependent variable) and the covariate is the same in each of our treatment groups" (Field, 2013, p. 486). Significance means non-homogenous regression slopes.
d) Covariates (compare with Chapter 4.4.3, p. 104ff, and Chapter 5.3, p. 139ff): (1) Sales (log), (2) Number of employees, (3) Industry type, (4) Ownership (a), (5) Ownership (b), (6) Internationalisation, (7) EU - customer, (8) EU - supplier, (9) EU - competitor, (10) EU - technology, (11) EU - regulation, (12) EU - economy, (13) Intensity of competition, (14) Interval of strategic revision, (15) Interval of strategic action revision, (16) Tenure, (17) UA_Organization, (18) FO_Organization, (19) PD_Organization, (20) Coll1_Organization, (21) Ass_Organization, (22) Home country.
e) The sign of the B-value expresses "the direction of the relationship between the covariate and outcome variable" (Field, 2013, p. 497-498).
f) MCS -->: values to the right side of this column show the effect of the covariate on the outcome variable (i.e. means of high and low cultural group, F-values, p-values and η^2 with regard to the effect of the covariate).
g) Significance levels: † p<0.10, * p<0.05, ** p<0.01, *** p<0.001.

Table 51: ANCOVA tests (3)

H	MCS item	CD	Homo-geneity	Covariate	B	F-value	η² (value)	MCS →	Mean High	Mean Low	F-value	η² (value)
30	D1a	UA	✓	12	0.17	4.39*	0.020		2.88	2.27	8.72**	0.038
30	D1a	UA	✓	13	0.10	1.53	0.007		2.90	2.25	9.78**	0.043
30	D1a	UA	RS**	16								0.056
30	D1a	UA	✓	22	-0.54	4.76*	0.021		2.93	2.21	12.90***	0.056
30	D1a	UA	RS***	18								
31	D1a	UA	✓	6	-0.04	2.30	0.010		1.83	1.47	14.64***	0.063
31	D1a	UA	RS*	12								
31	D1a	UA	✓	15	0.04	2.82 †	0.013		1.83	1.48	14.47***	0.062
31	D1a	UA	RS**	16								
5	D1a+b	FO	RS**	1								
5	D1a+b	FO	✓	5	-11.84	6.95**	0.031		62.09	77.82	12.55***	0.054
5	D1a+b	FO	✓	6	0.28	6.12*	0.027		64.14	75.41	6.57*	0.029
5	D1a+b	FO	RS*	12								
5	D1a+b	FO	✓	14	-3.04	5.61*	0.025		63.19	76.16	8.89**	0.039

a) H: hypothesis
b) CD: cultural dimension (UA: uncertainty avoidance, FO: future orientation, PD: power distance, IC: individualism/collectivism, Ass: assertiveness).
c) Homogeneity: homogeneity of regression slopes. This expresses whether "the relationship between the outcome (dependent variable) and the covariate is the same in each of our treatment groups" (Field, 2013, p. 486). Significance means non-homogenous regression slopes.
d) Covariates (compare with Chapter 4.4.3, p. 104ff., and Chapter 5.3, p. 139ff.): (1) Sales (log), (2) Number of employees, (3) Industry type, (4) Ownership (a), (5) Ownership (b), (6) Internationalisation, (7) EU - customer, (8) EU - supplier, (9) EU - competitor, (10) EU - technology, (11) EU - regulation, (12) EU - economy, (13) Intensity of competition, (14) Interval of strategic revision, (15) Interval of strategic action revision, (16) Tenure, (17) UA_Organization, (18) FO_Organization, (19) PD_Organization, (20) ColI1_Organization, (21) Ass_Organization, (22) Home country.
e) The sign of the B-value expresses "the direction of the relationship between the covariate and outcome variable" (Field, 2013, p. 497-498).
f) MCS →: values to the right side of this column show the effect of the covariate on the outcome variable (i.e. means of high and low cultural group, F-values, p-values and η² with regard to the effect of the covariate).
g) Significance levels: † p<0.10, * p<0.05, ** p<0.01, *** p<0.001.

Table 52: ANCOVA tests (4)

H	MCS item	CD	Homo-geneity	Covariate	B	F-value	η^2 (value)	MCS $\rightarrow$	Mean High	Mean Low	F-value	η^2 (value)
5	D1a+b	FO	✓	16	0.60	5.80*	0.026		63.30	76.39	9.11**	0.040
19	D1a+b	Coll	✓	1	6.68	3.93*	0.018		66.08	70.45	0.83	0.004
19	D1a+b	Coll	RS*	5								
19	D1a+b	Coll	✓	6	0.32	7.59**	0.034		65.09	72.14	2.49	0.011
19	D1a+b	Coll	✓	12	-3.04	2.84 †	0.013		65.48	71.89	1.92	0.009
19	D1a+b	Coll	RS*	14								
19	D1a+b	Coll	✓	16	0.59	5.52*	0.025		64.49	72.54	3.25 †	0.015
7	D1a+b	FO	✓	14	2.10	4.11*	0.018		25.18	8.10	23.69***	0.098
7	D1a+b	FO	✓	15	1.58	3.19 †	0.014		24.74	8.62	20.25***	0.085
16	D1a+b	Coll	RS**	14								
16	D1a+b	Coll	RS*	15								
27	D1a+b	UA	✓	14	2.10	4.11*	0.018		25.18	8.10	23.69***	0.098
27	D1a+b	UA	✓	15	1.58	3.19 †	0.014		24.74	8.62	20.25***	0.085
8	D1a+b	FO	✓	16	0.63	4.85*	0.022		41.20	42.63	0.08	0.000

a) H: hypothesis
b) CD: cultural dimension (UA: uncertainty avoidance, FO: future orientation, PD: power distance, I/C: individualism/collectivism, Ass: assertiveness).
c) Homogeneity: homogeneity of regression slopes. This expresses whether "the relationship between the outcome (dependent variable) and the covariate is the same in each of our treatment groups" (Field, 2013, p. 486). Significance means non-homogenous regression slopes.
d) Covariates (compare with Chapter 4.4.3, p. 104ff., and Chapter 5.3, p. 139ff.): (1) Sales (log), (2) Number of employees, (3) Industry type, (4) Ownership (a), (5) Ownership (b), (6) Internationalisation, (7) EU - customer, (8) EU - supplier, (9) EU - competitor, (10) EU - technology, (11) EU - regulation, (12) EU - economy, (13) Intensity of competition, (14) Interval of strategic revision, (15) Interval of strategic action revision, (16) Tenure, (17) UA_Organization, (18) FO_Organization, (19) PD_Organization, (20) Coll1_Organization, (21) Ass_Organization, (22) Home country.
e) The sign of the B-value expresses "the direction of the relationship between the covariate and outcome variable" (Field, 2013, p. 497-498).
f) MCS -->: values to the right side of this column show the effect of the covariate on the outcome variable (i.e. means of high and low cultural group. F-values, p-values and η^2 with regard to the effect of the covariate).
g) Significance levels: † p<0.10, * p<0.05, ** p<0.01, *** p<0.001.

Table 53: ANCOVA tests (5)

Appendix

H	MCS item	CD	Homo-geneity	Covariate	B	F-value	η² (value)	MCS →	Mean High	Mean Low	F-value	η² (value)
13	D1a+b	Ass	✓	16	0.42	2.08	0.009		34.97	51.77	10.93**	0.048
28	D1a+b	UA	✓	16	0.63	4.85*	0.022		41.20	42.63	0.08	0.000
2a	D1c	PD	✓	1	0.06	0.55	0.005		2.96	2.00	57.04***	0.319
2a	D1c	PD	✓	3	0.13	2.86 †	0.023		2.93	2.09	53.00***	0.299
2a	D1c	PD	✓	14	0.03	1.80	0.014		2.93	2.06	62.57***	0.337
2a	D1c	PD	✓	17	-0.21	15.11***	0.144		2.96	2.01	59.70***	0.399
17a	D1c	Coll	RS*	1								
17a	D1c	Coll	RS***	3								
17a	D1c	Coll	✓	14	0.06	5.37*	0.042		2.67	2.78	0.93	0.008
17a	D1c	Coll	✓	17	-0.18	7.01**	0.072		2.84	2.63	2.38	0.026
2b	D1c	PD	✓	1	-2.48	7.54**	0.081		2.79	1.69	48.27***	0.360
2b	D1c	PD	RS*	3								
2b	D1c	PD	✓	6	-0.01	6.15*	0.063		2.78	1.67	60.35***	0.396
2b	D1c	PD	✓	10	-0.09	3.02 †	0.032		2.78	1.65	60.53***	0.397

a) H: hypothesis
b) CD: cultural dimension (UA: uncertainty avoidance, FO: future orientation, PD: power distance, I/C: individualism/collectivism, Ass: assertiveness).
c) Homogeneity: homogeneity of regression slopes. This expresses whether "the relationship between the outcome (dependent variable) and the covariate is the same in each of our treatment groups" (Field, 2013, p. 486). Significance means non-homogenous regression slopes.
d) Covariates (compare with Chapter 4.4.3, p. 104ff, and Chapter 5.3, p. 139ff): (1) Sales (log), (2) Number of employees, (3) Industry type, (4) Ownership (a), (5) Ownership (b), (6) Internationalisation, (7) EU - customer, (8) EU - supplier, (9) EU - competitor, (10) EU - technology, (11) EU - regulation, (12) EU - economy, (13) Intensity of competition, (14) Interval of strategic revision, (15) Interval of strategic action revision, (16) Tenure, (17) UA_Organization, (18) FO_Organization, (19) PD_Organization, (20) Coll1_Organization, (21) Ass_Organization, (22) Home country.
e) The sign of the B-value expresses "the direction of the relationship between the covariate and outcome variable" (Field, 2013, p. 497-498).
f) MCS -->: values to the right side of this column show the effect of the covariate on the outcome variable (i.e. means of high and low cultural group.
F-values, p-values and η² with regard to the effect of the covariate).
g) Significance levels: † p≤0.10, * p≤0.05, ** p≤0.01, *** p≤0.001.

Table 54: ANCOVA tests (6)

H	MCS item	CD	Homo-geneity	Covariate	B	F-value	η² (value)	MCS →	Mean High	Mean Low	F-value	η² (value)
2b	D1c	PD	✓	18	0.18	3.47 †	0.045		2.73	1.65	41.01***	0.360
2b	D1c	PD	✓	20	0.10	1.13	0.015		2.75	1.59	51.08***	0.412
17b	D1c	Coll	RS**	1								0.013
17b	D1c	Coll	✓	3	0.26	4.11*	0.043		2.64	2.46	1.21	0.013
17b	D1c	Coll	RS**	6								
17b	D1c	Coll	RS †	10								
17b	D1c	Coll	RS***	18								
17b	D1c	Coll	✓	20	0.32	6.95*	0.087		2.62	2.37	2.16	0.029
34	D2+C4a	UA	✓	2	0.00	20.87***	0.087		5.50	4.70	36.37***	0.142
34	D2+C4a	UA	✓	10	-0.18	8.30**	0.036		5.44	4.77	24.28***	0.099
34	D2+C4a	UA	✓	13	0.10	3.21 †	0.014		5.44	4.77	22.22***	0.092
34	D2+C4a	UA	✓	15	0.04	1.15	0.005		5.45	4.76	24.05***	0.099
34	D2+C4a	UA	✓	22	-0.48	7.84**	0.034		5.47	4.74	29.40***	0.118
34	D2+C4a	UA	✓	18	0.32	8.73**	0.050		5.37	4.92	7.28**	0.042

a) H: hypothesis
b) CD: cultural dimension (UA: uncertainty avoidance, FO: future orientation, PD: power distance, I/C: individualism/collectivism, Ass.: assertiveness).
c) Homogeneity: homogeneity of regression slopes. This expresses whether "the relationship between the outcome (dependent variable) and the covariate is the same in each of our treatment groups" (Field, 2013, p. 486). Significance means non-homogenous regression slopes.
d) Covariates (compare with Chapter 4.4.3, p. 104ff., and Chapter 5.3, p. 139ff): (1) Sales (log), (2) Number of employees, (3) Industry type, (4) Ownership (a), (5) Ownership (b), (6) Internationalisation, (7) EU - customer, (8) EU - supplier, (9) EU - competitor, (10) EU - technology, (11) EU - regulation, (12) EU - economy, (13) Intensity of competition, (14) Interval of strategic revision, (15) Interval of strategic action revision, (16) Tenure, (17) UA_Organization, (18) FO_Organization, (19) PD_Organization, (20) Coll1_Organization, (21) Ass_Organization, (22) Home country.
e) The sign of the B-value expresses "the direction of the relationship between the covariate and outcome variable" (Field, 2013, p. 497-498).
f) MCS -->: values to the right side of this column show the effect of the covariate on the outcome variable (i.e. means of high and low cultural group. F-values, p-values and η² with regard to the effect of the covariate).
g) Significance levels: † p<0.10, * p<0.05, ** p<0.01, *** p<0.001.

Table 55: ANCOVA tests (7)

H	MCS item	CD	Homo-geneity	Covariate	B	F-value	η² (value)	MCS →	Mean High	Mean Low	F-value	η² (value)
24	D3a	Coll	RS*	3								
24	D3a	Coll	✓	6	0.02	8.06**	0.035		3.82	4.02	0.51	0.002
24	D3a	Coll	✓	9	0.38	9.64**	0.042		3.70	4.11	2.08	0.009
24	D3a	Coll	✓	10	0.29	5.04*	0.022		3.76	4.06	1.17	0.005
24	D3a	Coll	RS**	18								
22	D3b	Coll	✓	1	0.53	6.43*	0.029		2.84	4.18	19.96***	0.086
22	D3b	Coll	RS*	2								
22	D3b	Coll	✓	3	-0.77	13.25***	0.057		2.74	4.32	32.34***	0.128
22	D3b	Coll	✓	6	0.02	4.35*	0.019		2.71	4.34	33.31***	0.131
22	D3b	Coll	RS †	13								
22	D3b	Coll	✓	14	-0.19	5.30*	0.024		2.73	4.35	32.06***	0.128
22	D3b	Coll	✓	16	0.03	4.25*	0.019		2.68	4.36	35.58***	0.139
22	D3b	Coll	✓	17	-0.40	5.10*	0.030		2.73	4.58	29.19***	0.150
22	D3b	Coll	RS***	18								

a) H: hypothesis
b) CD: cultural dimension (UA: uncertainty avoidance, FO: future orientation, PD: power distance, I/C: individualism/collectivism, Ass: assertiveness)
c) Homogeneity: homogeneity of regression slopes. This expresses whether "the relationship between the outcome (dependent variable) and the covariate is the same in each of our treatment groups" (Field, 2013, p. 486). Significance means non-homogenous regression slopes.
d) Covariates (compare with Chapter 4.4.3, p. 104ff., and Chapter 5.3, p. 139ff.): (1) Sales (log), (2) Number of employees, (3) Industry type, (4) Ownership (a), (5) Ownership (b), (6) Internationalisation, (7) EU - customer, (8) EU - supplier, (9) EU - competitor, (10) EU - technology, (11) EU - regulation, (12) EU - economy, (13) Intensity of competition, (14) Interval of strategic revision, (15) Interval of strategic action revision, (16) Tenure, (17) UA_Organization, (18) FO_Organization, (19) PD_Organization, (20) Coll1_Organization, (21) Ass_Organization, (22) Home country.
e) The sign of the B-value expresses "the direction of the relationship between the covariate and outcome variable" (Field, 2013, p. 497-498).
f) MCS -->: values to the right side of this column show the effect of the covariate on the outcome variable (i.e. means of high and low cultural group.
F-values, p-values and η² with regard to the effect of the covariate).
g) Significance levels: † p<0.10, * p<0.05, ** p<0.01, *** p<0.001.

Table 56: ANCOVA tests (8)

H	MCS item	CD	Homo-geneity	Covariate	B	F-value	η^2 (value)	MCS →	Mean High	Mean Low	F-value	η^2 (value)
14	D3d-e	Ass	✓	1	-0.50	5.53*	0.025		1.00	0.83	0.33	0.002
14	D3d-e	Ass	RS*	12								
14	D3d-e	Ass	✓	18	0.37	3.59 †	0.021		1.25	0.70	3.52 †	0.021
14	D3d-e	Ass	✓	21	0.61	5.32*	0.031		1.27	0.67	4.28*	0.025
18	D3d-e	Coll	✓	1	-0.20	1.00	0.005		1.89	0.28	33.83***	0.138
18	D3d-e	Coll	✓	12	0.13	1.53	0.007		1.88	0.29	35.72***	0.140
18	D3d-e	Coll	RS †	18								
18	D3d-e	Coll	✓	21	0.55	4.65*	0.027		1.73	0.41	22.96***	0.122
21	D4d-f	Coll	✓	1	0.40	8.61**	0.039		5.03	5.14	0.31	0.001
10	D5b	FO	RS †	1								
10	D5b	FO	✓	2	0.00	4.21*	0.018		4.87	5.64	21.91***	0.085
10	D5b	FO	✓	4	-0.36	4.30*	0.018		4.86	5.65	23.06***	0.089
10	D5b	FO	✓	7	0.26	13.01***	0.052		4.86	5.65	24.18***	0.093
10	D5b	FO	✓	8	0.11	2.32	0.010		4.86	5.63	20.58***	0.081

a) H: hypothesis
b) CD: cultural dimension (UA: uncertainty avoidance, FO: future orientation, PD: power distance, I/C: individualism/collectivism, Ass: assertiveness).
c) Homogeneity: homogeneity of regression slopes. This expresses whether "the relationship between the outcome (dependent variable) and the covariate is the same in each of our treatment groups" (Field, 2013, p. 486). Significance means non-homogenous regression slopes.
d) Covariates (compare with Chapter 4.4.3, p. 104ff. and Chapter 5.3, p. 139ff): (1) Sales (log), (2) Number of employees, (3) Industry type, (4) Ownership (a), (5) Ownership (b), (6) Internationalisation, (7) EU - customer, (8) EU - supplier, (9) EU - competitor, (10) EU - technology, (11) EU - regulation, (12) EU - economy, (13) Intensity of competition, (14) Interval of strategic revision, (15) Interval of strategic action revision, (16) Tenure, (17) UA Organization, (18) FO Organization, (19) PD Organization, (20) Coll1 Organization, (21) Ass Organization, (22) Home country.
e) The sign of the B-value expresses "the direction of the relationship between the covariate and outcome variable" (Field, 2013, p. 497-498).
f) MCS →: values to the right side of this column show the effect of the covariate on the outcome variable (i.e. means of high and low cultural group. F-values, p-values and η^2 with regard to the effect of the covariate).
g) Significance levels: † p<0.10, * p<0.05, ** p<0.01, *** p<0.001.

Table 57: ANCOVA tests (9)

H	MCS item	CD	Homo-geneity	Covariate	B	F-value	η² (value)	MCS →	Mean High	Mean Low	F-value	η² (value)
10	D5b	FO	✓	10	0.16	4.42*	0.018		4.87	5.63	21.16***	0.082
26	D5b	Coll	RS**	1					5.03	5.31	2.65	0.011
26	D5b	Coll	✓	2	0.00	7.74**	0.032		5.09	5.27	1.06	0.004
26	D5b	Coll	✓	4	-0.41	5.13*	0.021		5.10	5.27	0.94	0.004
26	D5b	Coll	RS †	7	0.27	12.66***	0.051					
26	D5b	Coll	✓	8					5.07	5.29	1.68	0.007
26	D5b	Coll	✓	10	0.21	7.67**	0.031					
32	G2	UA	✓	10	-0.26	11.29***	0.046		2.61	2.22	5.05*	0.021
32	G2	UA	RS**	12								

a) H: hypothesis
b) CD: cultural dimension (UA: uncertainty avoidance, FO: future orientation, PD: power distance, I/C: individualism/collectivism, Ass: assertiveness).
c) Homogeneity: homogeneity of regression slopes. This expresses whether "the relationship between the outcome (dependent variable) and the covariate is the same in each of our treatment groups" (Field, 2013, p. 486). Significance means non-homogenous regression slopes.
d) Covariates (compare with Chapter 4.4.3, p. 104ff, and Chapter 5.3, p. 139ff.): (1) Sales (log), (2) Number of employees, (3) Industry type, (4) Ownership (a), (5) Ownership (b), (6) Internationalisation, (7) EU - customer, (8) EU - supplier, (9) EU - competitor, (10) EU - technology, (11) EU - regulation, (12) EU - economy, (13) Intensity of competition, (14) Interval of strategic revision, (15) Interval of strategic action revision, (16) Tenure, (17) UA_Organization, (18) FO_Organization, (19) PD_Organization, (20) Coll1_Organization, (21) Ass_Organization, (22) Home country.
e) The sign of the B-value expresses "the direction of the relationship between the covariate and outcome variable" (Field, 2013, p. 497-498).
f) MCS —>: values to the right side of this column show the effect of the covariate on the outcome variable (i.e. means of high and low cultural group, F-values, p-values and η² with regard to the effect of the covariate).
g) Significance levels: † p<0.10, * p<0.05, ** p<0.01, *** p<0.001.

Table 58: ANCOVA tests (10)

H	MCS item	CD	Homo-geneity	CV	MCS (Low CV) →	Mean High	Mean Low	F-value	η^2 (value)	MCS (High CV) →	Mean High	Mean Low	F-value	η^2 (value)
6	C3e-g	FO	RS*	13		4.92	5.19	2.16	0.018		5.00	4.45	6.84*	0.054
33	C4b-d	UA	RS*	1		3.26	4.15	12.05***	0.096		3.65	5.23	56.21***	0.330
33	C4b-d	UA	RS*	10		3.33	4.54	28.22***	0.178		3.57	5.15	44.54***	0.298
33	C4b-d	UA	RS***	12		3.21	5.13	90.77***	0.427		3.58	4.40	9.19**	0.075
33	C4b-d	UA	RS †	14		3.53	5.04	62.75***	0.279		3.18	4.53	18.29***	0.203
33	C4b-d	UA	RS †	15		3.44	5.11	65.10***	0.334		3.45	4.46	14.25***	0.122
11a	C6a	Ass	RS †	13		1.80	1.73	0.03	0.000		1.24	1.20	0.08	0.001
25a	C6a	Coll	RS*	13		2.56	1.23	11.98***	0.094		1.38	1.11	3.47 †	0.028
4b	C6b	FO	RS †	14		3.48	2.84	1.04	0.006		3.41	4.57	1.39	0.019
11b	C6b	Ass	RS*	1		3.91	5.50	2.88 †	0.025		2.94	2.57	0.33	0.003
11b	C6b	Ass	RS †	10		3.59	4.66	1.68	0.013		3.39	2.50	1.82	0.017
25b	C6b	Coll	RS**	10		6.81	2.03	48.75***	0.273		4.29	1.84	15.27***	0.127
35b	C6b	UA	RS †	14		3.48	2.84	1.04	0.006		3.41	4.57	1.39	0.019
30	D1a	UA	RS**	16		2.95	2.93	0.01	0.000		2.89	1.72	22.37***	0.166
30	D1a	UA	RS***	18		2.75	1.88	10.93**	0.118		2.91	3.03	0.10	0.001

a) H: hypothesis
b) CD: cultural dimension (UA: uncertainty avoidance, FO: future orientation, PD: power distance, I/C: individualism/collectivism, Ass: assertiveness).
c) Homogeneity: homogeneity of regression slopes. This expresses whether "the relationship between the outcome (dependent variable) and the covariate is the same in each of our treatment groups" (Field, 2013, p. 486). Significance means non-homogenous regression slopes.
d) CV: Covariates (compare with Chapter 4.4.3, p. 104ff., and Chapter 5.3, p. 139ff.): (1) Sales (log), (2) Number of employees, (3) Industry type, (4) Ownership (a), (5) Ownership (b), (6) Internationalisation, (7) EU - customer, (8) EU - supplier, (9) EU - competitor, (10) EU - technology, (11) EU - regulation, (12) EU - economy, (13) Intensity of competition, (14) Interval of strategic revision, (15) Interval of strategic action revision, (16) Tenure, (17) UA_Organization, (18) FO_Organization, (19) PD_Organization, (20) Coll1_Organization, (21) Ass_Organization, (22) Home country.
e) The sign of the B-value expresses "the direction of the relationship between the covariate and outcome variable" (Field, 2013, p. 497-498).
f) MCS -->: values to the right side of this column show the effect of the covariate on the outcome variable for both a low and high case scenario (i.e. means of high and low cultural group, F-values, p-values and η^2 with regard to the effect of the covariate).
g) Significance levels: † p<0.10, * p<0.05, ** p<0.01, *** p<0.001.

Table 59: ANCOVA tests – only heterogeneous regression slopes (1)

H	MCS item	CD	Homo-geneity	CV	MCS (Low CV)→	Mean High	Mean Low	F-value	η^2 (value)	MCS (High CV)→	Mean High	Mean Low	F-value	η^2 (value)
31	D1a	UA	RS*	12		1.88	1.32	22.04***	0.161		1.81	1.70	0.53	0.005
31	D1a	UA	RS**	16		1.86	1.86	0	0.000		1.81	1.18	46.78***	0.295
5	D1a+b	FO	RS**	1		66.13	53.80	2.85 †	0.028		59.72	88.42	32.98***	0.231
5	D1a+b	FO	RS*	12		60.35	83.74	17.47***	0.132		65.56	63.49	0.09	0.001
19	D1a+b	Coll	RS*	5		76.79	72.30	0.45	0.005		55.16	72.82	8.88**	0.065
19	D1a+b	Coll	RS*	14		65.12	77.06	5.23*	0.034		63.38	58.97	0.26	0.004
16	D1a+b	Coll	RS**	14		15.60	13.27	0.36	0.002		16.76	32.11	3.53 †	0.049
16	D1a+b	Coll	RS*	15		14.45	9.25	1.65	0.014		17.41	32.67	5.83*	0.057
17a	D1c	Coll	RS*	1		2.84	2.95	0.50	0.008		2.73	2.50	1.50	0.025
17a	D1c	Coll	RS***	3 [g]										
2b	D1c	PD	RS*	3 [h]										
17b	D1c	Coll	RS**	1		2.76	3.22	6.36*	0.154		2.60	2.16	4.20*	0.077

a) H: hypothesis
b) CD: cultural dimension (UA: uncertainty avoidance, FO: future orientation, PD: power distance, I/C: individualism/collectivism, Ass: assertiveness).
c) Homogeneity: homogeneity of regression slopes. This expresses whether "the relationship between the outcome (dependent variable) and the covariate is the same in each of our treatment groups" (Field, 2013, p. 486). Significance means non-homogenous regression slopes.
d) CV: Covariates (compare with Chapter 4.4.3, p. 104ff., and Chapter 5.3, p. 139ff.): (1) Sales (log). (2) Number of employees. (3) Industry type. (4) Ownership (a), (5) Ownership (b), (6) Internationalisation, (7) EU - customer, (8) EU - supplier, (9) EU - competitor, (10) EU - technology, (11) EU - regulation, (12) EU - economy, (13) Intensity of competition, (14) Interval of strategic revision, (15) Interval of strategic action revision, (16) Tenure, (17) UA_Organization, (18) FO_Organization, (19) PD_Organization, (20) Coll1_Organization, (21) Ass_Organization, (22) Home country.
e) The sign of the B-value expresses "the direction of the relationship between the covariate and outcome variable" (Field, 2013, p. 497-498).
f) MCS -->: values to the right side of this column show the effect of the covariate on the outcome variable for both a low and high case scenario (i.e. means of high and low cultural group. F-values, p-values and η^2 with regard to the effect of the covariate).
g) There are three categories for industry type: for H17a: Manufacturing (M(high)=2.86, M(low)=2.35, F-value=14.31***, η^2=0.166; Services (M(high)=2.69, M(low)=3.14, F-value=4.97*, η^2=0.116; Trade (M(high)=2.89, M(low)=3.38, F-value=2.56, η^2=0.189.
h) There are three categories for industry type: for H2b: Manufacturing (M(high)=2.69, M(low)=1.73, F-value=33.08***, η^2=0.331; Services (M(high)=2.97, M(low)=1.13, F-value=57.75***, η^2=0.762; Trade (M(high)=3.17, M(low)=n.a., F-value=n.a., η^2=n.a.
i) Significance levels: † $p<0$, 0, * $p<0.05$, ** $p<0.01$, *** $p<0.001$.

Table 60: ANCOVA tests – only heterogeneous regression slopes (2)

H	MCS item	CD	Homo-geneity	CV	MCS (Low CV) →	MCS (High CV) →	Mean High	Mean Low	F-value	η² (value)	Mean High	Mean Low	F-value	η² (value)
17b	D1c	Coll	RS**	6			2.75	2.86	0.26	0.006	2.52	2.11	3.65 †	0.073
17b	D1c	Coll	RS †	10			2.69	2.63	0.06	0.001	2.61	2.21	3.06 †	0.069
17b	D1c	Coll	RS***	18			2.60	1.92	7.63**	0.179	2.65	2.85	0.85	0.022
24	D3a	Coll	RS †	3 [g]										
24	D3a	Coll	RS**	18			3.97	4.94	5.07*	0.058	3.59	3.41	0.16	0.002
22	D3b	Coll	RS*	2			2.84	4.42	15.04***	0.124	2.48	4.32	20.98***	0.157
22	D3b	Coll	RS †	13			2.63	4.91	32.17***	0.231	2.71	3.78	7.58**	0.063
22	D3b	Coll	RS***	18			2.56	5.23	41.67***	0.337	2.88	3.86	4.56**	0.052
14	D3d-e	Ass	RS*	12			0.91	0.17	4.45*	0.037	1.24	1.41	0.15	0.001
18	D3d-e	Coll	RS †	18			1.64	0.04	16.67***	0.169	1.85	0.77	7.66**	0.084
10	D5b	FO	RS †	1			4.64	5.57	11.48***	0.092	5.14	5.78	9.32**	0.076
26	D5b	Coll	RS**	1			5.06	4.75	1.42	0.012	5.12	5.61	4.39*	0.037
26	D5b	Coll	RS †	8			4.63	5.21	5.42*	0.042	5.53	5.37	0.54	0.005
32	G2	UA	RS**	12			2.64	1.98	10.25**	0.077	2.65	2.50	0.24	0.002

a) H: hypothesis
b) CD: cultural dimension (UA: uncertainty avoidance, FO: future orientation, PD: power distance, I/C: individualism/collectivism, Ass: assertiveness).
c) Homogeneity: homogeneity of regression slopes. This expresses whether "the relationship between the outcome (dependent variable) and the covariate is the same in each of our treatment groups" (Field, 2013, p. 486). Significance means non-homogenous regression slopes.
d) CV: Covariates (compare with Chapter 4.4.3, p. 104ff., and Chapter 5.3, p. 139ff.): (1) Sales (log), (2) Number of employees, (3) Industry type, (4) Ownership (a), (5) Ownership (b), (6) Internationalisation, (7) EU - customer, (8) EU - supplier, (9) EU - competitor, (10) EU - technology, (11) EU - regulation, (12) EU - economy, (13) Intensity of competition, (14) Interval of strategic revision, (15) Interval of strategic action revision, (16) Tenure, (17) UA_Organization, (18) FO_Organization, (19) PD_Organization, (20) Coll1_Organization, (21) Ass_Organization, (22) Home country.
e) The sign of the B-value expresses "the direction of the relationship between the covariate and outcome variable" (Field, 2013, p. 497-498).
f) MCS -->: values to the right side of this column show the effect of the covariate on the outcome variable for both a low and high case scenario (i.e. means of high and low cultural group. F-values, p-values and η² with regard to the effect of the covariate).
g) There are three categories for industry type: for H24: Manufacturing (M(high)=3.81, M(low)=4.34, F-value=2.15, η²=0.015; Services (M(high)=3.52, M(low)=3.72, F-value=0.14, η²=0.002; Trade (M(high)=4.18, M(low)=2.25, F-value=5.98*, η²=0.260.
h) Significance levels: † p<0.10, * p<0.05, ** p<0.01, *** p<0.001.

Table 61: ANCOVA tests – only heterogeneous regression slopes (3)

References

Abdel-Maksoud, Ahmed; Dugdale, David & Luther, Robert (2005): Non-financial performance measurement in manufacturing companies. The British Accounting Review, Vol. 37, No. 3, pp. 261-297.

Abernethy, Margaret A.; Bouwens, Jan & van Lent, Laurence (2013): The role of performance measures in the intertemporal decisions of Business Unit managers. Contemporary Accounting Research, Vol. 30, No. 3, pp. 925-961.

Abernethy, Margaret A. & Brownell, Peter (1997): Management control systems in research and development organizations: The role of accounting, behavior and personnel controls. Accounting, Organizations and Society, Vol. 22, No. 3-4, pp. 233-248.

Abernethy, Margaret A. & Chua, Wai F. (1996): A field study of control system 'redesign': The impact of institutional processes on strategic choice. Contemporary Accounting Research, Vol. 13, No. 2, pp. 569-606.

Abrutyn, Seth & Turner, Jonathan H. (2011): The old institutionalism meets the new institutionalism. Sociological Perspectives, Vol. 54, No. 3, pp. 283-306.

Achouri, Cyrus (2011): Human Resources Management: Eine praxisbasierte Einführung, Gabler, Wiesbaden.

Acock, Alan C. (2005): Working with missing values. Journal of Marriage and Family, Vol. 67, No. 4, pp. 1012-1028.

Adcock, Robert & Collier, David (2010): Measurement validity: A shared standard for qualitative and auantitative research. American Political Science Review, Vol. 95, No. 3, pp. 529-546.

Adler, Ralph W. (2011): Performance management and organizational strategy: How to design systems that meet the needs of confrontation strategy firms. The British Accounting Review, Vol. 43, No. 4, pp. 251-263.

Aggarwal, Rajesh K. & Samwick, Andrew A. (1999): Executive compensation, strategic competition, and relative performance evaluation: Theory and evidence. The Journal of Finance, Vol. 54, No. 6, pp. 1999-2043.

Aguilera, Ruth V. & Jackson, Gregory (2003): The cross-national diversity of corporate government: Dimensions and determinants. Academy of Management Review, Vol. 28, No. 3, pp. 447-465.

Aguinis, Herman (2009): Performance management, 2. ed., Pearson/Prentice Hall, London.

Aguinis, Herman; Joo, Harry & Gottfredson, Ryan K. (2013): What monetary rewards can and cannot do: How to show employees the money. Business Horizons, Vol. 56, No. 2, pp. 241-249.

Ahrens, Thomas & Chapman, Christopher S. (2004): Accounting for flexibility and efficiency: A field study of management control systems in a restaurant chain. Contemporary Accounting Research, Vol. 21, No. 2, pp. 271-301.

Alas, Ruth; Kraus, Ants & Niglas, Katrin (2009): Manufacturing strategies and choices in cultural contexts. Journal of Business Economics and Management, Vol. 10, No. 4, pp. 279-289.

Albuquerque, Ana (2009): Peer firms in relative performance evaluation. Journal of Accounting and Economics, Vol. 48, No. 1, pp. 69-89.

Alchian, Armen A. & Demsetz, Harold (1972): Production, information costs, and economic organization. The American Economic Review, Vol. 62, No. 5, pp. 777-795.

Alda, Holger; Bellmann, Lutz & Gartner, Hermann (2008): Wage structure and labor mobility in the West German private sector, 1993-2000. in: Lazear, Edward P. & Shaw, Kathryn L. (Ed.): The structure of wages: An international comparison. University of Chicago Press, Chicago, pp. 261-313.

Aldrich, Howard E. & Fiol, C. M. (1994): Fools rush in? The institutional context of industry creation. Academy of Management Review, Vol. 19, No. 4, pp. 645-670.

Alvesson, Mats & Kärreman, Dan (2004): Interfaces of control. Technocratic and socio-ideological control in a global management consultancy firm. Accounting, Organizations and Society, Vol. 29, No. 3-4, pp. 423-444.

Angelé-Halgand, Nathalie; Helmig, Bernd; Jegers, Marc & Lapsley, Irvine (2010): Current research in non-profit organisations' management. European Management Journal, Vol. 28, No. 6, pp. 401-402.

Ansari, Shadid L. (1977): An integrated approach to control system design. Accounting, Organizations and Society, Vol. 2, No. 2, pp. 101-112.

Anthony, Robert N. (1965): Planning and control systems: A framework for analysis, Division of Research, Graduate Business School of Business Administration, Harvard University, Boston.

Anthony, Robert N. & Govindarajan, Vijay (2001): Management control systems, 10. ed., McGraw-Hill, Boston, Mass.

Anthony, Robert N. & Govindarajan, Vijay (2007): Management control systems, 12. ed., McGraw-Hill, Boston.

Antle, Rick & Smith, Abbie (1986): An empirical investigation of the relative performance evaluation of corporate executives. Journal of Accounting Research, Vol. 24, No. 1, pp. 1-39.

Armstrong, Michael (2009): Armstrong's handbook of performance management: An evidence-based guide to delivering high performance, 4. ed., Kogan Page, London.

Arora, Alka & Alam, Pervaiz (2005): CEO compensation and stakeholders' claims. Contemporary Accounting Research, Vol. 22, No. 3, pp. 519-547.

Arrow, Kenneth J. (1985): The economics of agency. in: Pratt, John W. & Zeckhauser, Richard (Ed.): Principals and agents : The structure of business. Harvard Business School Press, Boston, Mass, pp. 1183-1195.

Ashkanasy, Neal M.; Gupta, Vipin; Mayfield, Melinda S. & Trevor-Roberts, Edwin (2004): Future Orientation. in: House, Robert J.; Hanges, Paul J.; Javidan, Mansour; Dorfman, Peter W. & Gupta, Vipin (Ed.): Culture, leadership, and organizations: The GLOBE study of 62 societies. Sage, Thousand Oaks, CA, pp. 282-342.

Ashkanasy, Neal M.; Trevor-Roberts, Edwin & Earnshaw, Louise (2002): The Anglo cluster: Legacy of the British empire. Journal of World Business, Vol. 37, No. 1, pp. 28-39.

Atkinson, Anthony A.; Balakrishnan, Ramji; Booth, Peter; Cote, Jane M.; Groot, Tom; Malmi, Teemu; Roberts, Hanno; Uliana, Enrico & Wu, Anne (1997): New directions in Management Accounting Research. Journal of Management Accounting Research, Vol. 9, pp. 79-108.

Avalos, Alison & Cohen, Kathryn (2011): WorldatWork 2011-2012 Salary Budget Survey Results.

Awasthi, Vidya N.; Chow, Chee W. & Wu, Anne (1998): Performance measure and resource expenditure choices in a teamwork environment: The effects of national culture. Management Accounting Research, Vol. 9, No. 2, pp. 119-138.

Awasthi, Vidya N.; Chow, Chee W. & Wu, Anne (2001): Cross-cultural differences in the behavioral consequences of imposing performance evaluation and reward systems: An experimental investigation. The International Journal of Accounting, Vol. 36, No. 3, pp. 291-309.

Aycan, Zeynep (2000): Cross-cultural industrial and organizational psychology: Contributions, past developments, and future directions. Journal of Cross-Cultural Psychology, Vol. 31, No. 1, pp. 110-128.

Bacher, Johann (2004): Welch test. in: Lewis-Beck, Michael S.; Bryman, Alan & Liao, Tim F. (Ed.): The Sage encyclopedia of social science research methods. Sage, Thousand Oaks, Calif, pp. 1192-1193.

Bagozzi, Richard P. & Yi, Youjae (2012): Specification, evaluation, and interpretation of structural equation models. Journal of the Academy of Marketing Science, Vol. 40, No. 1, pp. 8-34.

Baiman, Stanley (1990): Agency research in managerial accounting: A second look. Accounting, Organizations and Society, Vol. 15, No. 4, pp. 341-371.

Bakacsi, Gyula; Sándor, Takács; András, Karácsonyi & Viktor, Imrek (2002): Eastern european cluster: Tradition and transition. Journal of World Business, Vol. 37, No. 1, pp. 69-80.

Baker, George P. (1990): Pay-for-performance for middle managers: Causes and consequences. Journal of Applied Corporate Finance, Vol. 3, No. 3, pp. 50-61.

Baker, George P.; Jensen, Michael C. & Murphy, Kevin J. (1988): Compensation and incentives: Practice vs. theory. The Journal of Finance, Vol. 43, No. 3, pp. 593-616.

Banker, Rajiv D.; Lee, Seok-Young & Potter, Gordon (1996): A field study of the impact of a performance-based incentive plan. Journal of Accounting and Economics, Vol. 21, No. 2, pp. 195-226.

Banker, Rajiv D.; Potter, Gordon & Srinivasan, Dhinu (2000): An empirical investigation of an incentive plan that includes nonfinancial performance measures. The Accounting Review, Vol. 75, No. 1, pp. 65-92.

Barnett, Vic & Lewis, Toby (1994): Outliers in statistical data, 3. ed., Wiley, Chichester, England.

Barrett, Paul (2007): Structural equation modelling: Adjudging model fit. Personality and Individual Differences, Vol. 42, No. 5, pp. 815-824.

Baskerville, Rachel F. (2003): Hofstede never studied culture. Accounting, Organizations and Society, Vol. 28, No. 1, pp. 1-14.

Baskerville-Morley, Rachel F. (2005): A research note: The unfinished business of culture. Accounting, Organizations and Society, Vol. 30, No. 4, pp. 389-391.

Baxter, Jane & Chua, Wai F. (2003): Alternative management accounting research - whence and whither. Accounting, Organizations and Society, Vol. 28, No. 2-3, pp. 97-126.

Bearden, William O.; Money, Richard B. & Nevins, Jennifer L. (2006): Multidimensional versus unidimensional measures in assessing national culture values: The Hofstede VSM 94 example. Journal of Business Research, Vol. 59, No. 2, pp. 195-203.

Becker, Fred G. (1994): Grundlagen betrieblicher Leistungsbeurteilungen: Leistungsverständnis und -prinzip, Beurteilungsproblematik und Verfahrensprobleme, 2. ed., Band 88, Schäffer-Poeschel, Stuttgart.

Beckstead, Jason W. (2012): To be, or to be two, the question of dichotomizing variables. International Journal of Nursing Studies, Vol. 49, No. 6, pp. 635-636.

Bergkvist, Lars & Rossiter, John R. (2007): The predictive validity of multiple-item versus single-item measures of the same constructs. Journal of Marketing Research, Vol. 44, No. 2, pp. 175-184.

Berry, Anthony J.; Coad, Alan F.; Harris, Elaine P.; Otley, David T. & Stringer, Carolyn (2009): Emerging themes in management control: A review of recent literature. The British Accounting Review, Vol. 41, No. 1, pp. 2-20.

Bhattacharyya, S. K. (1973): Management control systems and conflicts – A framework for analysis and resolution. International Studies of Management & Organization, Vol. 3, No. 4, pp. 43-63.

Bhimani, Alnoor (1999): Mapping methodological frontiers in cross-national management control research. Accounting, Organizations and Society, Vol. 24, No. 5-6, pp. 413-440.

Billiet, Jaak; Maddens, Bart & Frognier, André-Paul (2006): Does Belgium (still) exist? Differences in political culture between Flemings and Walloons. West European Politics, Vol. 29, No. 5, pp. 912-932.

Birnberg, Jacob G. & Snodgrass, Coral R. (1988): Culture and control: A field study. Accounting, Organizations and Society, Vol. 13, No. 5, pp. 447-464.

Bisbe, Josep & Otley, David T. (2004): The effects of the interactive use of management control systems on product innovation. Accounting, Organizations and Society, Vol. 29, No. 8, pp. 709-737.

Björkman, Ingmar; Fey, Carl F. & Park, Hyeon J. (2007): Institutional theory and MNC subsidiary HRM practices: Evidence from a three-country study. Journal of International Business Studies, Vol. 38, No. 3, pp. 430-446.

Bogsnes, Bjarte (2009): Implementing beyond budgeting: Unlocking the performance potential, John Wiley & Sons, Hoboken, N.J.

Bol, Jasmijn C. (2008): Subjectivity in compensation contracting. Journal of Accounting Literature, Vol. 27, pp. 1-24.

Bol, Jasmijn C. (2011): The determinants and performance effects of managers' performance evaluation biases. The Accounting Review, Vol. 86, No. 5, pp. 1549-1575.

Bol, Jasmijn C. & Moers, Frank (2010): The dynamics of incentive contracting: The role of learning in the diffusion process. Accounting, Organizations and Society, Vol. 35, No. 8, pp. 721-736.

Bol, Jasmijn C. & Smith, Steven D. (2011): Spillover effects in subjective performance evaluation: Bias and the asymmetric influence of controllability. The Accounting Review, Vol. 86, No. 4, pp. 1213-1230.

Bommer, William H.; Johnson, Jonathan L.; Rich, Gregory A.; Podsakoff, Philip M. & MacKenzie, Scott B. (1995): On the interchangeability of objective and subjective measures of employee performance: a meta-analysis. Personnel Psychology, Vol. 48, No. 3, pp. 587-605.

Bonache, Jaime; Trullen, Jordi & Sanchez, Juan I. (2012): Managing cross-cultural differences: Testing human resource models in Latin America. Journal of Business Research, Vol. 65, pp. 1773-1781.

Bond, Michael H.; Leung, Kwok & Wan, Kwok C. (1982): How does cultural collectivism operate?: The impact of task and maintenance contributions on reward distribution. Journal of Cross-Cultural Psychology, Vol. 13, No. 2, pp. 186-200.

Bonner, Sarah E.; Hastie, Reid; Sprinkle, Geoffrey B. & Young, S. M. (2000): A review of the effects of financial incentives on performance in laboratory tasks: Implications for management accounting. Journal of Management Accounting Research, Vol. 12, pp. 19-64.

Bonner, Sarah E.; Hesford, James W.; van der Stede, Wim A. & Young, S. M. (2006): The most influential journals in academic accounting. Accounting, Organizations and Society, Vol. 31, No. 7, pp. 663-685.

Bonner, Sarah E. & Sprinkle, Geoffrey B. (2002): The effects of monetary incentives on effort and task performance: Theories, evidence, and a framework for research. Accounting, Organizations and Society, Vol. 27, No. 4-5, pp. 303-345.

Boswell, Wendy R. & Bourdreau, John W. (2000): Employee satisfaction with performance appraisals and appraisers: The role of perceived appraisal use. Human Resource Development Quarterly, Vol. 11, No. 3, pp. 283-299.

Bourguignon, Annick (2004): Performance management and management control: Evaluated managers' point of view. European Accounting Review, Vol. 13, No. 4, pp. 659-687.

Bourguignon, Annick & Chiapello, Eve (2005): The role of criticism in the dynamics of performance evaluation systems. Critical Perspectives on Accounting, Vol. 16, No. 6, pp. 665-700.

Bourguignon, Annick; Malleret, Véronique & Nørreklit, Hanne (2004): The American balanced scorecard versus the French tableau de bord: the ideological dimension. Management Accounting Research, Vol. 15, No. 2, pp. 107-134.

Bourne, Mike (2005): Researching performance measurement system implementation: the dynamics of success and failure. Production Planning & Control, Vol. 16, No. 2, pp. 101-113.

Bourne, Mike; Kennerley, Mike & Franco-Santos, Monica (2005): Managing through measures: A study of impact on performance. Journal of Manufacturing Technology Management, Vol. 16, No. 4, pp. 373-395.

Bourne, Mike; Melnyk, Steven A.; Bititci, Umit; Platts, Ken & Andersen, Bjørn (2014): Emerging issues in performance measurement. Management Accounting Research, Vol. 25, No. 2, pp. 117-118.

Bourne, Mike; Mills, John; Wilcox, Mark; Neely, Andy & Platts, Ken (2000): Designing, implementing and updating performance measurement systems. International Journal of Operations & Production Management, Vol. 20, No. 7, pp. 754-771.

Bourne, Mike; Neely, Andy; Mills, John & Platts, Ken (2003): Implementing performance measurement systems: A literature review. International Journal of Business Performance Management, Vol. 5, No. 1, pp. 1-24.

Boyacigiller, Nakiye A.; Kleinberg, Jill; Phillips, Margaret E. & Sackmann, Sonja A. (2004): Conceptualizing culture: Elucidating the streams of research in international cross-cultural management. in: Punnett, Betty J. & Shenkar, Oded (Ed.): Handbook for international management research. University of Michigan Press, Ann Arbor, pp. 99-167.

Brauer, Markus & Chaurand, Nadine (2009): Descriptive norms, prescriptive norms, and social control: An intercultural comparison of people's reactions to uncivil behaviors. European Journal of Social Psychology, Vol. 40, No. 3, pp. 490-499.

Bredmar, Krister (2011): Theoretical foundations of the concept of management control: A references analysis. International Journal of Management, Vol. 28, No. 2, pp. 412-426.

Bretz Jr., Robert D.; Milkovich, George T. & Read, Walter (1992): The Current state of performance appraisal research and practice: Concerns, directions, and implications. Journal of Management, Vol. 18, No. 2, pp. 321-352.

Brewer, Paul & Venaik, Sunil (2010): GLOBE practices and values: A case of diminishing marginal utility? Journal of International Business Studies, Vol. 41, No. 8, pp. 1316-1324.

Brewer, Paul & Venaik, Sunil (2011): Individualism–Collectivism in Hofstede and GLOBE. Journal of International Business Studies, Vol. 42, No. 3, pp. 436-445.

Brews, Peter J. & Hunt, Michelle R. (1999): Learning to plan and planning to learn: Resolving the planning school/learning school debate. Strategic Management Journal, Vol. 20, No. 10, pp. 889-913.

Brick, Ivan E.; Palmon, Oded & Wald, John K. (2006): CEO compensation, director compensation, and firm performance: Evidence of cronyism? Journal of Corporate Finance, Vol. 12, No. 3, pp. 403-423.

Brignall, Stan & Modell, Sven (2000): An institutional perspective on performance measurement and management in the 'new public sector'. Management Accounting Research, Vol. 11, No. 3, pp. 281-306.

Brislin, Richard W. (1986): The wording and translation of research instruments. in: Lonner, Walter J. & Berry, John W. (Ed.): Field methods in cross-cultural research. Sage, Beverly Hills, CA, pp. 137-164.

Broadbent, Jane & Laughlin, Richard (2009): Performance management systems: A conceptual model. Management Accounting Research, Vol. 20, No. 4, pp. 283-295.

Brodbeck, Felix C.; Frese, Michael; Akerblom, Staffan; Audia, Giuseppe; Bakacsi, Gyula; Bendova, Helena; Bodega, Domenico; Bodur, MuzaVer; Booth, Simon; Brenk, Klas; Castel, Phillippe; Den Hartog, Deanne; Donnelly-Cox, Gemma; Gratchev, Mikhail V.; Holmberg, Ingalill; Jarmuz, Slawomir; Jesuino, Jorge C.; Jorbenadse, Ravaz; Kabasakal, Hayat E.; Keating, Mary; Kipiani, George; Konrad, Edvard; Koopman, Paul; Kurc, Alexandre; Leeds, Christopher; Lindell, Martin; Mączyński, Jerzy; Martin, Gillian S.; O'Connell, Jeremiah; Papalexandris, Athan; Papalexandris, Nancy; Prieto, Jose M.; Rakitski, Boris; Reber, Gerhard; Sabadin, Argio; Schramm-Nielsen, Jette; Schultz, Majken; Sigfrids, Camilla; Szabo, Erna; Thierry, Henk; Vondrysova, Marie; Weibler, Jürgen; Wilderom, Celeste; Witkowski, Stanislaw & Wunderer, Rolf (2000): Cultural variation of leadership prototypes across 22 European countries. Journal of Occupational and Organizational Psychology, Vol. 73, No. 1, pp. 1-29.

Bromley, Patricia & Powell, Walter W. (2012): From smoke and mirrors to walking the talk: Decoupling in the contemporary world. The Academy of Management Annals, Vol. 6, No. 1, pp. 483-530.

Bromwich, Michael (2014): Goodbye, It Has Been Good to Know You. Management Accounting Research, Vol. 25, No. 1, pp. 2-5.

Brown, Timothy A. (2006): Confirmatory factor analysis for applied research, Guilford Press, New York.

Brown, Timothy A. & Moore, Michael T. (2012): Confirmatory Factor Analysis. in: Hoyle, Rick H. (Ed.): Handbook of structural equation modeling. Guilford Press, New York, pp. 361-379.

Brühl, Rolf & Osann, Mathias (2010): Stakeholdertheorie und Neoinstitutionalismus und ihre Beiträge zur Erklärung der freiwilligen Berichterstattung am Beispiel der immateriellen Ressourcen. Zeitschrift für Planung & Unternehmenssteuerung, Vol. 21, No. 3, pp. 277-298.

Brutus, Stéphane (2010): Words versus numbers: A theoretical exploration of giving and receiving narrative comments in performance appraisal. Human Resource Management Review, Vol. 20, No. 2, pp. 144-157.

Bryman, Alan (2008): Social research methods, 3. ed., Oxford University Press, Oxford.

Bryman, Alan & Bell, Emma (2011): Business research methods, 3. ed., Oxford University Press, New York.

Buhk, Per N. & Malmi, Teemu (2005): Re-examining the cause-and-effect principles of the balanced scorecard. in: Jönsson, Sten & Mouritsen, Jan (Ed.): Accounting in Scandinavia - The Northern Lights. Liber and Copenhagen Business School Press, Malmo, pp. 87-113.

Burkert, Michael; Dávila, Antonio & Oyon, Daniel (2010): Performance consequences of balanced scorecard adoptions: Claim for large-scale evidence and propositions for future research. in: Epstein, Marc J.; Manzoni, Jean-François & Dávila, Antonio (Ed.): Performance measurement and management control: Innovative concepts and practices, Band 20. Emerald, Bingley, pp. 345-361.

Burkert, Michael & Lueg, Rainer (2013): Differences in the sophistication of Value-based Management – The role of top executives. Management Accounting Research, Vol. 24, No. 1, pp. 3-22.

Burns, Tom R. & Stalker, George M. (1961): The management of innovation, Tavistock, London.

Bushman, Robert M.; Indjejikian, Raffi J. & Smith, Abbie (1996): CEO compensation: The role of individual performance evaluation. Journal of Accounting and Economics, Vol. 21, No. 2, pp. 161-193.

Butler, Alan; Letza, Steve R. & Neale, Bill (1997): Linking the balanced scorecard to strategy. Long Range Planning, Vol. 30, No. 2, pp. 242-253,153.

Byrne, Barbara M.; Shavelson, Richard J. & Muthén, Bengt (1989): Testing for the equivalence of factor covariance and mean structures: The issue of partial measurement in variance. Psychological Bulletin, Vol. 105, No. 3, pp. 456-466.

Cadsby, Charles B.; Song, Fei & Tapon, Francis (2007): Sorting and incentive effects of pay for performance: An experimental investigation. Academy of Management Journal, Vol. 50, No. 2, pp. 387-405.

Campbell, Dennis (2008): Nonfinancial performance measures and promotion-based incentives. Journal of Accounting Research, Vol. 46, No. 2, pp. 297-332.

Caprar, Dan V. & Neville, Benjamin A. (2012): "Norming" and "conforming": Integrating cultural and institutional explanations for sustainability adoption in business. Journal of Business Ethics, Vol. 110, No. 2, pp. 231-245.

Cardinaels, Eddy & van Veen-Dirks, Paula M. (2010): Financial versus non-financial information: The impact of information organization and presentation in a Balanced Scorecard. Accounting, Organizations and Society, Vol. 35, No. 6, pp. 565-578.

Cardy, Robert L. (2004): Performance management: Concepts, skills, and exercises, M.E. Sharpe, Armonk, N.Y.

Carenys, Jordi (2010): Management control systems: A historical perspective. International bulletin of business administration, Vol. 7, pp. 37-54.

Carl, Dale; Gupta, Vipin & Javidan, Mansour (2004): Power Distance. in: House, Robert J.; Hanges, Paul J.; Javidan, Mansour; Dorfman, Peter W. & Gupta, Vipin (Ed.): Culture, leadership, and organizations: The GLOBE study of 62 societies. Sage, Thousand Oaks, CA, pp. 513-563.

Carr, Chris & Pudelko, Markus (2006): Convergence of management practices in strategy, finance and HRM between the USA, Japan and Germany. International Journal of Cross Cultural Management, Vol. 6, No. 1, pp. 75-100.

Carton, Robert B. & Hofer, Charles W. (2006): Measuring organizational performance: Metrics for entrepreneurship and strategic management research, Edward Elgar, Cheltenham, UK.

Cascio, Wayne F. (2012): Methodological issues in international HR management research. The International Journal of Human Resource Management, Vol. 23, No. 12, pp. 2532-2545.

Chakrabarty, Subrata (2009): The influence of national culture and institutional voids on family ownership of large firms: A country level empirical study. Journal of International Management, Vol. 15, No. 1, pp. 32-45.

Chandler Jr., Alfred D. (1962): Strategy and structure: Chapters in the history of the American industrial enterprise, MIT Press, Cambridge, Mass.

Chanegrih, Tarek (2008): Applying a typology of management accounting change: A research note. Management Accounting Research, Vol. 19, No. 3, pp. 278-285.

Chang, Sea-Jin; van Witteloostuijn, Arjen & Eden, Lorraine (2010): From the editors: Common method variance in international business research. Journal of International Business Studies, Vol. 41, No. 2, pp. 178-184.

Chen, Chao C. (1995): New trends in rewards allocation preferences: A Sino-U.S. comparison. Academy of Management Journal, Vol. 38, No. 2, pp. 408-428.

Chen, Y.S A.; Romocki, Timothy & Zuckerman, Gilroy J. (1997): Examination of U.S.-based Japanese subsidiaries: Evidence of the transfer of the Japanese strategic cost management. The International Journal of Accounting, Vol. 32, No. 4, pp. 417-440.

Chenhall, Robert H. (2003): Management control systems design within its organizational context: findings from contingency-based research and directions for the future. Accounting, Organizations and Society, Vol. 28, No. 2-3, pp. 127-168.

Chenhall, Robert H. (2007): Theorising contingencies in management control systems research. in: Chapman, Christopher S.; Hopwood, Anthony G. & Shields, Michael D. (Ed.): Handbook of management accounting research: Volume 1. Elsevier, Amsterdam, Oxford, pp. 163-205.

Chiang, Flora F. & Birtch, Thomas A. (2005): A taxonomy of reward preference: Examining country differences. Journal of International Management, Vol. 11, No. 3, pp. 357-375.

Chiang, Flora F. & Birtch, Thomas A. (2006): An empirical examination of reward preferences within and across national settings. Management International Review, Vol. 46, No. 5, pp. 573-596.

Chiang, Flora F. & Birtch, Thomas A. (2007): The transferability of management practices: Examining cross-national differences in reward preferences. Human Relations, Vol. 60, No. 9, pp. 1293-1330.

Chiang, Flora F. & Birtch, Thomas A. (2010): Appraising performance across borders: An empirical examination of the purposes and practices of performance appraisal in a multi-country context. Journal of Management Studies, Vol. 47, No. 7, pp. 1365-1393.

Chiang, Flora F. & Birtch, Thomas A. (2012): The performance implications of financial and non-financial rewards: An Asian Nordic comparison. Journal of Management Studies, Vol. 49, No. 3, pp. 538-570.

Chidlow, Agnieszka; Plakoyiannaki, Emmanuella & Welch, Catherine (2014): Translation in cross-language international business research: Beyond equivalence. Journal of International Business Studies, Vol. 45, No. 5, pp. 562-582.

Choi, Sue Y.; Lee, Heeseok & Yoo, Youngjin (2010): The impact of information technology and transactive memory systems on knowledge sharing, application, and team performance: A field study. MIS Quarterly, Vol. 34, No. 4, pp. 855-870.

Chong, Eric (2013): Managerial competencies and career advancement: A comparative study of managers in two countries. Journal of Business Research, Vol. 66, No. 3, pp. 345-353.

Chong, Vincent K. & Eggleton, Ian R. (2007): The impact of reliance on incentive-based compensation schemes, information asymmetry and organisational commitment on managerial performance. Management Accounting Research, Vol. 18, No. 3, pp. 312-342.

Chong Ju Choi (1994): Contract enforcement across cultures. Organization Studies, Vol. 15, No. 5, pp. 673-682.

Chow, Chee W. & Harrison, Paul D. (2002): Identifying meaningful and significant topics for research and publication: A sharing of experiences and insights by 'influential' accounting authors. Journal of Accounting Education, Vol. 20, No. 3, pp. 183-203.

Chow, Chee W.; Harrison, Paul D.; Lindquist, Timothy M. & Wu, Anne (1997): Escalating commitment to unprofitable projects: Replication and cross-cultural extension. Management Accounting Research, Vol. 8, No. 3, pp. 347-361.

Chow, Chee W.; Kato, Yutaka & Merchant, Kenneth A. (1996): The use of organizational controls and their effects on data manipulation and management myopia: A Japan vs U.S. comparison. Accounting, Organizations and Society, Vol. 21, No. 2-3, pp. 175-192.

Chow, Chee W.; Kato, Yutaka & Shields, Michael D. (1994): National culture and the preference for management controls: An exploratory study of the firm-labor market interface. Accounting, Organizations and Society, Vol. 19, No. 4-5, pp. 381-400.

Chow, Chee W.; Shields, Michael D. & Wu, Anne (1999): The importance of national culture in the design of and preference for management controls for multi-national operations. Accounting, Organizations and Society, Vol. 24, No. 5-6, pp. 441-461.

Chui, Andy C. & Kwok, Chuck C. (2009): Cultural practices and life insurance consumption: An international analysis using GLOBE scores. Journal of Multinational Financial Management, Vol. 19, No. 4, pp. 273-290.

Clark, Lee A. (1987): Mutual relevance of mainstream and cross-cultural psychology. Journal of Consulting and Clinical Psychology, Vol. 55, No. 4, pp. 461-470.

Cleveland, Jeanette; Murphy, Kevin R. & Williams, Richard E. (1989): Multiple uses of performance appraisal: Prevalence and correlates. Journal of Applied Psychology, Vol. 74, No. 1, pp. 130-135.

Coates, Jeff; Davis, Ted & Stacey, Ray (1995): Performance measurement systems, incentive reward schemes and short-termism in multinational companies: A note. Management Accounting Research, Vol. 6, No. 2, pp. 125-135.

Cohen, Jacob (1983): The cost of dichotomization. Applied Psychological Measurement, Vol. 7, No. 3, pp. 249-253.

Cohen, Jacob (1988): Statistical power analysis for the behavioral sciences, 2. ed., Lawrence Erlbaum Associates, Hillsdale, N.J.

Colakoglu, Saba; Lepak, David P. & Hong, Ying (2006): Measuring HRM effectiveness: Considering multiple stakeholders in a global context. Human Resource Management Review, Vol. 16, No. 2, pp. 209-218.

Collier, Paul M. (2005): Entrepreneurial control and the construction of a relevant accounting. Management Accounting Research, Vol. 16, No. 3, pp. 321-339.

Collins, Frank; Almer, Elizabeth D. & Mendoza, Roberto (1999): Budget games and effort: Differences between the United States and Latin America. Journal of International Accounting, Auditing and Taxation, Vol. 8, No. 2, pp. 241-267.

Conyon, Martin J. & Schwalbach, Joachim (2000): Excecutive compensation: Evidence from the UK and Germany. Long Range Planning, Vol. 33, No. 4, pp. 504-526.

Cooke, Fang L. & Huang, Kun (2011): Postacquisition evolution of the appraisal and reward systems: A study of Chinese IT firms acquired by US firms. Human Resource Management, Vol. 50, No. 6, pp. 839-858.

Cooper, Harris M. (2010): Research synthesis and meta-analysis: A step-by-step approach, 4. ed., Sage, Los Angeles.

Cooper, Harris M.; Hedges, Larry V. & Valentine, Jeff C. (Eds.) (2009): The handbook of research synthesis and meta-analysis, Russell Sage Foundation, New York.

Cornett, Marcia M.; Marcus, Alan J. & Tehranian, Hassan (2008): Corporate governance and pay-for-performance: The impact of earnings management☆. Journal of Financial Economics, Vol. 87, No. 2, pp. 357-373.

Cronbach, Lee J. & Meehl, Paul E. (1955): Construct validity in psychological tests,. Psychological Bulletin, Vol. 52, No. 4, pp. 281-302.

Cronqvist, Henrik & Fahlenbrach, Rüdiger (2013): CEO contract design: How do strong principals do it? Journal of Financial Economics, Vol. 108, No. 3, pp. 659-674.

Crossland, Craig & Hambrick, Donald C. (2007): How national systems differ in their constraints on corporate executives: A study of CEO effects in three countries. Strategic Management Journal, Vol. 28, No. 8, pp. 767-789.

Crossland, Craig & Hambrick, Donald C. (2011): Differences in managerial discretion across countries: How nation-level institutions affect the degree to which ceos matter. Strategic Management Journal, Vol. 32, No. 8, pp. 797-819.

Cunningham, Gary M. (1992): Management control and accounting systems under a competitive strategy. Accounting, Auditing & Accountability Journal, Vol. 5, No. 2, pp. 85-102.

Cusson, Maurice (2001): Control: Social. in: Smelser, Neil J. & Baltes, Paul B. (Ed.): International encyclopedia of the social & behavioral sciences. Elsevier, Pergamon, Amsterdam, pp. 2730-2735.

Cycyota, Cynthia S. & Harrison, David A. (2006): What (not) to expect when surveying executives: A meta-analysis of top manager response rates and techniques over time. Organizational Research Methods, Vol. 9, No. 2, pp. 133-160.

Czaja, Ronald & Blair, Johnny (2005): Designing surveys: A guide to decisions and procedures, 2. ed., Pine Forge Press, Thousand Oaks, Calif.

Daft, Richard L. & Macintosh, Norman B. (1984): The Nature and Use of Formal Control Systems for Management Control and Strategy Implementation. Journal of Management, Vol. 10, No. 1, pp. 43-66.

Daniel, Johnnie (2012): Sampling essentials: Practical guidelines for making sampling choices, Sage, Los Angeles.

Dávila, Antonio (2005): An exploratory study on the emergence of management control systems: formalizing human resources in small growing firms. Accounting, Organizations and Society, Vol. 30, No. 3, pp. 223-248.

Dávila, Antonio & Foster, George (2005): Management accounting systems adoption decisions: Evidence and performance implications from early-stage/startup companies. The Accounting Review, Vol. 80, No. 4, pp. 1039-1068.

Dávila, Antonio & Venkatachalam, Mohan (2004): The relevance of non-financial performance measures for CEO compensation: Evidence from the Airline industry. Review of Accounting Studies, Vol. 9, No. 4, pp. 443-464.

Davis, Stan & Albright, Tom (2004): An investigation of the effect of Balanced Scorecard implementation on financial performance. Management Accounting Research, Vol. 15, No. 2, pp. 135-153.

Dawes, John (2008): Do data characteristics change according to the number of scale points used? International Journal of Market Research, Vol. 50, No. 1, pp. 61-77.

Dawson, Neal V. & Weiss, Robert (2012): Dichotomizing continuous variables in statistical analysis: A practice to avoid. Medical Decision Making, Vol. 32, No. 2, pp. 225-226.

Day, George S.; Shocker, Allan D. & Srivastava, Rajendra K. (1979): Customer-oriented approaches to identifiying product-markets. Journal of Marketing, Vol. 43, No. 4, pp. 8-19.

De Geuser, Fabien; Mooraj, Stella & Oyon, Daniel (2009): Does the Balanced Scorecard Add Value? Empirical Evidence on its Effect on Performance. European Accounting Review, Vol. 18, No. 1, pp. 93-122.

DeCoster, Jamie; Iselin, Anne-Marie R. & Gallucci, Marcello (2009): A conceptual and empirical examination of justifications for dichotomization. Psychological Methods, Vol. 14, No. 4, pp. 349-366.

Deephouse, David L. (1996): Does isomorphism legitimate? Academy of Management Journal, Vol. 39, No. 4, pp. 1024-1039.

Den Hartog, Deanne (2004): Assertiveness. in: House, Robert J.; Hanges, Paul J.; Javidan, Mansour; Dorfman, Peter W. & Gupta, Vipin (Ed.): Culture, leadership, and organizations: The GLOBE study of 62 societies. Sage, Thousand Oaks, CA, pp. 395-436.

DeNisi, Angelo S. & Pritchard, Robert D. (2006): Performance appraisal, performance management and improving individual performance: A motivational framework. Management and Organization Review, Vol. 2, No. 2, pp. 253-277.

Deutsch, Morton (1985): Distributive justice: A social-psychological perspective, Yale University Press, New Haven, CT.

Devers, Cynthia E.; Cannella, Albert A.; Reilly, Gregory P. & Yoder, Michele E. (2007): Executive compensation: A multidisciplinary review of recent developments. Journal of Management, Vol. 33, No. 6, pp. 1016-1072.

DeVoe, Sanford E. & Iyengar, Sheena S. (2004): Managers' theories of subordinates: A cross-cultural examination of manager perceptions of motivation and appraisal of performance. Organizational Behavior and Human Decision Processes, Vol. 93, No. 1, pp. 47-61.

Dickson, Marcus W.; BeShears, Renee S. & Gupta, Vipin (2004): The impact of societal culture and industry on organizational culture. in: House, Robert J.; Hanges, Paul J.; Javidan, Mansour; Dorfman, Peter W. & Gupta, Vipin (Ed.): Culture, leadership, and organizations: The GLOBE study of 62 societies. Sage, Thousand Oaks, CA, pp. 74-90.

Dillman, Don A. (2007): Mail and internet surveys: The tailored design method, 2. ed., Wiley, Hoboken, N.J.

DiMaggio, Paul J. & Powell, Walter W. (1983): The iron cage revisited: Institutional isomorphism and collective rationality in organizational fields. American Sociological Review, Vol. 48, No. 2, pp. 147-160.

DiMaggio, Paul J. & Powell, Walter W. (1991): Introduction. in: Powell, Walter W. & DiMaggio, Paul J. (Ed.): The new institutionalism in organizational analysis. University of Chicago Press, Chicago, pp. 1-38.

Dimitrov, Dimiter M. (2006): Comparing groups on latent variables: A structural equation modeling approach. Work: A Journal of Prevention, Assessment and Rehabilitation, Vol. 26, No. 4, pp. 429-436.

Ding, Shujun & Beaulieu, Philip (2011): The Role of Financial Incentives in Balanced Scorecard-Based Performance Evaluations: Correcting Mood Congruency Biases. Journal of Accounting Research, Vol. 49, No. 5, pp. 1223-1247.

Donaldson, Lex (1996): The normal science of structural contingency theory. in: Clegg, Stewart R.; Hardy, Cynthia & Nord, Walter R. (Ed.): Handbook of Organiszation Studies. Sage, London, pp. 57-76.

Donaldson, Lex (2001): The contingency theory of organizations, Sage, Thousand Oaks, CA.

Donaldson, Thomas & Preston, Lee E. (1995): The stakeholder theory of the corporation: Concepts, evidence, and implications. Academy of Management Review, Vol. 20, No. 1, pp. 65-91.

Dorfman, Peter; Javidan, Mansour; Hanges, Paul; Dastmalchian, Ali & House, Robert (2012): GLOBE: A twenty year journey into the intriguing world of culture and leadership. Journal of World Business, Vol. 47, No. 4, pp. 504-518.

Dorfman, Peter W.; Stephan, Walter G. & Loveland, John (1986): Performance appraisal behaviors: Supervisor perception and subordinate reactions. Personnel Psychology, Vol. 39, No. 3, pp. 579-597.

Dossi, Andrea; Patelli, Lorenzo & Zoni, Laura (2010): The missing link between corporate performance measurement systems and chief executive officer incentive plans. Journal of Accounting, Auditing and Finance, Vol. 25, No. 4, pp. 531-558.

Douglas, Patricia C.; HassabElnaby, Hassan; Norman, Carolyn S. & Wier, Benson (2007): An investigation of ethical position and budgeting systems: Egyptian managers in US and Egyptian firms. Journal of International Accounting, Auditing and Taxation, Vol. 16, No. 1, pp. 90-109.

Dowling, John & Pfeffer, Jeffrey (1975): Organizational legitimacy: Social values and organizational behavior. The Pacific Sociological Review, Vol. 18, No. 1, pp. 122-136.

Dransfield, Robert (2000): Human resource management, Heinemann, Oxford.

Drogendijk, Rian & Holm, Ulf (2012): Cultural distance or cultural positions? Analysing the effect of culture on the HQ–subsidiary relationship. International Business Review, Vol. 21, No. 3, pp. 383-396.

Drogendijk, Rian & Slangen, Arjen (2006): Hofstede, Schwartz, or managerial perceptions? The effects of different cultural distance measures on establishment mode choices by multinational enterprises. International Business Review, Vol. 15, No. 4, pp. 361-380.

Dye, Ronald A. (2004): Strategy selection and performance measurement choice when profit drivers are uncertain. Management Science, Vol. 50, No. 12, pp. 1624-1637.

Earley, Christopher P. (2006): Leading cultural research in the future: a matter of paradigms and taste. Journal of International Business Studies, Vol. 37, No. 6, pp. 922-931.

Earley, Christopher P. & Singh, Harbir (1995): International and intercultural management research: What's next? Academy of Management Journal, Vol. 38, No. 2, pp. 327-340.

Efferein, Sujoko & Hopper, Trevor (2007): Management control, culture and ethnicity in a Chinese Indonesian company. Accounting, Organizations and Society, Vol. 32, No. 3, pp. 223-262.

Egelhoff, William & Frese, Erich (2009): Understanding managers' preferences for internal markets versus business planning: A comparative study of German and U.S. managers. Journal of International Management, Vol. 15, No. 1, pp. 77-91.

Egri, Carolyn P.; Khilji, Shaista E.; Ralston, David A.; Palmer, Ian; Girson, Ilya; Milton, Laurie; Richards, Malika; Ramburuth, Prem & Mockaitis, Audra (2012): Do Anglo countries still form a values cluster? Evidence of the complexity of value change. Journal of World Business, Vol. 47, No. 2, pp. 267-276.

Eisenberger, Robert & Cameron, Judy (1996): Detrimental effects of reward. Reality or myth? American Psychologist, Vol. 51, No. 11, pp. 1153-1166.

Eisenhardt, Kathleen M. (1989): Agency theory: An Assessment and review. Academy of Management Review, Vol. 14, No. 1, pp. 57-74.

Ember, Carol R. & Ember, Melvin (2009): Cross-cultural research methods, 2. ed., AltaMira Press, Lanham.

Emmanuel, Clive R.; Otley, David T. & Merchant, Kenneth A. (1990): Accounting for management control, 2. ed., Chapman and Hall, University and Professional Division, London.

Ennen, Edgar & Richter, Ansgar (2009): The Whole Is More Than the Sum of Its Parts-- Or Is It? A Review of the Empirical Literature on Complementarities in Organizations. Journal of Management, Vol. 36, No. 1, pp. 207-233.

Epstein, Marc J. & Manzoni, Jean-François (1997): The Balanced Scorecard and Tableau de Bord: A global perspective on translating strategy into action, INSEAD, France, Fontainebleau, INSEAD Working Papers

Euske, Kenneth J.; Hesford, James W. & Malina, Mary A. (2011): A social network analysis of the literature on management control. Journal of Management Accounting Research, Vol. 23, No. 1, pp. 259-283.

Evans, James R. (2004): An exploratory study of performance measurement systems and relationships with performance results. Journal of Operations Management, Vol. 22, No. 3, pp. 219-232.

Evanschitzky, Heiner & Armstrong, J. S. (2013): Research with In-built replications: Comment and further suggestions for replication research. Journal of Business Research, Vol. 66, No. 9, pp. 1406-1408.

Evanschitzky, Heiner; Baumgarth, Carsten; Hubbard, Raymond & Armstrong, J. S. (2007): Replication research's disturbing trend. Journal of Business Research, Vol. 60, No. 4, pp. 411-415.

Fenwick, Marilyn (2005): Extending strategic international human resource management research and pedagogy to the non-profit multinational. The International Journal of Human Resource Management, Vol. 16, No. 4, pp. 497-512.

Ferreira, Aldónio & Otley, David T. (2009): The design and use of performance management systems: An extended framework for analysis. Management Accounting Research, Vol. 20, No. 4, pp. 263-282.

Ferris, Gerald R.; Munyon, Timothy P.; Basik, Kevin & Buckley, M. R. (2008): The performance evaluation context: Social, emotional, cognitive, political, and relationship components. Human Resource Management Review, Vol. 18, No. 3, pp. 146-163.

Festing, Marion (2012): Strategic Human Resource Management in Germany: Evidence of convergence to the U.S. model, the European model, or a distinctive national model? Academy of Management Perspectives, Vol. 26, No. 2, pp. 37-54.

Festing, Marion; Dowling, Peter J.; Weber, Wolfgang & Engle, Allen D. (2011): Internationales Personalmanagement, 3. ed., Gabler, Wiesbaden.

Festing, Marion; Engle, Allen D.; Dowling, Peter J. & Sahakiants, Ihar (2012): HRM Activities: Pay and Rewards. in: Brewster, Chris & Mayrhofer, Wolfgang (Ed.): Handbook of research on comparative human resource management. Edward Elgar, Cheltenham, UK, pp. 139-163.

Field, Andy P. (2013): Discovering statistics using IBM SPSS statistics: And sex and drugs and rock 'n' roll, 4. ed., Sage, Los Angeles, Calif.

Fischer, Ronald (2004): Organizational reward allocation: A comparison of British and German organizations. International Journal of Intercultural Relations, Vol. 28, No. 2, pp. 151-164.

Fischer, Ronald & Smith, Peter B. (2003): Reward allocation and culture: A meta-analysis. Journal of Cross-Cultural Psychology, Vol. 34, No. 3, pp. 251-268.

Fischer, Ronald; Smith, Peter B.; Richey, Brenda; Ferreira, Maria C.; Assmar, Eveline M. L.; Maes, Jürgen & Stumpf, Siegfried (2007): How Do Organizations Allocate Rewards? The Predictive Validity of National Values, Economic and Organizational Factors Across Six Nations. Journal of Cross-Cultural Psychology, Vol. 38, No. 1, pp. 3-18.

Fisher, Joseph G. (1995): Contingency-based research on management control systems: Categorization by level of complexity. Journal of Accounting Literature, Vol. 14, pp. 24-53.

Fisher, Joseph G. (1998): Contingency theory, management control systems and firm outcomes: Past results and future directions. Behavioral Research in Accounting, Vol. 10 Supplement, pp. 47-64.

Flamholtz, Eric G. (1979): Behavioral aspects of accounting/control systems. in: Kerr, Steven (Ed.): Organizational behavior. Grid Pub., Columbus, Ohio, pp. 289-316.

Flamholtz, Eric G. (1983): Accounting, budgeting and control systems in their organizational context: Theoretical and empirical perspectives. Accounting, Organizations and Society, Vol. 8, No. 2-3, pp. 153-169.

Flamholtz, Eric G. (1996): Effective organizational control: A framework, applications, and implications. European Management Journal, Vol. 14, No. 6, pp. 596-611.

Flamholtz, Eric G.; Das, T. K. & Tsui, Anne S. (1985): Toward an integrative framework of organizational control. Accounting, Organizations and Society, Vol. 10, No. 1, pp. 35-50.

Flick, Uwe (2011): Introducing research methodology: A beginner's guide to doing a research project, Sage Publications, Thousand Oaks, Calif.

Flynn, Barbara B. & Saladin, Brooke (2006): Relevance of Baldrige constructs in an international context: A study of national culture. Journal of Operations Management, Vol. 24, No. 5, pp. 583-603.

Franco-Santos, Monica; Lucianetti, Lorenzo & Bourne, Mike (2012): Contemporary performance measurement systems: A review of their consequences and a framework for research. Management Accounting Research, Vol. 23, No. 2, pp. 79-119.

Franke, George R. & Richey, R. G. (2010): Improving generalizations from multi-country comparisons in international business research. Journal of International Business Studies, Vol. 41, No. 8, pp. 1275-1293.

Freeman, R. E. (1984): Strategic management: A stakeholder approach, Pitman, Boston.

Freeman, R. E.; Harrison, Jeffrey S. & Wicks, Andrew C. (2007): Managing for stakeholders: Survival, reputation, and success, Yale University Press, New Haven.

Freeman, R. E.; Harrison, Jeffrey S.; Wicks, Andrew C.; Parmar, Bidhan & de Colle, Simone (2010): Stakeholder theory: The state of the art, Cambridge University Press, Cambridge, UK.

Fullerton, Rosemary R. & McWatters, Cheryl S. (2002): The role of performance measures and incentive systems in relation to the degree of JIT implementation. Accounting, Organizations and Society, Vol. 27, No. 8, pp. 711-735.

Funk, Charles A.; Arthurs, Jonathan D.; Treviño, Len J. & Joireman, Jeff (2009): Consumer animosity in the global value chain: The effect of international production shifts on willingness to purchase hybrid products. Journal of International Business Studies, Vol. 41, No. 4, pp. 639-651.

Geertz, Clifford (1973): The interpetation of cultures, Basic Books, New York, NY.

Gehrke, Ingmar & Horváth, Péter (2002): Implementation of performance measurement: A comparative study of French and German organizations. in: Epstein, Marc J. & Manzoni, Jean-François (Ed.): Performance measurement and management control: A compendium of research, Band 12. Elsevier, Amsterdam, pp. 159-180.

Gelfand, Michele; Bhawuk, Dharm P.; Nishii, Lisa H. & Bechtold, David J. (2004): Individualism and Collectivism. in: House, Robert J.; Hanges, Paul J.; Javidan, Mansour; Dorfman, Peter W. & Gupta, Vipin (Ed.): Culture, leadership, and organizations: The GLOBE study of 62 societies. Sage, Thousand Oaks, CA, pp. 437-512.

Geppert, Mike; Matten, Dirk & Schmidt, Peggy (2004): Die Bedeutung institutionalistischer Ansätze für das Verständnis von Organisations-und Managementprozessen in multinationalen Unternehmen. Berliner Journal für Soziologie, Vol. 14, No. 3, pp. 379-397.

Gerhart, Barry (2008): Cross cultural management research: Assumptions, evidence, and suggested directions. International Journal of Cross Cultural Management, Vol. 8, No. 3, pp. 259-274.

Gerhart, Barry (2009a): Does national culture constrain organization culture and human resource strategy? The role of individual level mechanisms and implications for employee selection. Research in Personnel and Human Resources Management, Vol. 28, pp. 1-48.

Gerhart, Barry (2009b): How much does national culture constrain organizational culture? Management and Organization Review, Vol. 5, No. 2, pp. 241-259.

Gerhart, Barry & Fang, Meiyu (2005): National culture and human resource management: assumptions and evidence. The International Journal of Human Resource Management, Vol. 16, No. 6, pp. 971-986.

Ghosh, Dipankar & Lusch, Robert F. (2000): Outcome effect, controllability and performance evaluation of managers: some field evidence from multi-outlet businesses. Accounting, Organizations and Society, Vol. 25, No. 4-5, pp. 411-425.

Ghoshal, Sumantra & Bartlett, Christopher A. (1996): Rebuilding behavioral context: A blueprint for corporate renewal. Sloan Management Review, Vol. 37, No. 2, pp. 23-36.

Giacobbe-Miller, Jane K.; Miller, Daniel J. & Victorov, Vladimir I. (1998): A comparison of Russian and U.S. pay allocation decisions, distributive justice judgements, and productivity under different payment conditions. Personnel Psychology, Vol. 51, No. 1, pp. 137-163.

Giacobbe-Miller, Jane K.; Miller, Daniel J. & Zhang, Weijun (2003): Country and organizational-level adaptation to foreign workplace ideologies: A comparative study of distributive justice values in China, Russia and the United States. Journal of International Business Studies, Vol. 34, No. 4, pp. 389-406.

Gibbons, Robert & Murphy, Kevin J. (1990): Relative performance evaluation for Chief Executive Officers. Industrial and Labor Relations Review, Vol. 43, No. 3, pp. 30S-51S.

Gibbs, Michael (1995): Incentive compensation in a corporate hierarchy. Journal of Accounting and Economics, Vol. 19, No. 2-3, pp. 247-277.

Gibbs, Michael (2008): Discussion of Nonfinancial Performance Measures and Promotion-Based Incentives. Journal of Accounting Research, Vol. 46, No. 2, pp. 333-340.

Gibbs, Michael; Merchant, Kenneth A.; van der Stede, Wim A. & Vargus, Mark E. (2004): Determinants and effects of subjectivity in incentives. The Accounting Review, Vol. 79, No. 2, pp. 409-436.

Giddens, Anthony (1990): The consequences of modernity, Polity Press, Cambridge, UK.

Giglioni, Giovanni B. & Bedeian, Arthur G. (1974): A conspectus of management control theory: 1900-1972. Academy of Management Journal, Vol. 17, No. 2, pp. 292-305.

Glock, Christoph H. & Hochrein, Simon (2011): Purchasing organization and design: A literature review. BuR - Business Research, Vol. 4, No. 2, pp. 149-191.

Golman, Russell & Bhatia, Sudeep (2012): Performance evaluation inflation and compression. Accounting, Organizations and Society, Vol. 37, No. 8, pp. 534-543.

Gong, Guojin; Li, Laura Y. & Shin, Jae Y. (2011): Relative performance evaluation and related peer groups in executive compensation contracts. The Accounting Review, Vol. 86, No. 3, pp. 1007-1043.

Gooderham, Paul; Nordhaug, Odd & Ringdal, Kristen (2006): National embeddedness and calculative human resource management in US subsidiaries in Europe and Australia. Human Relations, Vol. 59, No. 11, pp. 1491-1513.

Gordon, Lawrence A. & Miller, Danny (1976): A contingency framework for the design of accounting information systems. Accounting, Organizations and Society, Vol. 1, No. 1, pp. 59-69.

Gordon, Lawrence A. & Narayanan, Vadake K. (1984): Management accounting systems, perceived environmental uncertainty and organization structure: An empirical investigation. Accounting, Organizations and Society, Vol. 9, No. 1, pp. 33-47.

Gosselin, Maurice (2005): An empirical study of performance measurement in manufacturing firms. International Journal of Productivity and Performance Management, Vol. 54, No. 5/6, pp. 419-437.

Govindarajan, Vijay & Gupta, Anil K. (2000): Analysis of the emerging global arena. European Management Journal, Vol. 18, No. 3, pp. 274-284.

Grabner, Isabella & Moers, Frank (2013): Management control as a system or a package? Conceptual and empirical issues. Accounting, Organizations and Society, Vol. 38, No. 6-7, pp. 407-419.

Graen, George B. (2006): In the eye of the beholder: Cross-cultural lesson in leadership from project GLOBE: A response viewed from the third culture bonding (TCB) model of cross-cultural leadership. Academy of Management Perspectives, Vol. 20, No. 4, pp. 95-101.

Grafton, Jennifer; Lillis, Anne M. & Widener, Sally K. (2010): The role of performance measurement and evaluation in building organizational capabilities and performance. Accounting, Organizations and Society, Vol. 35, No. 7, pp. 689-706.

Green, Stephen G. & Welsh, M. A. (1988): Cybernetics and dependence: Reframing the control concept. Academy of Management Review, Vol. 13, No. 2, pp. 287-301.

Greenwood, Royston & Hinings, Christopher R. (1996): Understanding radical organizational change: Bringing together the old and the new institutionalism. Academy of Management Review, Vol. 21, No. 4, pp. 1022-1054.

Greenwood, Royston; Oliver, Christine; Suddaby, Roy & Sahlin, Kerstin (2008): Introduction. in: Greenwood, Royston; Oliver, Christine; Suddaby, Roy & Sahlin, Kerstin (Ed.): The SAGE handbook of organizational institutionalism. Sage, Los Angeles, Calif., pp. 1-46.

Groen, Bianca A.; Wouters, Marc J. & Wilderom, Celeste P. (2012): Why do employees take more initiatives to improve their performance after co-developing performance measures? A field study. Management Accounting Research, Vol. 23, No. 2, pp. 120-141.

Gupta, Anil K. (1984): Contingency linkages between strategy and General Manager characteristics: A conceptual examination. Academy of Management Review, Vol. 9, No. 3, pp. 399-412.

Gupta, Vipin & Hanges, Paul J. (2004): Regional and climate clustering of societal cultures. in: House, Robert J.; Hanges, Paul J.; Javidan, Mansour; Dorfman, Peter W. & Gupta, Vipin (Ed.): Culture, leadership, and organizations: The GLOBE study of 62 societies. Sage, Thousand Oaks, CA, pp. 178-218.

Gupta, Vipin; Hanges, Paul J. & Dorfman, Peter W. (2002): Cultural clusters: methodology and findings. Journal of World Business, Vol. 37, No. 1, pp. 11-15.

Gupta, Vipin; Luque, Mary S. de & House, Robert J. (2004): Multisource construct validity of GLOBE scales. in: House, Robert J.; Hanges, Paul J.; Javidan, Mansour; Dorfman, Peter W. & Gupta, Vipin (Ed.): Culture, leadership, and organizations: The GLOBE study of 62 societies. Sage, Thousand Oaks, CA, pp. 152-177.

Haas, Marco de & Kleingeld, Ad (1999): Multilevel design of performance measurement systems: enhancing strategic dialogue throughout the organization. Management Accounting Research, Vol. 10, No. 3, pp. 233-261.

Hair Jr., Joseph F.; Wolfinbarger Celsi, Mary; Money, Arthur H.; Samouel, Phlipp & Page, Michael J. (2011): Essentials of business research methods, 2. ed., M.E. Sharpe, Armonk, N.Y.

Hall, Edward T. (1990): The silent language, Anchor Press/Doubleday, New York.

Hall, Peter A. & Soskice, David W. (2001): Varieties of capitalism: The institutional foundations of comparative advantage, Oxford University Press, Oxford.

Hammersley, Martyn (1987): Notes on the terms 'validity' and 'reliability'. British Educational Research Journal, Vol. 13, No. 1, pp. 73-81.

Handfield, Robert B. & Melnyk, Steven A. (1998): The scientific theory-building process: a primer using the case of TQM. Journal of Operations Management, Vol. 16, No. 4, pp. 321-339.

Hanges, Paul J. (2004): Appendix A: Societal-level correlations among GLOBE societal culture scales. in: House, Robert J.; Hanges, Paul J.; Javidan, Mansour; Dorfman, Peter W. & Gupta, Vipin (Ed.): Culture, leadership, and organizations: The GLOBE study of 62 societies. Sage, Thousand Oaks, CA, pp. 733-736.

Hanges, Paul J. & Dickson, Marcus W. (2004): The development and validation of the GLOBE culture and leadership scales. in: House, Robert J.; Hanges, Paul J.; Javidan, Mansour; Dorfman, Peter W. & Gupta, Vipin (Ed.): Culture, leadership, and organizations: The GLOBE study of 62 societies. Sage, Thousand Oaks, CA, pp. 122-151.

Hanges, Paul J. & Dickson, Marcus W. (2006): Agitation over aggregation: Clarifying the development of and the nature of the GLOBE scales. The Leadership Quarterly, Vol. 17, No. 5, pp. 522-536.

Hanges, Paul J.; Dickson, Marcus W. & Sipe, Mina T. (2004): Rationale for GLOBE statistical analysis. in: House, Robert J.; Hanges, Paul J.; Javidan, Mansour; Dorfman, Peter W. & Gupta, Vipin (Ed.): Culture, leadership, and organizations: The GLOBE study of 62 societies. Sage, Thousand Oaks, CA, pp. 219-233.

Hansen, Stephen C.; Otley, David T. & van der Stede, Wim A. (2003): Practice developments in budgeting: An overview and research perspective. Journal of Management Accounting Research, Vol. 15, pp. 95-116.

Hansen, Stephen C. & van der Stede, Wim A. (2004): Multiple facets of budgeting: an exploratory analysis. Management Accounting Research, Vol. 15, No. 4, pp. 415-439.

Hantrais, Linda & Mangen, Steen (1996): Method and management of cross-national social research. in: Hantrais, Linda & Mangen, Steen (Ed.): Cross-national research methods in the social sciences. Pinter, London, pp. 1-12.

Hanzlick, Michael & Brühl, Rolf (2013): Die Kopplung von Controlling-Systemen. Controlling & Management Review, Vol. 57, No. 2, pp. 66-70.

Harkness, Janet A. (2002): Questionnaire translation. in: Harkness, Janet A. (Ed.): Cross-cultural survey methods. Wiley-Interscience, New York, Chichester, pp. 35-56.

Harkness, Janet A. & Schoua-Glusberg, Alicia (1998): Questionnaires in translation. in: Harkness, Janet A. (Ed.): Cross-cultural survey equivalence. Zentrum für Umfragen, Methoden und Analysen (ZUMA), Mannheim, pp. 87-126.

Harkness, Janet A.; van de Vijver, Fons J. & Johnson, Timothy P. (2002): Questionnaire design in comparitive research. in: Harkness, Janet A. (Ed.): Cross-cultural survey methods. Wiley-Interscience, New York, Chichester, pp. 19-34.

Harrington, Donna (2009): Confirmatory factor analysis, Oxford University Press, New York.

Harris, Simon & Carr, Chris (2008): National cultural values and the purpose of businesses. International Business Review, Vol. 17, No. 1, pp. 103-117.

Harrison, Graeme L. (1992): The cross-cultural generalizability of the relation between participation, budget emphasis and job related attitudes. Accounting, Organizations and Society, Vol. 17, No. 1, pp. 1-15.

Harrison, Graeme L. & McKinnon, Jill L. (1999): Cross-cultural research in management control systems design: A review of the current state. Accounting, Organizations and Society, Vol. 24, No. 5-6, pp. 483-506.

Harrison, Graeme L. & McKinnon, Jill L. (2007): National culture and management control. in: Scapens, Robert W.; Northcott, Deryl & Hopper, Trevor (Ed.): Issues in management accounting. Pearson Education, Harlow, pp. 93-116.

Harzing, Anne-Wil; Reiche, B. S. & Pudelko, Markus (2013): Challenges in international survey research: A review with illustrations and suggested solutions for best practice. European Journal of International Management, Vol. 7, No. 1, pp. 112-134.

Henri, Jean-François (2006a): Management control systems and strategy: A resource-based perspective. Accounting, Organizations and Society, Vol. 31, No. 6, pp. 529-558.

Henri, Jean-François (2006b): Organizational culture and performance measurement systems. Accounting, Organizations and Society, Vol. 31, No. 1, pp. 77-103.

Hesford, James W.; Lee, Sung-Han; van der Stede, Wim A. & Young, S. M. (2007): Management accounting: A bibliographic study. in: Chapman, Christopher S.; Hopwood, Anthony G. & Shields, Michael D. (Ed.): Handbook of management accounting research: Volume 1. Elsevier, Amsterdam, Oxford, pp. 3-26.

Hill, Charles W. L. & Jones, Thomas M. (1992): Stakeholder-Agency theory. Journal of Management Studies, Vol. 29, No. 2, pp. 131-154.

Ho, Joanna L.; Wu, Anne & Wu, Steve Y. (2014): Performance measures, consensus on strategy implementation, and performance: Evidence from the operational-level of organizations. Accounting, Organizations and Society, Vol. 39, No. 1, pp. 38-58.

Hofer, Charles W. (1975): Toward a contingency theory of business strategy. Academy of Management Journal, Vol. 18, No. 4, pp. 784-810.

Hofstede, Geert (1980): Culture's Consequences: International differences in work-related values, Sage, Beverly Hills, CA.

Hofstede, Geert (1983): National cultures in four dimensions: A research-based theory of cultural differences among nations. International Studies of Management & Organization, Vol. 13, No. 1-2, pp. 46-74.

Hofstede, Geert (1984): Cultural dimensions in management and planning. Asia Pacific Journal of Management, Vol. 1, No. 2, pp. 81-99.

Hofstede, Geert (1998): Attitudes, values and organizational culture: Disentangling the concepts. Organization Studies, Vol. 19, No. 3, pp. 477-493.

Hofstede, Geert (2001): Culture's Consequences: Comparing values, behaviors, institutions and organizations across nations, 2. ed., Sage, Thousand Oaks, CA.

Hofstede, Geert (2002): Dimensions do not exist: A reply to Brendan McSweeney. Human Relations, Vol. 55, No. 11, pp. 1355-1361.

Hofstede, Geert (2003): What is culture? A reply to Baskerville. Accounting, Organizations and Society, Vol. 28, No. 7-8, pp. 811-813.

Hofstede, Geert (2006): What did GLOBE really measure? Researchers' minds versus respondents' minds. Journal of International Business Studies, Vol. 37, No. 6, pp. 882-896.

Hofstede, Geert (2010): The GLOBE debate: Back to relevance. Journal of International Business Studies, Vol. 41, No. 8, pp. 1339-1346.

Hofstede, Geert & Bond, Michael H. (1984): Hofstede's culture dimensions: An independent validation using Rokeach's Value Survey. Journal of Cross-Cultural Psychology, Vol. 15, No. 4, pp. 417-433.

Hofstede, Geert; Garibaldi de Hilal, Adriana V.; Malvezzi, Sigmar; Tanure, Betania & Vinken, Henk (2010): Comparing Regional Cultures Within a Country: Lessons From Brazil. Journal of Cross-Cultural Psychology, Vol. 41, No. 3, pp. 336-352.

Hofstede, Geert & Hofstede, Gert J. (2005): Cultures and organizations: Software of the mind, 2. ed., McGraw-Hill, New York, NY.

Hofstede, Geert; Hofstede, Gert J. & Minkov, Michael (2010): Cultures and organizations: Software of the mind. Intercultural cooperation and its importance for survival, 3. ed., McGraw-Hill, New York, NY.

Hofstede, Geert; Neuijen, Bram; Ohayv, Denise D. & Sanders, Geert (1990): Measuring organizational cultures: A qualitative and quantitative study across twenty cases. Administrative Science Quarterly, Vol. 35, No. 2, pp. 286-316.

Holmstrom, Bengt R. (1979): Moral hazard and observability. The Bell Journal of Economics, Vol. 10, No. 1, pp. 74-91.

Holmstrom, Bengt R. & Milgrom, Paul (1991): Multitask principal-agent analyses: Incentive contracts, asset ownership, and job design. Journal of Law, Economics, and Organization, Vol. 7, No. 1, pp. 24-52.

Holmstrom, Bengt R. & Tirole, Jean (1989): Chapter 2 The theory of the firm. in: Schmalensee, Richard & Willig, Robert (Ed.): Handbook of industrial organization, Band 1. North-Holland, Amsterdam, pp. 61-133.

Homburg, Christian; Klarmann, Martin; Reimann, Martin & Schilke, Oliver (2012): What drives key informant accuracy? Journal of Marketing Research, Vol. 49, No. 4, pp. 594-608.

Hope, Jeremy & Fraser, Robin (2003): New ways of setting rewards: The beyond budgeting model. California Management Review, Vol. 45, No. 4, pp. 99-119.

Höppe, Felix & Moers, Frank (2011): The choice of different types of subjectivity in CEO annual bonus contracts. The Accounting Review, Vol. 86, No. 6, pp. 2023-2046.

Hoque, Zahirul (2011): The relations among competition, delegation, management accounting systems change and performance: A path model. Advances in Accounting, Vol. 27, No. 2, pp. 266-277.

Hoque, Zahirul & James, Wendy (2000): Linking balanced scorecard measures to size and market factors: Impact on organizational performance. Journal of Management Accounting Research, Vol. 12, pp. 1-17.

House, Robert J. & Hanges, Paul J. (2004): Research design. in: House, Robert J.; Hanges, Paul J.; Javidan, Mansour; Dorfman, Peter W. & Gupta, Vipin (Ed.): Culture, leadership, and organizations: The GLOBE study of 62 societies. Sage, Thousand Oaks, CA, pp. 95-101.

House, Robert J.; Hanges, Paul J.; Javidan, Mansour; Dorfman, Peter W. & Gupta, Vipin (Eds.) (2004): Culture, leadership, and organizations: The GLOBE study of 62 societies, Sage, Thousand Oaks, CA.

House, Robert J. & Javidan, Mansour (2004): Overview of GLOBE. in: House, Robert J.; Hanges, Paul J.; Javidan, Mansour; Dorfman, Peter W. & Gupta, Vipin (Ed.): Culture, leadership, and organizations: The GLOBE study of 62 societies. Sage, Thousand Oaks, CA, pp. 9-28.

House, Robert J.; Javidan, Mansour; Hanges, Paul J. & Dorfman, Peter W. (2002): Understanding cultures and implicit leadership theories across the globe: an introduction to project GLOBE. Journal of World Business, Vol. 37, No. 1, pp. 3-10.

House, Robert J.; Quigley, Narda R. & Sully de Luque, Mary (2010): Insights from Project GLOBE: Extending global advertising research through a contemporary framework. International Journal of Advertising, Vol. 29, No. 1, pp. 111-139.

Hu, Li-tze & Bentler, Peter M. (1998): Fit indices in covariance structure modeling: Sensitivity to underparameterized model misspecification. Psychological Methods, Vol. 3, No. 4, pp. 424-453.

Hu, Li-tze & Bentler, Peter M. (1999): Cutoff criteria for fit indexes in covariance structure analysis: Conventional criteria versus new alternatives. Structural Equation Modeling: A Multidisciplinary Journal, Vol. 6, No. 1, pp. 1-55.

Huang, Fali (2013): Contract enforcement: A political economy model of legal development. Journal of Law, Economics, and Organization, Vol. 29, No. 4, pp. 835-870.

Hubbard, Raymond & Armstrong, J. S. (1994): Replications and extensions in marketing: Rarely published but quite contrary. International Journal of Research in Marketing, Vol. 11, No. 3, pp. 233-248.

Huber, George P. & Power, Daniel J. (1985): Retrospective reports of strategic-level managers: Guidelines for increasing their accuracy. Strategic Management Journal, Vol. 6, No. 2, pp. 171-180.

Hui, Harry C.; Triandis, Harry C. & Yee, Candice (1991): Cultural differences in reward allocation: Is collectivism the explanation. British Journal of Social Psychology, Vol. 30, No. 2, pp. 145-157.

Hult, G. T. M.; Ketchen, David J.; Griffith, David A.; Finnegan, Carol A.; Gonzalez-Padron, Tracy; Harmancioglu, Nukhet; Huang, Ying; Talay, M. B. & Cavusgil, S. T. (2008): Data equivalence in cross-cultural international business research: Assessment and guidelines. Journal of International Business Studies, Vol. 39, No. 6, pp. 1027-1044.

Ibrahim, Salma & Lloyd, Cynthia (2011): The association between non-financial performance measures in executive compensation contracts and earnings management. Journal of Accounting and Public Policy, Vol. 30, No. 3, pp. 256-274.

Ikramullah, Malik; Shah, Bahadar; Khan, Shadiullah; Ul Hassan, Faqir S. & Zaman, Tariq (2012): Purposes of performance appraisal system: A perceptual study of civil servants in district Dera Ismail Khan Pakistan. International Journal of Business and Management, Vol. 7, No. 3, pp. 142-151.

Indjejikian, Raffi J. & Nanda, Dhananjay (2002): Exectuive target bonuses and what they imply about performance standards. The Accounting Review, Vol. 77, No. 4, pp. 793-819.

Iselin, Anne-Marie R.; Gallucci, Marcello & DeCoster, Jamie (2013): Reconciling questions about dichotomizing variables in criminal justice research. Journal of Criminal Justice, Vol. 41, No. 6, pp. 386-394.

Ittner, Christopher D. & Larcker, David F. (1998): Innovations in performance measurement: Trends and research implications. Journal of Management Accounting Research, Vol. 10, pp. 205-238.

Ittner, Christopher D.; Larcker, David F. & Meyer, Marshall W. (2003): Subjectivity and the weighting of performance measures: Evidence from a Balanced Scorecard. The Accounting Review, Vol. 78, No. 3, pp. 725-758.

Ittner, Christopher D.; Larcker, David F. & Rajan, Madhav V. (1997): The choice of performance measures in annual bonus contracts. The Accounting Review, Vol. 72, No. 2, pp. 231-255.

Ittner, Christopher D.; Larcker, David F. & Randall, Taylor (2003): Performance implications of strategic performance measurement in financial services firms. Accounting, Organizations and Society, Vol. 28, No. 7-8, pp. 715-741.

Jackson, Dennis L.; Gillaspy, J. A. & Purc-Stephenson, Rebecca (2009): Reporting practices in confirmatory factor analysis: An overview and some recommendations. Psychological Methods, Vol. 14, No. 1, pp. 6-23.

Jackson, Terence; Amaeshi, Kenneth & Yavuz, Serap (2008): Untangling African indigenous management: Multiple influences on the success of SMEs in Kenya. Journal of World Business, Vol. 43, No. 4, pp. 400-416.

Janowitz, Morris (1975): Sociological theory and social control. American Journal of Sociology, Vol. 81, No. 1, pp. 82-108.

Jansen, E. P.; Merchant, Kenneth A. & van der Stede, Wim A. (2009): National differences in incentive compensation practices: The differing roles of financial performance measurement in the United States and the Netherlands. Accounting, Organizations and Society, Vol. 34, No. 1, pp. 58-84.

Javidan, Mansour (2004): Performance orientation. in: House, Robert J.; Hanges, Paul J.; Javidan, Mansour; Dorfman, Peter W. & Gupta, Vipin (Ed.): Culture, leadership, and organizations: The GLOBE study of 62 societies. Sage, Thousand Oaks, CA, pp. 239-281.

Javidan, Mansour & Dastmalchian, Ali (2009): Managerial implications of the GLOBE project: A study of 62 societies. Asia Pacific Journal of Human Resources, Vol. 47, No. 1, pp. 41-58.

Javidan, Mansour & House, Robert J. (2001): Cultural Acumen for the Global Manager: Lessons from Project GLOBE. Organizational Dynamics, Vol. 29, No. 4, pp. 289-305.

Javidan, Mansour; House, Robert J.; Dorfman, Peter W.; Hanges, Paul J. & Luque, Mary S. de (2006): Conceptualizing and measuring cultures and their consequences: A comparative review of GLOBE's and Hofstede's approaches. Journal of International Business Studies, Vol. 37, No. 6, pp. 897-914.

Jenkins Jr., G. Douglas; Gupta, Nina; Gupta, Atu & Shaw, Jason D. (1998): Are financial incentives related to performance? A meta-analytic review of empirical research. Journal of Applied Psychology, Vol. 83, No. 5, pp. 777-787.

Jensen, Michael C. & Meckling, William H. (1976): Theory of the firm: Managerial behavior, agency costs and ownership structure. Journal of Financial Economics, Vol. 3, No. 4, pp. 305-360.

Jensen, Michael C. & Murphy, Kevin J. (1990a): CEO incentives - it's not how much you pay, but how. Harvard Business Review, Vol. 68, No. 3, pp. 138-149.

Jensen, Michael C. & Murphy, Kevin J. (1990b): Performance pay and top-management incentives. Journal of Political Economy, Vol. 98, No. 2, pp. 225-264.

Jensen, Michael C.; Murphy, Kevin J. & Wruck, Eric G. (2004): Remuneration: Where we've been, how we got to here, what are the problems, and how to fix them. ECGI Working Paper Series in Finance

Jesuino, Jorge C. (2002): Latin Europe cluster: From South to North. Journal of World Business, Vol. 37, No. 1, pp. 81-89.

Johnson, H. T. & Kaplan, Robert S. (1987): Relevance lost: The rise and fall of management accounting, Harvard Business School Press, Boston, Mass.

Jong, Martijn G. de; Steenkamp, Jan-Benedict E.; Fox, Jean-Paul & Baumgartner, Hans (2008): Using item response theory to measure extreme response style in marketing research: A global investigation. Journal of Marketing Research, Vol. 45, No. 1, pp. 104-115.

Jordan, James L. & Nasis, Deovina B. (1992): Preferences for performance appraisal based on method used, type of rater, and purpose of evaluation. Psychological Reports, Vol. 70, No. 3, pp. 963-969.

Joshi, Prem L. (2001): The international diffusion of new management accounting practices: The case of India. Journal of International Accounting, Auditing and Taxation, Vol. 10, No. 1, pp. 85-109.

Kabasakal, Hayat; Dastmalchian, Ali; Karacay, Gaye & Bayraktar, Secil (2012): Leadership and culture in the MENA region: An analysis of the GLOBE project. Journal of World Business, Vol. 47, No. 4, pp. 519-529.

Kallunki, Juha-Pekka; Laitinen, Erkki K. & Silvola, Hanna (2011): Impact of enterprise resource planning systems on management control systems and firm performance. International Journal of Accounting Information Systems, Vol. 12, No. 1, pp. 20-39.

Kane, Jeffrey S. & Freeman, Kimberly A. (1997): A theory of equitable performance standards. Journal of Management, Vol. 23, No. 1, pp. 37-58.

Kaplan, David (1965): The superorganic: Science or metaphysics. American Anthropologist, Vol. 67, No. 4, pp. 958-976.

Kaplan, Robert S. (1984): The evolution of management accounting. The Accounting Review, Vol. 59, No. 3, pp. 390-418.

Kaplan, Robert S. & Norton, David P. (1992): The balanced scorecard - Measures that drive performance. Harvard Business Review, Vol. 70, No. 1, pp. 71-79.

Kaplan, Robert S. & Norton, David P. (1996a): Linking the Balanced Scorecard to strategy. California Management Review, Vol. 39, No. 1, pp. 53-79.

Kaplan, Robert S. & Norton, David P. (1996b): The balanced scorecard: Translating strategy into action, Harvard Business School Press, Boston, Mass.

Kaplan, Robert S. & Norton, David P. (1996c): Using the Balanced Scorecard as a strategic management system. Harvard Business Review, Vol. 74, No. 1, pp. 75-85.

Kaplan, Robert S. & Norton, David P. (2001a): The strategy-focused organization: How balanced scorecard companies thrive in the new business environment, Harvard Business School Press, Boston, Mass.

Kaplan, Robert S. & Norton, David P. (2001b): Transforming the Balanced Scorecard from performance measurement to strategic management. Accounting Horizons, Vol. 15, No. 1, pp. 87-104.

Kaplan, Robert S. & Norton, David P. (2004): Strategy maps: Converting intangible assets into tangible outcomes, Harvard Business School Press, Boston, Mass.

Kara, Aycan & Peterson, Mark F. (2012): The dynamic societal cultural milieu of organizations: Origins, maintenance and change. in: Tihanyi, László; Devinney, Timothy M. & Pedersen, Torben (Ed.): Advances in International Management / Institutional theory in international business and management. Emerald, Bingley, pp. 341-371.

Karen T. D'Alonzo (2004): The Johnson-Neyman procedure as an alternative to ANCOVA. Western Journal of Nursing Research, Vol. 26, No. 7, pp. 804-812.

Kärreman, Dan & Alvesson, Mats (2004): Cages in tandem: Management control, social identity, and Identification in a knowledge-intensive firm. Organization, Vol. 11, No. 1, pp. 149-175.

Kennedy, Jeffrey; Fu, Ping-Ping & Yukl, Gary (2003): Influence tactics across twelve cultures. Advances in Global Leadership, Vol. 3, No. 127-147

Kennerley, Mike & Neely, Andy (2002): A framework of the factors affecting the evolution of performance measurement systems. International Journal of Operations & Production Management, Vol. 22, No. 11, pp. 1222-1245.

Kieser, Alfred (1994): Book Reviews: Geert Hofstede (1991): Cultures and organizations: Software of the mind, McGraw-Hill, Maidenhead, U.K. Organization Studies, Vol. 15, No. 3, pp. 457-460.

Kim, Ken I.; Park, Hun-Joon & Suzuki, Nori (1990): Reward allocations in the United States, Japan, and Korea: A comparison of individualistic and collectivistic cultures. Academy of Management Journal, Vol. 33, No. 1, pp. 188-198.

Kinglake Tower, Rupert; Kelly, Caroline & Richards, Anne (1997): Individualism, collectivism and rewards allocation: A cross-cultural study in Russia and Britain. British Journal of Social Psychology, Vol. 36, No. 3, pp. 331-345.

Kirkman, Bradley L.; Lowe, Kevin B. & Gibson, Cristina B. (2006): A quarter century of Culture's Consequences: A review of empirical research incorporating Hofstede's cultural values framework. Journal of International Business Studies, Vol. 37, No. 3, pp. 285-320.

Kline, Rex B. (2005): Principles and practice of structural equation modeling, 2. ed., Guilford Press, New York.

Kline, Rex B. (2011): Principles and practice of structural equation modeling, 3. ed., Guilford Press, New York.

Kluckhohn, Clyde (1951): The study of culture. in: Lerner, Daniel & Lasswell, Harold D. (Ed.): The policy science. Stanford University Press, Stanford, CA, pp. 86-101.

Koopman, Paul; Den Hartog, Deanne; Konrad, Edvard & et al. (1999): National culture and leadership profiles in Europe: Some results from the GLOBE study. European Journal of Work and Organizational Psychology, Vol. 8, No. 4, pp. 503-520.

Kostova, Tatiana; Roth, Kendall & Dacin, M. T. (2008): Institutional theory in the study of Multinational corporations: A critique and new directions. Academy of Management Review, Vol. 33, No. 4, pp. 994-1006.

Kotha, Suresh & Orne, Daniel (1989): Generic manufacturing strategies: A conceptual synthesis. Strategic Management Journal, Vol. 10, No. 3, pp. 211-231.

Kressler, Herwig W. (2001): Leistungsbeurteilung und Anreizsysteme: Motivation, Vergütung, Incentives, Ueberreuter, Frankfurt/Wien.

Kreyer, Simone (2011): Multikulturelle Teams in interkulturellen B2B-Verhandlungen: Eine empirische Untersuchung am Beispiel der deutschen und französischen Kultur, 1. ed., Josef Eul, Lohmar.

Kroeber, Alfred L. & Kluckhohn, Clyde (1952): Culture: A critical review of concepts and definitions, Vintage Books, New York.

Kuper, Adam (2000): Culture: The anthropologists' account, Harvard University Press, Cambridge, Mass.

Kutschker, Michael & Schmid, Stefan (2011): Internationales Management, 7. ed., Oldenbourg, München.

La Porta, Rafael; Lopez-de-Silanes, Florencio & Shleifer, Andrei (1999): Corporate ownership around the world. Journal of Finance, Vol. 54, No. 2, pp. 471-517.

Lambert, Richard A. (2001): Contracting theory and accounting. Journal of Accounting and Economics, Vol. 32, No. 1-3, pp. 3-87.

Langfield-Smith, Kim (2007): A review of quantitative research in management control systems and strategy. in: Chapman, Christopher S.; Hopwood, Anthony G. & Shields, Michael D. (Ed.): Handbook of management accounting research: Volume 2. Elsevier, Amsterdam, Oxford, pp. 753-783.

Laplume, André O.; Sonpar, Karan & Litz, Reginald A. (2008): Stakeholder theory: Reviewing a theory that moves us. Journal of Management, Vol. 34, No. 6, pp. 1152-1189.

Lau, Chong M. & Eggleton, Ian R. (2004): Cultural differences in managers' propensity to create slack. Advances in International Accounting, Vol. 17, pp. 137-174.

Lau, Chong M. & Moser, Antony (2008): Behavioral effects of nonfinancial performance measures: The role of procedural fairness. Behavioral Research in Accounting, Vol. 20, No. 2, pp. 55-71.

Lawler III, Edward E. (2003): Reward practices and performance management system effectiveness. Organizational Dynamics, Vol. 32, No. 4, pp. 396-404.

Lawler III, Edward E.; Mohrman Jr., Allan M. & Resnick, Susan M. (1984): Performance appraisal revisited. Organizational Dynamics, Vol. 13, No. 1, pp. 20-35.

Lawrence, Paul R. & Lorsch, Jay W. (1967a): Differentiation and integration in complex organizations. Administrative Science Quarterly, Vol. 12, No. 1, pp. 1-47.

Lawrence, Paul R. & Lorsch, Jay W. (1967b): Organization and environment: Managing differentiation and integration, Harvard Business School Press, Boston, Mass.

Le Thang, Chien; Rowley, Chris; Quang, Truong & Warner, Malcolm (2007): To what extent can management practices be transferred between countries? Journal of World Business, Vol. 42, No. 1, pp. 113-127.

Leung, Angela K.- y; Kim, Young-Hoon; Zhang, Zhi-Xue; Tam, Kim-Pong & Chiu, Chi-yue (2012): Cultural construction of success and epistemic motives moderate American-Chinese differences in reward allocation biases. Journal of Cross-Cultural Psychology, Vol. 43, No. 1, pp. 46-52.

Leung, Kwok (2006): Editor's introduction to the exchange between Hofstede and GLOBE. Journal of International Business Studies, Vol. 37, No. 6, pp. 881.

Leung, Kwok (2008): Methods and measurements in cross-cultural management. in: Smith, Peter B.; Peterson, Mark F. & Thomas, David C. (Ed.): Handbook of cross-cultural management research. Sage, London, pp. 59-73.

Leung, Kwok; Bhagat, Rabi S.; Buchan, Nancy R.; Erez, Miriam & Gibson, Cristina B. (2005): Culture and international business: Recent advances and their implications for future research. Journal of International Business Studies, Vol. 36, No. 4, pp. 357-378.

Leung, Kwok & Bond, Michael H. (1984): The impact of cultural collectivism on reward allocation. Journal of Personality and Social Psychology, Vol. 47, No. 4, pp. 793-804.

Leung, Kwok & Iwawaki, Saburo (1988): Cultural collectivism and distributive behavior. Journal of Cross-Cultural Psychology, Vol. 19, No. 1, pp. 35-49.

Leung, Kwok & Park, Hun-Joon (1986): Effects of interactional goal on choice of allocation rule: A cross-national study. Organizational Behavior and Human Decision Processes, Vol. 37, No. 1, pp. 111-120.

Levy, Paul E. & Williams, Jane R. (2004): The social context of performance appraisal: A review and framework for the future. Journal of Management, Vol. 30, No. 6, pp. 881-905.

Leys, Christophe; Ley, Christophe; Klein, Olivier; Bernard, Philippe & Licata, Laurent (2013): Detecting outliers: Do not use standard deviation around the mean, use absolute deviation around the median. Journal of Experimental Social Psychology, Vol. 49, No. 4, pp. 764-766.

Li, Kai; Griffin, Dale; Yue, Heng & Zhao, Longkai (2011): National culture and capital structure decisions: Evidence from foreign joint ventures in China. Journal of International Business Studies, Vol. 42, No. 4, pp. 477-503.

Lillis, Anne M. (2002): Managing multiple dimensions of manufacturing performance - an exploratory study. Accounting, Organizations and Society, Vol. 27, No. 6, pp. 497-529.

Lindell, Michael K. & Whitney, David J. (2001): Accounting for common method variance in cross-sectional research designs. Journal of Applied Psychology, Vol. 86, No. 1, pp. 114-121.

Lindholm, Niklas (1999): National culture and performance management in MNC subsidiaries. International Studies of Management & Organization, Vol. 29, No. 4, pp. 45-66.

Lindsay, R. M. (1995): Reconsidering the status of tests of significance: An alternative criterion of adequacy. Accounting, Organizations and Society, Vol. 20, No. 1, pp. 35-53.

Lipe, Marlys G. & Salterio, Steven (2000): The Balanced Scorecard: Judgmental effects of common and unique performance measures. The Accounting Review, Vol. 75, No. 3, pp. 283-298.

Lipe, Marlys G. & Salterio, Steven (2002): A note on the judgmental effects of the balanced scorecard's information organization. Accounting, Organizations and Society, Vol. 27, No. 6, pp. 531-540.

Little, Roderick J. (1988): A test of missing completely at random for multivariate data with missing values. Journal of the American Statistical Association, Vol. 83, No. 404, pp. 1198-1202.

Little, Roderick J. A. & Rubin, Donald B. (2002): Statistical analysis with missing data, 2. ed., Wiley, Hoboken, N.J.

Liu, Xiaotao K. & Leitch, Robert A. (2013): Performance effects of setting targets and pay–performance relations before or after operations. Management Accounting Research, Vol. 24, No. 1, pp. 64-79.

Long, Richard J. & Shields, John L. (2005): Best practice or best fit? High involvement management and base pay practices in Canadian and Australian firms. Asia Pacific Journal of Human Resources, Vol. 43, No. 1, pp. 52-75.

Loo, Robert (2002): A caveat on using single-item versus multiple-item scales. Journal of Managerial Psychology, Vol. 17, No. 1, pp. 68-75.

Lorange, Peter & Scott Morton, Michael S. (1974): A framework for management control systems. Sloan Management Review, Vol. 16, No. 1, pp. 41-56.

Lounsbury, Michael (1997): Exploring the institutional tool kit: The rise of recycling in the U.S. solid waste field. American Behavioral Scientist, Vol. 40, No. 4, pp. 465-477.

Lowe, Ernest A. (1971): On the idea of a management control system: Integrating accounting and management control. The Journal of Management Studies, Vol. 8, No. 1, pp. 1-12.

Lowe, Kevin B.; Milliman, John; Cieri, Helen de & Dowling, Peter J. (2002): International compensation practices: A ten-country comparative analysis. Human Resource Management, Vol. 41, No. 1, pp. 45-66.

Luft, Joan & Shields, Michael D. (2003): Mapping management accounting: Graphics and guidelines for theory-consistent empirical research. Accounting, Organizations and Society, Vol. 28, No. 2-3, pp. 169-249.

Luft, Joan & Shields, Michael D. (2007): Mapping management accounting: Graphics and guidelines for theory-consistent empirical research. in: Chapman, Christopher S.; Hopwood, Anthony G. & Shields, Michael D. (Ed.): Handbook of management accounting research: Volume 1. Elsevier, Amsterdam, Oxford, pp. 27-95.

Luo, Yadong; Sun, Jinyun & Wang, Stephanie L. (2011): Comparative strategic management: An emergent field in international management. Journal of International Management, Vol. 17, No. 3, pp. 190-200.

Luque, Mary S. de & Javidan, Mansour (2004): Uncertainty Avoidance. in: House, Robert J.; Hanges, Paul J.; Javidan, Mansour; Dorfman, Peter W. & Gupta, Vipin (Ed.): Culture, leadership, and organizations: The GLOBE study of 62 societies. Sage, Thousand Oaks, CA, pp. 602-653.

Luque, Mary S. de & Sommer, Steven M. (2000): The impact of culture on feedback-seeking behavior: An integrated model and propositions. Academy of Management Review, Vol. 25, No. 4, pp. 829-849.

Lynch, Luann J. & Perry, Susan E. (2003): An overview of management compensation. Journal of Accounting Education, Vol. 21, No. 1, pp. 43-60.

MacCallum, Robert C.; Zhang, Shaobo; Preacher, Kristopher J. & Rucker, Derek D. (2002): On the practice of dichotomization of quantitative variables. Psychological Methods, Vol. 7, No. 1, pp. 19-40.

Machin, John L. J. (1979): A contingent methodology for management control. Journal of Management Studies, Vol. 16, No. 1, pp. 1-29.

Mączyński, Jerzy; Zamorska, Jolanta & Łobodziński, Andrzej (2010): Differences on organizational practices between Polish managers studied in 1996/1997 and 2008/2009. Journal of Intercultural Management, Vol. 2, No. 1, pp. 69-77.

Madapusi, Arun & D'Souza, Derrick (2012): The influence of ERP system implementation on the operational performance of an organization. International Journal of Information Management, Vol. 32, No. 1, pp. 24-34.

Malhotra, Naresh K.; Kim, Sung S. & Patil, Ashutosh (2006): Common method variance in IS research: A comparison of alternative approaches and a reanalysis of past research. Management Science, Vol. 52, No. 12, pp. 1865-1883.

Malina, Mary A. & Selto, Frank H. (2004): Choice and change of measures in performance measurement models. Management Accounting Research, Vol. 15, No. 4, pp. 441-469.

Malmi, Teemu (2001): Balanced scorecards in Finnish companies: A research note. Management Accounting Research, Vol. 12, No. 2, pp. 207-220.

Malmi, Teemu (2013): Management control as a package - The need for international research. Journal of Management Control, Vol. 23, No. 4, pp. 229-231.

Malmi, Teemu & Brown, David A. (2008): Management control systems as a package - Opportunities, challenges and research directions. Management Accounting Research, Vol. 19, No. 4, pp. 287-300.

Manas, Todd M. & Graham, Michael D. (2003): Creating a total rewards strategy: A toolkit for designing business-based plans, American Management Association, New York.

Maschke, Konstantin & Knyphausen-Aufseß, Dodo zu (2012): How the entrepreneurial top management team setup influences firm performance and the ability to raise capital: A literature review. BuR - Business Research, Vol. 5, No. 1

Maseland, Robbert & van Hoorn, André (2008): Explaining the negative correlation between values and practices: A note on the Hofstede–GLOBE debate. Journal of International Business Studies, Vol. 40, No. 3, pp. 527-532.

Maseland, Robbert & van Hoorn, André (2010): Values and marginal preferences in international business. Journal of International Business Studies, Vol. 41, No. 8, pp. 1325-1329.

Matlachowsky, Philip (2009): Implementierungsstand der Balanced Scorecard: Fallstudienbasierte Analyse in deutschen Unternehmen, Gabler, Wiesbaden.

Matsumura, Ella M. & Shin, Jae Y. (2006): An empirical analysis of an incentive plan with relative performance measures: Evidence from a postal service. The Accounting Review, Vol. 81, No. 3, pp. 533-566.

Matsunaga, Masaki (2010): How to factor-analyze your data right: Do's, Don'ts, and How-To's. International Journal of Psychological Research, Vol. 3, No. 1, pp. 97-110.

Mayrhofer, Wolfgang; Meyer, Michael; Steyrer, Johannes; Iellatchitch, Alexander; Schiffinger, Michael; Strunk, Guido; Erten-Buch, Christiane; Hermann, Anett & Mattl, Christine (2002): Einmal gut, immer gut? Einflussfaktoren auf Karrieren in ‚neuen' Karrierefeldern. Zeitschrift für Personalforschung, Vol. 16, No. 3, pp. 392-415.

McSweeney, Brendan (2002a): Hofstede's model of national cultural differences and their consequences: A triumph of faith - a failure of analysis. Human Relations, Vol. 55, No. 1, pp. 89-118.

McSweeney, Brendan (2002b): The essentials of scholarship: A reply to Geert Hofstede. Human Relations, Vol. 55, No. 11, pp. 1363-1372.

Mehran, Hamid (1995): Executive compensation structure, ownership, and firm performance. Journal of Financial Economics, Vol. 38, No. 2, pp. 163-184.

Melnyk, Steven A.; Bititci, Umit; Platts, Ken; Tobias, Jutta & Andersen, Bjørn (2014): Is performance measurement and management fit for the future? Management Accounting Research, Vol. 25, No. 2, pp. 173-186.

Melnyk, Steven A.; Stewart, Douglas M. & Swink, Morgan (2004): Metrics and performance measurement in operations management: Dealing with the metrics maze. Journal of Operations Management, Vol. 22, No. 3, pp. 209-218.

Merchant, Kenneth A.; Chow, Chee W. & Wu, Anne (1995): Measurement, evaluation and reward of profit center managers: A cross-cultural field study. Accounting, Organizations and Society, Vol. 20, No. 7-8, pp. 619-638.

Merchant, Kenneth A. & Otley, David T. (2007): A review of the literature on control and accountability. in: Chapman, Christopher S.; Hopwood, Anthony G. & Shields, Michael D. (Ed.): Handbook of management accounting research: Volume 2. Elsevier, Amsterdam, Oxford, pp. 785-802.

Merchant, Kenneth A. & Simons, Robert (1986): Research and control in complex organizations: An overview. Journal of Accounting Literature, Vol. 5, pp. 183-203.

Merchant, Kenneth A. & van der Stede, Wim A. (2003): Management control systems: Performance measurement, evaluation and incentives, Financial Times Prentice Hall, New York.

Merchant, Kenneth A. & van der Stede, Wim A. (2007): Management control systems: Performance measurement, evaluation and incentives, 2. ed., Prentice Hall, Harlow, England.

Merchant, Kenneth A.; van der Stede, Wim A.; Lin, Thomas W. & Yu, Zengbiao (2011): Performance Measurement and Incentive Compensation: An Empirical Analysis and Comparison of Chinese and Western Firms' Practices. European Accounting Review, Vol. 20, No. 4, pp. 639-667.

Meyer, Herbert H. (1975): The pay-for-performance dilemma. Organizational Dynamics, Vol. 3, No. 3, pp. 39-50.

Meyer, John W. & Rowan, Brian (1977): Institutionalized organizations: Formal structure as myth and ceremony. The American Journal of Sociology, Vol. 83, No. 2, pp. 340-363.

Micheli, Pietro & Mari, Luca (2014): The theory and practice of performance measurement. Management Accounting Research, Vol. 25, No. 2, pp. 147-156.

Miles, Jeremy & Shevlin, Mark (2007): A time and a place for incremental fit indices. Personality and Individual Differences, Vol. 42, No. 5, pp. 869-874.

Milliman, John; Nason, Stephen; Zhu, Cherrie & Cieri, Helen de (2002): An exploratory assessment of the purposes of performance appraisals in north and central america and the pacific rim. Human Resource Management, Vol. 41, No. 1, pp. 87-102.

Minkov, Michael & Hofstede, Geert (2011): The evolution of Hofstede's doctrine. Cross Cultural Management: An International Journal, Vol. 18, No. 1, pp. 10-20.

Mitchell, Ronald K.; Agle, Bradley R. & Wood, Donna J. (1997): Toward a theory of stakeholder identification and salience: Defining the principle of who and what really counts. Academy of Management Review, Vol. 22, No. 4, pp. 853-886.

Moers, Frank (2005): Discretion and bias in performance evaluation: the impact of diversity and subjectivity. Accounting, Organizations and Society, Vol. 30, No. 1, pp. 67-80.

Morrison, Elizabeth W.; Chen, Ya-Ru & Salgado, Susan R. (2004): Cultural differences in newcomer feedback seeking: A comparison of the United States and Hong Kong. Applied Psychology: An International Review, Vol. 53, No. 1, pp. 1-22.

Mueller, Ralph O. & Hancock, Gregory R. (2001): Factor analysis and latent structure, confirmatory. in: Smelser, Neil J. & Baltes, Paul B. (Ed.): International encyclopedia of the social & behavioral sciences. Elsevier, Pergamon, Amsterdam, pp. 5239-5244.

Murphy, Kevin J. (1999): Executive compensation. in: Ashenfelter, Orley & Card, David (Ed.): Handbook of labor economics, Vol. 3, Part B. Elsevier, Amsterdam, pp. 2485-2563.

Murphy, Kevin J. (2001): Performance standards in incentive contracts. Journal of Accounting and Economics, Vol. 30, No. 3, pp. 245-278.

Murphy, Kevin R. & Cleveland, Jeanette (1995): Understanding performance appraisal: Social, organizational, and goal-based perspectives, Sage, Thousand Oaks, Calif.

Murphy-Berman, Virginia & Berman, John J. (2002): Cross-cultural differences in perceptions of distributive justice: A comparison of Hong Kong and Indonesia. Journal of Cross-Cultural Psychology, Vol. 33, No. 2, pp. 157-170.

Murray, V. V.; Jain, Harish C. & Adams, Roy J. (1976): A framework for the comparative analysis of personnel administration. Academy of Management Review, Vol. 1, No. 3, pp. 47-57.

Myers, Michael D. & Tan, Felix B. (2002): Beyond models of national culture in information systems research. Journal of Global Information Management, Vol. 10, No. 1, pp. 24-32.

Myloni, Barbara; Harzing, Anne-Wil & Mirza, Hafiz (2004): Human resource management in Greece: Have the colours of culture faded away? International Journal of Cross Cultural Management, Vol. 4, No. 1, pp. 59-76.

Naor, Michael; Linderman, Kevin & Schroeder, Roger (2010): The globalization of operations in Eastern and Western countries: Unpacking the relationship between national and organizational culture and its impact on manufacturing performance. Journal of Operations Management, Vol. 28, No. 3, pp. 194-205.

Nathan, Barry R.; Mohrman Jr., Allan M. & Milliman, John (1991): Interpersonal relations as a context for the effects of appraisal interviews on performance and satisfaction: A longitudinal study. Academy of Management Review, Vol. 34, No. 2, pp. 352-369.

Neely, Andy (2007): Measuring performance: The operations management perspective. in: Neely, Andy (Ed.): Business performance measurement: Unifying theories and integrating practice. Cambridge University Press, Cambridge, UK, pp. 64-81.

Neely, Andy; Gregory, Mike & Platts, Ken (1995): Performance measurement system design: A literature review and research agenda. International Journal of Operations & Production Management, Vol. 15, No. 4, pp. 80-116.

Newman, Karen L. & Nollen, Stanley D. (1996): Culture and congruence: The fit between management practices and national culture. Journal of International Business Studies, Vol. 27, No. 4, pp. 753-779.

Nisbett, Richard E.; Peng, Kaiping; Choi, Incheol & Norenzayan, Ara (2001): Culture and systems of thought: Holistic versus analytic cognition. Psychological Review, Vol. 108, No. 2, pp. 291-310.

Nørreklit, Hanne (2000): The balance on the balanced scorecard a critical analysis of some of its assumptions. Management Accounting Research, Vol. 11, No. 1, pp. 65-88.

Nørreklit, Hanne & Schoenfeld, Hanns-Martin W. (2000): Controlling multinational companies: An attempt to analyze some unresolved issues. The International Journal of Accounting, Vol. 35, No. 3, pp. 415-430.

Nudurupati, Sai S.; Bititci, Umit S.; Kumar, Vikas & Chan, F.T.S (2011): State of the art literature review on performance measurement. Computers & Industrial Engineering, Vol. 60, No. 2, pp. 279-290.

Nunnally, Jum C. & Bernstein, Ira H. (1994): Psychometric theory, 3. ed., McGraw-Hill, New York.

Nurse, Lawrence (2005): Performance appraisal, employee development and organizational justice: exploring the linkages. The International Journal of Human Resource Management, Vol. 16, No. 7, pp. 1176-1194.

O'Sullivan, Sharon L. (2010): International human resource management challenges in Canadian development INGOs. European Management Journal, Vol. 28, No. 6, pp. 421-440.

O'Connor, Neale G. (1995): The influence of organizational culture on the usefulness of budget participation by Singaporean-Chinese managers. Accounting, Organizations and Society, Vol. 20, No. 5, pp. 383-403.

Ogbor, John O. & Williams, Johnnie (2003): The cross-cultural transfer of management practices: The case for creative synthesis. Cross Cultural Management: An International Journal, Vol. 10, No. 2, pp. 3-23.

Olivas-Luján, Miguel R.; Harzing, Anne-Wil & McCoy, Scott (2004): September 11, 2001: Two quasi-experiments on the influence of threats on cultural values and cosmopolitanism. International Journal of Cross Cultural Management, Vol. 4, No. 2, pp. 211-228.

Oliver, Christine (1991): Strategic responses to institutional processes. Academy of Management Review, Vol. 16, No. 1, pp. 145-179.

Olve, Nils-Göran; Roy, Jan & Wetter, Magnus (1999): Performance drivers: A practical guide to using the balanced scorecard, Wiley, Chichester, England.

O'Reilly III, Charles A.; Chatman, Jennifer & Caldwell, David F. (1991): People and organizational culture: A profile comparison approach to assessing person- organization fit. Academy of Management Journal, Vol. 34, No. 3, pp. 487-516.

Otley, David T. (1980): The contingency theory of management accounting: Achievement and prognosis. Accounting, Organizations and Society, Vol. 5, No. 4, pp. 413-428.

Otley, David T. (1999): Performance management: A framework for management control systems research. Management Accounting Research, Vol. 10, No. 4, pp. 363-382.

Otley, David T. (2003): Management control and performance management: whence and whither? The British Accounting Review, Vol. 35, No. 4, pp. 309-326.

Otley, David T. (2007): Accounting performance measurement: A review of its purposes and practises. in: Neely, Andy (Ed.): Business performance measurement: Unifying theories and integrating practice. Cambridge University Press, Cambridge, UK, pp. 11-35.

Otley, David T.; Broadbent, Jane & Berry, Anthony J. (1995): Research in management control: An overview of its developments. British Journal of Management, Vol. 6, No. Special Issue, pp. 31-44.

Otley, David T. & Fakiolas, Alexander (2000): Reliance on accounting performance measures: Dead end or new beginning. Accounting, Organizations and Society, Vol. 25, No. 4-5

Ouchi, William G. (1979): A conceptual framework for the design of organizational control mechanisms. Management Science, Vol. 25, No. 9, pp. 833-848.

Ouchi, William G. (1990): Markets, bureaucracies, and clans. Administrative Science Quarterly, Vol. 25, No. 1, pp. 129-141.

Palich, Leslie E.; Hom, Peter W. & Griffeth, Rodger W. (1995): Managing in the international context: Testing cultural generality of sources of commitment to multinational enterprises. Journal of Management, Vol. 21, No. 4, pp. 671-690.

Palmer, Donald; Biggart, Nicole & Dick, Brian (2008): Is the new institutionalism a theory? in: Greenwood, Royston; Oliver, Christine; Suddaby, Roy & Sahlin, Kerstin (Ed.): The SAGE handbook of organizational institutionalism. Sage, Los Angeles, Calif., pp. 739-768.

Parboteeah, K. P.; Addae, Helena M. & Cullen, John B. (2012): Propensity to support sustainability initiatives: A cross-national model. Journal of Business Ethics, Vol. 105, No. 3, pp. 403-413.

Park, Sanghee & Sturman, Michael C. (2012): How and what you pay matters: the relative effectiveness of merit pay, bonuses and long-term incentives on future job performance. Compensation & Benefits Review, Vol. 44, No. 2, pp. 80-85.

Pearse, Noel (2011): Deciding on the scale granularity of response categories of Likert type scales. The Electronic Journal of Business Research Methods, Vol. 9, No. 2, pp. 159-171.

Peng, Tai-Kuang & Peterson, Mark F. (2008): Nation, demographic, and attitudinal boundary conditions on leader social rewards and punishments in local governments. Journal of Organizational Behavior, Vol. 29, No. 1, pp. 95-117.

Pennings, Johannes M. (1993): Executive reward systems: A cross-national comparison. Journal of Management Studies, Vol. 30, No. 2, pp. 261-280.

Pepper, Alexander; Gore, Julie & Crossman, Alf (2013): Are long-term incentive plans an effective and efficient way of motivating senior executives? Human Resource Management Journal, Vol. 23, No. 1, pp. 36-51.

Peretz, Hilla & Fried, Yitzhak (2012): National cultures, performance appraisal practices, and organizational absenteeism and turnover: A study across 21 countries. Journal of Applied Psychology, Vol. 97, No. 2, pp. 448-459.

Petersen, Michael J. (2007): Using downstream revenue in a performance measurement system. Contemporary Accounting Research, Vol. 24, No. 4, pp. 1193-1215.

Peterson, Mark F. (2004): Review of culture, leadership and organizations: The GLOBE study of 62 societies by House R.J., Hanges P.J., Javidan M., Dorfman P.W. & Gupta V. Administrative Science Quarterly, Vol. 49, No. 4, pp. 641-647.

Podsakoff, Philip M.; MacKenzie, Scott B.; Bachrach, Daniel G. & Podsakoff, Nathan P. (2005): The influence of management journals in the 1980s and 1990s. Strategic Management Journal, Vol. 26, No. 5, pp. 473-488.

Podsakoff, Philip M.; MacKenzie, Scott B.; Lee, Jeong-Yeon & Podsakoff, Nathan P. (2003): Common method biases in behavioral research: A critical review of the literature and recommended remedies. Journal of Applied Psychology, Vol. 88, No. 5, pp. 879-903.

Popper, Karl R. (1972): Conjectures and refutations: The growth of scientific knowledge, 4. ed., Routledge and Kegan Paul, London.

Popper, Karl R. (2002): The logic of scientific discovery, Taylor & Francis Ltd., Hoboken.

Prendergast, Canice (1999): The provision of incentives in firms. Journal of Economic Literature, Vol. 37, No. 1, pp. 7-63.

Pudelko, Markus; Carr, Chris; Fink, Gerhard & Wentges, Paul (2006): Editorial for the Special Section: The convergence concept in cross cultural management research. International Journal of Cross Cultural Management, Vol. 6, No. 1, pp. 15-18.

Pudelko, Markus & Harzing, Anne-Wil (2007): Country-of-origin, localization, or dominance effect? An empirical investigation of HRM practices in foreign subsidiaries. Human Resource Management, Vol. 46, No. 4, pp. 535-559.

Pudelko, Markus & Harzing, Anne-Wil (2008): The Golden Triangle for MNCs: Standardization towards headquarters practices, standardization towards global best practices and localization. Organizational Dynamics, Vol. 37, No. 4, pp. 394-404.

Rajan, Madhav V. & Reichelstein, Stefan (2009): Objective versus subjective indicators of managerial performance. The Accounting Review, Vol. 84, No. 1, pp. 209-237.

Ralston, David A.; Gustafson, David J.; Cheung, Fanny M. & Terpstra, Robert H. (1993): Differences in managerial values: A study of U.S., Hong Kong and PRC managers. Journal of International Business Studies, Vol. 24, No. 2, pp. 249-275.

Ralston, David A.; Holt, David H.; Terpstra, Robert H. & Kai-Cheng, Yu (2008): The impact of national culture and economic ideology on managerial work values: A study of the United States, Russia, Japan, and China. Journal of International Business Studies, Vol. 39, No. 1, pp. 8-26.

Rappaport, Alfred (1998): Creating shareholder value: A guide for managers and investors, 2. ed., Free Press, New York.

Redding, Gordon; Bond, Michael H. & Witt, Michael A. (2014): Culture and the Business Systems of Asia. in: Witt, Michael A. & Redding, Gordon (Ed.): Oxford handbook of Asian Business Systems. Oxford University Press, Oxford

Reed, Jeffrey G. & Baxter, Pam M. (2009): Using reference databases. in: Cooper, Harris M.; Hedges, Larry V. & Valentine, Jeff C. (Ed.): The handbook of research synthesis and meta-analysis. Russell Sage Foundation, New York, pp. 73-101.

Reichenbach, Hans (1938): Experience and prediction: An analysis of the foundations and the structure of knowledge, University of Chicago Press, Chicago.

Rho, Boo-Ho & Yu, Yung-Mok (1998): A comparative study on the structural relationships of manufacturing practices, lead time and productivity in Japan and Korea. Journal of Operations Management, Vol. 16, No. 2-3, pp. 257-270.

Ribeiro, João A. & Scapens, Robert W. (2006): Institutional theories in management accounting change: Contributions, issues and paths for development. Qualitative Research in Accounting & Management, Vol. 3, No. 2, pp. 94-111.

Richardson, Hettie A.; Simmering, Marcia J. & Sturman, Michael C. (2009): A tale of three perspectives: Examining post hoc statistical techniques for detection and correction of common method variance. Organizational Research Methods, Vol. 12, No. 4, pp. 762-800.

Rosenstreich, Daniela & Wooliscroft, Ben (2009): Measuring the impact of accounting journals using Google Scholar and the g-index. The British Accounting Review, Vol. 41, No. 4, pp. 227-239.

Ross, Stephen A. (1973): The economic theory of agency: The principal's problem. The American Economic Review, Vol. 63, No. 2, pp. 134-139.

Rosseel, Yves (2012): lavaan: An R Package for Structural Equation Modeling. Journal of Statstical Software, Vol. 48, No. 2, pp. 1-36.

Roster, Catherine; Albaum, Gerald & Rogers, Robert (2006): Can cross-national/cultural studies presume etic equivalency in respondents' use of extreme categories of Likert rating scales? International Journal of Market Research, Vol. 48, No. 6, pp. 741-759.

Roth, Kendall & O'Donnell, Sharon (1996): Foreign subsidiary compensation strategy: An agency theory perspective. Academy of Management Journal, Vol. 39, No. 3, pp. 678-703.

Roush, Melvin & Mohammed, Baber S. (2008): Management Control Systems: Performance Measurement, Evaluation and Incentives. Journal of Accounting & Organizational Change, Vol. 4, No. 2, pp. 204-206.

Rubera, Gaia; Ordanini, Andrea & Griffith, David A. (2011): Incorporating cultural values for understanding the influence of perceived product creativity on intention to buy: An examination in Italy and the US. Journal of International Business Studies, Vol. 42, No. 4, pp. 459-476.

Said, Amal A.; HassabElnaby, Hassan & Wier, Benson (2003): An empirical investigation of the performance consequnces of non-financial measures. Journal of Management Accounting Research, Vol. 15, pp. 193-223.

Sandelin, Mikko (2008): Operation of management control practices as a package - A case study on control system variety in a growth firm context. Management Accounting Research, Vol. 19, No. 4, pp. 324-343.

Sarala, Riikka M. & Vaara, Eero (2010): Cultural differences, convergence, and crossvergence as explanations of knowledge transfer in international acquisitions. Journal of International Business Studies, Vol. 41, No. 8, pp. 1365-1390.

Scandura, Terri & Dorfman, Peter W. (2004): Leadership research in an international and cross-cultural context. The Leadership Quarterly, Vol. 15, No. 2, pp. 277-307.

Schafer, Joseph L. & Graham, John W. (2002): Missing data: Our view of the state of the art. Psychological Methods, Vol. 7, No. 2, pp. 147-177.

Schaffer, Bryan S. & Riordan, Christine M. (2003): A review of cross-cultural methodologies for organizational research: A best- practices approach. Organizational Research Methods, Vol. 6, No. 2, pp. 169-215.

Schäffer, Utz & Matlachowsky, Philip (2008): Warum die Balanced Scorecard nur selten als strategisches Managementsystem genutzt wird. Zeitschrift für Planung & Unternehmenssteuerung, Vol. 19, No. 2, pp. 207-232.

Schendera, Christian F. G. (2007): Datenqualität mit SPSS, Oldenbourg, München.

Schermelleh-Engel, Karin & Moosbrugger, Helfried (2003): Evaluating the fit of structural equation models: Tests of significance and descriptive goodness-of-fit measures. Methods of Psychological Research, Vol. 8, No. 2, pp. 23-74.

Schiff, Andrew D. & Hoffman, L. R. (1996): An exploration of the use of financial and nonfinancial measures of performance by executives in a service organization. Behavioral Research in Accounting, Vol. 8, pp. 134-153.

Schmid, Stefan & Kretschmer, Katharina (2010): Performance evaluation of foreign subsidiaries: A review of the literature and a contingency framework. International Journal of Management Reviews, Vol. 12, No. 3, pp. 219-258.

Schuler, Randall S. & Rogovsky, Nikolai (1998): Understanding compensation practice variations across firms: The impact of national culture. Journal of International Business Studies, Vol. 29, No. 1, pp. 159-177.

Schwartz, Shalom H. (1994): Beyond individualism/collectivism: New cultural dimensions of values. in: Kim, Uichol; Triandis, Harry C.; Kagitcibasi, Cigdem; Choi, Sang-Chin & Yoon, Gene (Ed.): Individualism and collectivism: Theory, method, and applications. Cross-cultural research and methodology series, Band 18. Sage Publications, Thousand Oaks, Calif, pp. 85-119.

Schwartz, Shalom H. (1999): A theory of cultural values and some implications for work. Applied Psychology: An International Review, Vol. 48, No. 1, pp. 23-47.

Schwartz, Shalom H. (2006): A theory of cultural value orientations: Explication and applications. Comparative Sociology, Vol. 5, No. 2, pp. 137-182.

Schwartz, Shalom H. & Bilsky, Wolfgang (1987): Toward a universal psychological structure of human values. Journal of Personality and Social Psychology, Vol. 53, No. 3, pp. 550-562.

Schwartz, Shalom H. & Bilsky, Wolfgang (1990): Toward a theory of the universal content and structure of values: Extensions and cross-cultural replications. Journal of Personality and Social Psychology, Vol. 58, No. 5, pp. 878-891.

Scott, William R. (1995): Institutions and organizations, Sage, Thousand Oaks, CA.

Scott, William R. (2001): Institutions and organizations, 2. ed., Sage, Thousand Oaks, CA.

Scott, William R. (2008): Institutions and organizations: Ideas and interests, 3. ed., Sage Publications, Los Angeles.

Scott, William R. (2009): Comparing organizations: Empirical and theoretical issues. in: King, Brayden G.; Felin, Teppo & Whetten, David A. (Ed.): Studying differences between organizations: Comparative approaches to organizational research. 26. Emerald, pp. 45-62.

Scott, William R. & Davis, Gerald F. (2007): Organizations and organizing: Rational, natural, and open system perspectives, Pearson Prentice Hall, Upper Saddle River, N.J.

Segalla, Michael; Rouziès, Dominique; Besson, Madeleine & Weitz, Barton A. (2006): A cross-national investigation of incentive sales compensation. International Journal of Research in Marketing, Vol. 23, No. 4, pp. 419-433.

Selznick, Philip (1996): Institutionalism "Old" and "New". Administrative Science Quarterly, Vol. 41, No. 2, pp. 270-277.

Shao, Liang; Kwok, Chuck C. & Guedhami, Omrane (2009): National culture and dividend policy. Journal of International Business Studies, Vol. 41, No. 8, pp. 1391-1414.

Sharma, Subhash; Durvasula, Srinivas & Ployhart, Robert E. (2011): The analysis of mean differences using mean and covariance structure analysis: Effect size estimation and error rates. Organizational Research Methods, Vol. 15, No. 1, pp. 75-102.

Shenkar, Oded (2001): Cultural distance revisited: Towards a more rigorous conceptualization and measurement of cultural differences. Journal of International Business Studies, Vol. 32, No. 2, pp. 519-535.

Shields, Michael D. (1997): Research in management accounting by North Americans in the 1990s. Journal of Management Accounting Research, Vol. 9, pp. 3-61.

Shim, Won S. & Steers, Richard M. (2012): Symmetric and asymmetric leadership cultures: A comparative study of leadership and organizational culture at Hyundai and Toyota. Journal of World Business, Vol. 47, No. 4, pp. 581-591.

Simon, Hermann (1996): Hidden champions: Lessons from 500 of the world's best unknown companies, Harvard Business School Press, Boston, Mass.

Simon, Hermann (2009): Hidden champions of the twenty-first century: The success strategies of unknown world market leaders, Springer, New York.

Simon, Hermann (2012): Hidden Champions - Aufbruch nach Globalia: Die Erfolgsstrategien unbekannter Weltmarktführer, Campus, Frankfurt, Main.

Simons, Robert (1987): Accounting control systems and business strategy: An empirical analysis. Accounting, Organizations and Society, Vol. 12, No. 4, pp. 357-374.

Simons, Robert (1994): How new top managers use control systems as levers of strategic renewal. Strategic Management Journal, Vol. 15, No. 3, pp. 169-189.

Simons, Robert (1995a): Control in an age of empowerment. Harvard Business Review, Vol. 73, No. 2, pp. 80-88.

Simons, Robert (1995b): Levers of control: How managers use innovative control systems to drive strategic renewal, Harvard Business School Press, Boston, Mass.

Simons, Robert (2005): Levers of organization design: How managers use accountability systems for greater performance and commitment, Harvard Business School Press, Boston, Mass.

Simons, Robert; Dávila, Antonio & Kaplan, Robert S. (2000): Performance measurement & control systems for implementing strategy, Prentice Hall, Upper Saddle River, N.J.

Singh, Kultar (2007): Quantitative social research methods, Sage, Thousand Oaks, CA.

Sivakumar, Kumar & Nakata, Cheryl (2001): The stampede toward Hofstede's framework: Avoiding the sample design pit in cross-cultural research. Journal of International Business Studies, Vol. 32, No. 3, pp. 555-574.

Skinner, Wickham (1974): The focused factory: New approach to managing manufacturing sees our productivity crisis as the problem of 'how to compete'. Harvard Business Review, Vol. 52, No. 3, pp. 113-121.

Smith, Peter B. (2002): Culture's Consequences: Something old and something new. Human Relations, Vol. 55, No. 1, pp. 119-135.

Smith, Peter B. (2006): When elephants fight, the grass gets trampled: the GLOBE and Hofstede projects. Journal of International Business Studies, Vol. 37, No. 6, pp. 915-921.

Snijders, Tom A. B. (2004): Multilevel analysis. in: Lewis-Beck, Michael S.; Bryman, Alan & Liao, Tim F. (Ed.): The Sage encyclopedia of social science research methods. Sage, Thousand Oaks, Calif, pp. 673-677.

Søndergaard, Mikael (1994): Research note: Hofstede's Consequences: A study of reviews, citations and replications. Organization Studies, Vol. 15, No. 3, pp. 447-456.

Sousa, Carlos M.; Ruzo, Emilio & Losada, Fernando (2010): The key role of managers' values in exporting: Influence on customer responsiveness and export performance. Journal of International Marketing, Vol. 18, No. 2, pp. 1-19.

Speckbacher, Gerhard; Bischof, Juergen & Pfeiffer, Thomas (2003): A descriptive analysis on the implementation of Balanced Scorecards in German-speaking countries. Management Accounting Research, Vol. 14, No. 4, pp. 361-388.

Speckbacher, Gerhard & Wentges, Paul (2012): The impact of family control on the use of performance measures in strategic target setting and incentive compensation: A research note. Management Accounting Research, Vol. 23, No. 1, pp. 34-46.

Spector, Paul E. (2006): Method variance in organizational research: Truth or urban legend? Organizational Research Methods, Vol. 9, No. 2, pp. 221-232.

Speklé, Roland F. (2001): Explaining management control structure variety: a transaction cost economics perspective. Accounting, Organizations and Society, Vol. 26, No. 4-5, pp. 419-441.

Steel, Piers & Taras, Vas (2010): Culture as a consequence: A multi-level multivariate meta-analysis of the effects of individual and country characteristics on work-related cultural values. Journal of International Management, Vol. 16, No. 3, pp. 211-233.

Steinmetz, Holger; Schmidt, Peter; Tina-Booh, Andrea; Wieczorek, Siegrid & Schwartz, Shalom H. (2009): Testing measurement invariance using multigroup CFA: Differences between educational groups in human values measurement. Quality & Quantity: International Journal of Methodology, Vol. 43, No. 4, pp. 599-616.

Stergiou, Konstantinos; Ashraf, Junaid & Uddin, Shahzad (2013): The role of structure and agency in management accounting control change of a family owned firm: A Greek case study. Critical Perspectives on Accounting, Vol. 24, No. 1, pp. 62-73.

Stevens, Douglas E. & Thevaranjan, Alex (2010): A moral solution to the moral hazard problem. Accounting, Organizations and Society, Vol. 35, No. 1, pp. 125-139.

Strauß, Erik & Zecher, Christina (2013): Management control systems: A review. Journal of Management Control, Vol. 23, No. 4, pp. 233-268.

Sturdy, Andrew (2004): The adoption of management ideas and practices: Theoretical perspectives and possibilities. Management Learning, Vol. 35, No. 2, pp. 155-179.

Suchman, Mark C. (1995): Managing legitimacy: Strategic and institutional approaches. Academy of Management Review, Vol. 20, No. 3, pp. 571-610.

Sunder, Shyam (2002): Management control, expectations, common knowledge, and culture. Journal of Management Accounting Research, Vol. 14, pp. 173-187.

Szabo, Erna; Brodbeck, Felix C.; Den Hartog, Deanne; Reber, Gerhard; Weibler, Jürgen & Wunderer, Rolf (2002): The Germanic Europe cluster: Where employees have a voice. Journal of World Business, Vol. 37, No. 1, pp. 55-68.

Tan, Sharon L. & Lau, Chong M. (2012): The impact of performance measures on employee fairness perceptions, job satisfaction and organisational commitment. Journal of Applied Management Accounting Research, Vol. 10, No. 2, pp. 57-72.

Tanning, Toivo & Tanning, Lembo (2013): Why Eastern European wages are several times lower than Western Europe. Global Business and Economics Research Journal, Vol. 2, No. 1, pp. 22-38.

Taras, Vas; Kirkman, Bradley L. & Steel, Piers (2010): Examining the impact of Culture's Consequences: A three-decade, multilevel, meta-analytic review of Hofstede's cultural value dimensions. Journal of Applied Psychology, Vol. 95, No. 3, pp. 405-439.

Taras, Vas; Rowney, Julie & Steel, Piers (2009): Half a century of measuring culture: Review of approaches, challenges, and limitations based on the analysis of 121 instruments for quantifying culture. Journal of International Management, Vol. 15, No. 4, pp. 357-373.

Taras, Vas; Sarala, Riikka; Muchinsky, Paul; Kemmelmeier, Markus; Singelis, Theodore M.; Avsec, Andreja; Coon, Heather M.; Dinnel, Dale L.; Gardner, Wendi; Grace, Sherry; Hardin, Erin E.; Hsu, Sandy; Johnson, Joel; Karakitapoglu-Aygun, Zahide; Kashima, Emiko S.; Kolstad, Arnulf; Milfont, Taciano L.; Oetzel, John; Okazaki, Sumie; Probst, Tahira M.; Sato, Toru; Shafiro, Maggie; Schwartz, Seth J. & Sinclair, H. Colleen (2014): Opposite ends of the same stick? Multi-method test of the dimensionality of individualism and collectivism. Journal of Cross-Cultural Psychology, Vol. 45, No. 2, pp. 213-245.

Taras, Vas; Steel, Piers & Kirkman, Bradley L. (2010): Negative practice–value correlations in the GLOBE data: Unexpected findings, questionnaire limitations and research directions. Journal of International Business Studies, Vol. 41, No. 8, pp. 1330-1338.

Tempel, Anne & Walgenbach, Peter (2007): Global standardization of organizational forms and management practices? What new institutionalism and the business-systems approach can learn from each other. Journal of Management Studies, Vol. 44, No. 1, pp. 1-24.

Tessier, Sophie & Otley, David (2012): A conceptual development of Simons' Levers of Control framework. Management Accounting Research, Vol. 23, No. 3, pp. 171-185.

Thompson, Lori F. & Surface, Eric A. (2007): Employee surveys administered online: Attitudes toward the medium, nonresponse, and data representativeness. Organizational Research Methods, Vol. 10, No. 2, pp. 241-261.

Tihanyi, László; Devinney, Timothy M. & Pedersen, Torben (2012): Introduction to part II: Institutional theory in international business and management. in: Tihanyi, László; Devinney, Timothy M. & Pedersen, Torben (Ed.): Advances in International Management / Institutional theory in international business and management. Emerald, Bingley, pp. 33-42.

Tosi, Henry L. & Greckhamer, Thomas (2004): Culture and CEO compensation. Organization Science, Vol. 15, No. 6, pp. 657-670.

Treiblmaier, Horst & Filzmoser, Peter (2010): Exploratory factor analysis revisited: How robust methods support the detection of hidden multivariate data structures in IS research. Information & Management, Vol. 47, No. 4, pp. 197-207.

Triandis, Harry C.; Bontempo, Robert; Villareal, Marcelo J.; Asai, Masaaki & Lucca, Nydia (1988): Individualism and collectivism: Cross-cultural perspectives on self-ingroup relationships. Journal of Personality and Social Psychology, Vol. 54, No. 2, pp. 323-338.

Trompenaars, Fons (1993): Riding the waves of culture: Understanding cultural diversity in business, Economist Books, London.

Trompenaars, Fons & Hampden-Turner, Charles (1998): Riding the waves of culture: Understanding diversity in global business, 2. ed., McGraw Hill, New York.

Trompenaars, Fons & Hampden-Turner, Charles (2012): Riding the waves of culture: Understanding diversity in business, 3. ed., Nicholas Brealey Publ., London [u.a.].

Tsui, Anne S.; Nifadkar, Ssuhsil S. & Ou, Amy Y. (2007): Cross-national, cross-cultural organizational behavior research: Advances, gaps, and recommendations. Journal of Management, Vol. 33, No. 3, pp. 426-478.

Tsui, Judy S. (2001): The impact of culture on the relationship between budgetary participation, management accounting systems, and managerial performance: An analysis of Chinese and Western managers. The International Journal of Accounting, Vol. 36, No. 2, pp. 125-146.

Tung, Rosalie L. & Verbeke, Alain (2010): Beyond Hofstede and GLOBE: Improving the quality of cross-cultural research. Journal of International Business Studies, Vol. 41, No. 8, pp. 1259-1274.

Uncles, Mark D. & Kwok, Simon (2013): Designing research with in-built differentiated replication. Journal of Business Research, Vol. 66, No. 9, pp. 1398-1405.

van de Schoot, Rens; Lugtig, Peter & Hox, Joop (2012): A checklist for testing measurement invariance. European Journal of Development Psychology, Vol. 9, No. 4, pp. 1-7.

van der Stede, Wim A. (2003): The effect of national culture on management control and incentive system design in multi-business firms: Evidence of intracorporate isomorphism. European Accounting Review, Vol. 12, No. 2, pp. 263-285.

van der Stede, Wim A.; Chow, Chee W. & Lin, Thomas W. (2006): Strategy, choice of performance measures, and performance. Behavioral Research in Accounting, Vol. 18, pp. 185-205.

van der Stede, Wim A.; Young, S. M. & Chen, Clara X. (2005): Assessing the quality of evidence in empirical management accounting research: The case of survey studies. Accounting, Organizations and Society, Vol. 30, No. 7-8, pp. 655-684.

van Veen-Dirks, Paula (2010): Different uses of performance measures: The evaluation versus reward of production managers. Accounting, Organizations and Society, Vol. 35, No. 2, pp. 141-164.

Vance, Charles M.; McClaine, Shirley R.; Boje, David M. & Stage, Daniel H. (1992): An examination of the transferability of traditional performance appraisal principles across cultural boundaries. Management International Review, Vol. 32, No. 4, pp. 313-326.

Vandello, Joseph A. & Cohen, Dov (1999): Patterns of individualism and collectivism across the United States. Journal of Personality and Social Psychology, Vol. 77, No. 2, pp. 279-292.

Vandenberg, R. J. & Lance, C. E. (2000): A review and synthesis of the measurement invariance literature: Suggestions, practices, and recommendations for organizational research. Organizational Research Methods, Vol. 3, No. 1, pp. 4-70.

Venaik, Sunil & Brewer, Paul (2010): Avoiding uncertainty in Hofstede and GLOBE. Journal of International Business Studies, Vol. 41, No. 8, pp. 1294-1315.

Venkatraman, N. Venkat & Ramanujam, Vasudevan (1986): Measurement of business performance in strategy research: A comparison of approaches. Academy of Management Review, Vol. 11, No. 4, pp. 801-814.

Walgenbach, Peter & Meyer, Renate E. (2008): Neoinstitutionalistische Organisationstheorie, Kohlhammer, Stuttgart.

Walumbwa, Fred O.; Avolio, Bruce J. & Aryee, Samuel (2011): Leadership and management research in Africa: A synthesis and suggestions for future research. Journal of Occupational and Organizational Psychology, Vol. 84, No. 3, pp. 425-439.

Webster, Cynthia & White, Allyn (2010): Exploring the national and organizational culture mix in service firms. Journal of the Academy of Marketing Science, Vol. 38, No. 6, pp. 691-703.

White, Howard D. (2009): Scientific communication and literature retrieval. in: Cooper, Harris M.; Hedges, Larry V. & Valentine, Jeff C. (Ed.): The handbook of research synthesis and meta-analysis. Russell Sage Foundation, New York, pp. 51-71.

Whitley, Richard D. (1991): The social construction of Business Systems in East Asia. Organization Studies, Vol. 12, No. 1, pp. 1-28.

Whitley, Richard D. (1992): Societies, firms and markets: The social structuring of business systems. in: Whitley, Richard D. (Ed.): European business systems: Firms and markets in their national contexts. Sage Publications, London, pp. 5-45.

Whitley, Richard D. (1999): Firms, institutions and management control: The comparative analysis of coordination and control systems. Accounting, Organizations and Society, Vol. 24, No. 5-6, pp. 507-524.

Wickramasinghe, Danture; Hopper, Trevor & Rathnasiri, Chandana (2004): Japanese cost management meets Sri Lankan politics: Disappearance and reappearance of bureaucratic management controls in a privatised utility. Accounting, Auditing & Accountability Journal, Vol. 17, No. 1, pp. 85-120.

Widener, Sally K. (2006): Human capital, pay structure, and the use of performance measures in bonus compensation. Management Accounting Research, Vol. 17, No. 2, pp. 198-221.

Widener, Sally K. (2007): An empirical analysis of the levers of control framework. Accounting, Organizations and Society, Vol. 32, No. 7-8, pp. 757-788.

Wiener, Norbert (1948/1994): Cybernetics or control and communication in the animal and the machine, 2. ed., MIT Press, Cambridge, Mass.

Williams, Christopher & van Triest, Sander (2009): The impact of corporate and national cultures on decentralization in multinational corporations. International Business Review, Vol. 18, No. 2, pp. 156-167.

Williams, John J. & Seaman, Alfred E. (2001): Predicting change in management accounting systems: national culture and industry effects. Accounting, Organizations and Society, Vol. 26, No. 4-5, pp. 443-460.

Williams, Larry J.; Hartman, Nathan & Cavazotte, Flavia (2010): Method variance and marker variables: A review and comprehensive CFA marker technique. Organizational Research Methods, Vol. 13, No. 3, pp. 477-514.

Wilson, David B. (2009): Systematic coding. in: Cooper, Harris M.; Hedges, Larry V. & Valentine, Jeff C. (Ed.): The handbook of research synthesis and meta-analysis. Russell Sage Foundation, New York, pp. 159-176.

Wilson, Dominic & Purushothaman, Roopa (2007): Dreaming with BRICs: The path to 2050. in: Jain, Subhash C. (Ed.): Emerging economies and the transformation of international business: Brazil, Russia, India and China (BRIC). Edward Elgar, Cheltenham, pp. 3-45.

Wilson, Dominic; Trivedi, Kamakshya; Carlson, Stacy & Ursúa, José (2011): The BRICs 10 years on: Halfway through the great transformation: Global Economics Paper No: 208

Wilson, Kathlyn Y. (2010): An analysis of bias in supervisor narrative comments in performance appraisal. Human Relations, Vol. 63, No. 12, pp. 1903-1933.

Wong-On-Wing, Bernard; Guo, Lan; Li, Wei & Yang, Dan (2007): Reducing conflict in balanced scorecard evaluations. Accounting, Organizations and Society, Vol. 32, No. 4-5, pp. 363-377.

Wooten, Melissa & Hoffmann, Andrew J. (2008): Organizational fields: Past, present and future. in: Greenwood, Royston; Oliver, Christine; Suddaby, Roy & Sahlin, Kerstin (Ed.): The SAGE handbook of organizational institutionalism. Sage, Los Angeles, Calif., pp. 130-147.

Yamawaki, Niwako (2012): Within-culture variations of collectivism in Japan. Journal of Cross-Cultural Psychology, Vol. 43, No. 8, pp. 1191-1204.

Youngcourt, Satoris S.; Leiva, Pedro I. & Jones, Robert G. (2007): Perceived purposes of performance appraisal: Correlates of individual- and position-focused purposes on attitudinal outcomes. Human Resource Development Quarterly, Vol. 18, No. 3, pp. 315-343.

Zeng, Yuping; Shenkar, Oded; Lee, Seung-Hyun & Song, Sangcheol (2013): Cultural differences, MNE learning abilities, and the effect of experience on subsidiary mortality in a dissimilar culture: Evidence from Korean MNEs. Journal of International Business Studies, Vol. 44, No. 1, pp. 42-65.

Zimmermann, Stefan (2009): Intern versus extern – eine personalökonomische Analyse Einflussfaktoren auf die Besetzung von Spitzenführungspositionen. Zeitschrift für Personalforschung,, Vol. 23, No. 3, pp. 195-218.

Zucker, Lynne G. (1977): The role of institutionalization in cultural persistence. American Sociological Review, Vol. 42, No. 5, pp. 726-743.